John M. Stowe

History of the Town of Hubbardston, Worcester County, Mass.

From the time its territory was purchased of the Indians in 1686, to the present :

with the genealogy of present and former resident families

John M. Stowe

History of the Town of Hubbardston, Worcester County, Mass.
*From the time its territory was purchased of the Indians in 1686, to the present : with the
genealogy of present and former resident families*

ISBN/EAN: 9783337304164

Printed in Europe, USA, Canada, Australia, Japan

Cover: Foto ©ninafisch / pixelio.de

More available books at **www.hansebooks.com**

HISTORY

OF THE

TOWN OF HUBBARDSTON,

WORCESTER COUNTY, MASS.

FROM THE TIME ITS TERRITORY WAS PURCHASED OF THE INDIANS IN 1686, TO THE PRESENT.

WITH

THE GENEALOGY

OF PRESENT AND FORMER RESIDENT FAMILIES.

BY REV. J. M. STOWE.

HUBBARDSTON, MASS.: PUBLISHED BY THE COMMITTEE.
1881.

PREFACE.

The preparation of the historical part of this work, from the material furnished by William Bennett, or gathered from other sources, was mainly completed by Rev. J. M. Stowe, even to writing the Introduction, in 1873. And at the same date the genealogical part had been reduced to the present tabular form, from the lists of names and dates received from Mr. Bennett, or collected by Mr. Stowe himself.

The general depression of business at that period led Mr. Bennett to regard the time as unfavorable for publication. The other members of the committee concurred in this view, and it was decided that expediency required delay. Consequently Mr. Stowe made no attempt to bring to completion the genealogical records, which from the nature of the case, were constantly changing; and for several years little was done in that direction besides recording whatever came to hand.

After the death of Mr. Stowe, no action was taken in reference to bringing the work before the public, till 1879, when the two vacancies in the publishing committee caused by the death of Levi Peirce and the removal from town of T. Sibley Heald, were filled by the appointment of Abel Howe and Horace Underwood in their places respectively. Of the others of the original committee, Lyman Woodward had become the only active member, in consequence of the declining health of William Bennett—now deceased— and the increasing years of Elisha Woodward; although the latter continued to be consulted upon unnumbered questions relating to the early history of the place and the people; and his retentive memory has proved an unfailing source of information upon all matters embraced within the range of his observation or experience.

At the April meeting in 1880, the reorganized committee reported to the town what progress was made by Mr. Stowe, and were instructed by vote of the town, "to have the manuscript history of the town completed, and cause the same to be printed as soon, and in such manner, as in their judgment seems proper, the whole matter being left in their care."

' By this time the changes in individual and family history had become so many that an entire revision of the records was necessary. Since so much had been done in that line, the committee were desirous of making the record of each family as complete as practicable notwithstanding the additional labor involved. And any one who has never attempted to collect or arrange the necessary items for such a purpose can have little idea of the greatness of the task, or of the care and patience required to avoid omissions and errors, which after all, are almost sure to be found when the whole is completed.

In the work of copying, Mr. Stowe had been aided by his wife, who thus became familiar with the method adopted in arranging the records. The committee therefore employed her to enter at once upon the effort to make them complete. The degree of success attained is indicated by the records themselves, as now presented.

To ascertain or verify the desired information respecting six or seven thousand individuals was not a rapid work. This reminder will account for any seeming delay.

The original plan embraced whatever was found in the town records regarding every one who had been at any time a citizen of the town. But the present committee thought best to abridge the work by omitting the records of families which by removal or death have become extinct. A manuscript copy of all which had been collated from the town records and other sources, will be preserved for reference with other documents in charge of the town clerk.

To reach those who have recently become residents, the committee posted a public notice in September, 1880, requesting all who wished to be represented in the genealogical records to be published with the history of the town, to furnish at once the requisite statements. No responsibility was felt in regard to those from whom nothing was received.

Mrs. Stowe was also employed to review the historical part, and so far as revision had become necessary, through the lapse of time and the consequent changes, to make whatever alterations and additions were required to bring the history down to the present date. Otherwise it is as Mr. Stowe left it.

The committee would hereby acknowledge the valuable services rendered by Mrs. Stowe, and bear their united testimony to the faithfulness and impartiality exercised in the performance of so arduous and important a task.

We desire also to express our gratitude to all others who have in various ways furnished us aid.

We claim no credit for superior ability or judgment in our efforts to bring this work to its completion, but are willing to submit it to the impartial criticism of all who have ever undertaken or borne a hand in a labor of this kind.

The illustrations are by the Lithotype Printing Company, 114 Nassau Street, New York; Printing works at Gardner, Mass.

ELISHA WOODWARD,
ABEL HOWE,
LYMAN WOODWARD,
HORACE UNDERWOOD,
} *Publishing Committee.*

Hubbardston, July, 1881.

CONTENTS.

CHAPTER I.

TOPOGRAPHY.

CHAPTER II.

EARLY HISTORY.

CHAPTER III.

INCORPORATION, NAME AND GROWTH.

CHAPTER IV.

CIRCUMSTANCES AND CUSTOMS OF SETTLERS.

CHAPTER V.

WAR OF THE REVOLUTION.

CHAPTER VI.

SHAYS' REBELLION.

CHAPTER VII.

COUNTY, STATE AND NATIONAL AFFAIRS.

B

CHAPTER VIII.

WAR OF 1812.

CHAPTER IX.

SCHOOLS AND EDUCATION.

CHAPTER X.

CHURCHES AND MINISTERS.

CHAPTER XI.

MEETING HOUSES.

CHAPTER XV.

VARIOUS LOCAL ORGANIZATIONS.

CHAPTER XVI.

NOTEWORTHY EVENTS.

CHAPTER XVII.

BIOGRAPHICAL.

CHAPTER XVIII.

CENTENNIAL CELEBRATION--STATISTICS.

CHAPTER XIX.

RETROSPECTIVE.

CHAPTER XX.

MUNICIPAL OFFICERS.

GENEALOGICAL RECORDS.

ILLUSTRATIONS.

PORTRAITS.

VIEWS.

INTRODUCTION.

On the approach of June 13, 1867, the one hundredth anniversary of the incorporation of the town of Hubbardston, much interest was felt in having the day appropriately observed. In November, 1866, the town appointed Levi Peirce, Elisha Woodward, William Bennett, Lyman Woodward and T. Sibley Heald, a committee of arrangements, and appropriated $300 to procure an historical address, and for the publication of that address, with other historical and statistical matter relating to the town.

William Bennett had been town clerk for many years, and being possessed of a remarkable memory, was well acquainted with the general history of the place and people. He entered with much enthusiasm into the work of preparing for the centennial anniversary, and spent a great amount of time in copying records and gathering facts and material from various sources.

A full account of the celebration, including the address, poem, toasts, speeches and letters, with a description of the ceremonies of the day, was published at the time in pamphlet form; from which an abridged account of the celebration is quoted in chapter XVIII of this work.

Only a small part of the interesting material that had been collected could be used on that occasion, and there was a desire on the part of many citizens that the whole should appear in a more permanent form. The subject was brought before the town in March, 1868, when an appropriation of $1000 was made for publishing a history of the town, and the committee above named were authorized to employ some one to complete the work already begun by Mr. Bennett, and to draw their warrant for the amount expended, when the history should be

C

completed and published. Mr. Bennett would not consent to arrange the material for publication, though he continued to gather facts and incidents to be used, especially in the line of the genealogical history. As there was no one in town who was willing to undertake the work, nothing was done for about a year, when Mr. John Clark proposed to pay Mr. Bennett for his papers and publish the work on his own responsibility. But as he was a stranger, this plan was not satisfactory to all the people and was not adopted.

After the writer returned to town, in the fall of 1870, he was solicited by the committee to take charge of the work; he entered upon it about the first of 1871, and carried it forward as he had time. On account of a variety of other duties it was impossible to complete the work at once, and do it with the care and thoroughness desirable. When he undertook it, he supposed there was little more to do than arrange the papers received from Mr. Bennett. But though these were found to be of great value and to save much labor, they were collected more with reference to the centennial ceremonies than for a full history, and many things of interest were not contained in them. Besides, in order to write intelligently in regard to matters which they contained, a personal acquaintance with the whole history was necessary to be able to look at all things in their relations to each other. Therefore all the town records and most of the church records have been carefully examined and re-examined; much new material has been inserted, but much more has been omitted, that the work might be kept within due limits.

The effort has been made to investigate every subject so thoroughly that what is stated may be reliable; and to deal with the utmost candor where there is room for difference of opinion. Yet it is not claimed that the work is free from imperfections; and as another has said,—" No one can so completely feel the imperfections of a work like this, as the one who has labored at every point to avoid or remove them; to compress the greatest amount of truth in the fewest words, and while reducing the scale, to preserve a just proportion in the details." It has

proved a very pleasant, though somewhat perplexing and difficult task.

In the plan of the work, the History of Winchendon, by Rev.
A. P. Marvin has been followed in part. Histories of other
neighboring towns have been carefully examined. Original
documents in the office of the Secretary of State, have been
consulted and some of them copied. Considerable time has
been spent in consulting various books in the State Library; and
much information has been obtained from private individuals.
The record relating to the soldiers in the recent war was copied
almost entirely from the "Rebellion Record" of the town.

Thus it will be seen that the credit of whatever there may be
of interest in the present work is largely due to others, especially to Mr. Bennett, who deserves the thanks of the town for
the part he has taken in it.

J. M. STOWE.

Hubbardston, 1873.

John M. Store

HISTORY OF HUBBARDSTON.

CHAPTER I.

TOPOGRAPHY.

PROBABLY most of the present generation, who read this history, are more or less acquainted with the natural features of the town, and will not attach importance to the description given in this chapter. But it may be pleasant for those who come after us, or live at a distance from us, to look at the old homestead as it was in the days of their fathers. We like sometimes to compare the pictures of our early life with the photographs of later years, to note the changes which time has wrought; so there may be those hereafter who will be grateful for an outline, though imperfect, of the face of the town as it is now.

Hubbardston is situated eighteen miles north of Worcester, and fifty-three miles from Boston. By railway it is sixty-two miles from Boston by way of Worcester, and seventy by way of Gardner. The latitude of the centre of the town is forty-two degrees, twenty-eight minutes, north; and the longitude is about five degrees east from Washington. The elevation of the common is 1015 feet above the level of the sea. Though we find the sides varying somewhat in length, it was evidently the original design that the township should be square, with boundary lines running about forty-five degrees from the meridian, so that a north and south line, through the centre, would cut it from corner to corner. It was also the design that it should be six miles on every side, and contain 23,040 acres; but from later surveys it is found that the lines over-run so much that the whole tract contains about 26,000 acres.

On the northeast side it is bounded by Gardner and Westminster; on the southeast by Princeton and Rutland; on the southwest by Barre, and on the northwest by Phillipston and Templeton. These boundaries are the same as at the first, except that in 1810 a tract of 500 acres, in the east corner, was set off to Princeton, for the greater convenience of the families living upon it, and possibly because the corner was so sharp as to be uncomfortable in the side of our neighbor.

Hills.—The general elevation of the town is high, compared with most other places in this part of the state. Its surface is broken and diversified, with a general slope toward the south; but, in accordance with a law which prevails throughout New England, and in general throughout the Western Continent, its ranges of hills extend north and south. In the northern portion of the town, these ridges are almost parallel. The hill which occupies the western part, and contains some of the best farms, has always been known as "Burnshirt." There are various traditions in regard to the origin of this name, but none of them seems very reliable.

Next towards the east is "Mount Jefferson," or "Muzzy Hill." This is also a ridge of good land. The Muzzy Place commands one of the finest views in the region. The steeples of fourteen churches, in eight different villages, can be seen scattered about in the wide reach of territory visible on all sides. Concerning an elevation in the northern part of this range, the following statement is made by Hobert B. Potter:—

"By actual levels, taken in connection with those of the Boston, Barre and Gardner Railroad, I find the highest point in Hubbardston to be 1325 feet above the ocean level. It is situated near the old Templeton road, not more than fifteen rods from the Templeton line, on the old Bennett farm. The only points that are as high as this, and visible to the naked eye from the same, are: Wachusett and adjacent hills on the east;

the hills in the north part of Ashburnham, New Ipswich and Peterboro', and Monadnock on the north; and the high land beyond Petersham, on the west.   In the southern view, from Petersham on the west, to Wachusett on the east, no land can be seen of so great height as this point."

Next in order is "Ragged Hill," so called from its rough appearance.   This general range extends through the village to the south corner of the town.   The next range is the one whose western side is followed by the Boston, Barre and Gardner Railroad.   One of its elevations is "Sherman Hill," near which the depot stands.   Still farther east is another range, but from its proximity to Wachusett, whose base reaches nearly to the border of Hubbardston, its prominences are not so noticeable.   In the south part of the town is "Corn Hill," and on the Worcester road, "Comet Hill," and farther west, "Fayerweather Hill," all spurs of the ranges before mentioned.

Plains and Meadows.—With so many ranges of hills within so short a distance, we cannot look for broad valleys or plains. The largest level tract lies south of the village, including what is known as the "Thicket," and extends to Rutland line. About one-twelfth of the township is meadow and interval.   Some of the meadows never had much timber on them, but were regarded by the first settlers as their most valuable lands, on account of the grass growing upon them.   In the division of land in some of the towns, one acre of meadow was considered equal in value to three acres of upland.   The meadows along the Natty-pond Brook are said to have produced quantities of hay of good quality, which was cut and stacked on the ground, and in spring was fed out to the cattle in the pasture, in case of storms or late vegetation.   Much of the land along the streams, once valuable for grass, is now nearly worthless.   In some of these places the cranberry grows, and probably many acres might be rendered profitable by its culture.

Streams.—The water sheds having been described, it is easy to see that the general course of the streams must be either north or south.   The ranges of hills are so near each other

there can be no large streams between them; and since the
north corner of the town slopes northward, while the main
portion slopes southward, it is plain there can be no stream
flowing through town, unless it be across the east or west corner.
Nearly all the streams rise either in town, or just over the
border. For this reason the water-power is not the most reliable, though there is so much fall in the streams that during
a large portion of the year, many mill privileges are available.

It has often been said, and perhaps is generally believed, that
all the water flowing from town reaches the Connecticut River,
either through Ware or Millers Rivers. But there is a swamp
in the extreme eastern corner of the town, from which the water
flows into Princeton, and helps form the South Wachusett Brook,
a tributary of the Nashua River.

Burnshirt River rises in Templeton and Phillipston, and passes
across the west corner of the town. Canesto Brook rises just
over the northern border, and flows between the two most
western ranges of hills. For a long distance it has no important
tributaries, but near the southern boundary unites with Natty-
pond Brook. The latter stream has all its sources in this town,
between the summits of Muzzy and Ragged Hills. One of its
sources is worthy of mention. It is the spring near the bridge
on the road to Templeton, which is often said to have no bottom.
The depth, current and purity of its waters is seldom equaled.
During the unparalleled drought of 1870, for several months all
the water used at the Crystal House, and by several private
families in the village, was obtained from this spring, a mile and
a half distant. For a time the steam mill was run by water
brought from the same spring.

Ware River branch also has its sources in town, the most
important of which is Moosehorn Pond. By the many brooks,
springs and ponds whose waters it receives, it drains a larger
surface than any other stream in town, and exceeds them all in
size. A small brook has its source in Comet Pond and flows
southward into Rutland. Another stream, which has one source
in the eastern corner of the town, and another in Westminster,

flows into the Ware River in Princeton. All the streams thus far described, with the single exception before mentioned, unite their waters in Ware River. Two small streams rise in the north part of the town and flow northwest into Otter River, a branch of Millers. Otter River rises in Templeton, runs into Hubbardston for a short distance, and thence into Templeton again.

Ponds.—Natty Pond, northwest from the village, is small in extent and so surrounded by bushes and wet, boggy meadows, that it is not a place of much resort. Such a tough, elastic quag has grown over the water in some places, that a heavy person standing upon it will soon find his foundations disappearing, and himself slowly sinking to his waist in clear water.

The deep, clear sheet of water, known as Comet Pond, is one of the most beautiful in town. How the name of this should be written, is difficult to determine. It probably came from some Indian word, and in various books and plans of the town, is written in the following different ways: Asnaconcomick, Asnecomcomit, Asnacomet, Commet and Comet. This pond is fed entirely by springs and water from the surrounding hills. It is bordered by gravel banks with natural curves and indentations that look like the work of man. It is remarkable for its elevation of ninety feet above the "Thicket Valley," only a little distance off, into which it might easily be drained. Its elevation above the sea is 910 feet. At a distance, from Muzzy Hill, for instance, it has the appearance of being upon a hill. For an area of twenty acres its depth is sixty feet. It is nearly a mile and a half long, and from five rods to half a mile wide, and covers 220 acres. Recently it has been enlarged beyond this extent, by a dam built for the purpose of making it a reservoir.

At a little distance is another large, natural pond, now known as Moosehorn, but formerly called the Little Asnacomet. This pond covers 130 acres, of which seventy are open water, twenty are covered by what is known as the "quag," and forty are partially flowed. It has no inlet of any size. It lies at an elevation of 980 feet, only thirty-five feet less than that of the village common. It may be observed that the figures given in this section concerning the elevation, area and depth of the ponds, and the elevation of the common, given in a former section, vary from statements recently published relating to the same points. Those given here were personally ascertained and furnished for this work by Hobert B. Potter.

There are several other natural ponds of greater or less extent, but of less importance. There are also several artificial ponds. The one so long known as Parker's Pond, with its beautiful islands and wooded hills mirrored in its clear surface, is a gem in itself, and one of the charming features in our village landscape. A fine view of it may be had from Underwood Hill, an elevation just off the village street, between the Barre and Worcester roads. One glances for a moment west and south at the long stretch of hills in Barre, Oakham, Rutland and Princeton, but as the eye sweeps eastward to Wachusett, it is caught and held by the beauty of the picture—the mountain in the background, the nearer hills covered with pleasing variety of orchard, woodland, waving fields, or rich verdure of mowing and grazing land, sloping here gently, there more abruptly, to the water's edge, only to seem to be continued in the equally varied islands of the miniature lake—all combine to make perhaps, the most beautiful view to be had within the limits of the township. In the great freshet of 1869, this pond broke away, and for many months was not restored. As the people of the village looked down upon its black, forsaken bed, they felt that they had met with personal loss. It hardly need be added that the restoration of the pond, by the rebuilding of the dam and bridge, in 1873, was hailed with joy.

The ponds and brooks abound with pickerel and trout, and have always been attractive to the angler. In winter, large quantities of pickerel are taken through the ice from Moosehorn and other ponds.

Forests.—With the exception of the few meadows mentioned above, the township was, at first, an unbroken wilderness. The primeval forest trees were regarded as the greatest incumbrance

VIEW OF MT. WACHUSETT, FROM UNDERWOOD'S HILL.

by the early settlers, who resorted to every means to destroy them. In spring, they set fires and burned over large tracts, in order that grass might grow for the cattle that were driven here for pasturage, from the lower towns. In clearing, they would fell the heavy timbers, cut off the limbs to dry, then burn over the tract, and after that, pile up the huge logs and burn them upon the ground. At one time, most of the money brought into town was received for potash, made from the ashes of these forest trees. These forests, so worthless in early times, have since become the great source of the business and wealth of the town. Indeed, the lumber trade has exceeded every other interest. It is probable that if this township had been secured from settlement, and all its timber left untouched to the present day, it would require five or six times the present valuation of the town to purchase the tract. Nearly the whole of the original growth of timber has fallen before the axe, and much of the land is now given up to a young growth of wood. There were large tracts covered with valuable pine timber, and now many acres are covered with saplings. In some parts of the town there was once a heavy growth of chestnut and oak, and many bushels of chestnuts were gathered every year. There have been but few walnut trees, except in the southwest part of the town. The sugar maple grows in some localities, but not to such an extent as to be of much value in the manufacture of sugar. In our woods may be found almost all varieties of trees which grow in our climate, and in our gardens and orchards, most kinds of fruit.

A few years ago double rows of maples and elms were set the whole length of the village street, many of which are now large trees, affording refreshing shade and contributing much to adorn the place, which is admitted to be one of the most beautiful in the county. The time may yet come when attention will be given to planting and cultivating trees for timber and the maple for sugar orchards.

Hubbardston Nonesuch.—Years ago, in an obscure pasture on one of the slopes of Burnshirt Hill, there sprang up, unplanted,

a little apple tree. For years it struggled for life against summer drought and winter storms, and the rough browsing of
cattle. At length it bore fruit, and of such quality as to attract
attention. Thus, it is claimed, originated the world renowned
" Hubbardston Nonesuch." This venerable tree is still standing, and until lately has borne barrels of apples in fruit-bearing
years.

Flowers.—The wild flowers of the town are similar to those
of other hill towns in New England. The trailing arbutus and
the mountain laurel are very abundant in places. The water
lily adorns many of the ponds, and in certain localities the rare
twin-flower *(Linnæa borealis)* carpets the forests with its creep-
ing vines and fills the air with its fragrance.

Early Wild Animals.—In early times the woods abounded
with wild animals, which attracted the hunter. For many years
after the settlement of the town, bears and wolves roamed
through these forests. At the March meeting in 1780, thirteen
years after the town was incorporated, the following vote was
passed: "That a bounty of one hundred pounds be paid for
every wolf, thirty pounds for every bear, and thirty pounds for
every wild cat killed, the head of each wild varmint to be
brought to one of the selectmen." This vote was reconsidered
afterwards, but it shows that these animals were not unknown
to the inhabitants. For many years deer reeves were among
the officers of the town.

Geology.—Bowlders of moderate size are scattered in abundance over the surface, and are a great hindrance in cultivating
the soil. In some places they are drifted and piled together in
such a way as to give the appearance of having been placed by
human agency. One old History of Worcester County says:
" Around Moosehorn Pond there is every appearance that there
was once a stone wall built, or building. In some places the
wall is two feet and a half high, as if laid up by men's hands,
and where there is not one stone left upon another, the appearance is of a large wall thrown down." The appearance remains
the same to this day, but good judges who have examined these

stones, are of the opinion that they show nothing more than might be produced by natural causes. As we can think of no reason for building such a wall, the presumption is that it is not artificial.

We have no mines of any special value, though many believe that they exist within our bounds. Just over our northern boundary, in what is known as "Mine Hill," is a remarkable cave, or room, extending fifty-seven feet into the solid rock, with a very narrow entrance. In the rocks inside, the marks of drills are plainly visible, and near by are the remains of an old well and *debris*, which prove the cave to be an excavation made long before there was any settlement here. When, and by whom, will probably forever remain a mystery; but from the appearance of the hill, it is probable that some persons expected to find valuable mines here, and kept their explorations secret till the matter was tested, and when the ore was found to be worthless, they did not care to publish their folly. There is an old tradition that after the settlement of Concord and Sudbury, while this whole region was a wilderness, some merchants in that vicinity traded largely with the Indians. At one time the Indians brought what seemed to be valuable ore, and the merchants, under their guidance, fitted out a company to go and explore the mine. They were gone three or four months, but where, was kept a secret. The next year they went again, and were gone about the same length of time, bringing back specimens of ore which, being sent to England and analyzed, proved worthless, consequently the place of their operations was never revealed. No spot has been discovered which seems more likely to be the scene of their fruitless labors than this cave.

Copperas Mine.—When the new county road to Templeton was built, in 1828, in cutting through a ledge, ore was discovered which was supposed to be of great value. It proved to be copperas. The mine was worked on a large scale for many years, but though the copperas was of good quality, the cost of its manufacture was so great the enterprise was at length

2

abandoned, and all the buildings of the settlement have now disappeared. This ledge is very extensive, though it comes to the surface in but few places.

The springs in some localities indicate the presence of iron, but probably it does not exist in sufficient quantity to be of much value.

CHAPTER II.

INDIANS.—We have no thrilling stories to relate about the Indians. There is no evidence that the red man ever had a home or settlement within the bounds of this town; but there are indications that he was acquainted with the whole region, and that he had hunting and fishing grounds here. Some of the ponds bore Indian names till corrupted by common speech. All the southern portion of what is now Worcester County, was owned and occupied by the Nipmucks. One or two large tribes seem to have had their headquarters at, or near, Wachusett Mountain. There they held councils of war. From there they sent out parties to burn and destroy white settlements. There they had great days of rejoicing, after some of their bloody adventures. Mrs. Rowlandson says: "At one time they built a great wigwam, large enough to hold a hundred Indians, which they did in preparation for a great day of dancing." "They began now to come from all quarters, against the merry dancing-day." They probably danced with the scalps of the murdered Englishmen adorning their wigwam.

At Nashaway (Lancaster) there was a large settlement of the Narragansett tribe, and later another at Nichewaug, now Petersham. From Nashaway to the foot of the "Great Wachusette," there was a path, or Indian trail. At the foot of the mountain it divided, one branch running on the north, the other on the south side, but both leading to Nichewaug. The south path undoubtedly lay through this town, running near Comet Pond, thence near the Thomas Temple place, thence to Burnshirt Hill, probably meeting the other path near Burnshirt River.

This path is still traceable on the farm of the late Oren Marean. Mrs. Rowlandson, mentioned above, the wife of the first minister of Lancaster, was taken captive by the Indians in 1676, during King Philip's War, and carried to Canada. When they returned with her, they probably passed down this path to Wachusett. There a council was held in which they consented to her release, Mr. Hoar having been sent out to treat with them for that purpose. There are still remains of an old chimney and rude fireplace, built of stone, near Comet Pond, supposed to be on this path. This trail seems to have been one of the thoroughfares of the country some years later, for in 1734 the proprietors of Petersham voted to give Capt. Jonas Houghton a certain sum of money, " For making the road so feasible from Lancaster along the north side of Wachusett, to the meeting of the other path, which goes from the aforesaid Lancaster along the south side of Wachusett, as to carry comfortably with four oxen, four barrels of cider, at once."

Soon after Mrs. Rowlandson's release, the General Court of the Province sent Seth Perry as a special messenger, to treat with the Indians, and his letters were directed to the " Sagamore about Wachusetts." Another record, made the same year, speaks of a plan to send a force " To visit the ennemye's headquarters at Wachusetts." From these, and other facts, it seems that Wachusett was a stronghold of the hostile Indians, and therefore we infer that this region was often traversed by them.

Purchase.—Wachusett seems to be the object which drew the attention of the first settlers of Massachusetts towards this region. As early as 1631, Governor Winthrop in his journal, speaks of going up Charles River, with some company, about eight miles above Watertown, and upon " A very high rock, where they might see a very high hill, due west about forty miles."

The first time the foot of civilized man trod any part of the soil of Worcester County, was in 1635, when an expedition crossed to the Connecticut. The first settlement in the county was at Lancaster, and began in 1643. In 1681 Mr. Stoughton and Joseph Dudley were appointed by the General Court to negotiate with the Nipmucks for their territory. The next year they reported that they had "Purchased of Black James, one tract for thirty pounds and a cart, and for fifty pounds, another tract, fifty miles long and twenty wide." This embraced the southern portion of the county, but they say, "The northern part towards Wachusett is still unpurchased, and persons yet scarcely to be found meet to be treated with thereabouts." Four years later, five Indians were found who claimed to be the owners and lords of this northern section. Their names were: Puagastion, Pompamamay, Qualipunit, Sassawannow and Wananapan. On the 22d of December, 1686, they deeded to Henry Willard, Joseph Rowlandson, Joseph Foster, Benjamin Willard and Cyprian Stevens, "A certain tract of land, meadows, swamps, timbers, etervils, containing twelve miles square," for twenty-three pounds. This seems to be a higher price than was paid for other lands four years before, though this was only a little more than one mill per acre. The general name given to the tract was "Naquag," and its boundaries were very indefinite— "Running along upon Great Wachusett," and the south corner "Butting on Muscopauge Pond." This deed, with the names of the above mentioned Indians attached to it, was entered for record April 14, 1714, and recorded in the Registry of Deeds for Middlesex County, vol. 16, p. 511, Worcester County not being incorporated till 1731. This purchase was undoubtedly made to keep the natives quiet, rather than in recognition of their right to convey the land. It is evident that the purchasers did not regard their deed as very valuable, for twenty-six years after it was given, and before they had taken the trouble to have it recorded, the sons and grandsons of Simon Willard of Lancaster, and other heirs of the original purchasers, petitioned the General Court for the confirmation of their title, which was granted February 23, 1713, on condition that within seven years sixty families be settled thereon, with a sufficient quantity of land reserved for the gospel ministry and for schools, excepting one thousand acres previously conveyed to Hon. Samuel

Sewall. Provided, also, that the grant should not encroach on any former grants, nor exceed twelve miles square. The town to be called Rutland, and to lie in the county of Middlesex. These provisions are similar to those made in reference to other townships. Our ancestors did not appear to regard it of any importance that settlements should be made, unless the institutions of the gospel and the means of education were also established. These were the first things they sought to secure, by laying the foundations in the very beginning of things. Even while the whole county was an unbroken wilderness, they made wise provision for the future, by stipulating the condition that a portion of the lands should be set apart for public uses, whenever settlements should be made. To this far-seeing policy we are indebted, in a great degree, for the present position and usefulness of the old Bay State.

Original Surveys and Assignments.—This tract of land was surveyed in 1715, by William Ward, and bounded as follows: " On Leicester, north 83 degrees west, seven and a half miles. On New Braintree farms and the country, north 41 degrees west, eleven miles. On the country, north 60 degrees east, thirteen miles; and on the country, south 39 degrees east, eleven miles, and by the line of Worcester about eight miles." It contained 93.160 acres, including what is now Rutland, Oakham, Barre, Hubbardston, a portion of Paxton and more than half of Princeton.

In December, 1715, the proprietors, who now numbered thirty-three, voted, " To survey and set off into lots, the contents of six miles square, to be granted to settlers, in order to secure the performance of the conditions in the original confirmation of the title." They then laid out sixty-two house lots of thirty acres each, which they offered to permanent settlers, with the promise that the remainder of the land should be divided among them, in case sixty families were settled there within the prescribed seven years. This was the case, and thus the proprietors gave up all their right to one-fourth of the original purchase, to encourage settlements. This fourth is now Rutland and part of Paxton. The remaining three-fourths were held in common, and managed according to the laws relating to proprietors, till 1749, when the northwest corner was incorporated into a separate district, taking the name of Rutland District, now the town of Barre. This is also six miles square, a favorite size and form, when these towns were laid out. What is now Oakham, was the West Wing, and the west part of Princeton, was the East Wing. What is now Hubbardston, bore the name of the Northeast Quarter. In 1737, the proprietors, in order to divide this Northeast Quarter among themselves, decided to lay out sixty-eight house lots of one hundred acres each, and thirty-three great farms of five hundred acres each, which would give one great farm and two house lots to each share, besides the reserved lands. House lots in those days, had quite a different meaning from the little, seven-by-nine patches, on the side of some narrow lane, called such, at the present day.

Abner Lee and Samuel Willard, Jr., made the survey. They laid out the house lots that year, and numbered them from one to sixty-eight, and one lot of seven acres and another of sixty. A plan of the whole was made out for the proprietors, who, before they proceeded to a division, ordered, " That lot No. 21 be assigned to the first learned and orthodox minister who shall be ordained and settled in the ministry, provided he shall continue seven years, or until the day of his death; to said minister, his heirs and assigns forever." This lot lay at the centre of the town, embracing what is now the common, the old cemetery, and the lots on which the buildings stand for a considerable distance around.

They also ordered that lot No. 30 be set apart and remain unalienated for the use of schools in town. The lot of sixty acres was given to Eleazer Brown, then living thereon, on condition " That he, or his heirs, dwell and keep a house thereon for the entertainment of travellers, for the space of seven years." This lot was the farm afterwards owned by Thomas Temple, and was the place of the first settlement in town. This first-

class hotel probably stood where W. E. Hammond now lives.
The seven acre lot, situated on the hill northeast of the old
burial ground, was granted for a meeting-house and common.
The reason why it was not used for that purpose will appear
hereafter.* These preliminaries having been settled, the division of house lots was made by drawing lots.

Early the next year the great farms were laid out, and finding that there was still a surplus of land, they ordered "That a
farm of 150 acres of the very choicest and best land remaining,
be given to the first minister, on the same conditions as before
mentioned." This lot was located on the south side of Comet
Pond, and contained very large measure. In all the old surveys, both of townships and farms, large allowance was made
for "sag of chain." As we have already seen, the township
over-ran its nominal amount of land by nearly 3,000 acres, and
the farms were surveyed on about the same scale. The
remainder of the land was divided into twelve small farms of
from fifty to ninety acres each, to be distributed, as the records
say, "to qualify the greater farms," which probably means to
equalize the shares in value. In this survey they also reserved
two strips of land, six rods wide, between the tiers of farms,
the whole length of the town one way, besides some shorter
pieces the other way, for roads. This land has since been
incorporated into the adjoining farms.

In June, 1738, when the final division of land was made, one
small farm of fifty-seven acres, was granted to Rev. Thomas
Prince, in consideration of great services performed for the
proprietors, and another of seventy acres, to Adam Winthrop,
for a similar reason. What these services were, does not appear
fully in the records, though Mr. Winthrop was for many years
moderator of the proprietors. Mr. Prince was the distinguished divine, for forty years pastor of the Old South Church,
Boston. By inheritance, he became the largest proprietor,
having for his share more than 3,000 acres, which was located

---

*See Chapter XI.

in the East Wing of Rutland. Governor Gill married a daughter of Mr. Prince, and probably caused the tract afterward to take the name of his distinguished father-in-law. Hence the name of Princeton. Most of the business of the proprietors was done in Boston, and Mr. Prince seems to have taken a great interest in the survey and settlement of this region, and did much towards procuring plans and giving intelligence in regard to it. After these grants were made, the ten other small farms were counted with the great farms, to make them as nearly equal in value as possible, and then the proprietors drew lots for their shares. At this division, such had been the changes in the twenty-five years since the confirmation of their title, that only two of the thirty-three original owners, remained to claim their shares, and only four others were claimed by the heirs of the original proprietors.

Thus the land passed out of the hands of the proprietors, as such, into the possession of individuals, though their organization was continued till 1770. Active measures were taken to encourage the settlement of what is now the town of Barre. Several grants of land were made on condition that houses should be erected upon them. Large appropriations were made to build a bridge over Ware River, " To clear out the road to Nichewaug," and to provide preaching. It does not appear that they ever made any special efforts, as proprietors, for the settlement of this Northeast Quarter, yet the course they pursued with their purchase as a whole, shows that they were men of large views and liberal policy. Their records show that they were educated and systematic business men. Not one of them ever settled here, yet their influence lives after them. They probably looked carefully after their own interests, but the policy they pursued in regard to these wild lands, has greatly affected the prosperity and welfare of all these towns. The same policy which led them to give away one-fourth of their land to actual settlers and make liberal outlays for other portions, was doubtless intended to apply to this part also. They foresaw that if the southerly and westerly portions were

3

settled, the tide of civilization, in the very nature of things, would soon flow over this tract. If personal interest prompted them in what they did, we should suppose they would have reserved the very choicest corner to the last, giving away the land least likely to be settled. However this may have been, the size and shape in which the town was laid out, with the reservation of land for schools, roads, parsonage and common, show that they intended and expected this to become as important a town as any of the others.

Settlement.—The old Romans, to conceal the meanness of their origin, claimed descent from the gods, and gloried in the brilliancy of their fabulous history. We claim no such high origin. Our ancestors were neither divinities nor very remarkable men, though we believe they were brave, honest and true. And we shall resort to no fiction in describing them, though we are not able to learn very much about many of them. Even their graves are unknown.

As before stated, Eleazer Brown was the first settler. He came here from Rutland, bringing his family, in 1737, and till the time of his death in 1746, was the only settler. He located on the farm of sixty acres given him by the proprietors on the condition already mentioned. We infer, from several circumstances, that this grant was made more for their own accommodation, than to encourage settlement. Of Mr. Brown we know but little, except that his business was to keep a hotel. For a man to move out here into a wilderness, inhabited only by deer, bears and wolves, with no roads but the path before described, and erect his log hut, six or seven miles from any human habitation, for the purpose of keeping a house of entertainment, would seem almost like Robinson Crusoe's keeping tavern on Juan Fernandez, with his man Friday for hostler. But when we reflect that this was the time when parties of men were surveying the country, and many were looking it over with reference to purchase or settlement; that forests abounding with game, and ponds with fish were attractive to sportsmen; and also remember that the valley of the Connecticut was regarded as the great west by those living east of us; and that the path which ran near Mr. Brown's house may have been the great thoroughfare for the conveyance of cider to the new settlements; we may suppose that his house had as many guests as some houses of larger pretensions. It seems he was faithful in his business, and exhibited true benevolence, for in the proprietors' records of June 1743, we find the following minute :—

"Whereas Eleazer Brown, for securing travellers from being lost in storms, was settled in the N. E. Quarter of Rutland, and has dwelt there for six years past, and has undergone considerable difficulty in so doing, therefore, voted, that for the encouragement of said Brown, Mr. John Caldwell be desired to purchase a good milch-cow for the use of said Brown, and notify said Brown thereof, and that he shall be paid therefor out of the proprietors' stock." In September of the same year, the record adds: "Mr. Caldwell informs that he is ready to deliver Mrs. Brown either of his own cows which she may choose, for sixteen pounds (old tenor,) pursuant to the vote passed at our last meeting." This shows human nature to have been the same among the early settlers as in some of their descendants. Mr. Caldwell improved the opportunity to make a good sale of one of his own cows, and Mrs. Brown appears as chief manager of the firm of Brown & Co., Innholders.

From all we can gather, we judge that Mrs. Brown was well fitted for her pioneer life —hardy, resolute and masculine in character. Mr. Read in his History of Rutland says: "Mrs. Brown had the resolution and fortitude to remain in the settlement for several years after her husband's death, before there was any other inhabitant, and for a number of years it was called 'Widow Brown's Farm.' Mr. Brown used to take cattle from the lower towns in the summer season, let them run in the woods, yard and salt them. After his death, Mrs. Brown would take her gun, mount her horse, and ride along the cattle paths, if necessary pass over Ware River to Rutland, and by the sound of a conch-shell, call the cattle together." We have no account of there being children or any other person in her family, and

infer that for several years she was sole inhabitant of the town.
How she displayed herself as polite landlady, will be best told
in the substance of a story which comes to us by tradition.   She
sometimes had distinguished guests from Boston, and on one
occasion, when several such gentlemen came to dine with her,
she prepared the best dinner in her power.   She was both cook
and table waiter.   They ate pudding first—which was the fashion till within sixty years—and one of them, more fastidious
than the rest, wanted a clean plate for his meat.   As she could
not furnish another, she quickly took his aside, washed it, and
returned it dripping to its place.   Observing that he was not
quite suited, she reached over his shoulder, took it again, wiped
it with the bottom of her short-gown and returned it once more.
Not having seen this operation, her guest now relished his dinner, and those on the other side of the table who did see it, did
not describe the dish-towel till dinner was over.   If we are
shocked by such rudeness, we must not forget that she was the
smartest, the handsomest and the most accomplished lady in
town, the very *élite* of the place.   And we are not sure but she
possessed those elements of true politeness, that with the oppor-
tunities and the culture of modern ladies, would have made her
their equal.   It was her evident purpose to fulfil faithfully the
conditions on which the grant of land was made ;   and this she
did to the evident satisfaction of the proprietors, for in December, 1749, they declared that these conditions had been fully
complied with, and confirmed the title of the land to the heirs
of said Brown and their assigns forever.

It has always been said that Mr. Brown was killed by a deer,
but all that is known about it is, that on the 25th of November,
1746, he left his home to hunt in the woods.   As he did not
return, search was made for him, and on the 17th of January,
fifty-three days after he left home, his dead body was found
about three miles from home, near the Barre line.   His gun
stood by the side of a tree, and a large buck lay dead by his
side.   All else is conjecture.   Of the death of Mrs. Brown
there is no record.   No stone marks her resting place.   The last

mention of her is in the proprietors' records of December, 1749.

Whether the town was left without an inhabitant after her departure or decease, we do not know, but there is no evidence that any one else came to live here before 1749. Probably one thing that prevented settlers from occupying these farms sooner, was the fear of the Indians, who often disturbed the people of Rutland, and other places near. As late as 1725, Capt. Brintnall was ordered to surround and protect with his company, the meadows in Rutland, while the farmers gathered their hay. Then as Barre and some of the other adjoining towns were previously settled, those who came from a distance would naturally locate where they would have nearer neighbors.

Molly Green, daughter of Israel Green, has always been reported to be the first child born in town. She died in 1826, supposed to be seventy-seven years old. If so, Mr. Green must have settled here as early as 1749. He lived on great farm No. 26, near the present residence of Luke Waite, and remained in town about twenty years. He was elected chairman of the first board of selectmen and assessors, and as long as he remained in town, held several other offices. In 1770, he moved to Winchendon, that part of it now within the limits of Gardner. His four sons, who served in the Revolutionary War, were probably born here. His daughter, Susannah, became the second wife of Josiah Baldwin, another early settler who moved from this town to Gardner. Many of their descendants are now living in Gardner. Before his death, Mr. Green moved to Westminster. The daughter, Molly, became enfeebled in body and in mind, and returned after an absence of about twenty years, to be supported by the town, coming, probably, from Westminster, as we find in the accounts of the selectmen of that time, a charge "for going to Westminster to get Molly Green."

Early in the settlement of the town, Charles Parmenter, Joseph Rist and Joseph Eveleth, resided here, but they came more for the purpose of hunting, than for clearing the land. Joseph Eveleth was the first one who united with the church after its formation, and was one of the first deacons.

In 1761, Joseph Grimes and four sons, one of whom was the noted Ephraim Grimes, came from Tewksbury.* In 1762, Stephen Heald came from Rutland. In 1764, Benjamin Hoyt built a large barn on the place now occupied by Mr. Lanphear. During the year 1766, several families came from Marlboro', Holden and Leicester and began settlements in different parts of the town. These latter came with a determination to make this place their home. They cleared land, erected permanent dwellings, and began to give attention to the formation of society and the building up of a town. Now things begin to take positive shape and character.

---

*See Genealogy.

CHAPTER III.

PREVIOUS to 1766, several efforts had been made to obtain a charter as a separate district, with the powers and privileges of a town, except in uniting with Rutland in the choice of a Representative to the General Court. About the only difference between towns and districts, as they were then incorporated, was in this matter of representation. But the families here were so few, their request had not been granted. After the accessions mentioned at the close of the last chapter, they renewed their petition with confidence and zeal, till their object was gained. The following is a copy of the petition taken from the state archives in Boston.

Petition of the Inhabitants of the N. E. Quarter of the Township of Rutland, in the County of Worcester.   Humbly Showeth :

That the said N. E. Quarter of Rutland, being of the contents of six miles square (of land capable of making a very good town,) and the inhabitants being incapable of transacting any affairs for promoting or forwarding the settlement of the township, as they are neither proprietary, district, nor parish ; that they have no roads laid out in said Quarter, neither are they able, under their present circumstances, to lay out any, or to raise money for repairing them ; that they are at a great distance from the public worship of God, and the greater part of the year are unable to travel so far, there being no roads for us to travel in ;—these and many other difficulties which might be mentioned, is a means of discouraging people from coming to settle among them.

They therefore pray your Excellency and Honors to take their case into your wise consideration, and be pleased to incorporate the said Northeast Quarter of Rutland into a town or district, as your Excellency or Hon⁵ shall see meet, and also grant a tax of one penny per acre upon all the non-resident proprietors' lands, in said Northeast Quarter, for three years, to enable the inhabitants to repair roads, and to assist them in settling the gospel among them ; or otherwise relieve the said inhabitants as your Excellency and Hon⁵ shall think proper, and as in duty bound shall pray.

JOHN MURRAY,
In behalf of the Inhabitants.

Dated, January 28, 1767.

This petition was read in the House of Representatives, February 16, 1767, and it was ordered, "That the petitioners notify the non-resident proprietors of the Northeast Quarter of Rutland, of this petition, by inserting the substance of it in one or more of the Boston newspapers, three weeks successively, that they may appear and show cause, if any they have, on the second Wednesday of the next sitting of the General Court, why the prayer thereof should not be granted."

June 5, 1767, it was read again in council. "And it appearing that the petitioners and the non-resident proprietors have come to an agreement that there shall be a tax of one penny per acre, laid upon all lands of the non-resident proprietors, lying in the Northeast Quarter of Rutland, for one year only, to enable the inhabitants to make and repair roads, Ordered, That the tax of one penny per acre be laid on these lands accordingly, and that the petitioners have liberty to bring in a bill to incorporate the said Quarter into a District."

Copy of the Act of Incorporation, taken from the town records, *verbatim et literatim et punctatim:*—

ANNO REGNI REGIS GEORGII TERTII SEPTIMO.

An Act for Incorporating the north East Quarter of the Township of Rutland, in the County of Worcester into a District By the Name of Hubbardston.

Whereas the Inhabitants of the north-east Quarter of the Township of Rutland in the county of Worcester Labour under Many and great Difficulties By Reason of their not Being Erected into a Distinct nad Separate District, wherefore

Be it Enacted By the Governor, Council and the House of Representatives, that the Said north-east Quarter of Rutland as hereafter Described viz.

Bounded Southerly on the town of Rutland, Easterly on Princetown, Northerly on Templeton, and Westerly on Rutland District, Be, and is hereby Incorporated into a District By the name of Hubbardston, and that the Said District .Be, and hereby is Invested with all the powers privileges and Immunities that towns in this Province By Law Do or May Enjoy, that of Sending a Representative To the General Court only Excepted and that the Inhabitants of Said District Shall have Liberty from time to time to join with the Town of Rutland in Chusing a Representative and Shall Be Notified By the Selectmen of Said Town of Rutland of the time and place of Election By Giving Seasonable notice to the Clerk of Said District for the time Being of the time and place of the Said Meeting to the end that the Said District may join them therein, and the Clerk of Said District Shall Set up in Some public place in Said District a Notification thereof accordingly, which Representative may Be Chosen Indifferently from Said Town or District, the pay and allowance of Such Representative to be Borne By Said Town and District in proportion as they Shall from time to time pay to the province Tax.

Provided, Nevertheless and be it further Enacted, that the Said District Shall pay their proportion of all Town, County and province Taxes, already Set on, or Granted to Be Raised By the Town of Rutland in Like Manner as if this act had not Been Made.

And Be it further Enacted, that there Be Laid a Tax of one penny per acre upon all the Lands Lying in Said District for one year only to Enable the Inhabitants of Said District to Make and Repair Roads.

And Be it further Enacted, that John Murray Esqr of Said Rutland Be, and hereby is Directed and impowered to issue his warrant Directed to some principal Inhabitant within Said District Requiring him to warn the Inhabitants of Said District qualified to vote in towns affairs to assemble at Some Suitable time and place in Said District to chuse all Such officers as are necessary to Manage the affairs of Said District.

And Be it further Enacted that the Town Clerk of the town of Rutland Before the first Meeting of the Said District of Hubbardston Shall Deliver to Said John Murray Esqr Copies of the Last List of Valuations of the Real and personal Estates of the Inhabitants of said District of Hubbardston in order to Determine the qualifications of Voters at Said

4

Meeting, and that the Inhabitants who Shall appear by Said Lists to be Voters according to Law Shall Be allowed to vote.

1767, June 12th Passed By the Representatives to Be Enacted.

June 12th Passed By the Council to Be Enacted.

June 13th Signed By the Governor.

Exam'd A. OLIVER *Sec'y*.

In accordance with the above act, John Murray, Esq., issued his warrant June 25, 1767, directed to Edward Rice, a principal inhabitant of the District, for a meeting for the choice of all necessary officers. This meeting was held on the 3d day of July following, at the house of Edward Rice, who lived near the place where W. E. Hammond now lives. The following list of officers was chosen :—

JOHN MURRAY, *Moderator*.

ISRAEL GREEN, ⎫ *Selectmen*
BENJ. NURSE, ⎬ *and*
BENJ. HOYT, ⎭ *Assessors*.

NATHANIEL UPHAM, ⎫ *Surveyors*
STEPHEN HEALD, ⎬ *of*
WILLIAM PAIN, ⎭ *Highways*.

DAVID SLARROW, ⎫ *Fence*
EBENEZER BOYNTON, ⎬ *Viewers*.
ROBERT CONVERSE, ⎭

JOHN LEBOURVEAU, *Clerk*.

EZEKIEL NEWTON, *Treasurer*.
JOSEPH GRIMES, *Constable*.
NATHANIEL UPHAM, *Warden*.

EPHRAIM RICE,
Tithing-man.

JOSEPH GRIMES,
Scaler of Boards and Shingles.

DAVID SLARROW, *Scaler of Weights and Measures*.

ROBERT CONVERSE, *Field Driver*. WILLIAM FOLLETT, ⎫ *Deer*
TIMOTHY NEWTON, *Hog Reeve*. ADAM WHEELER, ⎬ *Reeves*.

No other business was done at this meeting, though the selectmen issued a warrant the same day, for another to be held on the 15th of the same month, and several others were held before the year closed. Thus the District machinery was put in running order, and they could manage their own affairs.

This place was never incorporated as a town, but became such by a general act of the Legislature, passed March 23, 1786, by which all places incorporated as districts before January 1, 1777, were declared "to be towns to every intent and purpose whatever."

It does not appear that the people ever suggested a name for the place, and it was probably fixed by the House of Representatives, suggested, perhaps, by some interested individuals. It was given in honor of Hon. Thomas Hubbard, one of the proprietors. He was for many years a prominent man in Boston. Several years he was Speaker of the House of Representatives, and for seventeen years treasurer of Harvard College. As his name appears among the proprietors of some of the neighboring towns, and as treasurer of the proprietors of Royalston, we judge that he was an extensive landholder.

Tradition says that in view of the honor of giving his name to the town, he promised to give the glass for the first meetinghouse; and to make his liberality more conspicuous, the people planned for an extra number of windows. But he died in 1773, and his estate was so much involved that they received nothing, and were obliged to glaze their windows at their own expense.

Growth. — During the year 1771-2-3, Isaac Bellows from Rutland, John Woods from Marlboro' and William Muzzy from Lexington, came into the place, each bringing a large family. They were men of good education and general intelligence, and possessed those qualities which fitted them to become leading citizens. They did much towards forming the character of the town.

After its organization, the town rapidly increased in population, wealth and influence. The 150 people of 1767, had increased in 1776—the time of taking the first colonial census, after the incorporation—to 488; and in 1790, the date of the first United States census, to 933; in 1800, to 1113. This was a greater per cent. of increase than in any other town in the county.

FAMILIES IN TOWN BEFORE 1800.

So far as known, the families who were here before 1800, came from the following places at, or before, the given date; *m.* indicates marriage in the year named.

Elijah Adams, Medway,	1774
Issachar, bro. of Elijah, "	1778
Reuben, " " "	1786
Philemon Adams,	1780
Ralph Adams,	1780
Simeon Allen,	1776
Ephraim Allen, Rutland,	1788
John Ames, "	1769
Jonathan, son of John, m.	1795
Thomas Atwood,	1783
Isaac Balcom,	1795
Josiah Baldwin,	1768
Andrew Barber,	1777
Samuel Bartlett,	1795
Isaac Bellows, Rutland,	1772
Amasa, son of Isaac, m,	1790
Asaph, " " "	1796
David Bennett, Princeton,	1789
Abner Benson,	1790
Hugh Blair,	1773
Elijah Boyden,	1775
David Boynton,	1767
Ebenezer Boynton,	1767
Caleb Boynton,	1774
Isaac Bridges,	1773
Hosea Brigham,	1782
Asa Brigham,	1791
Samuel Britton,	1774
Eleazer Brown, Rutland,	1737
Ebenezer Brown, Sutton,	1788
Oliver, son of Ebenezer, m.	1798
Asa Brown, Rutland,	1787
John Browning, "	1785
Jesse Burditt, Marlboro',	1775
Thomas Caryl,	1773
Jonathan Caryl,	1773
Joseph Caryl,	1773
Stephen Church, Rutland,	1774
Asa, bro. of Stephen, "	1776
Ephraim, bro. of Stephen, "	1782

Reuben Clapp,	1791
John Clark, Hopkinton,	1774
John, son of John, "	1774
William, " " m,	1776
Moses, " " "	1778
Isaac, " " "	1784
Joseph, " " "	1784
Ezra, " " "	1790
Luther, son of John Jr. "	1791
John, " " " "	1798
Oliver, " " " "	1798
Ephraim, bro. of John, Hopkinton,	1782
Samuel, bro. of John, Hopkinton,	1796
Ely Clark, Barre,	1770
Benjamin Clark,	1782
Anthony Clark, Rutland,	1768
Peter, son of Anthony, m.	1788
Amos, " " "	1789
Jonathan Clifford, Southboro',	1778
Robert Converse,	1767
Abraham Cutting,	1795
Israel Davis, Holden,	1793
Asahel Davis,	1776
Asahel Davis, m.	1792
Bela Davis,	1777
David Davis,	1790
Oliver Davis,	1781
Benjamin Davis, Holden,	1798
Joel Earle, Leicester,	1783
Joseph Eveleth, Princeton,	1770
David, son of Joseph, m.	1790
Oliver Fairbanks,	1777
John H. Falis, Germany,	1785
Stephen Farrington,	1773
Elijah Farrington,	1773
William Follett, Attleboro,	1766
Samuel Follett, "	1775
Stephen Frost, Rutland,	1794

Daniel Gage,	1778	Daniel Howe, (d. 1810)	1799
Jonathan Gates, Rutland,	1770	Benjamin Hoyt, Rutland,	1767
Henry Gates, Framingham,	1787	Francis, son of Benjamin, Rut-	
Benjamin Gates,	1793	land, m.	1774
Abner Gay, Dedham,	1797	Asa, son of Benjamin, Rut-	
Bezaleel Gleason,	1790	land, m.	1776
Thomas Gleason,	1793	Alexander Hunting, Marlboro,	1795
Clark Gleason,	1797	Stephen Hunting, Needham,	1779
Seth Gleason,	1787	William, son of Stephen, " m.	1779
Peter Goodnough,	1773	Stephen, " " " "	1790
Isaac Goodspeed, Barnstable,	1782	Converse," " "	1788
Isaac, son of Isaac, " m.	1782	Moses, " " " m.	1792
Luther, " " " "	1794	John Jones,	1778
Heman, " " " "	1793	Silas Jones,	1788
Elijah, " " " "	1793	Ebenezer Joslin, Marlboro,	1770
Israel Green,	1749	William, son of Ebenezer, m.	1797
Joseph Green, Lexington,	1773	Silas, " " "	1789
Abijah Greenwood, Holden,	1770	Daniel Kinsman,	1770
Moses, bro. of Abijah, "	1770	Samuel, son of Daniel, m.	1793
Levi, " " "	1770	James Lamb, Spencer,	1796
Joseph Grimes, Tewksbury,	1761	James Lake,	1790
Bill, son of Joseph, " m.	1767	John LeBourveau,	1767
Joseph, son of Joseph, Tewks-		Joseph Lovewell, Needham,	1798
bury, m.	1771	Bezaleel Lyon, Barre,	1771
Ephraim, son of Joseph, Tewks-		Asa, son of Bezaleel, m.	1799
bury, m.	1791	Ebenezer Mann, Wrentham,	1777
Calvin Hale, Leominster,	1788	William Marean, Barre,	1768
Luther Hale, "	1788	Timothy P., son of William, m.	1797
Thomas Hapgood, Shrewsbury,		Paul Matthews,	1787
Vt.	1795	John W. McClenathan, Rutland,	1774
Caleb Harrington,	1771	Israel Mead,	1768
Abel Harrington,	1782	John Mead,	1768
Ephraim Harrington,	1789	Levi Mead,	1768
Stephen Heald, Rutland,	1762	David Merriam, Westminster,	1782
Timothy, son of Stephen, m.	1785	Asa Metcalf, Wrentham,	1768
Howard Hinds, Barre, m.	1778	George Metcalf, "	1768
Cornelius, bro. of Howard,		Phineas G. Miller,	1790
Barre,	1789	Paul Mirick,	1790
Eli, son of Cornelius, m.	1789	John Morse,	1768
Nathan Holden,	1781	Samuel Morse, Medfield,	1782
Ephraim Holt, Holden,	1797	Samuel, son of Samuel, m.	1785
Jonathan How,	1771	William, " " "	1791
Daniel How, (d. 1776)	1775	Alpheus Morse, Marlboro,	1775
Israel How, Sudbury,	1770	Robert Murdock, Newton,	1776
Buckley, bro. of Israel, Sud-		Abiel, bro. of Robert, Brookfield,	1791
bury,	1770	Joshua Murdock, Newton,	1790
Micah Howe, Rutland,	1781	William Muzzy, Lexington,	1773

Timothy Newton, Shrewsbury,	1766
Joel, son of Timothy, m.	1793
Timothy, " " "	1799
Jonas Newton,	1785
Josiah Newton,	1797
John E. Newton,	1789
Joseph Newton, Northboro,	1777
Ebenezer, son of Joseph, m.	1798
Jonathan Nichols, Athens, Vt.,	1780
William Nightingale,	1771
William, son of William, m.	1788
Nehemiah Parker,	1768
Thomas H., son of Nehemiah, m.	1799
Hollis Parker,	1774
Levi Parker,	1786
Amos Parker, Shrewsbury.	1781
Daniel Parkhurst,	1782
Charles Parmenter, Rutland.	1767
Levi, son of Charles, m.	1792
Joseph Parmenter,	1774
Thomas Peirce,	1778
Moses H., son of Thomas, m.	1792
Eliab Pierce, Chester. m.	1789
John Phelps, Rutland.	—
Moses, son of John, "	1776
Joshua Phillips, Smithfield, R. I.	1764
James, son of Joshua, Smithfield, R. I., m.	1767
Richard, son of Joshua, Smithfield, R. I., m.	1779
Gideon, son of Joshua. Smithfield, R. I., m.	1786
Joel Pollard, Rutland.	1770
Ezra Pond, Wrentham.	1768
Levi, son of Ezra, m.	1785
Joseph, " " "	1778
James Potter, Holden,	1787
Josiah Procter.	1778
Edward Rice, Rutland,	1767
Ephraim Rice, Holden,	1766
Silas Rice, "	1775
Ebenezer Rice, "	1784
Edmond Rice, Marlboro,	1782
Abel Rice, Barre,	1791
Job Richardson,	1788
Solomon Rolph, Princeton.	1782

Thomas Sargent, Leicester,	1773
Samuel, son of Thomas, "	1774
John. " " " m.	1776
Ebenezer," " " "	1785
John, son of John, m.	1797
Edward Selfridge, Rutland,	1788
Joseph Shattuck.	1772
David Slarrow, Rutland,	1767
Samuel Slocomb, Medway,	1779
James, son of Samuel, m.	1786
Peleg. " " "	1797
John Smith,	1774
Jonathan W. Smith, Boylston,	1782
Elisha Snell,	1779
Samuel Spring, Newton,	1785
John Spring,	1790
Nathan Stone, Rutland,	1768
Jeduthan, son of Nathan, m.	1790
William Stone, Watertown,	1774
Ebenezer Stowe, Concord,	1796
Joseph Tabor,	1799
Joseph Tame.	1785
Abel Tenney, Northboro',	1778
James Thompson, Holden.	1773
Samuel Thompson, "	1791
Timothy Underwood, Holliston.	1771
Israel Underwood, Princeton,	1770
Nathaniel Upham, Leicester,	1776
Calvin, son of Nathaniel, m.	1797
Nathaniel Waite, Leicester,	1766
Nathaniel, son of Nathaniel, m.	1792
Jacob. " " "	1797
Joseph Waite, Marlboro,	1782
Benjamin Warren,	1774
Ebenezer Warren, Rutland,	1781
Luke Warren, Northboro',	1798
Adam Wheeler, Rutland,	1766
Silas, son of Adam, m.	1786
Asa, " " "	1791
Stephen Wheelock,	1781
John Whipple,	1781
Isaac Whittemore, N. H.	1797
Oliver Wight,	1793
Joshua Willard, Winchendon,	1785
John Williams, Lancaster,	1783
Jude, bro. of John, "	1783

David Winch,	1770	Edward, son of John, m.	1795
Zenas Winslow,	1793	Elisha Woodward, Newton,	1774
Oliver Witt, Paxton,	1787	Daniel Woodward, "	1776
Daniel, son of Oliver, Paxton,	1788	Philemon Woodward, "	1776
Oliver, " " "	——	Joseph Wright, Woburn,	1773
John Woods, Marlboro'.	1771		

CHAPTER IV.

CIRCUMSTANCES AND CUSTOMS OF THE SETTLERS.

IT may be interesting to pause in our annals and take a look at the old town, as it was in the beginning of its corporate life, that we may realize more fully the changes which have since occurred.

We should like to look into the homes of these early settlers, and see what household conveniences they had; how they dressed and how they lived. We should like to look at them at their daily toil, to see what they were doing and what tools they used. We should like to know where they all lived; how far from neighbors; and when they went abroad, what roads they had to travel; what conveyances they used, and how they appeared "in society." But with all the *data* available, it is possible to reproduce only faint outlines of the picture.

So far as can now be ascertained, there were at that time about thirty families, and 150 people in town. We do not know whence they all came, on what farms they all settled, nor how much land was then cleared; but we know they were scattered in all parts of the town. For obvious reasons, the hills were settled first; then paths were made from one settlement to another, or to the centre of the town, for traveling on horseback. There was, then no road through town, and no public travel; no bridges over the streams, no mills, no stores, no post office, no meeting-house, no schoolhouse. Where our beautiful village now stands, were only a few rude dwellings, which have all passed away. A dense forest covered these streets. There is but one building in town that was erected before the incorporation — the house where Charles Hinds afterward lived, now occupied by George E. Morse.

NORTH MAIN STREET

The people of that day were strangers to many of the comforts and luxuries which are now enjoyed. Their dwellings, many of them, were cabins, without glass or paint, and ill-fitted to exclude the cold. Had it not been for the roaring fires kept up by the huge logs that could not be burned fast enough, their inmates must have suffered. Friction matches were unknown. They depended upon keeping the fire constantly alive upon the hearth. Sometimes, however, they would lose it, and then they must either go to a neighbor's for " seed-fire," or resort to the tinder box, flint and steel. The old flint-lock " Queen's-arm," was sometimes used in this service. Tow, or some other light substance, was ignited by " flushing " powder upon it, and thus the fire of a cold winter's morning was started.

" Those fire-places were so immense as to allow a path to the oven on one side, and on the other would be a wooden bench or ' settle,' on which, in cold winter evenings, sat a row of buxom boys and girls, eking out a perhaps scanty supper of bean-porridge, by parching corn, and roasting potatoes or chestnuts in the embers. Their farming utensils were clumsy, and many of them would seem to us intolerable. Their clothing was home-spun and coarse, yet durable. The men wore tow shirts, striped woolen frocks, and leather aprons. The best suit, of home-made woolen, was for Sundays, funerals and special occasions, and lasted many years, as little attention was paid to the changes of fashion. Great-coats and boots were rare. In winter, the men wore shoes, excluding the snow by woolen leggins fastened over the mouth of the shoe by a leather or tow string. Neither men nor women wore shoes in summer. On Sundays, the women and girls, to save the wear, sometimes carried them in their hands, walking barefoot, or perhaps wearing an old pair, till they came near the meeting-house, where they would stop and put on their ' meeting shoes' of coarse, thick leather."*

Customs differ. The orientals, to this day, on entering sacred places, take off their shoes and leave them in rows outside, while they scrupulously keep their heads covered.

---

*Dr. Whiton, History of Winchendon.

The first women of the place, while about their work—which was nearly all the time—were dressed in short gowns, and striped aprons, of coarse material. Calico was too dressy and too expensive to be thought of. All the materials for the dress and bedding of the household were home products. The flax and the wool were raised on the farm and carded, spun and woven, by hand in the house. The brake, the swingling knife, the hatchel, the cards, the wheel, the loom, now known as antiquarian curiosities, were then among the most essential implements of the home. Carpets, sofas and pianos were unknown. The music of their homes was "the æolian cadence of the spinning wheel," the clatter of the loom, and the merry voices of children. Stools and blocks often took the place of the straight-backed "kitchen chairs." Instead of silver in the cupboard, was an array of wooden and pewter plates, and pewter spoons, often made in moulds by their own firesides. Candles were scarce, and oil hardly known. Their lamps were often of the most primitive style—a linen rag placed in a cup, or saucer, of lard, and made to burn over the edge. But more often the light of the home was the blazing pine knot in the great open fire-place of the kitchen, or living-room of the family. Here, many a winter's evening, the men shaved shingles, or peeled brooms, while mother and daughters knit or spun, and the boys of the family read, if anything could be procured to read; or, lying on the floor, gazed into the fire, laying large plans for the future, and building air-castles, to see them disappear in the black smoke. But alas! for those cheerful fire-sides. They are no more. There are few hearthstones now save in poetry. The pine knots are all consumed. Huge, black, iron cells imprison the free blaze of the fire, and shut off the light. We could almost wish the country always new, if we could only retain the cheerful open fire, and plenty of pitch pine, or "pich pain," as it is often spelled in the old records. If some of our youth do not grow up with as large ideas and noble purposes as those of that time, let us remember that they have no place now, as then, where they may muse while the fire burns.   .

The viands of the table were almost exclusively the products of their own land. Few luxuries were bought. Tea and coffee were kept, if at all, only for company. Corn bread, journey (or Johnny) cake, baked beans, bean porridge, fried pork, hasty pudding, potatoes, milk and eggs, were the great staples of living. They employed little foreign labor. If they had any occasion for assistance in making bonnets, clothes, or boots and shoes, the work was all done at home.

In winter, they often rode to meeting on ox sleds. In summer, they walked, or rode on horseback, the man on the saddle with a child on a pillow before him, and his wife on a pillion behind, with another child in her arms. We are led to believe that the snows in those days lay much deeper than since the forests were cleared. Yet they were traversed, without regard to roads, by means of snow-shoes, or "rackets," which were flat, perhaps fifteen inches wide and twenty-five long, and made of strips of wood bent into an elliptical form, and filled in with a net work of leather strings. These were bound to the soles of the shoes, to keep them from sinking into the snow. But how those people used them, without the one interfering with the other, is a mystery to some of their descendants who have tried the experiment.

But that age of home-spun, hard work, and simple fare, was not without its advantages. There was an independence in living within their own resources. They did not have the bother and vexation of servants. They did not depend for very existence upon the butcher, the merchant, the tailor, or the milliner. They were capable of doing for themselves. Their life was enlivened by various social gatherings, trainings, musters, raisings, huskings, quiltings, carding bees, and the like; and so far as known, they seldom had the *blues*, except externally, from the dye-pot in the chimney corner. Living in the free air of heaven, with plenty of work, and the disposition to do it, and free from many of the habits of luxurious living, and the diseases thereby induced, their life was not a sad or gloomy one.

They had few books or papers to read, and thus escaped the

overwhelming floods of literary trash which have drowned the senses of so many of the present generation. They thought for themselves, and were not lacking in sound common sense and practical intelligence. The character of the people in regard to education, morals, and religion, will appear in what will be said upon these separate topics. That they were industrious, and did not squander their time, appears from various items in the records, as well as from tradition. At one time, a town meeting was held at seven o'clock in the morning. At another time, at five in the afternoon, which shows that they meant to do a day's work on their farms besides attending to public business.

Support of the Poor.—There were few then who were not able to provide for themselves. Such persons had not the health or enterprise to engage in pioneer life. The first mention of any one helped by the town was in 1776, when a son of Edward Rice was put out to board for six shillings, six pence per week.

Few but the healthy and hardy were among the first settlers. Others were not encouraged to come, lest they should be burdensome. In fact, much was done to prevent their coming. We find several instances in which the town voted to receive certain individuals as citizens. By this vote the town became liable to their support if they should become paupers. But they took care to receive only persons that were expected never to be in need. It was also the custom for the selectmen to instruct the constable to warn new comers out of the town. They were not always expected or desired to leave, but the law was such that persons thus warned could not gain a settlement. In case they became paupers, they must look for help to the towns from which they came. Through such precautions, the "poor list" was kept very small for many years. Often those who needed help were supplied by the contributions of generous neighbors. The few that were provided for at public expense were boarded in private families, till 1832, when the present town farm was purchased. Here the poor have been well cared for, at large expense.

A few items are inserted here, which do not properly classify elsewhere, that will in some degree illustrate early methods of doing business. The spelling of the records is retained in the extracts which follow :—

1767. "Voted to procure a plain of the town."

"Voted to choose a committee to collect the penny text."

1768. "Voted to allow Benj. Nurs 3s. for making the rats (rates) of the town."

"Voted to pay Adam Wheeler for Bording ye Rev. Nehemiah Parker Four Sabbaths 6s. 8d."

"For bording ye Rev. Nehemiah Parker from April ye 1, 1770 to June ye 13 following 13s. 4d."

Dec. 1775. "Voted to pay Wm. Muzzy for attending Provincial Congress thirteen days and expenses 1£. 5s. 7d." (about fifty cents a day.)

1779. "Voted to choose a committee to prevent monopolizing, agreeably to act of General Court." Which we understand to mean to prevent speculation in the sale of provisions and other necessaries of life, by fixing the prices of those articles. This the towns were authorized to do once in three months, by the act referred to above.

Sept. 30, 1776. One article in the town meeting warrant was, "To see if it be the mind of the town that John Woolson, Esq., should set up a hospital for innoculating the small pox, according to the order of the Court of General Sessions of the peace of the county." "Passed in the negative."

Oct. 12, 1796. "Voted to allow Dr. C. Wilson and Dr. Reuben Walker to innoculate for the small pox."

Mar., 1797. "Voted not to have a pest house."

In 1771, it was discovered that the records of the town had not been legally kept, and the authorities were petitioned, as follows :—

Province of Massachusetts Bay.

To his Excellency Thomas Hutchinson, Esqr Captain General, Governor in chief of the Said Province, and to the Honble his majestys councel and House of Representatives at Cambridge, march, A. D., 1771.

The Petition of the Subscribers in behalf of the Inhabitants of ye District of Hubbardston in ye county of worcester humbly sheweth—that the Said Inhabitants finding themselves in a bad situation of affairs by reason of their Records in ye town Book, being not according to Law for this reason, viz. for a very few of ye Records are signed attested by the moderator as moderator or attested or signed by ye clerks, and a great part of the Roads that are laid out being not Recorded according to Law whith if Said meeting Should be broke up it would be very detrimental to S^d District—Wherefore your Petitioners in behalf of S^d District humbly pray your Excellency and Honors to take the Subject matter of the foregoing Petition under your wise consideration, and order the S^d meetings Shall be established good and Valid or otherwise grant relief as your Excellency and Honors in your known wisdom and goodness shall see meet and your Petitioners in behalf of themselves and Said District in duty bound shall ever pray.

STEPHEN HEALD,   *Selectmen*
JOSEPH EVELETH,   *of*
WILL$^{m.}$ MAREAN.   *Hubbardston.*

CHAPTER V.

THE loyalty and patriotism of the town has never been questioned except in one instance, yet to be related. Through all the bloody struggles of the nation, the people have met their responsibilities with heroic courage, and have borne their part with unflinching resolution. The first settlers came here amidst the exciting scenes of the French and Indian War. Before the charter was obtained, signs of an approaching revolution were too distinct to be mistaken, and the ears of the people here were quick to catch the first notes of alarm. Two years before the incorporation, the famous Stamp Act was passed by Parliament. This roused the indignation of all the American Colonies, so that Franklin wrote to his friend, Charles Thompson, "the sun of American liberty is set; the Americans must light the lamps of industry and economy." "Be assured," was his friend's reply, "we shall light torches of a very different character."

The almost superhuman eloquence of Patrick Henry had sounded the tocsin through the land. The people resisted, or evaded, the Stamp Act and other revenue laws of the mother country, often destroying the articles on which the duty was laid. They would never have refused to pay their share towards supporting the home government, if they had been allowed a voice in levying the taxes, but taxation without representation they regarded as striking at the very foundation of liberty. Their ancestors had fled from the cruel hand of oppression and persecution, and braved the untold hardships of the wilderness for the blessings of civil and religious liberty. Through in-

credible suffering, by their own undaunted industry and perse-
verance, with the divine blessing, they had toiled up to strength
and prosperity, and they determined not to surrender their
priceless heritage.

In 1768, the year following the act of incorporation, Great
Britain sent troops to Boston, to reduce the people to submission. A day of fasting and prayer was appointed, town
meetings were called, and a general convention of delegates
from all parts of the province, was held in Faneuil Hall. After
the troops landed, they were in constant collision with the
populace, which resulted in the Boston Massacre in 1770. The
following quotation will bear repetition : —

" Even the boys of Boston caught the spirit of their sires.
They were wont to amuse themselves, in winter, by building
snow forts and skating on the pond on the common. The
soldiers wantonly interfered with their forts, and when they
complained to the inferior officers, they were treated with contempt and ridicule. At last a number of the larger boys waited
upon Gen. Gage himself, and told him they had come for satisfaction. 'What,' said Gage, 'have your fathers been teaching
you rebellion, and sent you here to exhibit it?' 'Nobody sent
us,' answered the leader with a flashing eye. 'We have never
injured your troops, but they have trampled down our snow
forts, and broken the ice of our skating pond. We complained,
and they called us young rebels, and told us to help ourselves
if we could; we told the captain, and he laughed at us. Yes-
terday, our works were destroyed for the third time, *and we
will bear it no longer!*' The British general could not restrain
his admiration. 'The very children here,' he exclaimed, 'draw
in a love of liberty with the very air they breathe. Go, my
brave boys, and be assured, if my troops trouble you again,
they shall be punished.'"

Those were trying days for a town just out of its cradle, but
one cannot fail to see that the air of these forest hills was
vibrating with liberty. Every pulsation from the heart of the
province was met by patriotic throbbings from this new settle-

ment. Boston was then only a town, but in the autumn of 1772, the selectmen sent out a circular to the other towns in the province, calling for an expression of opinion upon public affairs. In response to this circular, this town called a meeting December 30, and chose a committee of nine, with John Woods, chairman, to draw up an answer to the letter from the town of Boston. They then voted to "adjourn, to meet at the house of John Ames, Innholder, on the 20th of January next." At that meeting, January 20, 1773, the committee made the following report:—

1ly We are of opinion that Rulers first Derive their Power from the Ruled by Certain Laws and Ruls agreed upon by Ruler and Ruled, and when a Ruler Breaks over Such Laws and Rules as agreed to by Ruler and Ruled, and makes new ones that then the Ruled have a Right to Refuse Such new Laws and that the Ruled have a Right to Judge for themselves when Rulers Transgress.

2ly We think the Parliment of Great Britton have Taxed us Contrary to our Charter Right, they have made our governor independent of the people by appointing him a Salary from home, and the Judges of the Superior Court, we hear, have a Salary appointed from home, and have reason to believe it, which appears to us so big with Slavery that we think it enough to arouse Every Individual (that has any Ideas of arbitrary Power above the Brutal Creation) to use his utmost indeavors in a lawfull way to Seek Redress for our Injured Rights and Priveleges.

3ly we think we aught immediately, vigorously, and unanimously, to xert our Selves in the most firm, but most peaceable manner, for obtaining Relief. The Cause of liberty is a cause of too much dignity to be Sullied by Turbulence and Tumult. It ought to be maintained in a manner sutable to her Nature ; those who ingage in it should breathe a Sedate yet Fervent spirit animating us to actions of Justice and Bravery : a free people Cant be too Quick in observing, nor too firm in opposing the beginings of alterations in a Constitution.

Signed,

	JOHN WOODS,	JOSEPH SLARROW,
	GEORGE METCALF,	JOSEPH EVELETH,
Committee Men	EZEKIEL NEWTON,	NATHANIEL UPHAM,
	WILLIAM MAREAN,	EZRA POND,
	STEPHEN HEALD.	

The record continues :—

After being Twice Read the vote was called for and passed in the afermitive.

Voted to put this Draught on the Town Book of Records. Voted the Clerk Transmit a Coppy of the Proceedings of the Destrict of Hubbardston to the Selectmen of the Town of Boston.

Atts.   JOHN WOODS, *District Clerk*.

Atts.   GEORGE METCALF, *Moderator*.

Thus, more than three years before the Declaration of Independence, the people of this town expressed their views of public affairs, in language which, if not the most elegant, shows that they clearly comprehended their situation, and understood the true principles of a republican government. Though they were desirous of peace, there is a boldness and decision in these declarations which indicates the spirit of independence already working in them. Soon after this, the several towns in this county had standing committees of correspondence, safety, and inspection, who often met and consulted, or corresponded, in relation to public affairs. Hubbardston chose such a committee, August 22, 1774, consisting of the following men: William Muzzy, John Woods, Stephen Heald, Joseph Eveleth and John Clark. Two years later, Joseph Shattuck and William Stone were added to this committee. September 23rd, they voted to send John Clark to represent them in a convention to be held at Concord, in the month of October following. At that convention, active preparations were made for the war, which was seen to be inevitable.

At a meeting held December 24th, 1774, the following article was considered. "To see if the District will Chuse one person to represent them in the Provential Congress to set the first of February next at Cambridge, and to be Dissolved the Tuesday before the last Wednesday in May, 1775, and to give him Such Instructions as they Think proper." No action was taken upon it.

The following is the copy of another article, and the action thereon. "Art. 6. To see if the District will Chuse a com^{tte} to Draw up a Covenant for the Inhabitants to sign, in order to put in force the Resolves of the Continental Congress."

"The com^{tte} that was Chose agreeably to the Sixth Article at the adjournment, presented the Association Drawed up by the Continental Congress, with the additional Resolve of the provential Congress, that is, not to by aney thing that is Imported from Great Britton after the first of October Next, let it be Imported when it would, it being put to Vote and voted in the affirmitive."

March 7, 1775, voted "To make void the Worcester Covenant signed last fall." Up to this time all town meetings were warned in His Majesty's name.

In March, 1775, the town voted to raise thirty minute men, and if they should be called out they were to have two dollars bounty, when they should march. Some of these men were called out at the time of the Lexington massacre which so soon followed.

On the 14th of June, 1776, a meeting was held "to see if it be the minds of the Town that Continental Congress should Declare Independence of the Colonies to Great Britain, and whether the Town will stand by the above said Congress in So Doing."

"The Question being put whether it be the minds of this Town that the Hon. Continental Congress should Declare the Colonies Independent of Great Britain, it passed unanimously in the Affirmative,—then voted, Should the Hon. Congress Declare the Colonies Independent of Great Britain as above Said, we the Said Town Solemnly Engage with our Lives and fortunes to Support them in the measures."

This action was taken in response to the General Court, which body had assured Congress of the support of the people of this colony. The question was sent out for each town to act upon individually, and thus this town was enabled to record its Declaration of Independence nearly three weeks before it was declared by the Continental Congress. We think the signers of the Declaration of Independence were bold men, but such records as the above, show us that they knew the will of the people before they took the step. They followed, rather than led public sentiment.

We are unable to learn the names of all the men who first enlisted in the Continental Army, or to what extent they were in active service. But to a call that was made before the battle of Bunker Hill, thirty men responded, one of the first of whom was Isaac Bellows. Other prominent men soon followed.

In the engagement at Bunker Hill, Henry Gates received a wound in the face, by which he was so disfigured that he was afterwards known as "Twist-mouth Gates."

In February, 1777, the town voted to send two delegates, John Woods and John Clark, to a convention to be held in Worcester agreeably to a call from the town of Sutton, to form a County Congress.

At this period large sums of money were needed to meet public expenses, which were voted and assessed upon the inhabitants, and the tax bills committed to the collectors, but nearly one tenth part of the people were totally unable to pay, and long lists of taxes were abated every year. The treasury was without funds, and the selectmen were obliged to borrow from abroad, whenever they could do so, on the credit of the town. So great were their burdens that the minute men, to whom had been promised two dollars bounty, were not paid till nearly three years after they were called out, although in January, 1776, the selectmen were directed to give them orders upon the treasury for their money. March 2, 1778, we find the following record: "2ly. Paid to the minute men that marcht after Lexenton fite, Israel Skinner, Joseph Shattuck, Abijah Greenwood, Asa Hoyt, Hugh Blair, Joseph Write, Stephen Farrington, John Ames, Isaac Bellows, Joseph Caryl, Asa Metcalf, Daniel Kinsman, Stephen Church, Silas Rice, Nathan Stone, Bezaleel Lyon, Enoch Devenport, Seventeen in Number, at Twelve Shillings each man. — — — — — — 10^L — 4^S — 0^D."

There is no evidence that the thirteen others of the thirty, were called out at that time, and the probability is that those who went found they were not needed then and returned.

When it became evident that the war must continue for a long time, calls were made for men to enlist for three years; then larger bounties were required. On the 11th of May, 1778, a meeting was called to see what bounty the town would give to the men who were then to be raised. Voted "To give 30 pounds to each man. Then voted to adjourn the meeting to Moses Clark's, Inholder's, to seven o'clock this day, and there the meeting Died a natural death." Very likely the reason for such a record is that they did not succeed in getting the men to volunteer, for on the 25th of the same month, another meeting was held, at which they voted to raise three Continental men, and also voted that the men who should be called into the service in the future, should be hired, and the town taxed for the same. Then adjourned to seven o'clock, when it was voted to give a bounty of 140 pounds to each of the three men. At an adjourned meeting, on the next Wednesday, this vote was reconsidered, and 100 pounds was voted, "and no more," and a committee was chosen to hire the men, and borrow the money. Then adjourned to June 5th. But probably this committee did not find it easy to get either the men or the money, for June 5th they reconsidered the last vote, and voted 120 pounds. Then adjourned to June 15th, when they voted to raise 800 pounds, to be assessed on the town, to hire men as needed. These records indicate that they were in straits in regard to those calls for men. At the meeting May 25th it was voted "To make an Everidge of what has been Done by the Inhabitants of the Town Since the Continental men have been Raised—then voted to Chuse a Com^te of five men to make an Everidge, then voted John Woods, Thomas Sergant, Joseph Eveleth, Ezra Pond, Capt. John Clark, be a Com^te for the above said purpose to make ye Everidge and hire men into ye service."

This committee made their report in August of the same year, which was not accepted. But on the 15th of October,

their report was adopted in substance, and is inserted here because it shows in what kind of service the men from this town
had been engaged.

"2ly. Voted six pounds p' month for the two months to
Rhode Island, May and June 1777—then voted Ten pounds
p' month for the men that went to Bennington, gon five weeks
July 20th then voted fifteen Shillings p' Day to the men that
went over ye Mountain on horseback—then Voted Twenty
pounds for the Three months Service Sept. 2^d—then Voted Ten
pounds p' man that went for thirty Days to Take Genl. Burgoyne—then Voted Twenty pounds p, man that went for three
months under Capt Marean to gard Burgoynes men to Cambridge—then Voted four pounds p' month for ye Six months
Service at ye Barracks in Rutland—then Voted three pounds
p' month for the Turn to Brookfield to Keep Stores—then
Voted Twelve Shillings p' Day for ye twenty Days men that
went with Leut Muzzy."

It is probable these sums were for special service rendered by
men who were not soldiers, and who had gone without any
bounty stipulated by the town. At the same meeting they also
voted "To chuse a Com^{tte} whose bisiness Shall be (when there
is orders comes for men) to Set the price they will give for men
to go that turn if men will Turn out and go for said price then
to hire them if they will turn out, then to Draft ye highest
payers, and to Draft in proposion to what a man possesses."

What is meant here by "drafting the highest payers," we are
at a loss to understand. How many men this committee hired,
is not on record. It seems some of the leading citizens of the
town had hired men on their own account, whether to shield
themselves from an anticipated draft, or because individual
credit was better than that of the town, does not appear, but
October 26, 1778, the town voted to exempt several men from
paying taxes, for bounties, because they had hired men for the
army, and also voted to give credit to all those who had done
more than their part. In June, 1780, four men, Ezekiel Pond,
Thomas Durant, William Nightingale and Timothy Nightingale,

were hired for the army, and the sum of 10,000 pounds was raised to aid them and others who might be called for Then voted "To give ten dollars per month, the old way, to the militia men who enlisted for six months, to be stated in Rye, Indian Corn, Beef, and Sole Leather, and also voted to add $500 in paper, to each of the militia now hired." And those who enlisted for three years or for the war were to have "twenty head of three years old cattle, Heifers and Steers, of average value."* This was done because the currency had so far depreciated that they found it difficult to fix upon any definite sums. Up to this time the several quotas had been filled without a draft. But the summer of 1781 was probably the darkest in the whole history of the town. Calls for men had been so often made that probably nearly three-fourths of all who were fit for soldiers, had been, or were then in the service. There seemed to be no men who could be spared and their means had become almost exhausted in paying the war taxes. Every measure was resorted to which offered any hope of escaping a draft. April 30, 1781, they voted "To divide the town into two parts, by the Templeton and Rutland road and each part shall furnish a man for the army for three years." Whether these men were raised does not appear, but it is evident that they failed to furnish all the men called for, as the order soon came to Captain Slocomb, commander of the militia, for a draft. The selectmen and militia officers made every possible effort to obtain the men, but failed. Another town meeting was called, the 2d of July, to decide what measures should be adopted. They then chose a committee to consult as to the best means to be adopted. After conferring together for an hour, they reported that in their opinion it was best to " class the town." This report was accepted, and it was voted " To class the town into four classes." Then voted "That Capt.

---

*The following record shows the value of stock as estimated December 19,1777, voted "That a yoke of oxen five or six years old that measure six foot be Set at 13£ and all other cattle in proportion. Voted a good horse five years old at 12£ and all others in proportion. Voted Store Sheep at 6s. Voted Swine one year old at one pound and all others in proportion."

Slocomb postpone the draft till next Monday, and the town clear him of all damage in so doing." All their efforts were fruitless, and when they came together on Monday it was voted "That Capt. Slocomb draft for six months into the Continental Army." The names of the drafted men are not recorded.

On the 16th of the same month a meeting was held "to see what bounties the town will give to the men that are detailed from the militia for six months, five months, and three months, into the service, and what means the town will adopt to furnish the men with spending money." Voted "To give the three months men nine pounds the old way, stated in beef and Indian corn." After an adjournment of two hours it was voted "That the treasurer give his security to the six months, five months, and three months men, and that Lieut. Nathan Stone give his security to such of the men as choose it.

There is nothing in all the records that more clearly shows the exigencies of the times than this. All they attempted to do was to furnish spending money for the men, and to do this, required the assembled wisdom of the town. And the fact that they thought indemnity from Nathan Stone was better than from the town, as such, shows how low their credit had fallen. It is probable that only one other call for men was made. At a meeting held February 11, 1782, "to see if the town will raise the remainder of the men for the three years service, and procure money for marching the same," it was voted "to accept of four men which Lieut. Jones of Charlton has offered at 75£ per man. Then voted "to set off to Lieut. Eli Clark, one seventh part of the town to pay Levi Parmenter, as a soldier, to serve three years in the Continental Army." It is probable that the remainder of the men volunteered.

Occasionally an individual presented a claim for services in the army, which the town would not recognize. November 19, 1781, there was an article in a warrant for town meeting "To see if the town will make any consideration to Oliver Fairbanks for the service he has Don in the army, extraordinary as he may make it appear." Voted "in the negative."

During all these years the families of soldiers were faithfully provided for at the expense of the town. They received no state aid, as in the War of the Rebellion. As early as 1777, a committee was appointed to provide for these families, and 100£. raised for the purpose. Each succeeding year, during the war, some action was taken in relation to this matter, and several appropriations were made, but such was the state of the treasury that few of the bills were presented before 1782. A few specimens of these accounts are inserted here to show the names of some of the soldiers, and how their families were taken care of.

Town of Hubbardston indebted to me for supplying the women whose husbands were in the service of the U. S., for 1778.

Delivered to the wife of Asa Church five ½ Bushels of Indian corn, eight bushels of Rie 117lb. of fresh pork and 100lb. of Beef.

Delivered to the wife of Israel mead Seven Bushels Indian corn four ½ Bushels Rie 38lb. cheese 83lb. Beef one pair Shooes half Bushel malt one peck salt five Bushels Potatoes.

Delivered to the wife of Andrew Barber two Bushels Indian Corn one Bushel Rie 7½lb. cheese which I delivered in behalf of the town, for which I now pray for allowance for the same.

WILLIAM MAREAN.

Hubbardston, october 8th, 1781.

"The above account was voted as it stands without any price anext to sd articles."

At the same meeting it was voted to allow "Capt. Adam Wheeler for geting three Beriels of Sider by the Desire of the Selectmen for Mr. Stephen Churchs wife at 3s. per Beriel——9s.

For transport of sd Sider from Rutland —— —— ——4s."

Besides the calls for men as stated above, and the expense of providing for their families, frequent demands were made upon the town to furnish beef for the army. In 1780, the General Court sent an order for 3420 pounds. The town voted to comply with the request, and the currency had so far depreciated that they raised 5130£. to pay for it, which would make the cost over seven dollars per pound. On the 1st of January,

7

1781, another committee was chosen to purchase beef and
10,000£. was raised to pay for it. This would make more than
$60,000 raised in less than a year, for the purchase of beef.
In estimating the sacrifices of those times we must remember
that this money had cost them as much as good money costs in
ordinary times. Several other calls were made for beef, and
were met, and accounts were allowed for driving cattle to Rutland, for the army. Some of the men who took these contracts
for beef, and received pay in continental money, were totally
ruined. The currency continued so to depreciate in value, that
at one time the town voted to allow one silver dollar for $75
paper money. Then it decreased so that $90 would pay only
one dollar taxes, and finally the town voted not to receive any
more paper money. The following extract from an old mem-
orandum book of Capt. John Woods, will illustrate still further
the worth of money at that time :—

For doing some writing (probably a deed,) .	$30.00
For flip (drank, perhaps, while doing it,) .	8.00
For an almanac.	6.00

One year, the town voted to pay $50 per day for work on the
highways. At length the old continental scrip became almost
as worthless as the confederate bonds of later times, but it was
long a perplexity and annoyance.

In 1782, a vote was passed to hear the report of Daniel Sumner in regard to the paper money his son took of the town for
his services in the army. The same year an article was inserted
in the town meeting warrant, "To see what the town will do
with the old average tax that was to raise bounties for the men
levied in 1777." Voted "All persons behind in sd average,
pay up." The same year it was also voted "To set off one
seventh part of the town to John Woods to pay Thomas Durant
for three years service in the army." Also voted "To set off
one seventh to Abijah Greenwood to pay Caleb Newton for
three years service in the army." That was the third seventh
of the town set off for this purpose. Just what is meant, we do
not know.

In some respects the records of this period of the revolution are meager and obscure. Those men sought rather to meet the stern demands of their time, than to put their sacrifices and hardships upon parchment for future generations. The historian searching these records will often find the exclamation rising to his lips, why did they not tell us more about this! or why did they not record that! He finds just enough of the plain, stern facts to make him feel that the broad margin of unwritten history would furnish themes far more interesting and thrilling than any that can be drawn from these dry records.

Could we lift the veil and look upon the private burdens and personal heroism of those dark, sad days, we should more fully appreciate the cost of our freedom. For eight long, dreary years the war cloud enveloped the nation in gloom, and the effect was peculiarly severe upon these infant towns.

We cannot furnish a full list of the men who went into the army, nor of those who died there. But from the facts already stated, it is clear that the war consumed the bone and sinew of the town. The men endured untold privations and sufferings in the service. Widows and orphans were left to be cared for by the public. The means of the people were so exhausted that they were overwhelmed with debts they could not pay. The state tax was excessively burdensome, and many lawsuits were brought against the town. Yet there was not a lisp of repudiation. With the same manly courage, and noble sense of justice which led them to support the government, they set about adjusting their debts almost as soon as the last gun was fired. They voted to instruct the selectmen to borrow money to pay all just demands, if it could be done at a rate of interest not exceeding twenty-five per cent.

The following are the names of some of the Hubbardston men who served in the army in the War of the Revolution. Those whose names are in *italics* are known to have been in the army, but it is not known whether they were residents of this town at that time or came here after the war :—

Elijah Adams,
Issachar Adams.
Ephraim Allen.
John Ames,
Andrew Barber,
Isaac Bellows.
Isaac Bellows, Jr., '
David Bennett,*
Hugh Blair,
Thomas Brintnall.
Ebenezer Brown,†
Joseph Caryl,
Asa Church,
Stephen Church.
Isaac Clark,
William Clark.
Robert Converse.
Enoch Davenport.
Stephen Farrington.
Henry Gates,
Abijah Greenwood.
Thomas Hapgood.

Stephen Heald.
Ephraim Holt,
Daniel How,
Asa Hoyt.
Converse Hunting.‡
Moses Hunting.‡
Daniel Kinsman,
Bezaleel Lyon,
Ebenezer Mann.
William Marean.
Israel Mead,
Asa Metcalf,
Timothy Metcalf,
Samuel Morse.
John Moulton.
Robert Murdock.
Joshua Murdock.
William Muzzy.
William Nightingale.
Joseph Norcross,
Charles Parmenter.
Joseph Parmenter.

Levi Parmenter,
Richard Phillips.
Joshua Phillips,§
Gideon Phillips,§
Paine Phillips, §
Ezekiel Pond,
Ezra Pond,
Joseph Pond.
Silas Rice.
Joseph Shattuck.
Israel Skinner,
Jonathan W. Smith.
Nathan Stone,
Nathaniel Upham.
Joseph Waite,
Nathaniel Waite.
Adam Wheeler.
John Williams,‖
Daniel Witt.⸿
Daniel Woodward,
Joseph Wright.

---

*Went from Princeton.   †Went from Sutton.   ‡Went from Needham.   §Went from Rutland.
‖Went from Lancaster.   ⸿ Went from Paxton.

CHAPTER VI.

THE historian is sometimes brought face to face with facts that are strange and unlooked for. Facts so abnormal and so out of harmony with the general current of events that he is at a loss to know what causes to assign, or what motives to ascribe to the actors in the scenes. He must trust, in great measure, to the accounts given by those who lived near the time, and were familiar with the attending circumstances. Yet he does not always thus obtain the exact and unvarnished truth. The true and honest history of some events cannot be written till the public mind has outgrown the biases and prejudices which the events themselves awakened. Those who stand nearest the scene, partake too deeply of the general sentiment to be the most candid judges of the merits of the case, especially if it be an unsuccessful and unpopular cause.

We have found nothing else in the history of Hubbardston to which these remarks so fully apply, as to the affair which is the subject of this chapter. After such proofs of heroic patriotism and self-sacrificing loyalty as we were permitted to record in the last chapter, it seems unaccountable that the very next thing we are called upon to relate of these same people, is that they are plotting and carrying out schemes of rebellion against the very government for which they had pledged their lives and their fortunes, and for which so many had bled and died. Yet it is a fact which cannot be denied or disguised, that this town took an active and prominent part in Shays' Rebellion. Public sentiment was in its favor; all the best men were enlisted in it. It is said that only one man in the town expressed any opposition to it. This has always been regarded as a foul blot on the otherwise fair name of the town; a reproach and dishonor which could never be removed; and it would be a fruitless task to attempt now to reverse the record of the past, and vindicate entirely the honor of the town and the course of these men. Yet although we have no occasion to question the veracity or honesty of those who have given us the history of the affair, we think there is a more favorable side than has usually been presented, and that these men had better reasons for their course than have been ascribed to them. For when we look at the character of the men, honest yeomen, peace-loving citizens, many of them devout, God-fearing men, and see what they had done to secure the freedom and sustain the institutions of their country, it does not seem possible that they were so fickle-minded, so reckless, or so devoid of reason, as seriously to contemplate the destruction of their own government, and to take up arms against the civil authorities, without any excuse. They were not tories, but true patriots, and the unanimity and earnestness with which they embarked in the enterprise, is evidence that they thought they had good reasons for their course.

Our aim in this chapter is not to give a full account of this movement, nor to justify the men engaged in it, but to place before the reader the facts, so far as they relate to this town, and the causes and occasions of the uprising among the people, so far as we are able to obtain them from history and tradition. In Lincoln's History of Worcester County may be found a much more detailed account than we shall be able to give. From that account many things here stated, are taken. We get little help from the records of the town, for the course of the citizens required caution in the expression of their designs. They understood their own records, but we must make out their meaning by the light of concurrent history.

Before the close of the Revolutionary War, there began to be uneasiness and discontent among the people of the central and western portions of the state, in regard to the acts of the Legislature, and the operations of many of the laws. There was a jealousy of Boston influence, especially over the General Court, and it was felt that many of the enactments worked unfairly toward the small, rural towns.

On the 9th of April, 1782, twenty-six towns in this county met in convention at Worcester, to consider their grievances. William Muzzy was the delegate from this town. This convention expressed dissatisfaction with the state officers, in regard to the disbursement of large sums of money, and recommended instructions to representatives to require immediate settlement with all officers entrusted with the funds of the commonwealth, and if adjustment was refused, or delayed, to withdraw from the General Court and return to their constituents. They also recommended that the compensation of the members of the House, and the fees of lawyers be reduced; the revival of the confession of debt; the enlargement of the jurisdiction of justices of the peace to twenty pounds; contribution to the support of the Continental Army in specific articles, instead of money; and the settlement of accounts with Congress.

At an adjourned meeting, they also recommended that account of the public expenditures should be annually rendered to the towns; the removal of the General Court from Boston to some country town; and the separation of the business of the Court of Common Pleas and the Sessions.

In March, 1784, this town voted "That William Muzzy meet the convention at Worcester in behalf of the town, at the time set forth in the letter from Sutton." There is no explanation of this letter from Sutton, nor of the object of the convention, but it is a matter of history that a proposition was made by the town of Sutton in 1784, to the other towns in the county that a convention should be called to consider grievances and the means of redress. May 19, they voted "To comply with what the county convention did at Worcester, and chose John Woods to draw off the petition that is laid before the town, and to sign in behalf of the town, and that the selectmen forward the petition." But there is no record of this petition, of its aim, nor where it was sent. In these transactions the people were seeking redress for their wrongs in a legitimate and peaceable way, probably without any design of open resistance. But they did not obtain what they sought, and in 1786, matters began to assume a warlike aspect. Other conventions were held, in Concord, Paxton, Hatfield, and Leicester. To this last, held in August, 1786, this town sent as delegates, Elisha Woodward and Joseph Wright. The next month, they chose a committee to give instructions to these delegates, but left no record of what these instructions were. In November, they voted "To continue the same delegates at Worcester." At these conventions they enumerated the evils they wished to have remedied: "1. Sitting of the General Court in Boston; 2. the want of a circulating system; 3. the abuses in the practice of the law, and the exorbitance of the fee table; 4. the existence of the Court of Common Pleas in their present modes of administration; 5. the appropriating the revenue arising from the impost and excise to the payment of the interest of the State Securities; 6. the unreasonable and unnecessary grants made by the General Court to the Attorney General and others; 7. the Servants of the government being too numerous, and having too great salaries; 8. the existence of the Senate."

In all this there is no threat or intimation of a purpose of open resistance to authorities. The conventions expressed their devotion to their government. At Paxton, November 3, 1786, they declared that however they might suffer in their character, person or estate, they should think themselves "Happy if they could, in the least degree, contribute to restore the harmony of the commonwealth, and to support the weight of a tottering empire."

On the 27th of December, this town was called together "To see if they will send a petition to the General Court similar to that sent by the body at Worcester, together with the addition recommended by the committee at Worcester to be sent in by the several towns in this and the two upper counties." It was voted to send such a petition if the other towns should do the same. There is nothing in these proceedings which shows a

MAIN STREET LOOKING SOUTHEASTERLY.

hostile or defiant spirit. Yet during the whole of this autumn, bands of armed men were being organized, and other warlike preparations were going on. In August, when the delegates to the Leicester convention were appointed, this town instructed the selectmen to request the militia officers to discipline the soldiers, and if they refused, to get some one else to do it; also that they inquire into the state of the town stock of ammunition. In November, they met again to see if they would raise an independent company, and increase the town stock. They voted not to raise the company, and referred the other matter to the selectmen. The moderator then withdrew, and when requested to dissolve the meeting, he said it was "dead of itself." They had gone so far that they probably began to have doubts as to their success in this appeal to arms.

The rebellion took its name from Daniel Shays of Pelham, who had been an officer in the Continental Army, not because he was the instigator or prime-mover in it—there was an armed force before he had any connection with it—but for some reason he was chosen to take command of the insurgents, or "Regulators," as they styled themselves. Their badge was a sprig of evergreen worn in the cap. Their operations were chiefly confined to this county and the northern parts of Middlesex and Hampshire Counties (the latter then included Franklin and Hampden). Their plans were never very systematic, nor were all their forces concentrated upon any one point. Their object, so far as appears, was to stop the proceedings of the courts, for reasons that will be given hereafter.

The man who was next to Shays in position, and figured almost as largely, was Capt. Adam Wheeler of this town, a highly esteemed citizen. He served in the French and Indian War and was a brave officer in the War of the Revolution, displaying much heroism in the battle of Bunker Hill. He now raised and commanded a company of nearly a hundred men, mostly from this town, in the interests of the rebellion. Early in September, 1786, with eighty men, he marched to Worcester, and took possession of the Court House. The next day their

8

number was increased to more than a hundred, besides as many
more without arms.   A sentinel was placed on the verge of the
hill.   On the steps were stationed a file of men with fixed bayonets, while in front stood Capt. Wheeler, with drawn sword.
This was their preparation to meet the court, which was to
begin its session that morning.   Chief Justice Artemas Ward
was possessed of intrepid firmness, and a resolute and manly
bearing.   He had been an officer in the army, and as he advanced at the head of the court officers and members of the
bar, he recognized the sentinel as one of his old soldiers, and
sternly ordered him to withdraw his leveled musket.   Awed by
the voice he had been accustomed to obey, the sentinel instantly
complied.   As they came to the Court House, the crier was
ordered to open the doors, which he was allowed to do, reveal-
ing a party of infantry, with guns leveled as if ready to fire.
Judge Ward then advanced till the bayonets, turned against him,
pierced his clothes, demanding repeatedly to know who commanded the people there ; by what authority and for what purpose they were met.   Wheeler at length replied that he was
not a leader, but he had come to relieve the distresses of the
people by preventing the sittings of the court until they could
obtain redress of grievances.   The judge answered that he
would satisfy them that their complaints were groundless.   He
was told that any communication he had to make might be
reduced to writing, which he indignantly refused to do.   He
said he did not value their bayonets ; they might plunge them
into his heart, but while that heart beat, he would do his duty ;
when opposed to duty his life was of little consequence.   If
they would take away their bayonets, and give him a place
where he could be heard by his fellow-citizens, and not by the
leaders alone, who had deluded and deceived them, he would
speak, but not otherwise.   The insurgent officers, fearing the
influence of his words on their followers, interrupted.   They
said they did not come there to hear long speeches, but to resist oppression, and demanded an adjournment without day.
The judge peremptorily refused to answer any proposition un-

less accompanied by the name of him who made it. He was
then ordered to fall back. The drum was beat, and the guard
ordered to charge. The soldiers advanced till their bayonets
pressed hard upon the breast of the chief justice, who stood
immovable as a statue. His intrepidity so over-awed the
soldiers, that the guns were removed. The judge ascended the
steps and addressed the assembly. In a clear and forcible manner he examined their supposed grievances, exposed their
fallacy, explained the dangerous tendency of their rash measures, told them they were imperiling the liberty acquired by the
efforts and sufferings of years, plunging the country in civil
war, and involving themselves and their families in misery; that
the measures they had taken would defeat their own wishes, for
the government would never yield to force what would readily
be accorded to respectful representations, and warned them that
the majesty of the law would be vindicated, and their resistance
of its power avenged. He spoke nearly two hours amidst frequent interruptions. But argument and remonstrance were
unavailing. The insurgents declared that they would hold their
ground till they had obtained satisfaction. Judge Ward then
addressed himself to Capt. Wheeler, advising him to allow his
troops to disperse. They were waging war which was treason,
and its end would be—a momentary pause, and he added—the
gallows! He then retired unmolested, through the armed files.
The court was opened at the United States Arms Tavern, and
adjourned till the next day, and a demand was made upon the
militia of the county to rally and sustain the courts. But they
were so much in sympathy with the movement, that the officers
were obliged to report that it was not in their power to muster
their companies. This encouraged the insurgents, and they
gathered in larger forces. The Court House was guarded in
martial form, and the men not on duty, bivouacked in the halls
of justice. They again demanded that the court should adjourn
without day, but were met with the same stern refusal as before.
They now numbered about four hundred, and marched through
the streets with music, inviting all who sought relief from op-

pression, to join them. But they obtained no recruits. The court, finding there was no reliance to be placed on the support of the military force, adjourned, continuing all the cases to the next term. After some further parleying and parading, the "Regulators" dispersed.

At the next session of the court, on the 21st of November, they gathered again, and went through about the same manœuvers. The high sheriff, Col. William Greenleaf, addressed the company of men with fixed bayonets who had taken possession of the steps of the Court House, and remarked with great severity on the conduct of the armed party. One of the leaders, not improbably Capt. Wheeler, told him they sought relief from grievances, and among the most intolerable of them was the sheriff himself, and next to his person were his fees, which were excessive and intolerable, especially in criminal executions. "If you consider fees for execution excessive," replied the sheriff, irritated by the attack, "you need not wait long for redress, for I will hang you all for nothing, gentlemen, with great pleasure." Some one in the crowd secretly placed a sprig of pine in his hat, and thus the sheriff retired with the court, wearing the badge of the rebellion.

Up to this time, the government had been very indulgent toward this movement. Several acts were passed for the purpose of affording relief, and to satisfy the clamors of the people. It was supposed that the excitement would soon subside, and the men return to their allegiance. Then there was so much of the comic about it, that it seemed hardly credible that they could be in earnest. But now it had come to be too serious to be trifled with longer, and it was determined to raise an army sufficient to crush out the rebellion. This only led the insurgents to rally in greater force. Capt. Wheeler enlisted about thirty new men and made Shrewsbury his headquarters. Their determination now was to interrupt the courts, not only in Worcester, but in Concord and other places. But hearing, on November 30th, that a force was marching against them which had already captured some of the leaders, they abandoncd their expedition into Middlesex County, and retreated in great alarm to Holden. Capt. Wheeler secreted himself in a house which his pursuers passed by, and he escaped capture only by accident.

It was about this time that Daniel Shays, the reputed commander-in-chief, and nominal leader of the force, first joined the troops of this county. The plans of the insurgents were now interrupted. They had not sufficient clothing to protect them from the extreme cold; they were without food and without money. About one hundred went to Grafton, while Shays' company and one other, retired to the barracks in Rutland, and large numbers were dismissed with the order that they all assemble in Worcester, on the Monday following.

From this point in the narrative, we are unable to follow the men from this town in distinction from others, though we know that Capt. Wheeler, and some others, continued with Shays till the final dispersion of the forces. Large plans were further made to interrupt most of the courts of the state, and to liberate the prisoners from the jails, and great exertions were made to enlist new men. But a series of disasters followed them. In Worcester, they were overtaken by a severe snow storm, and as they were compelled to retire, their sufferings were intense. If they sought shelter, they were refused, for the current of public opinion had now set in favor of the government. Shays and his men were driven from post to post by the state troops. His forces were separated, diminished, and disheartened. On the second of February, 1787, he, with his men, left Pelham for Petersham. They began their march on Saturday evening with mild weather and a cloudless sky, but were soon overtaken by a driving snow storm. They could find no shelter and pressed on all night. Sabbath morning they halted for rest and to prepare breakfast. The snow was piled in drifts, and the weather severely cold. They felt sure that the troops in pursuit would not follow them in such a storm. But these troops had kept moving all night, to save themselves from freezing, and came upon the insurgents while engaged in preparing food, and

captured two hundred and fifty of them, while the others fled
in different directions; some of them went to Winchester,
N. H., and from there scattered to other places, but more went
to their homes, hiding their arms by the way, though their rags
and their shame could not be hidden. Thus ends a rebellion
which finds no parallel in history. In this county not a man fell,
not a gun was fired, and no blood was shed, except from a
sabre cut in the hand of one of the insurgents. The insurgents
probably never numbered more than 2000, and these were but
poorly equipped. For a time, some of the state troops were
stationed in the old centre schoolhouse in this town to watch
the movements of the people. Dr. Moses Phelps said that
when he was called out in the night to visit patients, he was
obliged to go to the commandant and get leave, or he would be
challenged. This became so much of an annoyance that he
finally said to them that they knew him and his business, and
he should not come again. If they wanted to fire upon him,
they must do so.

Capt. Wheeler fled to Canada, and remained there four years,
till a proclamation of amnesty was issued by the governor. In
1791, we find the following record: "Art. 2. To see if the
town will grant the petition of Adam Wheeler, which is as follows, viz: 'The petition of Adam Wheeler to the town of
Hubbardston. Humbly showeth that your said petitioner was
at Pelham about four years ago, in the unhappy disturbance
that happened in this county; and that Dr. Hinds has commenced an action against me which is gone to execution, which
is not in my power to discharge. Gentlemen, friends, fellow-
citizens and neighbors; your petitioner prays for help to discharge said debt and cost, which is 9^L 4^S 9^D, and your petitioner as in duty bound will ever pray.'

ADAM WHEELER."

"Voted that the selectmen settle the debt of Capt. Wheeler,
in the best and easiest manner possible."

Thus we find that the people upheld their leaders even in an
unpopular cause.

A few of the insurgents were tried, and found guilty of treason, and sentenced to be hung. Even the day of their execution was fixed, but after thus being frightened, and disgraced, they were reprieved. Probably the extent of the disaffection was not fully known till after the troubles were over, and the insurgents had been disqualified from holding civil office. It was then found that some towns had not enough other men to fill the necessary town offices, and further legislation was had, to meet the difficulty. Full amnesty was at length offered to all who would return to their allegiance. This nearly all were glad to do, and were ever after, good and loyal citizens. The government was lenient and forbearing towards these men. It sought, in a measure at least, to redress their grievances, instead of taking the ground that the insurrection was wholly without cause.

Sometime before June, 1785, the General Court established a "Scale of Depreciation," by which debts, contracted on the basis of the continental currency, might be reduced to their specie value. During the winter after the outbreak, "The Tender Act," "An Act of Indemnity," "An Act Reducing Fee-bills," "An Act for the More Easy Payment of Taxes," and an "Act Regulating the Courts of Common Pleas and Sessions of the Peace," were passed with the design of affording some relief to the people. It is evident that the people of that time pronounced a tolerant judgment upon this whole affair. In less than a year after the dispersion of Shays' forces at Petersham, the Massachusetts convention for the ratification of the United States Constitution was held, and a large number of the delegates from the northern part of Worcester County, were avowed and active insurgents. These men were not in disgrace or humiliation among their fellow-citizens, after the excitement had so far subsided as to allow a candid judgment. Such facts shed light upon the motives, spirit, and characters of those who embarked in this scheme.

It may now be asked, what was the real cause of all this trouble? What did they expect to accomplish by stopping the courts? And why was this town more unanimous in it than other places?

The causes usually assigned for this movement, do not seem to afford a sufficient explanation of such a course, on the part of men of such character as we know these men to have been. If the taxes were burdensome, they were mostly voted by the town, to meet the exigencies of the times. Did honest, industrious yeomen leave their farms and their families, shoulder their guns and march to Worcester, and the whole town sustain them in it, because a majority in town meeting had voted too much money to meet expenses? It is true they complained of the inequality of the state tax. In 1783, this town voted " To try for some abatement of this tax, and William Marean, John Woods and Elisha Woodward were chosen a committee to draft a petition to the General Court to this effect." Their draft was adopted, and William Marean was chosen to lay it before the General Court, but probably no relief was granted. This, however, of itself, was not a sufficient cause for rebellion. If salaries of state officers did seem high, to these poor laboring men ; if fees of lawyers were exorbitant ; if they were jealous of the influence of Boston over the General Court ; it does not seem possible that to redress such wrongs, they should be led into open insurrection against the people's government just established. It is probable that these things had more influence than they ought. They may have been guided and led on, in some measure by ambitious and designing men, who did not openly espouse their cause, but who magnified their grievances, and led them to feel that their burdens were the result of oppression, or mismanagement on the part of the government. They were driven almost to desperation by their distresses, and were probably led to take false views in regard to the true causes of their burdens.

We can see here the reflex wave of the revolution. Something of the same spirit animated these men, now, as then. They had successfully resisted the oppression of the mother country, and, at fearful cost of blood and treasure, had gained their liberty, and now, when they thought they saw that liberty encroached upon, they were just as ready to suffer in its behalf, as before. They determined to resist their own government when that became oppressive. Some of the old English colonial laws were still in force, in all their stringency. They were greatly disappointed in the direct results of the war for independence. Lincoln, in his History of Worcester County, says: "Massachusetts stood in the splendor of triumph, in republican honesty, bankrupt in resources, with no revenue but an expiring currency, and no metal in her treasury more precious than the continental copper, bearing devices of union and freedom. The country had been drained by taxation for the support of the army of independence, to the utmost limit of its means; public credit was extinct; manners had become relaxed, trade decayed, manufactures languishing, money depreciated to worthlessness, claims on the nation accumulated, with a heavy pressure of debt resting on the commonwealth, towns and citizens. The first revivings of commerce overstocked the markets with foreign luxuries and superfluities sold to those who trusted to the future for ability to pay. The temporary act of 1782, making property a tender in discharge of pecuniary contracts, instead of affording the designed remedy, only enhanced the evil of general insolvency, by postponing collections. At length floods of suits broke out. In 1784, more than two thousand actions were entered in the county of Worcester, with a population of less than 50,000. Lands and goods were seized and sacrificed on sale, when the general difficulties drove away purchasers. [Tracts of the best land in this town were sold at auction for ten or eleven cents per acre, to pay taxes, and few were able to purchase at that price; some of those who did, were unable to pay the taxes assessed to them upon the same land, and it was sold several times over.] Amid the universal distress, artful and designing persons, discerning the prospect for advancement, fomented discontent by inflammatory publications and seditious appeals to every excitable passion and prejudice. Driven to despair by the actual evil of enormous debt,

9

and irritated to madness by the increasing clamor about supposed grievances, it is scarcely surprising that a suffering and deluded people should have attempted relief, without considering that the misery they endured was the necessary result of the confusion of eight years of war."

The scarcity of money and the overwhelming debts of the people were evils from which they were striving to extricate themselves. One of the principal things demanded was the issue of paper money. The doctrine of inflation did not originate with the present generation. The views of the people of this town appear in the action taken in a town meeting called January 5, 1786: "To see what instructions the town will vote to send to the Great and General Court under our distressed circumstances, occasioned by the scarcity of cash, whether by making a bank of paper money, or any other method." Voted unanimously "That there be a bank of paper money emitted on certain conditions." Dea. Elisha Woodward, Lieut. Robert Murdock, Edward Selfridge, Jonathan Gates and Capt. Adam Wheeler, were chosen committee to draft and report on what conditions the said bank be emitted. The town adopted the report of the committee, which was as follows: "That there be a bank of paper money made sufficient to redeem all of this state's securities, and after said bank is issued, all securities of this state shall cease to draw interest within three months, and if said securities are not returned into the treasury in the term of one full year, then the said securities to be forfeited. Also, voted that said money shall be a lawful tender to pay all debts and assessments, and if any person refuse to take said money when tendered before witness, he shall be deprived of bringing an action against said debtor, provided said debtor pays the same into the state treasury, there to be applied to the use of the state, unless redeemed by the creditor in the term of six months. Voted that there be a severe punishment inflicted, as well as penalty annexed, on all such as shall counterfeit said currency, or undervalue the same." Voted "That the town clerk transmit a copy of the above report to Capt. Lee of Barre, or John Fessenden, Esq. of Rutland, that the same may be forwarded to court."

Their object in preventing the sessions of the courts, and in attempting to liberate the prisoners in the jails, evidently was, not to prevent conviction or punishment of crime, but to stay the action of the courts in suits for payment of debts. The law then was such that men could be imprisoned for debt, even when they had no means for paying. The jails were filled with these poor debtors. Some of them were men who had made contracts for provisions for the army, and taking pay in continental money had lost their all. The "Regulators" considered these things cruel and oppressive and sought to liberate their suffering neighbors, and to prevent the courts from issuing any farther executions till some means for relief could be devised. Their indignation was excited against the lawyers because they regarded them as seeking to multiply these suits. A neighboring town instructed its delegate to the Paxton convention to " Use his influence that the lawyers and inferior courts be entirely annihilated."

The reason why this town engaged in the scheme more generally than other towns, was probably because they were poorer, and their misfortunes greater. Those who came and settled here were mostly young men with families, and many of them in debt for their land. The War of the Revolution was upon them before they had time to get ahead in the world. The calls for soldiers were for able-bodied men, which affected unequally such a town as this, and excited their jealousy of older, larger towns. The Continental Army took most of the men from this town, leaving their families to be provided for at public expense. They were poorly paid by the government, even in the old continental scrip, which became almost worthless, so that when they were discharged from the ranks, they found themselves in the deepest straits of poverty, and they entered into this movement as a forlorn hope.

In view of all the facts, we think that their descendants have as much occasion to pity them in their distress, and admire their heroic self-denial, as to blush with shame at their deeds.

CHAPTER VII

COUNTY, STATE, AND NATIONAL AFFAIRS.

NEW COUNTY.—It will be remembered that when this township and the adjacent territory, was purchased of the Indians, in 1686, it was included within the limits of Middlesex County. The General Court, in confirming the title of these purchasers, in 1713, stipulates: "The town to be called Rutland, and to lie in the county of Middlesex."

In 1731, Rutland, with seven other towns from Middlesex County, five from Suffolk, and one from Hampshire, "With certain grants and unsettled territory, were erected into the county of Worcester."

Before the close of the War of the Revolution, the towns in the northern part of Worcester County, began to agitate the question of forming a new county. In 1781, this town chose a committee to meet a committee of the town of Warwick, in Petersham, in reference to the subject. These committees met and voted to invite other towns. There is no record of any further action till 1791, when a delegate was sent to a convention in Warwick with instructions to favor the forming of a new county, "If it could be done without expense; otherwise, not." In 1796, Edward Selfridge was chosen to meet with others in Templeton, to see about dividing the county. In 1798, a memorial of delegates of Templeton, Barre, Petersham, Athol, Winchendon, Hubbardston, Adams, Gerry, now Phillipston, Gardner, Royalston, and Warwick, was sent to the Legislature, asking that these towns might be incorporated into a new county. Again, in 1800, the town voted "To accept the report of the gentlemen who had attended the convention in Templeton in reference to dividing the county." What the report was, does not appear. In 1803, Major Daniel Parkhurst was authorized to sign a petition in behalf of the town for a division of the county. In 1810, a committee was chosen to meet with several other towns in reference to the same matter. These facts indicate that up to that time, the people of this town were strongly in favor of a new county. But when the subject was again agitated, in 1828, and the Legislature submitted to the towns the question of forming a new county, to be composed of sixteen towns from Worcester County, and five from Middlesex, as asked for in "The petition of Ivers Jewett and others," this town voted yeas, two; nays, one hundred and forty-four. Every time the question came up afterwards, they voted against the division. In 1853, they remonstrated against it, and once or twice afterward chose an agent to oppose it. In November, 1874, a resolution was unanimously passed opposing a division and instructing the representative in the Legislature to oppose it.

State Constitution.—A town meeting was held September 30th, 1776, "To see if the inhabitants of the town that are free, and twenty-one years of age, will give their consent that the present House of Representatives in this State of Massachusetts Bay, in New England, together with the Council, shall consult, agree, and enact such a constitution and frame of government for this State as the said House of Representatives and Council, on the fullest and most mature deliberation, shall judge will most conduce to the safety, peace, and happiness of the State, in the after investigations and generations; and if they, the inhabitants, would direct that the same be made public for the inspection and perusal of the inhabitants before the ratification thereof, by the Assembly." "Passed in the negative."

Whether their objection was to forming a constitution, or to the existing General Court, does not appear.

In 1778, a form of constitution for the "State of Massachusetts Bay," drawn up by the General Court assembled in convention, was submitted to the people and rejected. The vote of this town, as returned was, "affirmative, none; negative,

fifty-three." Their unanimous objection seems to have been to
the property qualification of voters; they were unwilling to
recognize the principle of measuring the man by his possessions.

In 1779, the subject of calling a convention to frame a new
constitution, was brought before the people of this town, and
they voted in the affirmative, on the following conditions: "The
convention shall be called solely for this purpose, and the delegates shall be chosen agreeably to the old mode of representation; [in 1776, the Legislature passed an act by which the
people were to have one representative for every one hundred
free-holders; it had been one for every thirty; this is the "old
mode" referred to; it was probably thought that the change
operated against the small towns.] Also that the convention
be held as near the middle of the state as is convenient; and
when they have formed a constitution and frame of government, it be laid before the whole people, and if it receive a two-
thirds vote in its favor, it be adopted, but if it fail of such a
majority, then the convention to sit again, and make another
attempt."

But the majority of the voters in the state expressed their
desire for such a convention, without these conditions, and the
General Court ordered such a convention to be assembled at
Cambridge, on the first of September, of the same year. Capt.
John Woods was appointed delegate from this town. James
Bowdoin presided. A committee of thirty was appointed to
propose a "Declaration of Rights, and a Constitution," and
then the convention adjourned to October 28th. The committee of thirty appointed John Adams to draft the Declaration
of Rights, and James Bowdoin, Samuel Adams and John Adams
to prepare a Form of Government. This committee assigned
this part also to John Adams, and thus he became the author
of the whole work, which, after some amendments, was adopted
by the convention. This convention completed its work March
2d, 1780, and submitted the whole to the people for acceptance or rejection. It was approved and adopted by the state;
the people of this town voted for it, with but one dissenting

voice. It would seem that the inhabitants generally without regard to property had a voice in the matter, for the call was issued to "All free-holders and other inhabitants of the town, being free, and twenty-one years of age." The same form was used in calling meetings for the choice of representatives. We do not suppose the women voted in those days, but under such a call as this we do not see how they could consistently be refused, if they claimed the right.

In 1820, Ephraim Allen was appointed delegate to a convention called to revise the constitution. Fourteen articles of amendment were proposed. The town accepted all but three, and those three were rejected by the state.

Several other amendments were proposed prior to 1852, and the vote of the town was almost unanimous in favor of each.

In 1852, a call was issued for another convention, which met in 1853, and proposed eight articles of amendment. These were accepted by the town, though rejected by the state. William Bennett was the delegate to the convention. All the later amendments received the approval of this town.

National Constitution.—We find no record of the action of the town upon the constitution of the United States, after it was adopted in convention, nor any instructions to their delegate.

In 1787, Capt. John Woods was chosen delegate to the convention held in Boston, for the purpose of considering the proposed national constitution, and, with the entire northern part of Worcester County except Athol, he voted against it, assigning as a principal reason, that too many of the rights of the citizen were not well guarded, and that a more explicit enumeration of the rights of the individual states, and the United States, should be definitely expressed in that instrument.

As a general rule, those towns and individuals who favored the Shays' movement, opposed the constitution, from the fear that there would be too much power in the central government. They were jealous of state rights. Others probably objected on the ground of the compact made with slavery, and the toleration of the slave trade. Not a slave ever breathed the air of

Hubbardston, and slavery was formally abolished in the state in 1780. We may believe that these men were governed by their love of freedom and equal rights, in rejecting this instrument.

The first election under the new constitution, was held December 18th, 1788. Two persons were to be chosen as electors of president, and the record of the vote of this town is as follows: "Timothy Fuller, forty-three votes; Amos Singletery, forty-three; Peter Pennyman, one." This shows the unanimity with which the people here gave their support to Washington.

CHAPTER VIII.

THE WAR OF 1812.

THE records of the transactions of this town in reference to the last war with England, are very meager, and the little we have ascertained upon this topic, has been derived mostly from other sources.

The majority of the people of Massachusetts, in common with the other eastern states, were opposed to the war, believing it uncalled for and detrimental to the welfare of the country. Caleb Strong was one of the most influential leaders of the opposition in the state, and on this ground was several times elected governor. The sentiment of this town was very equally divided on this subject, and political excitement probably never ran higher in all its history, than at this period. At the election in 1812, Caleb Strong had 106 votes, for governor, and Elbridge Gerry, 101. But the opposition party grew as the war went on. In 1813, the vote of the town was for Caleb Strong, 113; for J. B. Varnum, 83; in 1814, for Caleb Strong, 116; for ———— Dexter, 82.

In October, 1812, a meeting was held to see if the town would give any additional sum to those who are detached, in case they should be called into actual service. This meeting was adjourned to November, and then dissolved with no action upon this article. Whether the town met the requirements made upon it, or furnished the men called for, does not appear, but there is no doubt that they avoided, as far as possible, all action which would give countenance to the war. Men did not volunteer, and at one time a draft was made.

. 10

In November, 1814, they voted "To make up the sum of $18 per month, with what the government allows, to those soldiers who have been detached into the service, viz: Otis Hale, Lowell Leland, Asa Lyon. Daniel Thompson, and Bildad Wright." These are the names of all that appear in the records, as having served in the army during this war, though we know that others went.

At the time the draft was ordered, the men liable to do military duty, were organized in two companies. These companies were called out, meeting at the old meeting-house, which was the headquarters of the town, in almost all respects. Plenty of grog was distributed among them, and when they had "well drunk," earnest appeals were made to them, to volunteer. The fife and drum struck up stirring strains, and the men marched in double file through the aisles of the meeting-house, and any who were willing to volunteer, were requested to fall into a certain pew. Only one or two could be found to go, and the remainder of the quota was raised by draft. These men were ordered to Fort Warren in Boston Harbor, and guard duty was probably the only service they rendered. Some others, who were afterwards citizens of this town, or who enlisted from other places, were in the service. Abijah Clark, going from Rhode Island, was out a few months; Luther Goodspeed was in some of the most bloody battles of the war. He was with Com. McDonough at the bloody victory of Plattsburg and Lake Champlain, and used to tell thrilling stories of the scenes of that day.

CHAPTER IX.

SCHOOLS AND EDUCATION.

THE founders of the Massachusetts Bay Colony were men of liberal ideas in regard to education, though their standard was somewhat different from ours. Among the earliest acts of legislation we find stringent laws requiring every town of fifty householders to build a schoolhouse and maintain a school for the instruction of all the children in the rudiments of the English language. They declared "the good education of children is of singular behoof and benefit to any commonwealth," and asserted the right of the state to cause every child within its jurisdiction to be so far educated as to be capable of becoming a good citizen; and they declare what that education shall be, as follows: "First, the ability perfectly to read the English tongue; second, a knowledge of the capital laws; and third an acquaintance with the grounds and principles of religion." And every town with one hundred householders was required to maintain a Grammar School in which young men might be fitted for college. This is the substance of an act passed in 1647, and the following quaint preamble shows their reasons for such enactments :—

"It being yᵉ chiefe project of yᵉ ould deluder, Sathan, to keepe men from yᵉ knowledge of yᵉ Scripture as in formʳ times, by keeping yᵐ in an unknowne tongue, so in these lattʳ times by perswading from yᵉ use of tongues, yᵗ so at least yᵉ true sence and meaning of yᵉ originall might be clouded by false glasses of said seeming deceivers, yᵗ learning may not be buried in yᵉ graves of our fathʳˢ in yᵉ church and Commonwealth, yᵉ Lord assisting our endeavors, it is therefore ordered," etc.

The year in which the town was incorporated, Plymouth Colony passed a similar act, premising " that the maintainance of good literature doth much tend to the advancement of the weal, and flourishing estate of societies and republicks."

Town School Fund.— This town was not behind others in these matters; as we have seen, in the division of the land among the original proprietors, lot No. 30 was set apart, and to remain unalienated for the use of schools. In 1796, this lot was sold for $1,276, and was the origin of the present school fund of the town. The annual income has been applied to the schools, amounting in the aggregate to more than $6,000.

First Public School.—July 22, 1767, or about five weeks after the town was incorporated, a meeting was held to see if the town would " take measures to procure schooling," but there is no record of any action being taken at that time. On the first day of the following February, another meeting was held, at which time they made provisions for a school to be kept three months during the same winter and spring—one month at the house of Joseph Slarrow on " Muzzy Hill," one month at the house of Edward Rice, near the present residence of W. E. Hammond, and one month at the house of Adam Wheeler, the residence of the late Oren Marean. This was probably the first public school in town. It was attended by nearly all the boys of suitable age, and when the school was too far from their homes, they boarded in the vicinity, and thus obtained the benefit of the whole. Why the girls did not also attend, we do not know, but we suspect they were not sufficiently well clad to protect them in such long walks at that uncomfortable season, as tradition says some of the large girls were without shoes.

Appropriations.—There is no record that any money was raised by the town for the purpose of defraying the expenses of schooling for 1767, or the two following years; mention is made only of spending what was allowed them by the " quarter sessions at Worcester." In 1768, Benjamin Hoyt was allowed " three shillings for one day and a half in going to Worcester to see how much school money there was."

After 1768, appropriations for schools were made annually, except for two or three years during the darkest period of the revolution, the sums ranging from five to one thousand pounds. The latter amount was in 1780, when the currency had become of little value. For several years after 1784, the amount raised was sixty pounds. From 1792 to the close of the century, it was one hundred pounds. In 1800, it was $300; in 1810, $500; 1820, $800; 1830, $700; 1840, $1200; 1850, $1200; 1860, $1600; 1870, $2500; 1880, $2000. Nine times the amount reached $2500, but fell in 1879, to $2000. Sometimes the amount appropriated is exclusive of that derived from the town fund for schools, but in general, the income of the fund is included.

Building of Schoolhouses.—In 1770, the town voted to build a schoolhouse twenty-six feet by twenty. This was the first in town, and stood near the southwest corner of the old burial ground, and was for some time used also as a town-house and church. Prior to this the schools and town meetings had all been held in private houses.

In 1771, the town chose a committee to "squadron out the school places;" that is, provide places for schools in other parts of the town. Before 1781, nothing had been done to build other schoolhouses. At their March meeting that year, a committee of seven was chosen "To squadron out the town for schooling, and to see how many schoolhousen to build" The next year this committee made their report, dividing the town into seven squadrons, and recommended building a schoolhouse in each squadron. The report was accepted, but no further action was taken till March, 1784, when it was voted to build the seven schoolhouses, to be completed by the first of June, 1785. The sum of 105 pounds was raised to pay expenses, and a building committee appointed in each squadron, but it was from three to five years before these houses were all completed; probably because the town was found to be much more in debt than was supposed. In 1786, there was an article in the town-meeting warrant, "To see if the town will reconsider the vote

formerly passed, granting 105£. to build schoolhouses." The
vote to reconsider was in the negative; a new committee was
appointed, and $50 additional appropriated to each squadron to
complete its schoolhouse. It is probable that most of them
were finished during the next two years.

Squadrons.—The squadroning process, referred to above, was
simply assigning places where the children of different families
should attend school. The whole was under the supervision of
the town, there being no law authorizing the establishment of
school-districts till 1789. The report of the committee made
in 1782, is here inserted to show what families were then in
town, and in what parts of the town they lived.

Squadron No. 1.

Hugh Blair,
Moses Clark,
Stephen Church,
Joseph Eveleth,
Joseph Grimes,
Bill Grimes,
Ephraim Grimes,

Abijah Greenwood,
Clark Haven,
Micah Howe,
Ebenezer Joslin,
William Marean,
Robert Murdock,
William Nightingale,

Moses Phelps,
Ezra Pond,
Ebenezer Warren,
Adam Wheeler,
John Whipple,
John Woods,
Joseph Wright.

Squadron No. 2.

Isaac Bellows,
Jesse Burditt,
Jonathan Clifford,
Oliver Fairbanks,
Samuel Follett,
Jonathan Gates,
Bezaleel Gleason,
Daniel Gleason,

Peter Goodnough,
Joseph Green, Jr.,
Daniel Kinsman,
Ebenezer Mann,
Alpheus Morse,
William Muzzy,
Joseph Newton,

Daniel Parkhurst,
Amos Parker,
Thomas Sargent,
Reuben Totman,
Nathaniel Upham,
Nathaniel Waite,
Elisha Woodward.

Squadron No. 3.

Joseph Caryl,
Moses Greenwood,
Joseph Grimes, Jr.,
Dependence Haywood,

Howard Hinds,
Stephen Hunting,
William Hunting,
Samuel Morse,

Adam Peters,
Abel Tenney,
Lemuel Warren,
Stephen Wheelock.

Squadron No. 4.

Elijah Adams,
Issacher Adams,
Philip Boynes,
Hosea Brigham,
John Clark,
Ephraim Clark,

John Clark, Jr.,
William Clark,
Isaac Clark,
Stephen Heald,
John McClenathan,

Thomas Peirce,
Henry Rice,
Elisha Snell,
J.-Warren Smith,
Timothy Underwood.

Squadron No. 5.

Anthony Clark,
Eli Clark,
Timothy Darling.
Buckley Howe,
Israel Howe,

Samuel Lewis,
Timothy Newton,
Jonathan Nichols,
Charles Parmenter,
Joseph Parmenter,

William Prentiss,
Joseph Shattuck,
Nathan Stone,
James Thompson.

Squadron No. 6.

Philemon Adams,
Asa Church,
Caleb Harrington,
Abel Harrington,
Daniel Gage,

Daniel Gage, Jr.
Asa Gage,
Joseph Green,
Asa Hoyt,
John Mead,

Joel Pollard,
Samuel Slocomb,
Joseph Waite.

Squadron No. 7.

Simeon Allen,
Benjamin Clark,
Bela Davis,
Stephen Farrington,

Elijah Farrington,
Bezaleel Lyon,
David Merriam,
Hollis Parker,

Josiah Proctor,
Solomon Rolph,
Samuel Underwood.

The northwest squadron at first included Burnshirt and Muzzy Hills. The people requested a division, which was granted, Canesto Brook being made the dividing line. Burnshirt became the west squadron, and the other part the northwest. The names of the several schools then were, the Centre, Northwest, North, Northeast, East, Southeast, South and West. But in a few years the name of squadron was abandoned, the term district adopted, and the cardinal numbers from one to eight, inclusive, were applied, in the order above stated.

Changes in Districts.—In 1816, a part of district No. 7 was made district No. 9. In 1820, district No. 10 was set off from No. 8. In 1823, district No. 11 was formed from parts of Nos. 1 and 3. In 1828, district No. 12 was formed from parts of Nos. 1, 4, and 5.

In 1837, the town was redistricted by a committee of three (Silas Greenwood, Justus Ellinwood, and Moses Waite), and carefully defined territorial limits and boundaries were established. Previously, the schoolhouses had been erected and repaired by the town. Since then, with the exception of the time when all districts were abolished, each district has repaired and rebuilt its own house, which is done by a separate tax, granted by the voters of the district, and assessed upon its inhabitants.

In 1851, district No. 13 was formed from parts of Nos. 2, 3, and 11, and new boundaries established between the several districts Nos. 2, 3, and 11.

These thirteen districts continued till 1869, when the state passed a law abolishing the district system.

It was never designed that the districts should be independent organizations. From the establishment of the district system to the present time, an article has been inserted in the March meeting warrant, every year (except the two years when the new law was in force), "To see if the town will allow the several school districts to appoint their own committees to divide the school-money, call school-meetings and hire teachers." Yet the system has been very popular in this town. In 1866, a decided vote was passed against abolishing the districts, and when compelled by law to do so in 1869, much feeling was awakened. When the law was so amended in 1871, as to allow a return to the district system, the town at once voted to do so, ninety-six to fourteen. A committee was appointed to redistrict the town. This committee recommended that the town be divided into nine districts, giving the bounds of each. Their report was adopted.

Description of Schoolhouses.—The schoolhouses when first built were rough structures, some of them costing less than $100, and they soon became dilapidated. The tooth of time and the knives of the boys, made deep and lasting impressions upon them. They were built with huge fireplaces, which were enormous consumers of fuel, and some of them, as enormous producers of smoke which often filled the schoolroom, while the heat escaped through the chimney. There was no lack of ventilation, though we have never heard of any application for a patent for the method. The seats were long, in some cases extending half the length of the house, one above another on an inclined plane so that every apple or inkstand which chanced

to fall, rolled down to the feet of the teacher. Some of the
scholars, we fear, had a greater ambition to be promoted to the
back seats than to climb the heights of learning. Some of the
boys still retain vivid impressions of their first experiences in
these houses, when they were compelled to sit all day, with
nothing to do, on the front seat, with no desk before them, and
the seat so high that their feet dangled in the air, and perhaps
so near the roaring fire that they were compelled to turn round
like a chicken on the spit. To sit was an active verb.

These old structures have nearly all departed, or been so
transformed as to leave few traces of their early services. To-
day most of the houses are in good repair. The change in the
number and territory of the districts in 1871 required a new
location for the schoolhouse in the central district, and a new
house was built the following year, at a cost of about $12,000.
It has four rooms above the basement, of which three are occupied by the Primary, Intermediate and Grammar Schools.

Wages of Teachers.—We find it difficult to ascertain from the
records, what wages teachers generally received in the early
days, but we know they must have been small, or the schools
short, for some of the districts did not receive more than $25 a
year as their portion. The money raised was divided, as the
record has it, "According to the number of Pools in each district, between four and twenty-one years of age." In one case
Philip Boynes was paid $13.00 for a whole term, and another
year Reuben Walker was paid $7.50 per month for teaching
school. Whether they paid their female teachers so little as
not to be worthy of record, we do not know, but we find no
account of their wages, though in several instances, persons
were paid about fifty cents per week "For boarding the school-
mistress."

Description of Schools.—As no school-registers were kept in
those days we do not know the names of many of the teachers,
nor what was the method or character of the instruction given.
Doubtless the schools were similar in other rural towns, and the
school books nearly the same. An extract is therefore given

11

from Dr. Whiton's History of Winchendon, as a probable description of the schools in this town. "In the earliest times the only books found were the old New England Primer, small, but rich in value ; Dilworth's Spelling Book and Psalter, including the Psalms, Proverbs, and the New Testament. In some places the scholars learned to write on white birch bark, for lack of paper, and were taught in rotation a week each by all the men who could read, some of whom cut a sorry figure as teachers. In 1790, a decided advancement was made in school books. Perry's Spelling Book, superseded Dilworth's. Pike's Arithmetic was introduced, and afterwards superseded by Adams'. Webster's Third Part came into use as a reading book, followed, not long after, by the American Preceptor. The study of English Grammar began to be thought of, Alexander's Grammar finding its way into the schools. Not the least attention was given to Geography till 1795, when a small abridgment of Morse's Geography began to be called for. These books held possession of the schools for many years till better and more modern ones expelled them. It was scarcely known that such sciences as Chemistry, Natural Philosophy, Botany, Rhetoric, Physiology, or Algebra, were in existence ; of their introduction into common schools no one ever dreamed. To read, spell, and write decently, and acquire enough of Arithmetic for the transaction of ordinary business, was all the young aspired to."

Singing Schools and Church Music.—In 1799, we find the first appropriation made by the town for singing. They then voted "To allow $9.50 for teaching a singing-school." For many years afterward, an article was inserted in each March meeting warrant to see what sum of money the town would raise for singing. Sometimes no action was taken ; when any sum was voted, it was usually $30, but occasionally amounted to $75, or $80. One year the record runs, "Voted to raise $75 for singing, to be appropriated by the Singing Society." Another year, "Voted to raise $80 for the support and encouragement of singing the present year." It was evidently the design to stimulate and assist individual effort.

In earlier times, no instrumental music was allowed in the churches. Its ultimate admission was not without deep-seated opposition. It is recorded of Jesse Burditt: "He was so much disturbed by the use of musical instruments by the choir, that for a long time, he absented himself from public worship. Being called to account by the church, the protracted controversy was settled by his consenting to withdraw his opposition to the use of the bass viol, provided no other instrument should be used, and the choir should take no part in singing at the communion service."

The people in general were not furnished with hymn books, in those days. The hymns were "deaconed out," that is, after the minister read the hymn, one of the deacons repeated the first two lines ; the choir, or the whole congregation sung them ; in the same way, the next two lines were repeated and sung, and so on through the hymn.

Much attention has always been given to church music ; there have been one or two singing schools nearly every winter, and we usually have good singing in all our places of worship. The service of song has been a voluntary one ; rarely has any one received remuneration, though invaluable aid has been rendered by individuals connected with the different choirs, as choristers, or otherwise, for long periods of time ; in one case for thirty-seven years ; in another, forty-eight years.

The Lyceum.—Among the educational influences of the past, a town Lyceum had its share. It was organized in 1844. Meetings were held weekly during the fall and winter. The largest hall in the place was filled to overflowing. It was sustained entirely by home talent. Questions were proposed for discussion, often embracing the most exciting topics of the day ; and once in two weeks, a paper called the Winter Wreath, composed of original articles, was prepared by the ladies. There was no lack of those who were ready to take part in these exercises. The interest in them sometimes rose to the pitch of enthusiasm. The effect was not transitory. Many were led to exercise their powers in speaking, writing or lecturing, to their own great

profit, as well as to the interest of others. For ten or twelve
years, this Lyceum furnished pleasant entertainment for the
young, and by it many were probably kept from places of idle
resort. It also helped to form, or unify, public sentiment upon
great moral questions; the people were led to examine the
topics presented, and form more intelligent opinions than they
would otherwise have done; vices and foibles were often trans-
fixed by keen shafts from the quiver of the Winter Wreath;
and the general tone of morals was elevated.

In later years, the young men have sometimes had private
debating clubs, which were sustained with spirit.

CHAPTER X.

IN former times all the towns in Massachusetts were required by the General Court to supply their inhabitants with good preaching; the penalties for neglect of this requirement were in force as late as the year 1800. Provision for meeting-houses and parsonages was also required by law; mention has been made of the lots reserved for these purposes, in the first surveys of this township. Originally, the towns were legal parishes and had charge of raising funds to build meeting-houses and to support preaching, and in Hubbardston there are no parish records separate from the town records, till within the last sixty years. The churches were Congregational, and though associated with the towns, and in some degree, dependent on their action, they were distinct bodies so far as regards the choice of officers, and determining the principles and by-laws by which they were governed. They nominally selected their pastors, though often acting in connection with the town, because all the money needed must come from the town treasury. All the people were taxed to support the institutions of the gospel, as well as to support schools, or build roads. The practical working of this system was, that the town at length came to have the virtual control of the whole matter of settling and dismissing ministers.

As we have already seen, it was the design of the original proprietors of the town to make provision for a permanent "learned and orthodox ministry." But there were so few people here at the time of the incorporation, it was difficult to support preaching or even to gather a congregation, regularly.

Some of the families connected themselves with churches in adjoining towns.

The first effort to gather a church here was made by Joseph Grimes about the year 1766; but it failed, because only four or five church-members could be found in town. In 1770, another effort proved more successful, and a church was organized February 14, consisting of six male members. All the records state that the number of members was seven, but a careful examination of dates affords proof that one, Joseph Eveleth, whose name was included in the original number, did not join the number till January 13, 1771. The names of the six are, Nehemiah Parker, pastor-elect; Adam Wheeler, from the church in Rutland; Nathaniel Upham, from the church in Leicester; Joseph Grimes, from the church in Tewksbury; Nathaniel Waite and Ephraim Rice, from the church in Templeton.

It is probable that the wives of the last two, and perhaps of the others, united about the same time, for we find that Nathaniel Waite and wife united with the church in Templeton in 1767, and Ephraim Rice and wife, in 1769, though both families lived in this town, and the Templeton records show that five persons were dismissed from that church, to unite here, in 1770.

The following Covenant is copied from the church records.

The first Covenant (in consistency with, and subserving to the Covenant of grace in general), that gives form to the church of Christ in Hubbardston.

Agreed to and signed Feb. 14, 1770.

We, whose names are hereunto subscribed, apprehending ourselves called of God to compose and make up a particular constituted church of Christ, upon the plan of the gospel:—do, in the first place, acknowledge our utter unworthiness of any favor from God, whatever. Yet as He has been pleased to offer in His covenant of grace and peace, in Jesus Christ, to be our God, and the God of our seed, requiring us to be His people, we desire to lay hold of this covenant of His, for ourselves and ours, giving up our seed and selves to Him in the covenant of His grace; begging Him to accept us and them, promising by His grace to live in all sincere obedience before Him, and to look for the coming of our Lord Jesus Christ unto eternal life.

We believe Christianity to be the only true religion in the world ; that it is contained entirely in the Holy Scriptures, the only standard of truth and duty, which therefore we solemnly accept as our only Rule. Yet we acknowledge the "Westminster and New England Confession of Faith," the longer, and especially the shorter Catechisms (with which we are fully acquainted,) as good theories of christian knowledge.

And as thus we give up ourselves and seed to God, in the gospel of His Son, to serve and glorify Him in all the duties of a well-ordered life, as exhibited in the Bible ; and to look and wait for His salvation ; so we give up ourselves—one with the other, to live in holy fellowship and communion, one with the other, in a church standing—to Jesus Christ.

We will by God's grace, diligently and severally attend the public reading and preaching of the word of God, at all fit times and seasons— as the Lord's days and otherwise ; the administration of the seals of the covenant—Baptism and the Lord's Supper ; the admonitions and censors of the church.

We will obey them that rule over us in Christ, watching over one another for the good of each other. We will thankfully accept seasonable reproof, and do what in us lies, to approving this Covenant. We will endeavor to follow the directions given us in the Holy Scriptures in this as in all matters, and do what in us lies to build each other up in comfort and holiness, through faith.

These promises are to bind us to all that may be of our communion and fellowship, and to all others.

And we purpose and promise all, in reliance on the Head of the church for assistance and acceptance ; for pardon of our failings ; grace, and glory, and every really good thing ; humbly looking to Him to enable us to keep these resolutions, and to worship Him with the holiness which becomes His house, forever. Amen.

     Signed,

             NEHEMIAH PARKER, *Pastor-elect.*

ADAM WHEELER,	NATHANIEL UPHAM.
NATHANIEL WAITE,	JOSEPH GRIMES,
EPHRAIM RICE,	JOSEPH EVELETH.

It is evident that public worship was held in town, two or three years before there was a church. October 24, 1767, the town voted "to hire one month's preaching," and two days later, Benjamin Hoyt was chosen "to provide a minister, and to provide for the minister." February 29, 1768, 5£. 6s. 8d. was

voted "for Mr. Parker's preaching," which shows he was here at
the beginning of 1768.   In June of the same year it was voted
"to pay Mr. Parker's sallery out of the land tax granted at
March meeting," but it would seem he preached here only a
part of the time.   Another vote, February, 1769, was "to raise
five and one half pounds for one month's preaching."

August 15, 1769, a formal call was voted to Mr. Parker, with
the offer of a salary of forty pounds a year for the first three
years, fifty pounds a year for the next three years, and after
that sixty pounds yearly.   But it was not till September 9,
that a committee was raised to carry this call to Mr. Parker.
This committee consisted of Ezekiel Newton, Benjamin Hoyt,
and Moses Rice.   Mr. Parker's reply bears date December 14,
1769, and is as follows : —

Inasmuch as you have manifested an affectionate regard to me, and
have unanimously invited me to settle with you in the work of the gospel
ministry. I have taken the matter into serious consideration. and having
sought to God for direction. I am very sensible that the work of the
gospel minister is great and arduous ; but I hope and trust that my dependence is upon the grace and strength of the great Redeemer. Your
offers with regard to my support. are not large, but I consider your circumstances. and depend upon your generosity : it is not your money, but
your souls that I have a desire for.   I hope for the continuance of that
regard which you have manifested towards me. in reliance upon which,
and above all, in dependence upon divine assistance, I accept your
invitation.

NEH. PARKER.

Mr. Parker was ordained June 13, 1770, under a large oak on
the south side of the common.

He seems to have been a man of decided theological opinions and conscientious convictions, though not of superior in-
tellectual gifts.   He was gentle in spirit, of tender sympathies,
and unaffected piety.   Like Abraham of old, he was a man of
peace, and could not endure controversy.   He was a graduate
of Harvard College, in the class of 1763, and according to his
own report was somewhat given to college pranks.

His ministry was one of sore trials, on account of the newness of the place, and the distracted state of the country. But for more than twenty years, there existed the kindest feelings between him and the people of the town. During the days of the Revolution, he manifested a truly noble and generous spirit. He asked for no additional aid, though the people showed a willingness to grant it. November 19, 1781, the town voted "to get Mr. Parker's wood the present year, in consideration of his having suffered by the depreciation of the old continental money, on his giving a receipt for his salary for 1781." "Then voted to squadron into five squadrons, according to their pay, to get Mr. Parker's wood."

When the town was embarrassed for want of funds, he waited long for the payment of his small salary. During these years he sold the 150 acres of land near Comet Pond, and nearly one half of his farm, and had spent the proceeds in living, and still found himself in debt. In 1792, he made known his circumstances to the town, and asked for aid. They very coldly added fifteen pounds to his salary "for that year." The next May he was obliged to ask further aid, and offered to sell his place for a parsonage, or give them security for money on his real estate. After discussing many propositions, the meeting was dissolved without action, showing that the feeling toward him had changed. His friends now moved for another meeting, at which it was voted "to add fifteen pounds to Mr. Parker's salary, annually." Subsequently the attention of the town was twice called to this subject, but no aid was granted. According to the expressed desire of Mr. Parker, a town meeting was held June 5, 1800, and a committee consisting of Robert Murdock, John Clark and Edward Selfridge, was appointed to wait on Mr. Parker and ask him to be present. He complied with the request and made the following communication : —

To the Inhabitants of Hubbardston Assembled in Town Meeting.

Gentlemen : Considering the many infirmities of my body, and other important reasons, I think it most for the glory of God that I be dismissed, and give up my ministerial office. I therefore request that you vote my dismission, and that the pastoral relation be dissolved.

12   NEH. PARKER.

His request was granted, and so far as appears, this action was regarded as ultimate, no mention being made of a council.

"Thus was dissolved that connection between Rev. Nehemiah Parker and the inhabitants of Hubbardston which was formed in the open air, under the spreading branches of a lofty oak tree, on the 13th of June, 1770; that connection which so happily continued for more than twenty-two years, when each party seemed ready to lay down its life for the other, to spend and be spent for their mutual benefit and happiness. But when the prime and vigor of manhood was beginning to depart from that faithful servant, and other troubles, over which he had no control, were pressing heavily upon him, that sympathy which he had formerly received, and now more than ever needed, was beginning to be withheld, and so continued by slow degrees, till he was forced to believe his usefulness had departed. Now in the evening of life, with ruined health, and poverty before him, he felt willing 'for the glory of God,' to relinquish that small salary, which for the last few years, had been so grudgingly paid him, and cast himself entirely upon the mercy of that Heavenly Friend and Master whom he had so faithfully served, and who, he no doubt trusted, would soon take him home.

We would, in charity to our ancestors, withhold this narrative from the people of the present day, but as faithful historians we feel bound to make it public. No truer illustration of the fable of 'the old Hound and his Master' was ever acted out in real life."[*]

Mr. Parker died August 20, 1801, aged fifty-nine, and his remains sleep in the old burial ground, among the voiceless congregation to which he ministered. The stone over his grave was erected by the town. The expenses of his funeral—$18.58—were paid from the same treasury.

His ministry was, in some respects, a prosperous one, and left permanent impressions for good, upon the people. Ninety-three were added to the church by profession, and nineteen by

---

[*] William Bennett, as quoted in Centennial Address.

letter; total 112; besides this number, 106 were received in the "half-way covenant," so called, and 740 were baptized.

The "half-way covenant" was a plan adopted, and for many years followed, by the New England churches, by which parents who had been baptized in their infancy, and who sustained a good moral character, were permitted to "own a covenant" similar to the church covenant, and to have their children baptized. Its object was to extend the privileges of church membership beyond the pale of actual communicants at the sacramental table. It originated about 1660, in the days of complete union of church and state. How close that union was in 1631, appears from the enactment that no man should " be admitted to the freedom of this body politic, but such as are members of some of the churches within the limits of the same."*

For some time after the death of Mr. Parker, there was no stated minister, though liberal appropriations were made for preaching, and there was a standing committee to supply the pulpit. In June, 1802, the town voted to call Rev. Mr. Allen, "if he please to tarry," and "that the committee hire preaching for the winter, or discontinue it as they please." Mr. Allen did not "please to tarry."

On the first day of July following, they voted to concur with the church in giving a call to Mr. David Kendall to settle with them with a salary of $400, so long as he should perform the work of the gospel ministry. At an adjourned meeting on the 12th of the same month, a committee was chosen to consult with Mr. Kendall, to see on what terms he would settle with them. Their report was that he be paid his yearly salary, "until a majority of the town, or Mr. Kendall, for reasons that either party may set forth, see cause to call a mutual council of seven churches, the result of which shall be decisive." This

---

*This necessity of being a church-member in order to be a voter, or eligible to office, naturally led to a strong desire on the part of all men to enter the church. Hence an act was passed by the synod of Boston in 1663, which recognized all baptized persons as members of the church, and their children were entitled to baptism. Still they made no profession of their faith in Christ, and did not partake of the Lord's Supper This was called the half-way covenant.—[Brown's Religious Encyclopedia.]

report was adopted, though not without opposition. They "polled the house" to decide the vote. It stood fifty-three for, and thirteen against adopting it.

MR. KENDALL'S LETTER OF ACCEPTANCE.

To the Church and People of Hubbardston.

Beloved in the Lord Jesus Christ : Your invitation requesting me to settle with you in the gospel ministry, has been taken into serious and deliberate consideration ; counsel has been sought of heaven, and christian advice received. Thus far there appears no obstacle in the way of my compliance with your wishes, but as it is a duty enjoined by the gospel that "every one should provide for his own, especially those of his own house ;" and as it is required that "they who preach the gospel should live of the gospel," and that he who ministers to a people "in spiritual things, should be partaker of their temporal things," it is highly fit and proper that the means for a comfortable and decent support should be taken into consideration, when we deliberate on a subject of so much importance as the devoting one's self to the service of a people in the work of the ministry. Candid deliberation and friendly advice have accordingly been taken on this part of the subject. From which it appears that the stipulation proposed for an annual salary would of itself alone, be rather inadequate to the numerous expenses incident to a clerical life, taking into view, at the same time, the propriety of making suitable provision for those whom it may please God to give us the care of, together with the very high price of land, which is the foundation of all temporal subsistence. But I have further taken into account the friendly and benevolent disposition of the people of this town, heretofore manifested toward their pastor, and the assurances which have been given me, that the same would be continued toward his successor. Particular encouragements have been specified, upon which I am requested to rely with implicit confidence, and I do not scruple the sincerity of these proposals, and it would no doubt be deemed a want of christian candor to anticipate a dereliction from them, so long as the relation of pastor and people should continue between us, provided it be once formed.

The above particulars being duly weighed and considered, I have seen fit, with submission to divine Providence, to accept of your invitation and encouragements, so long as these encouragements are realized. And I do therefore make known to you by these presents, my willingness to serve you in the work of the gospel ministry, according to the grace

which is, or may be given unto me, to enable me to fulfil this arduous
and important service. And may this decision in all its effects and con-
sequences be attended with the blessing of Almighty God, "to whom I
now commend you and to the word of his grace, and to the Spirit of all
truth, which are able to build you up in faith and holiness, to stablish you
in every good word and work, and to give you an inheritance among all
them that are sanctified." That this may be your happy lot and portion
may God of his infinite mercy grant, through Jesus Christ our Lord.
Amen.

DAVID KENDALL.

Note.—The liberty of being absent three or four Sabbaths in a year, if
need so require, is usually reserved by ministers, at the time of their settlement : this indulgence will also be expected by me.

Soon after, the town voted to raise a committee to provide
for a council, and raised $100 to pay the expenses of the ordi-
nation of Mr. Kendall, which took place October 20, 1802.
The council met at the house of Dr. Moses Phelps, and was composed of pastors and delegates from the following churches:—

First church in Cambridge, Rev. Abial Holmes, pastor;
church in Weston, Rev. Samuel Kendall, pastor; first church in
Brookfield, Rev. Ephraim Ward, pastor; church in Westminster, Rev. Asaph Rice, pastor; church in Templeton, Rev. Ebenezer Sparhawk, pastor; church in Athol, —— —— ——;
church in Rutland, Rev. Hezekiah Goodrich, pastor; church in
Gardner, Rev. Jona. Osgood, pastor.

After examination, they voted they "were fully satisfied." It
would seem from the assignment of parts for the public service
that they had no sermon.

Mr. Kendall was a graduate of Harvard College and a man
of sound principles, but apparently of very different temper
and spirit from his predecessor. Mr. Parker declared that he
desired "the souls, not the money," of his people. Mr. Kendall
dwelt with most emphasis on the importance of his having a
comfortable and respectable support. When they wanted to
get rid of him, they did not find him the man to sacrifice all his
own interests to accommodate them. The relation between

pastor and people did not long remain harmonious. Complaints began to be made on both sides. Grievances were magnified by prejudice, and bitter criminations followed. The people charged the minister with a want of sympathy for them generally, and he complained of their neglect to fulfil their implied, though unwritten, promises of pecuniary aid, made at the time of his settlement. It was long the custom of the town, or individuals, to supply the minister with wood. The amount carried to Mr. Parker was sometimes thirty cords a year. It is a matter of tradition that they neglected to supply Mr. Kendall, till he preached from the text, "Where no wood is, the fire goeth out." If this did not bring the wood, it fanned the flame in the parish.

Thus matters continued. The opposition increased till September, 1808, when a town meeting was called "to see if the town will choose a committee to wait on Rev. David Kendall, to see on what terms he will agree to take a dismission from his ministerial charge, or act anything in relation to said article, agreeable to a petition presented to us, the selectmen."

At the meeting it was voted "to act on the article, forty-nine in the affirmative, twenty-six in the negative," and a committee of nine was chosen who made an elaborate report at a meeting held three weeks later, which is as follows:—

Whereas, apprehensions have arisen between the town and minister, that the mutual agreements and engagements entered into by the said parties at the time of his settlement among them in the gospel ministry, have not been duly observed and faithfully fulfilled, it is hereby mutually agreed that whatever injury may have been sustained by either of the contracting parties, through the neglect or failure of the other, just and reasonable satisfaction shall be made and reformation duly engaged for the future. As all the agreements are mutual, and both the contracting parties equally obliged to fulfil their mutual stipulations, so likewise all after settlements with respect to such agreements, should be mutual. Also, it is further agreed between the town and minister, that the following mode and method be adopted for searching into and settling all matters of complaint which now subsist between the parties. A committee shall

be organized for this purpose, and in order that it may be a mutual committee, it is agreed that the minister shall add by his own appointment an
equal number to the committee chosen by the town, and one of the parties shall nominate three settled ministers, of which three, the other party
shall select one who shall be the moderator or president, of the said
mutual committee. The committee being thus organized shall make a
regular draft or statement of all matters of complaint which the town has
against the minister, and a correct copy of said draft or statement being
signed by the committee shall be handed to the minister, a suitable time
before the committee meet to make up their result. The committee shall
also receive from the minister a draft or statement of any matter of complaint which he may have to lay before them. And after due and serious
deliberation on all matters on both sides, the committee shall make up
their report, a true copy of which shall be presented to the minister, and
another copy of said report laid before the town, and the said report being approved and accepted by both the town and minister, shall be a final
settlement and burial of all past matters of complaint between the town
and minister. But in case either of the said parties shall see cause to
dissent from the said report, the party so dissenting shall state his, or
their, objections in writing, and the committee shall proceed to revise
their report, and the said report so revised shall be set up in the same
manner as above prescribed. But should either of the parties still see
cause to dissent from the revised report, the party so dissenting shall have
a right to appeal to a mutual council, for a final decision upon all matters
of complaint, according to the original agreement and stipulations entered into between the town and the minister at the time of his settlement among them in the office of a gospel minister.

Signed,

ELISHA WOODWARD,	JAMES THOMPSON,	SAMUEL MORSE,
EPHRAIM ALLEN,	MOSES PHELPS,	LUKE WARREN,
OTIS PARKER,	MOSES GREENWOOD.	EBENEZER STOW.

This report, on being presented to the town, was summarily
rejected, but after further consideration and deliberation, the
vote was reconsidered and the report accepted.

The town then chose a committee of seven, agreeably to the
suggestion in said report, consisting of Elisha Woodward,
Ephraim Allen, Abijah Greenwood, Moses Greenwood, Moses
Phelps, Samuel Thompson and Luke Warren. Rev. Mr. Kendall appointed James Thompson, David Merriam, Otis Parker,

William Muzzy, John McClenathan, Nathan Stone and Ebenezer Newton as his part of the committee. The town then nominated three settled ministers, viz: Rev. Mr. Estabrook, Rev. Mr. Osgood, and Rev. Mr. Bascom, of whom Rev. Mr. Kendall selected Rev. Mr. Estabrook as moderator.

On the 12th of December following, this committee made report to the town, which was accepted, but not adopted, nor recorded. Another committee was then appointed, consisting of five ministers; Rev. Mr. Estabrook of Athol, was selected as chairman; Rev. Mr. Osgood of Gardner, and Rev. Mr. Bascom of Gerry, now Phillipston, were chosen by the town, and Rev. Mr. Goffe of Sutton, and•Rev. Mr. Barton of Fitchburg, were chosen by Mr. Kendall. Elisha Woodward, Ephraim Allen, and Moses Phelps were chosen to bring allegations before said committee. The day fixed for the meeting of this committee was January 24, 1809, but there is no evidence that they ever met, or in any way considered the case.

February 13, 1809, the town chose a committee of seven (Elisha Woodward, Moses Phelps, Ephraim Allen, Abijah Greenwood, Moses Greenwood, Samuel Morse and Luke Warren) to wait on Mr. Kendall and see on what conditions he would be dismissed. The efforts of this committee also were fruitless, and two weeks later, the town chose still another committee to make proposals to Mr. Kendall. They were Israel Davis, Samuel Swan, and Moses Greenwood. This committee proposed to the town to pay Mr. Kendall's salary to the 20th of October, amounting to $258.33, in case he consented to an immediate dismission. The town accepted the proposition, but Mr. Kendall declined the offer.

Elisha Woodward, Ephraim Allen, and William Marean were next appointed to try to agree with Mr. Kendall on terms of separation. March 6, they reported that they were unable to agree upon any terms with Mr. Kendall. The town then voted to offer Mr. Kendall $500 if he would take dismission, and further voted that if he declined to accept this offer, to proceed to a reference or council.

MAIN STREET LOOKING NORTHWESTERLY, 1870.

Mr. Kendall refused the offer. March 20, the town voted to choose one man, and invite Mr. Kendall to select another, to agree on terms of settlement. The town chose William Marean, and Mr. Kendall, John McClenathan. After consultation these men reported they were unable to agree. Mr. Kendall being further urged to make proposals, agreed to accept $800, in addition to his salary to that date. The town offered him $600, which he refused. The town next offered him $700, on condition that he would give twenty dollars of it to the poor, the selectmen to say who should receive the charity. This proposition Mr. Kendall accepted. The notes and papers embodying the terms of the agreement, were duly signed by Mr. Kendall and the authorities of the town, and placed in the hands of Reuben Wheeler, to be kept until the formal dismission of Mr. Kendall. One item in the agreement was that all allegations on both sides should be withdrawn. It was voted that Mr. Kendall should not supply the pulpit after the date of the agreement.

On the 7th of April, Mr. Kendall called a church meeting, and after rehearsing the difficulties in a long speech, in which he asserted that there were "more than forty who had made this conspiracy," he called upon any who had any objection to giving him a "christian recommendation to the work of the gospel ministry," to make it known then and there. No one offering any objection, he put the following question to the church, viz: "Brethren, are you willing to recommend your pastor as a gospel minister, in case a dismission takes place?" They voted in the affirmative. He then asked: "Brethren, will you consent to the dismission of your pastor, from motives of hope and trust in God that he may be more useful to the church and cause of Christ in some other part of the vineyard?" The question was put in this form, the record says, because it was well understood that the church as a body were unwilling to part with their pastor. Their answer was in the affirmative, and they then voted to unite with him in calling a council for his dismission; the council to consist of representatives of five

13

churches; the pastor to name two, the church, two, and the town committee, one.

This council met April 26. The churches represented were: Royalston, by Rev. Joseph Lee; Worcester, by Rev. Samuel Austin; Athol, by Rev. Joseph Estabrook; Gardner, by Rev. Jonathan Osgood; and Sutton, by Rev. Joseph Goffe. The council ratified the mutual agreement, dismissed Mr. Kendall, and said: "Whereas the church in Hubbardston have voted to recommend their pastor as a gospel minister, in case his dismission should take place, and nothing appearing against either his moral or ministerial character, this council do also hereby cordially recommend him to the churches, as a man of good character, and as far as we know, a faithful preacher of the gospel." After expressing sympathy with Mr. Kendall in his trials, their Result goes on to say: "This council regrets the convulsed state of the church and the town, and hopes that in future, the glorious doctrines of the cross will be more generally received, and have a more uniting influence in this place. We beseech the people to take heed that they do not receive the grace of God in vain; that they embrace the glorious overtures of the gospel in the obedience of faith; that they seek the re-establishment of a faithful and regular ministry; that they avoid offences and divisions; that they wait upon God with spirituality and diligence in the worship of his house, and in every respect seek those things which make for peace, and the things wherewith one may edify another.

Brethren and friends, farewell. Live in peace, and the God of peace shall be with you. Joseph Lee, Moderator; Joseph Goffe, Scribe."

The council also voted to advise Mr. Kendall not to hold religious meetings in town unless requested by a committee of the town or by a particular friend on a funeral occasion. Mr. Kendall acceded to this advice. During his ministry twenty-five were added to the church and forty-six were baptized.

After his dismission, Mr. Kendall removed to Augusta, N. Y., where he was installed in 1810, and dismissed in 1814. He was never settled again, and sixteen years later he was deposed from the ministry and excommunicated from the church. He died February 19, 1853, aged eighty-five. His pastor thought he gave evidence of repentance in his last days. It appears from subsequent records that Mr. Kendall sued the town for the amount pledged to him at the time of his dismission, and recovered it on execution.

After the close of Mr. Kendall's ministry there is no record of any effort to obtain a minister till the next March meeting, when it was voted "to poll the house to see if the town wishes to hear either Mr. Randall or Mr. Nourse, before they hear a new candidate." The vote stood, yeas, thirty-six; nays, thirty-six. "Then voted to drop the matter, and leave it to the committee to hear whom they please."

A meeting of the church was held August 13, 1810, to see if they would invite Mr. Samuel Gay to become their pastor. On taking an informal vote, it was found that they were equally divided, five in favor of giving him a call, and five opposed. The reason for the opposition on the part of these members, was that they thought Mr. Gay too liberal in his doctrinal views. After this failure to obtain a majority, they voted "to give brethren of other churches, who reside in town, liberty to sit and vote with the church in this meeting." The vote then taken resulted as follows; yeas, Dea. Ephraim Allen, Timothy Newton, Nathaniel Waite, Joseph Grimes, Abijah Greenwood; brethren from "other churches," Abial Murdock, and Joshua Willard (these two were formally admitted to the church during the same year,)—seven; nays, Dea. Otis Parker, James Thompson, Ebenezer Newton, Aaron Grimes, Jonathan Ames; from "other churches," David Merriam,—six.

At a meeting of the town held the same day, it was voted to concur with the action of the church, one hundred and one in favor, two opposed. At an adjourned meeting on the 20th of the same month, the town voted "to pay Mr. Gay an annual salary of $500 so long as his ministry shall continue, and provided that whenever two-thirds of the qualified voters of the town shall vote his dismission, his salary shall cease in one year thereafter; and the said town shall be at the expense of dismissing him in ecclesiastical form. And the said town give the said Gay liberty to be dismissed at any time upon his giving them one year's notice of such intention ; and he shall relinquish his salary when he shall be dismissed, which dismission shall be at his own expense." "And it was further voted to give Mr. Gay in addition to his salary, the sum of $500, one half in one year, and one half in two years, to be absolutely his own, if he should continue in his ministry for ten years ; but if he leave within ten years at his own request, he shall refund to the town in proportion to the time wanting of the said ten years." Mr. Gay signed his acceptance in the following letter :—

To the Church and Congregation in the Town of Hubbardston.

Grace, mercy and peace be with you, from God our Father and from the Lord Jesus Christ.

I thank you for the honor you have done me, by so unanimously inviting me to settle with you in the gospel ministry. The work of the ministry, though an honorable calling, is nevertheless an arduous work, and attended with many discouragements ; it has, however, from my youth, been the object of my choice, though it has been my fixed determination not to take the pastoral charge of any flock, till an effectual door was apparently opened for my happiness and usefulness. You have not only honored me, but you have done equal honor to yourselves as a town, by so unanimously voting a salary, which in this vicinity, is considered an honorable support. I should beg the favor of a larger settlement, did I not anticipate considerable from your liberality, in the way of firewood and lumber, should it be my lot to build in town. Your former character, the example of neighboring societies, and the attachment you have already evinced, are to me sure pledges of your future attention and assistance. Such help, though much less burdensome to you than raising a sum of money for a settlement, may be of equal advantage to me, and any favor that any individual shall see fit to confer, will be received with gratitude, and considered as an evidence of the giver's respect and affection.

The division in the church is a matter of my sincere regret, but considering the character of those who voted against me, I do in charity hope and believe, that they will not endeavor by their observations to hinder my usefulness in this place, but though they may differ from me in some opinions, which in every period of the christian church, have been subjects of controversy, I hope they will exercise that love and forbearance towards me, which ever becometh the disciple of the blessed Jesus, and that by divine assistance I shall be enabled to do the same towards them.

Upon condition that two Sabbaths a year be allowed me to visit friends, I do declare my compliance with your request to be your minister, and give myself up to spend and be spent in your service, so long as mutual love shall continue with us, which I hope will be as lasting as our lives.

Confiding in your friendship and liberality under divine providence, and requesting an interest in your prayers for me, that the blessing of Almighty God may rest upon me, rendering me happy and useful among you, and that the great Head of the church will watch over me, and preserve me from error in doctrine, in discipline and in practice, and enable me at all times rightly to divide the word of truth, and to discharge the duties of my office, I subscribe myself,

Your devoted servant and brother in the common faith,

SAMUEL GAY.

The town accepted this letter, and "chose a committee of nine to confer with Mr. Gay in regard to the council; a committee of three to lay the proceedings before the council; a committee of eight to keep order on the day of ordination; a committee of three to procure suitable vocal and instrumental music; and a committee of three for the purpose of supporting the meeting-house." The entertainment of the council was let out to the lowest bidder, Jacob Waite, for $35.

Mr. Gay was ordained October 17, 1810, which was a high day through the town. At five P. M. of the day previous, the council met at the house of Jacob Waite for the examination of the candidate. At the ordination service, Rev. Joseph Chickering of Woburn offered the introductory prayer, Rev. Jabez Chickering of Dedham preached the sermon, Rev. Mr. Osgood of Gardner offered the ordaining prayer, Rev. Mr. Thatcher of Dedham gave the charge, Rev. James Thompson of Barre the right hand of fellowship, and Rev. Mr. Goodrich of Rutland offered the concluding prayer. Before these public services commenced, the church assembled at the house of Jacob Waite and received Mr. Gay into its membership.

· The following Church Covenant and Declaration was adopted May 3, 1811 :—

CHURCH COVENANT.

You believe that there is one God, self-existent, independent ; the Creator and Governor of all things ; that He made man at first holy, in His image, and happy in His favor. That man being placed in honor, abode not, but apostatized by sinning against his Maker, and thus involved all the human family in guilt and ruin ; that the Son of God came into the world to recover them from the deplorable effects of the apostasy ; that to this end He expiated for human guilt by dying on the cross ; that He rose from the dead for the justification of believers, and is now exalted at the right hand of God, as a Prince and a Savior, to give repentance and remission of sins. You believe the Christian religion to be from heaven ; that it consists in the exercise of true love to God, and sincere benevolence to men ; and sensible of its vast importance, you do now, so far as you know your own heart (or hearts,) choose God as your everlasting Portion, the Lord Jesus Christ as your Mediator and Savior, the Holy Spirit as your Sanctifier and Guide. Sensible of your many errors and imperfections you profess humbly and penitently to implore the pardon of your sins, and the divine aid to enable you henceforth to walk before God in love and holy obedience. Convinced of the importance of early instruction in piety and virtue, you promise conscientiously to educate all committed to your care, agreeably to the prescriptions of God's holy word ; and that you will, in all respects endeavor to maintain a daily walk with God. You likewise promise to attend to the ministrations of the word and ordinances with us, submitting yourself to our christian watch and discipline, while it shall please God to continue your life and abode among us.

DECLARATION.

In behalf of the church, I acknowledge you a member of this same body with us, and promise that we will treat you with that affection, watchfulness and tenderness, which so sacred a relation calls for, praying God, now and ever, to build up you and us, and all His saints, a spiritual build-

ing. an holy house, a living temple unto Himself, the Lord and God.
Amen.

For some time after the settlement of Mr. Gay there was a
good degree of harmony and prosperity, and many were added
to the church. But he was a man of uncompromising principles; fearless in the utterance of what he believed to be right,
and, as fearless in rebuking wrong, he sometimes gave offence
by his plainness of speech. During the war of 1812, a large
party in town became dissatisfied with him because he took a
bold, firm stand against the administration, and did not hesitate
to speak his sentiments plainly in his sermons. Twenty-seven
families withdrew and joined the Baptist Society at Coldbrook,
filing their certificates of membership in that society, with the
town clerk, according to law. The assessors, however, still
assessed upon them a tax for the support of the minister, and
committed it to the collector with warrants for collection, in due
forms of law. Jacob Waite, one of the leading dissenters, in
their behalf, refused to pay, and notified the assessors and collector accordingly. The collector as promptly notified them
that unless they voluntarily paid these taxes, he should proceed
to collect them according to law. They were not intimidated
by the threat. The collector commenced with Jacob Waite,
giving as a reason, that when the others should become acquainted with the majesty of the law, they would pay the small
tax. He accordingly seized Mr. Waite's horse, which was not
only a valuable one, but a great pet of the family, thinking he
would not allow it to be sold. But the tax was not paid. The
horse was advertised and sold, "for cash, lawful currency of the
United States." As specie was then very scarce, there were
but few bidders, and the horse was bought for a small sum, by
Isaac Follett. As soon as the horse could be delivered and
settled for, it was again seized as the property of Follett (who
was another dissenter,) to pay his tax. The horse was sold on
the same conditions as before, and was bought by his first
owner. The collector next seized and sold a horse belonging
to Silas Wheeler. Mr. Waite having employed able counsel,
now commenced a suit against the assessors, and the collector

was requested to postpone further action till the town could take legal advice. The result was that at the next town meeting, a committee was appointed to compromise with the dissenters. This committee obtained the signatures of seven of the disaffected ones to a writing in which they declared that they were " desirous to promote the harmony and peace of the Congregational Society, and not to secede therefrom, nor to support any other religious society," and they agreed to return and become members of the society again, and support the present pastor, on condition that their ministerial tax for 1813 and 1814 should be abated, pledging their " consciences that they will forever pay their proportional part for the support of said pastor, unless some new cause, good and sufficient shall arise between us and said pastor, for us to secede from said society, of which we agree to give seasonable notice to the town clerk." This committee also arranged the conditions of settlement with Jacob Waite, Isaac Follett and Silas Wheeler; Mr. Waite agreeing to take $24.83 as costs and expenses. Mr. Follett was to receive $30, and Mr. Wheeler agreed to submit his claim to the decision of James Thompson, as one condition of the paper just mentioned, and which he signed, was that they should not be holden for any cost in this lawsuit, and they were to recover damages incurred in the illegal sale of their property. This committee then gave a bond to these three men, in the sum of $500 that the town should settle these claims within a reasonable time. The settlement was made, the dissenters returned, and the excitement abated, at least for a time. But entire harmony did not long continue, for we find in the records of 1818, a certificate from the town clerk of Barre, stating that Nathan Stone had paid one dollar that year, for preaching, in the Baptist Society in the town of Barre. Also two other certificates declaring that Amos Hartwell and Isaac Underwood had become members of said Baptist Society. We suppose this was done to comply with the forms of law in order to avoid paying ministerial tax in this town.

Soon after this there began to be complaints of the doctrinal sentiments of the minister, and in 1821, the "First Restoration Society of Hubbardston" was formed, and thirty-eight families joined it at first, and several more every spring till 1825. As we understand it, this society was organized as a mere form, to avoid supporting the minister, as the law required every citizen to pay for the support of some religious society. We do not learn that they ever did more than to keep their society alive, so as to answer the requirements of law.

April 3, 1826, a direct vote was taken in town meeting on the question of dismissing Mr. Gay, and stood, affirmative, forty-eight; negative, one hundred and one. · The disaffected party now seeing that they were too few to avail anything, used all the means in their power, to increase and concentrate the opposition ; the Restoration Society disbanded on the first of May, and most of the members returned to the Congregational Society in order to vote upon this question, when it should come up again.

The following is a copy of a petition to the selectmen for the insertion of certain articles in the March meeting warrant for 1827 :—

HUBBARDSTON, Feb. 5, 1827.

To the Gentlemen, Selectmen of Hubbardston.

The subscribers, considering the present difficulties and disputes about religious matters, and which have existed for a number of years between the town and their minister, would represent, that in their opinion, these difficulties, disputes, strife and contention, in families and society, have in a great measure arisen from the doctrines preached by their minister ; that there is no prospect of a favorable termination, so long as he continues to preach the Calvinistic doctrine. For preaching this doctrine, the Rev. David Kendall was dismissed from the ministry in this place : a grant of $700 was made him ; and afterwards, $500 settlement, and $100 an increase of salary, among other things, was bestowed on the present minister, to obtain preaching which corresponded with the sentiments of the people ; that great unanimity existed between Mr. Gay and his people at the time of his settlement, almost without opposition, except in the church ; but since, the said Gay has upheld and supported religious doctrines wholly different from those holden by him and the

14

Society at the time of his settlement, and are now such, as in our opinion his Society neither approve nor believe, thereby abandoning his old friends and principles, attaching himself to a religious party once opposed to him, and, with a zeal unbecoming his former professions, is endeavoring to form and establish a religious party in town, whose opinions, at best, as we think, are not only speculative, but subversive of that practical religion which ought to be inculcated by a minister, and conformed to by every man who would wish to bear the name of a christian. That notwithstanding an attempt was made last May, by a committee of the town, to settle the differences between the town and their minister, as to his preaching, we do not find that he has complied with the propositions then made to him, but on the contrary has been more zealous to propagate his peculiar doctrines, exhibiting a conduct indicating a determination to put down all opposition to what he deems orthodoxy.

Without particular remarks on his doctrines and preaching, but regarding our own religious principles and views, regarding also the religious education of our children, and wishing to promote the peace and harmony of the town, we cannot longer forbear requesting you to insert in your next March meeting warrant the subjoined articles for the consideration of the town, hoping they will in some way or manner, meet the wishes of its inhabitants, and praying the people of the town will act thereon, agreeably to the principles of their religion, and the dictates of an unbiased conscience.

1st. To see if the town consider that the Rev. Samuel Gay preaches the same religious doctrines that he preached at the time of his settlement in this town, or whether he has changed his religious doctrines in preaching to his Society, from what they were at that time.

2nd. To see if the town consider that the Rev. Samuel Gay has complied with the propositions made him by the committee last May, to settle the then existing difficulties between the town and him as to his preaching and other matters contained in those propositions, or act anything relative thereto.

3rd. To see if the town are satisfied with the doctrines preached by the Rev. Samuel Gay, or act anything thereon.

4th. To see if the town will vote to dismiss the Rev. Samuel Gay from his ministerial charge in said town, on account of his religious doctrines, or act anything thereon.

5th. To see if the town will vote to grant the Rev. Samuel Gay's salary the present year, or act anything thereon.

6th. To see what religious doctrines the town are willing to support, or act anything thereon.

7th. To see if the town will vote that any number of persons who may form themselves into any religious society, may have the use and occupation of the meeting-house the present year according to taxation, or polls, as shall be agreed on by the town, or act anything thereon.

Signed,

ABIJAH CLARK,	DELPHOS GATES,	CHARLES P. GAY,
AARON GATES,	ELISHA SPRING,	JAMES H. WHEELER,
JOHN CHURCH,	JOHN PHELPS,	MOSES GAY,
JOSEPH WAITE,	JONAS HEALD,	LEWIS POND,
MOSES CLARK.	DEXTER PHELPS,	ASA MAREAN,
BENJAMIN C. FROST,	ELIJAH WARREN,	AARON POND,
CHARLES WRIGHT,	NATHAN WRIGHT,	WILLIAM RICE,
SAMPSON STONE,	HAVEN PEIRCE.	SIMEON HOLT,
JOTHAM STONE,	JOSEPH CLARK, JR.,	GARDNER BROWN.
ELIPHALET STONE.	STEPHEN CLARK,	ASA ALLEN,
ELIAS HOLT.	MARTIN CLARK,	EMORY SMITH,
ROWLAND WOODWARD,	REUBEN PARTRIDGE.	SAMUEL DYKE,
SEWELL WHEELER.	ELISHA WHITTEMORE,	MOSES PHELPS.
WILLIAM BENNETT.	ISAAC LOVEWELL,	JOHN PARMENTER.
JAMES H. PEIRCE.	STEPHEN CHURCH,	WILLIAM JOSLIN,
JOSEPH BARTLETT,	STEPHEN FROST, JR.,	JONATHAN M. FOLLETT,
RUSSELL BROWN,	DANIEL CLARK.	AMOS J. RICE,
ELLA SLOCOMB,	JONATHAN KENDALL,	JOSHUA BROWNING,
FREEMAN BROWN,	SIMPSON CLARK,	DANIEL WOODWARD, JR.,
RICHARD MORSE,	WILLIAM HOBBS,	ELISHA WOODWARD.
BILL GRIMES,		ABNER GAY.—62.

Copy of the application for another article in the same warrant.

HUBBARDSTON, Feb. 9, 1827.

To the Selectmen of Hubbardston.

Gentlemen : Having seen several articles respecting the minister and the meeting-house, to be inserted in the next March meeting warrant, and considering that the hearts of all men are in the hands of God, and that he can turn them as the rivers of water are turned, and that the effectual. fervent prayer of the righteous availeth much, and that out of the abundance of the heart the mouth speaketh, I would request you, gentlemen, to insert the following article in the said warrant :—

To see if the town will vote to appoint a certain time in each week, for the year ensuing. to be in secret, concert prayer to God that He would make the hearts of both minister and people right with him ; that the minister may preach, and the people hear the truth of the gospel of Christ in the love of it, and that God would grant us His Spirit to enable us to practice according to the precepts of the Bible, that we may all live together as a band of brothers in the unity of the Spirit, and in the bonds of peace, while here in time, and in eternity all unite in singing the praises of redeeming love.

By inserting the above article you will oblige a well-wisher to the peace and harmony of the inhabitants of Hubbardston.

Yours respectfully,

OTIS PARKER.

The articles in both these applications were inserted as requested, but the one suggested by Mr. Parker was dismissed without action by the town.

On the first article in the other application, they voted sixty-four to two, "that Mr. Gay has changed his doctrines."

Of action upon the second, there is no record.

On the third they voted, "Eighty-eight to sixty-four, that they are not satisfied with the doctrines preached by Mr. Gay.

"Fourth—Voted ninety-nine to sixty-five to dismiss Mr. Gay.

"Fifth—On motion of Abijah Clark to raise $300 to pay Rev. Samuel Gay up to this time for his ministerial services, and if any be left, that it be in the funds of the town. Voted fifty-two for and twenty-one against.

"Sixth—Dismissed.

"Seventh—Voted, any persons who may form themselves into a religious society, may have the use of the meeting-house the present year, their proportional part of the time, according to taxation. Yeas, one hundred; nays, eight."

The vote on the fourth article, according to the terms of Mr. Gay's settlement, was not a sufficient majority to dismiss him, and another meeting was held on the 16th of April, at which the vote stood for dismissing Mr. Gay, one hundred and six; against it, sixty-five. Still the majority was insufficient, and the town voted that the selectmen call another meeting, to be held on the first Monday in May, and the warrant was immediately issued with a similar article. But in the mean time, April, 1827, the friends of Mr. Gay organized the First Calvinistic Society of Hubbardston, the same that now bears the name of the Evangelical Congregational Society. Eighty-eight persons joined it at first, and filed their certificates of membership, with the town clerk, before the first of May. Consequently, when this town meeting was held, May 7, the vote stood for dismissing Mr. Gay, one hundred and fourteen ; against it, none. A committee appointed to inform Mr. Gay, reported at the same meeting that Mr. Gay considered the vote to be in accordance with the contract between the parties, and that he would be satisfied to take his dimission at any time the town should choose, provided they pay his salary to April 17, 1828. Another committee was then chosen to confer with Mr. Gay in regard to his dismission, who reported at an adjourned meeting that they had not been able to effect anything with Mr. Gay in regard to the matter, except that if it was the pleasure of the town, he would consent to be dismissed without a council. A committee was next appointed to invite Mr. Gay to attend the meeting called in reference to his dismission. He met the former committee and they agreed that he should be dismissed by a mutual council of three ministers, on or before the first Monday in October, from his pastoral relation to the town and the church connected with the town ; and that he supply the pulpit till that date. Also that he be paid the sum of $750 in full. These propositions were accepted by the town, and the meeting adjourned to the first Monday in October.

September 3, 1827, four weeks before the time appointed for the council, the church held a meeting in the Centre School-house and passed the following resolutions, viz :—

1. *Resolved,* That with a view to perpetuate good feelings and promote christian charity, we mutually agree to divide, and from this time be two distinct churches ; those connected with the Calvinistic Society one, and those remaining with the old society, the other ; each church as a separate body, to relinquish all claim to discipline, and all obligation to watch over the members of the other.

2. To grant all sisters who wish to be connected with the church associated with the town, to withdraw their names from the other church

at any time within one year, and to be at liberty during that time to attend public worship where they please and commune with which church they please.

3. That the church furniture be kept by Dea. Justus Ellinwood, for the use of both churches, until the two churches shall otherwise agree ; and that we will hold communions on different Sabbaths, so as to accommodate such an arrangement.

4. That the church records, for the present, be kept by Rev. Mr. Gay, to be consulted by both churches, as occasion may require.

5. That we will request the council which is to be called to ratify the agreement between Rev. Mr. Gay and the town, to recognize the church remaining with the town, as the First Church in Hubbardston, and the members who have seceded from the town, as the church associated with the Calvinistic Society in Hubbardston, and Rev. Mr. Gay as their pastor.

According to the records ninety-four members of the church went with the new society, and thirty remained with the town.

The letters missive for the council to dismiss Mr. Gay were issued by the pastor and the committee of the town, the church, as such, taking no part. This council met October 1, 1827, and was composed of the following pastors and delegates : Rev. Aaron Bancroft, D. D., and Dea. Benjamin Butman of Worcester ; Rev. John Fisk and Mr. Amasa Bigelow of New Braintree ; Rev. Samuel Clark and Dea. Charles Russell of Princeton.

There is no evidence in the records that any documents were presented for their consideration, except the paper showing the agreement between Mr. Gay and the town. Their result is recorded as follows : " Voted *nem. con.* that this council, after due deliberation, deem it expedient to give an ecclesiastical sanction to the proceedings of said respective parties, and by authority with which said respective parties have invested them, the council do hereby pronounce the ministerial and pastoral relation between Rev. Samuel Gay and the town of Hubbardston, and the church associated with the town, to be dissolved.

The council, without qualification, express their gratification in reviewing the christian temper manifested by the pastor and people in the whole transaction. No allegation has been made against Mr. Gay, and the members of the original church and congregation, though differing in speculative opinion, have discovered a disposition to maintain the unity of the spirit in the bonds of peace."

It is evident from this result that this council did not take any action upon the request of the church in regard to recognizing the two bodies, and Mr. Gay as the pastor of those associated with the new society. Probably they did not even consider the subject.

It will also be seen from the reference here to differences in speculative opinions, and from the petition above introduced, that the cause of the separation was the same that was agitating almost the entire state at that time, by which the old churches of the towns were broken up into those bearing the names of Orthodox and Unitarian.

On the 13th of the same month, those members who had gone with the Calvinistic Society, voted to call a council to consider their state as a church, and to state publicly their view of their standing and of the standing of their pastor.

The ministers upon this council were, Rev. Joseph Chickering of Phillipston, Rev. Cyrus Mann of Westminster, Rev. Josiah Clark of Rutland, Rev. Horatio Bardwell of Holden, Rev. Alonzo Phillips of Princeton, and Rev. Sumner Lincoln of Gardner. They, with their delegates, met October 31, 1827, and after a careful examination of various documents relative to the division of the church, and the formation of the Calvinistic Society, unanimously adopted the following resolutions :—

1. *Resolved*, That the majority of a church seceding from the society with which they have been connected, continue to be the church.

2. *Resolved*, That though we are satisfied that the church in Hubbardston were actuated by the most pacific feelings in passing certain resolves relating to dividing itself into two churches, yet, in our estimation, their resolves are not warranted by ecclesiastical usage, and imply a principle of dangerous tendency.

3. *Resolved*, That as an ecclesiastical council we do hereby recognize and declare Rev. Samuel Gay pastor of the church and minister of the Calvinistic Society of Hubbardston.

This Result was read at the dedication of the meeting-house Nov. 1, 1827. The church being thus publicly recognized as the same body which had been associated with the town was never reorganized; and, though at first it received the name of Calvinistic Church from being associated with the society then called the Calvinistic, its name was never changed. And as the pastor was declared to hold to the church the same relation which was formed in 1810, he was not reinstalled.

In the controversy which followed, the validity of these transactions was called in question. It was claimed that Mr. Gay was not, *de facto*, the pastor of any church after his dismission from the town; and an attempt was made to have him indicted for solemnizing marriages contrary to law. But when the proceedings of this last council were presented to the Grand Jury, the case was summarily dismissed.

For the next ten or twelve years much harmony and prosperity attended the ministry of Mr. Gay, and there were many additions to the church, two hundred being added in ten years. At length he was guilty of growing old, and much dissatisfaction began to be manifested, and efforts were made to have him dismissed. This was effected December 1, 1841, and the same day Rev. Oliver B. Bidwell was settled in his place; the ordination sermon was preached by Hubbard Winslow, D. D.

During the entire ministry of Mr. Gay, 340 were added to the church and 740 were baptized. Mr. Gay was born in Dedham, March 16, 1784, and graduated at Harvard College in 1805. After his dismission, he retired to his farm in Hubbardston, where he died very suddenly, October 16, 1848, thirty-eight years, lacking one day, after his ordination.

The first part of Mr. Bidwell's ministry was successful, but the anti-slavery agitation which so widely prevailed, caused serious jars and divisions in the church. A part became much dissatisfied with the course of the pastor; the result was that after a pastorate of four years, he was dismissed. During that time sixty were added to the church.

Rev. Dana B. Bradford was installed June 17, 1846; sermon by Prof. Warner of Amherst College. He was dismissed April

22, 1852. Forty were received to the church during his stay.

Rev. Cyrus W. Allen was installed December 29, 1852, and dismissed December 31, 1860. Thirty-nine were added to the church.

From this time to the settlement of Rev. Henry C. Fay in 1868, there was no settled pastor; two or three were called who declined. Rev. J. E. Wilkins, Rev. C. F. Boynton and Rev. David Cushman, each acted as stated supply for some time. From 1860 to 1868, twenty-two were added.

Soon after the settlement of Mr. Fay, the pecuniary resources of the parish were so much reduced by losses from removals, and the great freshet of October, 1869, that it was found impossible to pay the amount of salary which had been promised, and he remained only till the spring of 1870. During his ministry twenty-five were added to the church. He was dismissed September 14, 1870, by the same council which installed Rev. John M. Stowe, who received forty to the church and baptized seventeen. His ministry was abruptly terminated by his death May 9, 1877.* From July of that year to the present time the pulpit has been occupied by Rev. John F. Norton.

Including the ninety-four of the separation, the whole number of persons who have belonged to the church since that time, is 545.

The deacons of the church from its beginning to the time of the separation, were the following:—

Joseph Eveleth, elected September 2, 1771 ; dismissed Jan. 13, 1788.
Adam Wheeler, elected September 2, 1771 ; died August 24, 1802.
Elisha Woodward, elected April 11, 1778 ; died March 18, 1810.
Ebenezer Rice, elected November 8, 1787 ; removed.
Ephraim Allen, elected April 21, 1796 ; declined official duties 1818.
Otis Parker, elected May 6, 1805 ; went with the Calvinistic Society ; resigned April 13, 1840, and was dismissed to the Methodist Church.
Justus Ellinwood, elected September 11, 1818, also went with the Calvinistic Society ; declined official duties in 1842 ; died in 1844.

---

*A fuller account of Mr. Stowe is given in Chapter XVII.

After the formation of the Calvinistic Society, those church members that remained with the town, continued to call themselves the "First Congregational Church in Hubbardston." In the records of Rev. A. D. Jones, their next pastor, the following note is subjoined to the names of the thirty who remained:—

"It may be proper to mention here that with these members of the 'church,' about three-fourths of the inhabitants of the town, held the original ground, and were, of course, the First Church and Society in Hubbardston."

Their parish affairs remained under the control of the town as before. They never assumed or claimed any other name than the one given above, though in later years their church has often been designated as the Unitarian Church, because associated with Unitarian Churches and holding similar sentiments.

Thus we find two churches growing from the roots of the one old church, without any new organization, and neither assuming a new name, though widely different in doctrinal belief.

It was nearly eleven months after the dismission of Mr. Gay from the town, before the town voted a call to Mr. Abner D. Jones, though the pulpit was supplied all the time. Mr. Jones was only twenty-three years of age when he came, but the people were so much pleased with his appearance and his preaching, that when the question of giving him a call was brought up in town meeting, the vote was one hundred and five in the affirmative, and none in the negative. The church, according to previous request, acted with the town, and not in their separate capacity. The salary offered Mr. Jones was $550, "to be continued so long as he should supply the pulpit with the consent of the majority of the voters of the First Congregational Society, and for six months after notice should be given him that a majority desired his dismission." If he should desire to leave, he was to give them three months' notice. Mr. Jones reserved to himself five Sabbaths in a year, and with that condition, accepted the call by writing a very affectionate letter.

In these days a parish society is an organization entirely separate from the town or city in which it exists; but allusion has already been made to the fact, apparent all through the records, that the legal parish in Massachusetts was formerly the town itself, which therefore acted in the double capacity of town and parish; when acting in the latter capacity it is often referred to as a "society," or a "religious society;" and when the time came that distinct religious societies began to be organized, the town, here, as in other places, began to be spoken of as "The First Parish," "The First Society;" or, since originally all churches in New England were Congregational, as "The First Congregational Society." This fact explains the circumstance that the record of the doings of "The First Congregational Society," which was copied and sent to Mr. Jones in giving him a call, is identical with the town records of the same date, and was an attested copy of the same by the town clerk.

Mr. Jones was ordained November 13, 1828. Fourteen churches were invited on the council. Rev. Dr. Thayer of Lancaster preached the sermon. On the 11th of November, 1832, Mr. Jones publicly, but very unexpectedly to the people, requested a dismission without supplying the three months agreed upon. The town voted to grant his request, and at the same time passed a vote "that the First Congregational Society approve his religious sentiments, express their deep regret that he should leave them, and recommend him to the people of their denomination, wishing him in their mutual and friendly separation, peace, prosperity, and happiness on earth, and a blessed immortality in the world to come." "At the close of the meeting, Mr. Jones entered the house, and the vote was read to him, when he addressed those present in an affectionate and pathetic manner, recommending to them union, tranquility and harmony, in their continued efforts for the preaching of the gospel in the unity and truth thereof, and lastly commending the society to the Almighty, who careth for and regardeth all true and sincere worshippers." When he preached his farewell sermon, the house was crowded. Those who had never attended his meeting before came in large numbers to hear what he would say. He looked over his audience as he rose to address them, and said there were so many itching ears present, he should not preach the sermon prepared, and spoke extemporaneously.

At a meeting held January 22, 1833, the town voted unanimously to call Rev. Ebenezer Robinson of Beverly, the church as before, taking no separate action. He was offered a salary of $500. His reply was as follows:—

BEVERLY, Feb. 4, 1833.

To the First Congregational Society in Hubbardston.

Gentlemen : Having received through your committee an invitation to settle with you in the work of the gospel ministry, I have prayerfully considered the solemn and important subject, and taken the counsel of a number of my friends, and come to the conclusion to give, and do hereby give you an affirmative answer, and accept your call on the conditions you have proposed, reserving to myself two Sabbaths in each year.

As my object in preaching to you will be the glory of God in the salvation of men, I sincerely request your most fervent prayers that he will enable me to come unto you in the fullness of the blessing of the gospel of Christ, and assist me to preach the truth as it is in Jesus ; to preach experimental religion and practical persevering holiness ; thus may his enemies become reconciled, and strangers become fellow-citizens with the saints, and of the household of God, and thus may his name be praised, and his cause advanced. And may the Lord graciously smile upon us and make our connection profitable, lasting, and happy.

Yours in the bonds of the gospel,

EBENEZER ROBINSON.

He was installed February 20; seven churches were represented in the council, and Mr. Gay and Mr. Jones were invited to be present at the installation. The sermon was preached by Rev. Mr. Thayer of Beverly. About this time the connection of the church with the town ceased.

Mr. Robinson preached his farewell sermon October 9, 1836.

Concerning the pastors during the next thirty years, the following was furnished by Rev. B. F. McDaniel:—

"In 1838–9, Rev. W. H. Kingsley supplied for one year. At a meeting of the church, April 15, 1840, it was unanimously voted to extend an invitation to Rev. Claudius Bradford to become their pastor, the parish having previously extended a like invitation.   He was ordained the same day, April 15, 1840. He closed his ministry April 13, 1845.   Soon after, Rev. S. H. Lloyd was settled, but remained only one year.   April 14, 1847, Mr. George T. Hill was ordained over this society.   He closed his labors September 1, 1852.   This pastorate is represented as being most happy and beneficial.   For a little more than a year after this, Rev. Stillman Barber supplied the pulpit, but was not settled.   June 20, 1855, Rev. A. S. Ryder was ordained as pastor of the church and parish.   He was an earnest worker and made many friends.   He was dismissed December 1, 1860.   He was succeeded by Rev. Mr. Brown, Rev. H. F. Edes, and Rev. Seth Saltmarsh, each of whom supplied from one to two years, but were not installed."

October 20, 1869, Rev. Benjamin F. McDaniel was ordained. His ministry continued till April 28, 1871.   After that Rev. W. A. P. Willard supplied about two years, Rev. J. R. Johnson nearly two years, and Rev. H. W. Morse a year and a half; Rev. Alfred C. Nickerson of Templeton preached here six months in 1879, and Rev. D. W. Morehouse three months in the summer of 1880.   The remainder of the time—when there has been preaching—has been filled by temporary supply from Sabbath to Sabbath.   Rev. N. A. Haskell, the present acting pastor, began his labors with February, 1881.

From statements above recorded it will be seen that both branches of the church have been distinguished for brief pastorates.   For the causes of this fact, we do not feel called upon to inquire at length.   The ministers have generally been worthy and faithful men, and in but few cases, has there been any serious bitterness or opposition on the part of the people.   Though these churches have heaped to themselves teachers, it has not been altogether because they could not endure sound doctrine, nor because of itching ears ; but ministers have not been so firmly settled in the minds and hearts of the people, in late years, as formerly, and they have not looked upon the acceptance of a call as entering upon a life service, as did the earlier pastors; consequently the relation has been more easily disturbed.

Since the first jar of the separation of the church was over, the two branches have flourished side by side, with a good degree of friendliness.

The Methodist Church.—Down to the year 1839, there was no church in town besides the two branches of the original church, just described, and there was no preaching by any other denomination. In the early autumn of 1838, Rev. Benjamin Paine, a Methodist preacher stationed at Princeton, appointed a meeting at five o'clock, on Sabbath afternoon, at the schoolhouse in the west part of Princeton, near Valley Village; but when he arrived, he found the house closed against him, and held his meeting in the open air. Meetings were held on several succeeding Sabbaths, under the shade trees in front of Mr. Isaac Lovewell's house. Many assembled and listened attentively, who had seldom attended any meeting before, and who not only heard, but received the word gladly, and brought forth fruits meet for repentance. Among the converts at these meetings and others held during the fall and winter, were about twenty of the inhabitants of Hubbardston, mostly from the sixth school district. These persons were desirous that there should be preaching at the centre of the town, under the auspices of the Methodists. The hall at the Star Hotel was engaged, and Rev. Joseph Whitman was transferred from his appointment at Grafton, to this town. His first sermon was preached in the hall, Thursday, April 2, 1839, and lectures were continued on Thursday and Sabbath evenings, till May 12, when regular Sabbath services were commenced and continued till the meeting of the conference, June 5, when at the earnest request of the people, Mr. Whitman was stationed here. The meetings were continued in the hall for about a year and a half, constantly increasing in numbers and interest. Mr. Whitman was a young man of great energy, of much talent and promise, and an interesting preacher. He remained two years, the longest term then allowed by the conference, and awakened a deep interest. During the time, he was married to Miss Eleanor Wheeler of Concord, who entered heartily into the work with him and won the respect and affection of the whole congregation. It was with great pain and regret that the people parted with them. In the time of Mr. Whitman's stay here, 171 were received as church members, 158 of them on probation.

In the spring of 1841, Rev. Stephen Cushing was appointed to this place. He found the young church in a prosperous condition, and labored with general acceptance for one year. Six were added to the church by certificate and thirty-one on trial, twenty-two of whom were received in full communion.

The next man sent here was Rev. Willard Smith, who remained two years. At this time there was a general awakening in the Methodist denomination, and this place shared in that interest to a considerable extent. Seven were added to the church by certificate and fifty-nine on trial, of whom forty-one were received into full communion. Several who had united with this church came from Templeton; about the time Mr. Smith left, a church was formed there, and sixteen were dismissed from this church to join them, and Mr. Smith was appointed their preacher.

He was followed in his ministry here, by Rev. George W. Bates, who remained two years. His efforts were directed mainly to the cultivation of christian character among the present members, and to the promotion of the purity of the church. During his two years, ten were admitted by certificate, and five on probation. In the same time, the number of those who died, removed, withdrew, or were dropped or expelled, amounted to eighty-five, leaving the church with seventy members less than at the beginning of this term.

Mr. Bates was followed by Rev. Wm. Gordon, for two years, during which time twenty were added to the church.

His successor was Rev. Samuel Tupper, who remained two years, and by his discreet and earnest labors endeared himself, not only to the people of his own charge, but to all who became acquainted with him. Nine were received to the church by certificate, and sixteen on probation, seven of whom, came into full communion.

After he left, Rev. George Q. Poole came for one year, and was followed by Rev. Moses P. Webster, who remained one year. In this time six came into the church, five of whom had before been members, but had left town, and now returned; the church now numbered 128.

Rev. Burtis Judd was the next minister, during whose labors there were forty-seven additions, though it appears that fifteen of the probationers never came into full fellowship.

Mr. Judd was followed by Rev. Freeman Q. Barrows, one year. After the close of his engagement, he remained in town till December 5, 1854, when he went to Gardner and preached, returning in a severe snow storm. After leaving his horse at the stable, he walked to his house, and as he was entering the yard, he fell into the snow and almost instantly expired.

In the spring of 1854, Rev. Charles Baker came, who remained two years. He was a man of much vivacity and activity. Thirty-four were added to the church during his stay, most of them by certificate.

After he left, Rev. Mr. Atkinson labored here for one year and was succeeded by Rev. N. H. Martin, who remained till 1859, two years. In this period the church received large accessions, many of whom were from the church in Templeton. These were transferred to the church in East Templeton, after its organization in 1860, and Mr. Martin was appointed to that station.

He was succeeded here by Rev. H. R. Parmenter, for one year, who was followed by Rev. Rodney Gage. Early in his second year Mr. Gage was appointed chaplain in the United States Army.

Rev. Charles H. Newell supplied the pulpit with acceptance during the remainder of that year, and was appointed by the conference in 1863. At the close of his year the church numbered one hundred and thirty-two, twenty-two less than three years before.

In 1864, Rev. Charles H. Vinton became the pastor, and remained two years. His pastorate was a successful one. During his first year there was an interesting and somewhat extensive revival, and before he left, the church increased to one hundred and seventy-five.

Rev. I. B. Bigelow commenced his labors in 1866, and remained two years. The parsonage was purchased about the time he came, and he did a good work in securing the enlargement and extensive repairs of the meeting-house. At the close of his ministry the church numbered one hundred and seventy-one.

He was succeeded by Rev. Porter M. Vinton, who remained three years, during which time the church continued in the "even tenor of its way." When he left, in 1871, the church numbered one hundred and fifty.

His successor, Rev. J. S. Day, remained but one year, during which several were added to the church; but by correction of the records, and dropping the names of back-sliders, the whole number was considerably reduced. It was then one hundred and twenty-four.*

Rev. T. B. Treadwell began his labors in 1872, and remained for two years, a faithful pastor and a good man. Though the church did not make that advancement in divine things that was desirable, yet much good was done, and he left the charge in 1874 the same in membership as when he became its pastor.

Rev. O. W. Adams was next appointed to serve this church, which he did for one year with much zeal, faith and success. A revival sprang up and some sixteen souls were saved. The number in church fellowship at this time was one hundred and forty.

Rev. William R. Tisdale followed Mr. Adams, in the spring of 1875. During this year the church fell off some ten in membership.

---

*The account of the last ten years just given, was furnished by Rev. J. S. Day. That which follows, from 1872 to the present time, is in the language of Rev. Charles H. Vinton.

16

Rev. J. J. Woodbury, the next preacher in charge, bears the name of a faithful minister, among the people, and for two years, with extra means and help, much interest was manifest. The church was built up in the gospel and about fifty joined on probation, but for some reason, not a large company joined the church in full membership.

Rev. W. E. Dwight became the next pastor; the minutes show a falling off in membership, from one hundred and thirty to one hundred and ten, owing to deaths, withdrawals and the dropping of several unworthy persons, during his pastorate of two years.

In 1880, Rev. C. H. Vinton was again appointed to this charge. And as in his former pastorate he received over fifty persons into this church, so may it be in his present pastorate.

CHAPTER XI

SOON after the organization of the church and the settlement of Mr. Parker, in 1770, the question of building a house of worship began to be agitated. We infer that the schoolhouse, where the meetings were held, had become too strait for them, for the town voted to " build seats *above* in the schoolhouse."

It had become evident that the seven-acre lot, set apart by the proprietors for a meeting-house and common, would not become the natural business centre of the town, and arrangements were made to exchange with Mr. Parker, giving him the seven acres and receiving three and a half acres where the common and burial-ground now are.

In October, 1771, an article was inserted in the town meeting warrant " to see if the town will build a meeting-house." " Dismissed." September 8, 1772, the town voted " to build a meeting-house the present year," and " to set it betwixt Mr. Parker's and the burying-ground, on the height of land;" also, " to build it fifty foot in length and forty in wedth;" but at the next meeting they voted that the meeting-house should " be forty-five foot in length, and forty-five foot in wedth," and a building committee was appointed.

The erection of the frame was let, by the job, for eighty pounds, to be completed during the month of June next. In May, arrangements were made for raising the house, and it was voted "to provide entertainment, vitals and drink, for one hundred men, and no more," as this was regarded a sufficient number. During the next winter, the window frames and sashes were made, and the lower floor was laid. On the 8th of May, 1774, a committee was chosen to purchase the glass, and other

materials necessary to finish the outside of the house, and to
have it done the same year. Thus in a little more than two
years from the time they began, they had the outside of a meeting-house. If we think them unreasonably dilatory in this
work, we must remember that they were few in numbers and
of small means, and that the events of the Revolution were
already crowding thickly upon them.

December 14, 1775, the town voted to build the body seats
of the meeting-house the same winter "leaving ground for one
row of pews in the hind seats," and chose a committee to do
the work. But it was not done. It is probable, that in this
house, without paint or ceiling, pulpit or pews, or even seats—
except of rough boards laid on blocks—and with no fire, they
worshipped for nine or ten years, though during that time, one
or two attempts were made to finish it. We learn that the men
sat on one side, and the women on the other.

Pew-Plots.—In April, 1778, after much voting and reconsid-
ering, it was decided "to plot out the pew-ground and number
the pews," which was done. At another meeting they voted to
sell these pews at auction, and appropriate the money to finish
the house. Each man who bought a space for a pew, was to
pay eight dollars, earnest money, which was to be forfeited if
he did not appear within two months and pay the balance.
Those who bought wall pews were to finish them as high as the
bottom of the windows. One condition of the sale was, "that
each man who buys a pew shall set on his own pew-ground
after one year." This method of deeding to individuals certain
portions of the floor of the meeting-house, for the purpose of
building the family pews thereon, was not uncommon. In this
case it is evident that they expected to realize a considerable
sum of money, and that many pews would soon be erected,
which was not the case. Whether the pew-ground was sold
and each family sat on temporary seats, on the square patch
marked off to them, does not appear.

At the same meeting, it was voted "to let out the meeting-
house to be finished complete," the inside to be finished in three

years. To guide the committee in some parts of their work, they were instructed to build a pulpit and deacons' seats as good as those in the Rutland meeting-house. These instructions were afterwards modified. In 1781, an article was inserted in the town meeting warrant "to see if the town will insist on having the pulpit of the meeting-house, built according to the fashion of the pulpit in the old Rutland meeting-house, or will comply to have it built according to the rest of the work in the meeting-house." The vote upon this article is recorded as follows: "Voted to accept of a pulpit in Hubbardston meeting-house, equal to the pulpit in the meeting-house in the first parish in Shrewsbury."

Several times in 1781, the question came up why the house was not finished according to contract, but no definite reason is recorded. Probably the inevitable burdens of the times were all they could carry. In June of that year, Joel Pollard and Isaac Bellows were chosen a committee to seat the meeting-house, and the time for finishing it was extended one year. As soon after the close of the Revolution as they could take breath, they began again the work of finishing the inside, but it went forward slowly. A pulpit and the deacons' seats were first built, and then permanent seats on the lower floor, which soon began to give place to pews, though it was many years before all these pews were built. As early as 1794, the wall pews on the lower floor, one tier in the rear of the body of the house, and one tier in the gallery, had been completed. In April 1802, it was voted "to take up the two hind seats to build pews." In September of the next year they voted "to sell ground for a row of pews in the gallery at each end."

Pews Sold.—The following is a copy from the town records:

At public vendue December 2, 1793, the following pew spots were sold to the persons whose names are prefixed thereto, at the prices annexed :—

No. 1. First pew east of the middle alley, reserved for a town pew. - - - - - - -

No. 2. Second pew east of the middle alley, to Nathaniel £. s. Waite for - - - - - - - 12 10

No. 3. Adjoining Mr. Waite's pew on the one side and £. s.
    the east alley on the other, to Asa Church, -   - 16 5
No. 4. Adjoining the middle alley on the east side, to John
    McClenathan, - - - - - - - 20
No. 5. Second pew west of the middle alley, Ebenezer
    Mann, - - - - - - - - 12 5
No. 6. Joining Ebenezer Mann's on the one side, and the
    west alley on the other, Joseph Green, -   - 13
N. B. the above pews are the same for bigness as the pews behind.

GALLERY PEWS ON THE WALL OF THE FRONT GALLERY.

                                                £. s.
No. 1. At the head of the men's stairs, Ebenezer Joslin, 7
No. 2. Paul Matthews,   -   -   -   -   -   - 6 5
No. 3. Ebenezer Warren,   -   -   -   -   -   6
No. 4. Micah Howe, -   -   -   -   -   -   - 5 15
No. 5. John Newton, -   -   -   -   -   -   - 6 5
No. 6. William Nightingale,   -   -   -   -   6 15
N. B. the above pews are of equal bigness, about five feet three inches
by five feet.   £. s.
No. 1. Over men's stairs, six feet six inches by seven feet
    two inches, Nathaniel Waite,   -   -   -   - 5 15
No. 2. Over the women's stairs, same bigness, Nathaniel
    Upham, -   -   -   -   -   -   -   - 4 5

In 1816, a meeting was called to see if the town would allow
the body seats to remain for the benefit of aged and infirm
persons, but it was voted to make them into pews. In February,
1817, there was a sale of several pews. The first on the right
hand of the broad aisle was sold to Nathaniel Waite for $101.
The second, on the left hand, to William Marean for $93. The
third, on the west aisle, to Maj. Moses Greenwood, for $66.
The fourth, on the east aisle, to Daniel Woodward for $58.

In 1794, they voted to paint the meeting-house outside and
inside.

Porch and Belfry.—Two years later the question came up
whether they would build porches, but the article was dismissed.
In September, 1803, they voted to build a belfry at the west end
and a porch at the east end, but they did not choose a com-

mittee to do the work till a year later, and it was not completed till the early part of 1806, when a committee was appointed to inspect the porch and cupola. They reported that every part was thoroughly done, and that the undertakers had done themselves honor by their faithful performance, and deserved the thanks of the town.

Bell.—In 1805, a vote was passed to procure a bell and a lightning rod, the bell to weigh 800 lbs., 3 qrs. The committee were instructed to get the bell, as soon as they pleased, but not to call for pay for it, for one year. It cost $400.

The Clock was a gift of the proprietors of the town, received in 1808.

Stoves.—In 1815, there was an article in the town meeting warrant to see if the town would procure a stove. Rejected. In 1827, the town voted to accept of stoves, if put in at individual expense. In 1830, stoves were put in.

Thus by slow degrees came into being, the "old meeting-house," which is so closely interwoven with the childhood memories of many of us. It was so long in building, that it was several times necessary to make appropriations for repairs, before it was finished. In 1818, a committee was chosen "to dress the pulpit anew."

This house as we remember it, was a large square structure, with double rows of windows, and on the south side, double doors, opening into the broad middle aisle. On the east end was the projecting entrance, or porch. On the west end, the huge belfry with another entrance. The towering pulpit was in the middle of the north side, and the sounding board hung like a huge extinguisher over the minister. There were galleries with pews, on three sides. The pews were square and high, with lattice work at the top. The seats were provided with hinges that they might be raised when the people stood in prayer, which was then the custom. Great was the clatter, when they were let down again. One row of these pews was built round against the walls and raised a step above the main floor.

In front of the pulpit was the famous deacons' seat, which they were expected to occupy with grave dignity. Underneath was an open space, into which, our grandmothers told us, the deacons would put us, if we whispered or played in meeting time.

In this house the people of the whole town gathered for worship till the time of the division of the church.

Order of Exit.—They seem to have had a due sense of propriety in regard to entering and leaving the place of worship. In 1803, the town chose a committee " to consult what method the people should take to come out of the meeting-house in a regular way, after divine service." The report of this committee, as follows, was adopted :—

" We being appointed a committee to consider what method will be decent to be observed in going out of the meeting-house on Sundays after divine survice is ended, report as follows : That all and every person keep their seats, till the minister come down from the Desk, then to move in regular succession, beginning at the fore seats, and so in succession till the body seats and pews on the lower floor have passed out of their seats and pews ; then the galleries to follow in regular succession, by two in the procession, till the gallery is clear ; and it is recommended for every person to move from the door, when out of the house, so that those who are coming out may not be crowded."

Changes.—This house stood in its place without change, and was used as a town house, as well as for a house of worship, till 1842, when the belfry and the porch were torn down, and the body of the house, removed a few feet from its original site, was made into the house at present occupied by the Unitarian people. It was rededicated, January, 1843.

In 1869, it was again remodeled, and rededicated.

The Second Meeting-house in Town, that of the Evangelical Society, was dedicated November 1, 1827. It was enlarged a few years later. The pulpit was, at first, in front of the high gallery, but in the winter of 1841–2 the pews were turned, and

FIRST CONGREGATIONAL CHURCH, (UNITARIAN).
Erected 1773. Remodeled in 1842.

the pulpit placed at the opposite end in its present position. In the repairs of 1868 the high gallery gave place to the present arrangement.

The semi-centennial anniversary of its dedication was observed in 1877, with appropriate exercises, including a historical address by Rev. J. F. Norton, followed by a social reunion of the church with former members and other friends who had assembled from far and near to commemorate the day.

The Methodist Meeting-house was built in 1840 and dedicated September 25 of that year. It was enlarged and thoroughly repaired in 1867.

17

CHAPTER XII

CEMETERIES.

IN early times, the burial-places of the dead were neglected, desolate and lonely enclosures, if indeed they were even enclosed. They were not often entered except on funeral occasions. To the minds of children they were enveloped in gloom; and if they had occasion to pass the church-yard at night, they did so with the trembling apprehension of seeing the ghosts of the departed walking there in white robes.

The first spot occupied as a burial-place in this town, was the southwest corner of the common; and it is probable that the bodies buried there were never all removed.

Soon after the exchange of land with Rev. Mr. Parker,* the northeasterly portion of the three and a half acres received from him, was laid out for a burial-ground. In 1773, an article was inserted in the town meeting warrant "to see if the District will vote what way or manner they will come into for clearing up the common for burial-place and meeting-house." But no action was taken, and it was many years before much was done even toward fencing the burial-ground. After the meeting-house was built, a row of horse sheds extended the entire length of the south side; the remainder was fenced with stone wall, built at several different times.

· The following vote shows what care was taken of the resting places of the dead: May, 1804, "Voted, that Jona. Cutting have all he can get off the burying-field, and that he shall not turn any creature larger than a calf into said field, for the term of

---

*See Chapter XI.

ten years, for getting a lock and key for the gate, and repairing the wall, and keeping it in repair for the same term of years."

In 1818, the question of enlarging this ground was considered, and a committee was appointed to select grounds in different parts of the town for the same purpose. But we do not find any report of this committee, nor any further action in relation to the subject, except that the town voted "to accept the burying-ground." What ground it was is not designated in the record, but it is now known to be the cemetery in the easterly part of the town. A small piece of land on the Gardner road was enclosed for the same purpose, many years ago; very few were ever buried there.

About the year 1849, several plans were discussed for laying out a new and larger cemetery for the town, but none of them were carried out. Instead, several grounds were laid out in different parts of the town, by private associations which own and control them. They are located as follows: One in the north part, near Warren Pond; one in the south part near "Tilton's Mills;" Forest Hill Cemetery, a mile and a half west of the village; Rural Glen Cemetery, on the Worcester road; Pine Grove Cemetery, on the Barre road; and Greenwood Cemetery, on the farm (then) of Hon. E. A. Greenwood.

In 1869, the town appropriated $500 to repair the old cemetery, and the ground is now kept in much better condition than formerly.

The town tomb was built in 1872; the new one at the Pine Grove Cemetery in 1877.

CHAPTER XIII.

WAR OF THE REBELLION.

ANTI-SLAVERY AGITATION.—Probably few towns in the state were more deeply agitated than Hubbardston, by the great anti-slavery contest which preceded the outbreak of the civil war in 1861. In the beginning of that movement, there was a party of active, earnest, persistent men and women in this town, who were in sympathy with William Lloyd Garrison and his coadjutors. Prominent abolitionists,—Wendell Phillips, Frederick Douglass, S. S. Foster, Abby Kelly, and others—often came to address the people here. Sometimes three or four of these speakers came together, and held conventions for several successive days. And though their words of bitter denunciation and biting sarcasm were often like barbed arrows to the people, large numbers came to hear. When opportunity was given for free discussion, these meetings frequently became excited and stormy, and were liable to be protracted far into the night. These reformers were especially severe in their denunciations of the churches, sometimes formally declaring that the churches in Hubbardston were "compacted in blood and in league with hell," because·they did not adopt the radical measures of the anti-slavery leaders. As leading members of the churches joined with them, divisions arose that led to sad results; churches, families, and neighborhoods were divided against themselves. Though the majority of the people were indignant and often irritated by the measures of the reformers, yet the spirit of freedom, and abhorrence of the whole system of human bondage, was widening and deepening all the while.

When the third political party—the Liberty Party—was organized, sufficient numbers entered into it in this town, to hold the balance of power between the two old parties, the Whig and Democratic, all officers then being elected by a majority instead of by a plurality of votes. The election of representative in 1843, was probably the most exciting political contest ever known in town. The Liberty Party was smaller than either of the others, but large enough to prevent any man from receiving the majority of votes. For two successive days, the three parties continued their balloting, each endeavoring to rally every man whom it was possible to bring to the polls, and each supporting its own candidate, hoping that one of the others would yield.

Repeated motions were made, "not to send," "to dissolve the meeting." When the sun went down on the second day there was little or no change in the position of affairs, but as they could no longer vote legally, a motion was carried to dissolve the meeting. The selectmen were immediately petitioned to call another meeting, which was held two weeks later, each party holding its ground as before. That was their last opportunity, according to the limitations of the law. As the day drew towards the close, an attempt was made to effect a union of the Whig and Liberty Parties. The result was that Sylvanus Dunton the Liberty Party candidate received a majority of one vote, and was declared elected. Thus this town had the credit of sending the first anti-slavery representative, elected on that ground, to the Massachusetts Legislature. When he took his seat, he found the other two parties were equally divided in the Legislature, and there was no choice of governor. For many days he voted for Mr. Sewall, the candidate of his own party, and prevented a choice, but finally yielded and allowed George N. Briggs, the candidate of the Whig party, to be elected.

The next two years the town was not represented, it being impossible to elect any man for that purpose. Thus the people of this town were agitated by every new feature of the great contest for freedom, and were not behind in doing their part when the bugle call rang through the land rousing the nation to arms.

Government Sustained.—After the fall of Sumpter and the Massacre of Massachusetts men in Baltimore, the flame of patriotic sentiment which swept through every loyal state, kindled high among the people here. Party names were forgotten. All came forward with alacrity to sustain the government. Not as many public meetings were held as in some places, for there were few men who coveted the privilege of making speeches, and speeches were not needed to inspire their patriotism; nor were they tardy in responding to demands made upon them. At the first call for men in 1861, a town meeting was called and a committee appointed to obtain subscriptions for the benefit of a military company, and to provide for the families of soldiers. How much was raised, we do not know.

The town was represented in the first regiment that went from the state, and more largely in the second. During the summer and autumn of this first year of the war, fifty men enlisted for three years, without bounty, and most of them doubtless went from patriotic motives, in response to the call of their imperiled country. Though they were quiet, peace-loving citizens, they were ready to follow the old flag to victory or to death. Probably they did not realize all that was before them, but most of them met their duties and dangers like true and faithful soldiers, and like heroes endured untold sufferings in camp and hospital, on the march or in the bloody strife. The same is true of those who enlisted afterward; they were an honor to the town. A few perhaps, were shirks; a few may have been reckless, caring little for the cause, but the great majority did good service. The regiments which included these first fifty men, were soon called into active service, and were in many of the most terrible battles of the war.

25th Massachusetts Regiment.—Many of them went into the 25th Regiment, Company I, of which T. Sibley Heald was chosen second lieutenant. He was soon afterward promoted to first lieutenant, but declined. This regiment joined Butler's expedition, and was in the battles of Newbern, and Roanoke Island.

In the summer of 1862, after the call for 300.000 three years' men, the town offered a bounty of one hundred dollars, to every man who would enlist, and chose a committee of five to act in concert with the selectmen, in obtaining volunteers· Twenty or more were recruited, most of them entering the 25th Regiment, in place of those who had fallen or been discharged for disability. During the war, forty-three men entered this regiment, a larger number than was connected with any other. Of this number, seventeen were killed or died of disease, and seven others were wounded. Twenty men, who enlisted in 1861 and 1862, re-enlisted when their three years had expired, and some of them went through the whole service without sickness or casualty, while others sickened and died before seeing any active service. A few endured the horrible barbarities of the rebel prison.

53rd Regiment.—When the 53rd Regiment of nine months' men was being recruited in the fall of 1862, twenty-two men from this town entered Company H., and three Company C. If we give here more particulars of this regiment than of others, it is not because they did better service or suffered more than others, but because more particulars have been furnished. A. B. Sawyer of Winchendon, was chosen captain of Company H. but soon resigned, and First Lieutenant Lyman Woodward of this town was promoted to the place, and commanded the company through the term of service. Oren Marean was first sergeant. The date of enlistment of most of the men was September 3, 1862. In October, the company went into camp at Groton Junction. On the 29th of November they started for New York. After a tedious delay and much suffering from storm and cold in that city, and an exhausting march to Long Island and back, they embarked on board the Transport Mississippi for the Gulf of Mexico, December 16. But so many of their number were sick, that they were put on shore again.

One from this town, Henry F. Russell, died in the barracks. On the 16th of January they took ship for New Orleans in the steamer Continental. They had a rough passage, and suffered much, in the storms, from their close quarters. Once the ship took fire and all on board were threatened with immediate destruction. They reached New Orleans on the last day of January, and after a few weeks spent in drilling, went into active service. Company H. took part in several severe engagements. They were in the siege, and at the fall of Port Hudson, and rendered effective service. Though they were in imminent peril and suffered extremely, the company did not lose a man. During this siege, July 1863, an attack from the rebels upon Fort Butler was anticipated, and men were ordered from the convalescent hospitals to defend it, some of them with scarcely strength enough to work the guns. Three of these men were from this town. About one hundred and twenty of those sick men held the fort against a concerted attack of 2000 rebels, and repulsed them with great slaughter. Sixty or seventy of the enemy, who came inside the palisades, demanding the surrender of the fort and attempting to scale the walls, were all taken prisoners. When they marched in to lay down their arms, they saw that they had been captured by pale, sickly men who had become so completely exhausted that nearly all of them had sunk down just where they stood. This exploit was most highly complimented by the superior officers. One of our men, James Earle, lost an eye at that time.

There was much sickness in this company during its stay. Some of the men were never able to be in the ranks. Three from this town—William Gates, Isaac N. Rice and Samuel H. Hastings—died and were buried on the bank of the Mississippi. About the first of August the regiment was ordered to return. Many of the men were taken from the hospital to start for home. The invalids were put on board the Transport St. Mary's for New York. Three from this town—Calvin Allen, Asa B. Browning and John N. Kendall—died and were buried at sea. The regiment came by way of the river and the north-

WEST MAIN STREET

ern railroads. One of our men, Hobart L. Hale, was left at Cleveland, Ohio, and died there. One, Levi Flagg, who came with the company to Fitchburg, and was mustered out, died a few days after in Lunenburg, unable to reach home. One who reached home, Edson A. Greenwood, lived but a few days, making six, who started with the hope of meeting their friends, but died before or just after reaching home. Two, Leonard S. Day and Oren Marean, who never recovered from the effects of the service, have since died, leaving of the twenty-five in that regiment, thirteen survivors.

A public reception was given the regiment in Fitchburg; a day of great joy to many, a day of deep sadness to others. They were mustered out September 2, 1863, after a service of just a year.

Substitutes.—As has been stated, fifty enlisted from this town in 1861. In 1862, there was the same number of enlistments. After this it was difficult to obtain volunteers among our own citizens. March, 1863, the town voted $125 bounty to volunteers or substitutes, and a committee was appointed to hire substitutes. From this time to the close of the war the quota of the town was filled principally by men hired from abroad, or by draft. Only one conscripted man, Davis Holt, went into the service. A few furnished substitutes. Ten paid the $300 commutation fee.

The amount paid in bounties, by the town, was $8,625, and $2,405 was raised by private subscription.

The following table, prepared mainly from the Rebellion Record of the town, contains, as far as known, the names of all the men from Hubbardston who served in the army, with date of enlistment, name of regiment and company, date of discharge or death, and a brief statement of such other items as were at hand. The names marked with a * are mentioned more particularly in the preceding pages:—

18

HUBBARDSTON IN THE WAR OF THE REBELLION.

Name.	Enlisted.	Reg't.	Co.	Discharged.	Remarks.
*Allen, Calvin	Sept. 3, 1862	53	H	Died Aug. 14,	1863, Transport St. Mary's, on the way home.
Allen, George	July 26, 1862	25	G	Aug. 20, 1864	Wounded.
Banks, Prentiss J.	July 19, 1861	21	K	Trans'd to 36th	Reg. Co. K, Jan. 2, '64. Died Feb. 11, '65.
Barnes, Francis	Oct. 8, 1861	25	I	Oct. 20, 1864	Expiration of service.
Barnes, George H.	Aug. 11, 1862	25	I		Killed battle of Cold Harbor, June 3, '64.
Bartlett, Charles A.	May 18, 1861	12	B		Killed May 8, 1864.
Bates, George S.	Sept. 3, 1862	53	H	Sept. 2, 1863	Corporal.
Blood, George W.	Sept. 30, 1861	25	I		Captured at Cold Harbor, June 1, 1864.
Re-enlisted,	Feb. 7, 1864	25	I		Died in the hands of the enemy.
Blood, Joseph W.	Aug. 4, 1862	25	I	June 21, 1865	Expiration of service.
Brizzee, William A.	Aug. 4, 1862	27	B	Sept. 20, 1864	Wounded at Cold Harbor June 2, 1864.
Brown, Welcome E.	May 16, 1861	Navy			Ship Brooklyn; re-enlisted for 9 months.
	Aug. 15, 1862	46	A	Nov. 11, 1864	Re-enlisted for one hundred days.
	July 9, 1864	8	A		Expiration of service.
*Browning, Asa B.	Sept. 3, 1862	53	H	Died Aug. 8, 1863	near mouth of Miss. river on the way home.
Browning, James	Sept. 3, 1862	53	H	Sept. 2, 1863	Corporal of Color Guard.
Butler, Eli H.	Sept. 3, 1862	53	H	Sept. 2, 1863	Sergeant. Captured at Thibodeaux, La., in the summer of '63, but at once paroled.
· Re-enlisted summer of 1864		4th	H. A.	June 17, 1865	Expiration of service.
Childs, Addison	July 30, 1862	25	G	Oct. 20, 1864	For disability.
Childs, Walter	July 30, 1862	25	I	May 9, 1863	
Churchill, Eber F.	May 25, 1861	2	F	Died	May 25, 1862, of wounds, Winchester, Va.
Clark, Almond W.	July 30, 1862	25	I	Died	Sept. 17, 1862, of fever, Newbern, N. C.
Clark, Alson W.	Sept. 21, 1861	25	K	Corporal.	Wounded at Drewry's Bluff, May 9, 1864.
Re-enlisted,	Oct. 4, 1864	25	K	July 13, 1865	Died April 18, 1868.
Clark, Asa G.	July 30, 1862	25	I	May 9, 1863	For disability. Died March 20, 1870.

				Trans'd to Co.	
Clark, Eli E.	Sept. 21, 1861	25	K		C. Died Andersonville prison, Sept. 12, 64.
Cleveland, Alvin A.	Sept. 3, 1862	53	H	Sept. 2, 1863	Expiration of service.
Clifford, Josephus, Jr.	Sept. 3, 1862	53	H	Sept. 2, 1863	Expiration of service.
Cole, Stephen T.	May 18, 1861	12	B	Feb. 1, 1863	For disability.
Re-enlisted,	Jan. 27, 1864	4th Cav.	E	Nov. 14, 1865	Expiration of service.
Coleman, Oliver B.	Sept. 3, 1862	53	H	Sept. 2, 1863	Re-enlisted in Frontier Cavalry and served on borders of Ca., Vt. and N. Y.
Conant, Levi W.	Sept. 3, 1862	53	H	Sept. 2, 1863	Captured in the summer of '63 at Thibodeaux, La., but immediately paroled.
Coleman, Darius	July 31, 1862	34	C	Dec. 27, 1862	For disability.
Davis, Myron W.	Sept. 17, 1861	25	K	July 13, 1865	Wounded at Cold Harbor, June 3, 1864.
Day, Leonard S.	Sept. 22, 1862	53	C	Sept. 2, 1863	Died Oct. 7, 1863.
Devereaux, John H.	Sept. 10, 1861	25	K	Died of	wounds, Petersburg, Va., July 22, 1864.
*Earle, James	Sept. 3, 1862	53	H	Sept. 2, 1863	Wounded at Donaldsonville, July, 1863.
Eaton, John H.	Dec. 10, 1863	25	I		Deserted at Cold Harbor, June 2, 1864.
Felton, George W.	Dec. 10, 1863	4 Mass.	Cav. G	Nov. 14, 1865	Expiration of service.
Fisk, Addison W.	July 30, 1862	25	I	Oct. 15, 1864	Expiration of service.
Flagg, Joel S.	Aug. 7, 1862	25	I	Oct. 20, 1864	Transferred to Co. G, Jan. 20, 1863.
*Flagg, Levi	Sept. 27, 1862	53	H	Sept. 2, 1863	Died at Lunenburg, Sept. 8, 1863.
Flagg, Silas	Aug. 7, 1862	25	I		Wounded and captured at Drewry's Bluff.
					Died in Libby Prison, June 16, 1864.
Frost, Sumner	Sept. 20, 1861	25	I	Oct. 20, 1864	Captured at Drewry's Bluff, May 16, 1864.
				Paroled	and died Annapolis, Md., Dec. 28, 1864.
					Chaplain at Washington.
Gage, Rev. Rodney	Oct. 10, 1861	11	C	June 10, 1862	For disability.
Gates, Irving C.	Sept. 3, 1862	53	H		at Baton Rouge, La., April 18, 1863.
Gates, William	June 29, 1861	13	D	Died	Wounded at Antietam, Sept. 17, 1862.
Greenwood, A. Hobart				Feb. 14, 1863	Died at Alexandria, Va., Feb. 21, 1863.
Greenwood, Chester	Feb. 25, 1864	25	D	July 8, 1865	Wounded June 3, '64 and March 10, '65.
Greenwood, Edson A.	Sept. 3, 1862	53	H	Sept. 2, 1863	Died Sept. 28, 1863, after reaching home.

HUBBARDSTON IN THE WAR OF THE REBELLION—*Continued.*

Name.	Enlisted.	Reg't.	Co.	Discharged.	Remarks.
Greenwood, George	Aug. 7, 1862	25	I	Died May 10, '64,	of wounds rec'd Point of Rocks, Va.
Greenwood, Morrill A.	July 9, 1864	42	G	Nov. 11, 1864.	Expiration of service.
Greenwood, Thomas E.	May 7, 1862	25	I	Oct. 20, 1864.	Expiration of service.
*Hale, Hobart L.	Sept. 3, 1862	53	H		Died at Cleveland, O., Sept. 12, '63, on the way home.
Hale, Seth P. H.	Jan. 4, 1864	4	G	June 7, 1865	From the hospital.
Hallett, Charles O.	May 25, 1861	2	F		Sergeant.
Re-enlisted,	Dec. 30, 1863				Promoted to 1st Lieut. March 20, 1864.
Hartwell, Cyrus W.	Oct. 14, 1862	42	K	Aug. 20, 1863	Expiration of service.
Harty, James	Sept. 3, 1862	55	H		
Hastings, Samuel H.	Sept. 24, 1861	53	L		Died at Baton Rouge, July 23, 1863.
*Heald, T. Sibley	May 25, 1861	2	F	Oct. 20, 1864	2d Lieut. Wounded in the face.
Heald, Wm. H.	Sept. 30, 1861	25	I		Died at Baltimore, Dec. 17, 1861.
Herrick, James W.		25	I	Dec. 1, 1863	'Re-enlist. Promoted to Corp'l Sept. 6, '62.
Re-enlisted,	Dec. 2, 1863				Died in hospital, Ft. Schuyler, N. Y., Aug. 6, 1864.
Holt, Davis Drafted,	June 1, 1864	19	D	June 30, 1865	Died July 11, '65, from effects of service.
Holt, Oscar E.	July 30, 1862	25	K	Sept. 11, 1863	For disability.
Holt, W. Irving	July 30, 1862	25	L	Killed	Killed at Cold Harbor, June 3, 1864. Corporal.
Hunting, Daniel A.	July 19, 1861	21	K	Oct. 21, 1862	For disability.
Hunting, Eli	May 25, 1861	2	F	May 25, 1864	Expiration of service.
Hunting, John W.	Aug. 4, 1862	25	I		Captured at Drewry's Bluff, May 15, 1864. Died in Andersonville prison, July 29, 1864.
Howard, James C.	Aug. 7, 1862	1st Cav	B	Oct. 24, 1864	Expiration of service.
Joslin, Wm. H.	July 9, 1864	42	G	Nov. 11, 1864	Expiration of service.
Kendall, Edward J.	Aug. 28, 1861	22	D	Dec. 30, 1862	For disability.
*Kendall, John N.	Sept. 13, 1862	53	C	Died Aug. 13, '63,	Transport St. Mary's, on the way home.

Name	Enlisted	Reg.	Co.	Date	Remarks
Kendall, James P. E.	June 29, 1861	13	D		Died Hagerstown, Md., Oct. 1, '62, of wounds received [at Antietam.
Laughna, Terrence	Aug. 16, 1861	21	C	Aug. 30, 1864	To re-enlist.
	Oct. 10, 1864	2d N.Y.	D	July 17, 1865	Expiration of service.
Lewis, George M.	Sept. 20, 1861	25	K	June 27, 1864	Killed near close of war. Color-bearer.
Lewis, Seth E.	May 27, 1862	7			Died at Washington, N. C., Oct. 1, 1863.
Lincoln, Wm. H.	Sept. 3, 1862	53	H	Sept. 2, 1863	Ass't Surg. Promoted Surg. Sept. 10, '63.
Marean, Oren	Nov. 4, 1861	53	H	June 29, 1865	1st Sergeant. Died Oct. 27, 1879.
Martin, George W.	Sept. 3, 1862	Ft. Warren Bat	H	Sept. 2, 1863	Trans'd to 32d Reg. Co. B, spring of '62.
Maynard, Edward S.	Feb. 29, 1864	25	K	July 13, 1865	Expiration of service.
Maynard, Fred W.	July 19, 1861	21	K	Mar. 16, 1863	Expiration of service.
Maynard, George S.	Oct. 28, 1864	10th Battery	I		For disability. Died June 14, 1863.
Maynard, John C.	Oct. 14, 1862	42	K	June 9, 1865	Expiration of service.
Minms, James	Sept. 25, 1861	25	G	Aug. 20, 1863	Expiration of service.
Moore, Joseph W.	July 19, 1861	21	H	Oct. 20, 1864	Expiration of service.
Moore, Rufus D.	July 19, 1861	42	B	Aug. 5, 1862	For disability.
Re-enlisted,	July 19, 1864	53		Nov. 11, 1864	Expiration of service.
Murdock, Leander L.	Sept. 3, 1862	12	I	Sept. 2, 1863	Expiration of service.
Newton, Isaac	June 17, 1862	25	F		For disability. Died Dec. 1, 1862.
Orr, Jesse H.	Aug. 4, 1862	2	F		Died Point of Rocks, Va., May 10, 1864, of wounds [received May 9. Corporal.
Parker, Alfred R.	May 25, 1861	2	F		Killed Averysboro', N. C., March 16, '65.
Re-enlisted,	Dec. 31, 1863			June 18, 1862	Expiration of service.
Parker, Stephen S.	May 25, 1861	Ft. Warren Bat	C	May 25, 1864	Trans'd to 32d Reg. Co. B, spring of '62.
Parsons, Willard	Nov. 4, 1861	25	K	Nov. 27, 1864	Expiration of service.
Pollard, Henry G.	Sept. 13, 1862	25	I	Sept. 2, 1863	Wounded at Drewry's Bluff, Va., May 16, '64
Pond, George H.	Sept. 21, 1861	25	I	July 13, 1865	Expiration of service.
Pond, Lowell	Oct. 2, 1861	25	K		Killed at Drewry's Bluff, Va., May 16, '64.
Pond, Rowland	Sept. 21, 1861	25	I	Oct. 20, 1864	Expiration of service.
Pond, Wm. G.	Sept. 21, 1861	25		July 13, 1865	Expiration of service.
Rice, Francis	July 20, 1862	25	I	Oct. 20, 1864	Expiration of service.
Rice, Isaac N.	Sept. 3, 1862	53	H		Died at Baton Rouge, La., May 13, 1863.

HUBBARDSTON IN THE WAR OF THE REBELLION—*Continued.*

NAME.	ENLISTED.	REG'T.	CO.	DISCHARGED.	REMARKS.
Richardson, George, P.	Feb. 23, 1864	12th Ill.	A.†	Sept. 26, 1865	1st Lieut. 3rd Reg.Co. H, H.A., June 25,'65
Richardson, James M.	July 19, 1861	21	C	July 2, 1862	To re-enlist. Raised a Co. for 44th Reg.
Capt. Nov. 16, '63				Nov. 16, 1864	Raised a Co. of H. A. which afterwards
Lieut. Col. Mar. 13,'65				Sept. 18, 1865	became Co. H of 3rd Reg. of H. A.
Richmond, Wm. S.	July 30, 1862	25			Rejected recruit.
*Russell, Henry F.	Sept. 3, 1862	53		Died	Barracks, N. Y. City, Jan. 9,1863. Corporal.
Sargent, Sydney H.	Nov. 4, 1861	Ft.Warren Bat		Died Oct.	27, 1862, Alexandria, Va., Co. B 32rd Reg.
Sargent, Wm. H.	Nov. 19, 1861	32	B	Nov. 20, 1864	Trans'd to Vet. Reserve Corps, Sept.15,'63
Savage, Samuel K.	Sept. 3, 1862	53	H	Sept. 2, 1863	Expiration of service.
Shaffer, Jacob	Aug. 7, 1862	25	K	Oct. 20, 1864	Expiration of service.
Smith, Benj. F.	Sept. 21, 1861	25	K	Nov. 28, 1862	For disability.
Smith, Charles A.	July 19, 1861	21	K	Jan. 1, 1864	To re-enlist. Corporal.
	Jan. 2, 1864	36	K	July 12, 1865	Transferred to 56th Reg.Co.D, June 8,'65
Smith, John A.	July 19, 1861	21	K	Jan. 1, 1864	To re-enlist.
	Jan. 2, 1864	36	K	July 12, 1865	Transferred to 56th Reg. Co. B, [Harbor.
Stone, Asa	Jan. 2, 1864	36	L	July 12, 1865	Died at Washington, June 20, '64, of wounds rec'd at Cold
Stone, J. Franklin	Sept. 30, 1861	25	H	Killed at	battle of White Hall, N. C., Dec. 16, 1862.
Stowe, Charles E.	July 12, 1862	23	K	Jan. 23, 1863	For disability.
Stowe, Charles R.	July 19, 1861	21	K	Died July 4,	'64, of wounds received near Petersburg,Va.
Stowe, George W.	Mar. 16, 1864	25	C	May 14, 1864	For disability.
Tenney, Charles F.	Aug. 15, 1862	36	K	Jan. 18, 1864	To re-enlist. Corporal.
Tenney, Geo. A. Serg't.	Sept. 21, 1861	25	C	July 21, 1865	Wounded at Drewry's Bluff, May 9, '64.
Tyler, W. H. Frederick	May 23, 1861	1	E	Oct. 28, 1863	Disability.‡
Whitney, Jerry	Aug. 2, 1864	58	F	July 14, 1865	Capt'd at Petersburg, Apr. 2, '65, released in
	May 25, 1861	2			Deserted Sept. 15, 1862. [9 days.

Name	Enlisted	Reg.	A. M	Discharged	Remarks
Whitney, Jona. W.	Sept. 5, 1864	2d H.		June 30, 1865	Trans'd to 17th Reg. Co. F, Jan. 16, '65.
Witt, Clayton,	July 30, 1862	25	K		Died at Florence, N. C., Nov. 20, 1864.
Woodward, Daniel H.	Aug. 18, 1862	25	K		Died at Camp Nelson, Ky., Sept. 15, 63.
Woodward, Lyman	Sept. 3, 1862	53	H	Sept. 2, 1863	1st Lieut. Promoted Captain, Oct. 31, '62. Killed at Gaines Hill, Va., June 27, 1862.
Wright, Parker S.	Aug. 28, 1861	22	D		Transferred to 32d Reg., Co. B.
Young, Makepeace	Nov. 4, 1861	Ft. Warren Bat			Killed at Cold Harbor, June 3, 1864.
Young, Sumner C.	Nov. 4, 1861	Ft. Warren Bat		June 29, 1865	Transferred to 32d Reg. Co. B.

†Unattached Company.

‡Wounded at Gettysburg July 2, 1865. Died May 14, 1865.

The following are the names of those who were drafted or furnished substitutes, and their substitutes :—

John C. Clark,	John R. Green, substitute.
William C. Hale,	James Smithers, substitute.
Milton Stone,	William G. Rowelson, substitute.

The following were hired from abroad to fill the quotas of the town, most of whom re-enlisted from the regular army :—

Barnes, Willard G.	Foster, John K.	Oakler, Frederick
Bignall, Henry	Gibson, Geo. W.	O'Brien, Michael
Brooks, William H.	Gilbertson, James	O'Brien, William
Corey, John	Gleaves, John W.	O'Toole, Francis
Crandell, George M.	Gribbin, Daniel	Pevel, Leon
Cunningham, Paul	Jenkins, Michael	Reiser, Andreas
Dawson, Jeremiah	Kelley, Thomas	Sullivan, Patrick
Denovan, Lloyd S.	McCabe, John	Tracy, James
Denton, George	McCarrick, John	Ucher, William
Eagan, Eugene	McCormick, John	Walker, David
Eberle, Frank	McGuly, Patrick	Witzman, William

Eight went into the Navy, viz :—

Atkins, Firth B.	Smith, George	Williams, John
Hogan, Dennis	Snow, Fred C.	Wilson, John
Watson, Alexander		Woodward, Thomas F.

SUMMARY.

Number of Hubbardston men,	120
Whole number furnished by the town, besides the twenty who re-enlisted and were counted twice,	164
Excess above the number required to fill all the quotas,	10
Volunteers,	120
Died in the service or very soon after (of the 120 residents),	44

The last figures show that more than one-third of the Hubbardston men laid down their lives in their country's cause.

The bodies of those who were brought home for burial, with those of their comrades who have since died, are buried in the following places :—

North Cemetery, Leonard S. Day ; East Cemetery, Asa G. Clark ; Greenwood Cemetery, Isaac Newton and Alfred R. Parker ; South Cemetery, Levi Flagg ; Rural Glen Cemetery, Sumner Frost, George S. Maynard and Oren Marean ; Forest Hill Cemetery, William Gates, Edson A. Greenwood, Henry R. Russell, George A. Tenney; Pine Grove Cemetery, Almond W. Clark, Alson W. Clark, Hobart A. Greenwood, George Greenwood, Hobart L. Hale, Davis Holt, Charles R. Stowe, Makepeace Young.

Burnside Post.—The returned soldiers formed themselves into the Burnside Post, G. A. R. During the ten years of their organization, May 30, or "Decoration Day" was observed, under their direction, with appropriate public services, at the close of which, processions visited the different cemeteries to decorate the graves of soldiers with flags and flowers.

Soldiers' Aid Society.—During the war, provision was made by the town for the families of the soldiers, and much was done by individual effort for the men in the hospital and in the field. An efficient Ladies' Soldiers' Aid Society was constantly at work for the same object. A large number of boxes and barrels were sent to the army by this society.

The following list, prepared by the secretary, will show what those packages contained, and their estimated value. It is a summary of the work of the society during the war:—

109 bed quilts, at $1.00	$109 00
140 sheets, at 75c.	105 00
18 blankets, at $2.50	45 00
226 pillows, at $1.50	339 00
30 pillow-cases, at 50c.	15 00
97 flannel shirts, at $2.50	242 50
100 print shirts, at $1.25	125 00
205 shirts, at 75c.	153 75
93 pairs drawers, at $1.30	121 35
46 dressing-gowns, at $3.00	138 00
23 thin coats, at $1.00	23 00
42 vests, at 50c.	21 00
15 pairs pants, at $1.00	15 00
310 pairs socks, at $1.00	310 00
222 handkerchiefs, at 15c.	33 30
31 pairs slippers, at 75c.	23 25
26 pairs mittens, at 33c.	8 58
166 towels, at 20c.	33 20

19

42 napkins, at 17c.	$7 14
50 pin cushions, at 10c.	5 00
Bandages,	65 00
50 comfort bags,	50 00
9 yards netting.	2 25
7 lbs. cocoa, at 50c.	3 50
51 lbs. corn starch,	8 67
11 papers farina,	2 00
5 bars castile soap,	1 25
64 bottles blackberry cordial,	1 25
Cider, jelly and pickles,	9 25
Horse radish, tea, sugar, rice,	15 25
Dried apple,	15 00
Postage stamps, Testaments and other books, papers, chair-cushions. table-covers, combs, brushes, sponges. ointment, coffee, crackers, rice, shells, cloves, &c.	50 00
Money,	99 00
Total	——$2350 74

Soldiers' Monument Proposed.—After the war closed, the operations of this society continued till $282.23 had been accumulated and deposited in the Savings Bank, which the society proprosed to appropriate towards a soldiers' monument. In November, 1865, the town voted $800, for the same purpose, and chose Moses Greenwood, John F. Woodward and Lyman Woodward to act in conference with the selectmen and the Soldiers' Aid Society, with power to procure a site and receive proposals for a suitable monument. But nothing further was done. In discussing the matter, it was found to be the opinion of many that a Memorial Hall would be a more suitable tribute to the fallen soldiers, and an effort was made to build a town-house with such a room in it. All these plans failed in consequence of the enormous expense of building a county road just at that time. The debt of the town has so increased since then, by the building of railroads and other roads, that we have no present prospect of having either the monument or hall. Yet the heroic deeds and patient sufferings of the men who filled the quotas of the town, are not forgotten. Though their names should never be chiseled in granite or marble, they are written deep in the hearts of a grateful people, and will there remain while the town retains its place on the map of the old Bay State. So long as we or our children live beneath the clear, calm sky of freedom which bends its genial arch above us, we will delight to honor the men who sealed with their blood the emancipation of all races in America.

CHAPTER XIV

HIGHWAYS, HOTELS, AND RAILROADS.

HIGHWAYS.—It has seemed strange to many people who have traveled the roads of this town, that they were made over the highest hills, when in many instances shorter roads might have been made through the valleys, with less expense; and that they were made so crooked when they could be made straight more easily. We might infer that the early settlers had not the foresight and appreciation of the wants of succeeding generations in this matter, that they showed in most things. But we must remember that many of these roads never were built. Like Topsy they "growed." For obvious reasons, the hills were the first portions to be cleared and settled, and then paths were made from one dwelling, or settlement, to another. There was no foreign travel. The pioneer settler in going to the mill or to the house of his neighbor, would select the most "feasible" way, avoiding rocks and fallen trees. Then as he used the path more and more, and had the time, he would begin to clear away some of the obstructions; and as neighbors came and settled near, they joined him in making improvements year by year, still following the original route. Thus the roads came into existence by degrees. When the town and county roads were laid out, these paths were followed, as far as practicable, because it was a saving of labor. Just as the man who makes the first track through the newly fallen snow, is followed by all travelers through the winter, even though he may have gone far one side of the right track.

When the town was incorporated, there were no public roads running through it, and those in town were mere bridle paths (or "bridal-roads," as some of the old records have it), followed by the help of "blazed" trees. There were no bridges over the streams. Very soon the county road from Templeton to Rutland was laid out. This was the old road, leading over Muzzy Hill, through the village, and by the present residence of Isaac Mundell. At a town meeting held July 15, 1767, sixteen pounds, or about $53 was raised to build this road, which could not have been more than eight dollars to the mile. Though the road was indirect, very hilly, and poorly built, it continued to be the great thoroughfare for stages and teams from Keene to Worcester for about sixty years, till the building of the new Templeton road by the copperas mine.

In May, 1768, a contract was made with Stephen Heald, which was afterwards taken and executed by Joshua Phillips, to build a bridge over Ware River, for $33. This was at the place where Howe's mills were washed away in 1869.

The town also voted at this time to allow "for men to work on the highways three shillings per day till October, and two shillings four pence till November; one shilling four pence for oxen, and eight pence per day for chart." In 1780, ten pounds per day was allowed to each man, equaling $50 in continental currency.

Almost every year from the incorporation, some piece of road was laid out and built. As a specimen of the manner in which these roads were described, the following copy from the records of 1768 is inserted:—

"Voted and Laid out By us the Subscribers a Road or way of three Roods wide, Begining at a Small pich pain tree on the County Road at the river market on Lot No. 23, to a whit pain tree, runing esterly to Lot No. 27 to a Black oak, and to a pich pain tree runing true Lot No. 50 to a Black oak; and true Adam Wheelers Land runing true Lot No. 57 to a Black oak and to a hemlog runing true Lot No. 53 to a Black oak and to a chenest tree runing true Lot No. 54 to a Black oak and to a pich pain tree runing true Lot No. 55 to a pich pain tree and to a Black oak, runing true Lot No. 58 to a pich pain tree and to a nother pich pain tree ; runing true Lot No. 59 to a Black oak tree, runing true a Great Farm No 15 with market trees Near Said Road till it Com's to princetown Line."

Signed by the Selectmen.

This was the road to Princeton over the Joslin Hill, north of Comet Pond. Also on the same day :—

"Voted and Laid out By us the Subscribers a Road or way of three Roods wide Begining at a pich pain tree on the County Road in the Ministre Lot and runing true Lot No. 29, 32, 31, to a Great Farm No. 32 to a nother Great Farm, No. 11, upon the Line Between Joseph Grimes and Bill Grimes till it Com's to Joseph Grimes Jun'. three Roods wide with market trees on the Northerly Side of Said Road."

Signed by the Selectmen.

This was the road to Westminster.

There was strong opposition to the "new county road" from Templeton. The town chose committees, year after year to resist it, and it was several years after the subject was first agitated before the road was completed, which was in 1828. There was similar opposition to the building of several other roads after they had been laid out, probably on account of the expense, but according to the records, nearly all of them were "excepted."

Turnpikes.—In 1804, they voted not to have a turnpike through town. A turnpike was a common road, built by private capital, or a chartered company, and was supported by toll, collected at gates along the way. At one period such roads were common in New England. But they were never profitable, and were at length given up to the towns to keep in repair, and became public highways. Notwithstanding the vote above referred to, such a road was built through this town—the road now leading from Barre to Princeton. In 1825, they opposed the erection of a half-toll gate on this turnpike. In 1832, it became a public county road, under the care of the town.

Scarcely a year has passed without some changes being made in the highways, new roads opened, or old roads discontinued, but it would be of little consequence to describe all these changes.

Sidewalks.—Till within the last forty years we had no sidewalks. The credit of building those we now have is due in a great measure, to the ladies, who held a festival and took other measures to raise money for this purpose and for planting shade trees.

For many years there was a great amount of travel through the town, north and south. Two or three stages and many four and six-horse teams were running regularly. The old turnpike in the south part of the town, leading from the western towns towards Boston, was also an important thoroughfare.

Hotels.—Our village then had a much more lively appearance than at present, especially about the two hotels. Both these and also one at the "Reed Place" were well supported. Now, there is little *legitimate* business for even one, but fifty or sixty years ago these country hotels were very important places. Most of the farmers of those days carried their own produce to Boston market and brought home their year's stock of groceries and dry goods. The trip would occupy several days, and though they usually carried with them their own rations, and provender for their horses, they must find lodging places on the way. After the opening of the railroads all this was changed.

Since the burning of the Crystal House in 1880, the Star Hotel has been the only public house in town.

Surveys for Canals.—In 1824, the town chose a committee to meet the commissioners and engineers appointed to view a route for a canal through this part of the county, and to give them information in regard to the best location. This was during the building of the Blackstone canal from Worcester to Providence, and it was proposed to extend this canal to Keene. It was thought that Moosehorn Pond and some of the higher streams in this town would help furnish the water supply. About the same time, two surveys were also being made to find a route for a canal from Boston to the Hudson, one of which passed through Ashburnham and thence followed Millers

River to its mouth. It is possible that the vote above referred to may have had some reference to this latter survey. Both were made by Loammi Baldwin, an engineer of high reputation.

Very soon after this, public attention was turned towards building railroads, and all canal projects were abandoned.

Railroads.—The State Board of Directors of Internal Improvements, of which Levi Lincoln was chairman, considered the plan of a railroad from Boston to Albany. In 1827 and 1828, they caused surveys to be made of two general routes. One was that which was adopted and followed by the present Boston and Albany Railroad. The other passed through Waltham, Sudbury and Boylston to Princeton. Thence two routes were surveyed, both through this town; one to the line of Mr. Baldwin's canal survey in Templeton; the other followed the course of the Ware River towards Northampton, and passed through Hubbardston near the crossing of the stream from Comet Pond by the road to Princeton, and thence to North Rutland. The route through this town to Millers River was shorter by eight miles than either of the others, but in places, the grade was higher, and it was estimated that the amount of business would be greater on the southern route.

In 1845, the town appropriated $250 towards surveying a railroad route from Worcester to Baldwinsville. In 1846, petitions were presented to the Legislature for a road through the western part of the town, and another through the southern part, to Barre. Hubbardston voted in favor of the road to Baldwinsville, but asked for an open charter for a road through this vicinity. The next year the town passed resolutions in favor of a road from Worcester to Barre, and a branch from it to South Gardner. This road was chartered April 26, 1847, taking the name of the Barre and Worcester Railroad. By the charter, the corporation was allowed to construct a road from some convenient point on the Nashua and Worcester Railroad, in the city of Worcester, through Holden, Rutland, Princeton, Hubbardston and Oakham, to some convenient point in the centre of Barre; and also from some convenient point in the route in

Princeton, to the Vermont and Massachusetts Railroad in Gardner. The location of the road was to be filed within one year, and the road to be completed in three years. The next year an extension of the time was granted by the Legislature; and again in 1849, when the name was changed to "Boston, Barre and Gardner Railroad." In 1851, the time was again extended for two years, and the corporation was released from the obligation to build the portion of the road leading to Barre. In 1853, the time was extended to 1856, and liberty was granted to build the road in sections; the first section to extend from Worcester to Princeton; the second from Princeton to Gardner; the third from Princeton to Barre. The capital stock needed for building the road could not be raised, and the road was not built, but the charter was kept good by the extension of time granted about once in two years till 1869, when some of the towns subscribed to the stock to the amount of five per cent of their valuation. The needful funds were now soon obtained, and the work of construction from Worcester to Gardner commenced in the spring of 1870. The first passenger train ran over the road on the 4th of July, 1871. After so long waiting—twenty-four years—the screech of the whistle and the rumbling of the wheels were very pleasant sounds.

An extension of this road, from Gardner to Winchendon, to connect with the Cheshire and Monadnock Railroads, was granted by the Legislature in February, 1872. The last rail was laid November 27, 1873. Regular trains from Worcester to Winchendon and Peterboro N. H., began to run February 2, 1874.

The Barre branch of this road, as surveyed, ran very near Tilton's mills; but there is now no probability that it will ever be built.

Other projects for railroads through town have been on the tapis at different times. In 1847, the town voted in favor of a railroad from Ware to South Gardner, and in 1848, against one from Winchendon to Worcester, through the west part of the town. In 1851, a town meeting was called in reference to a

20

petition for a railroad from Palmer to New Hampshire line, but no action was taken upon it.

The following statements concerning the Ware River Railroad were furnished by the chief engineer of the company, W. A. Heywood of Springfield :—

Through the combined efforts of Messrs. George Williams, father and son, together with others in towns along the route, the charter of Ware River Railroad was originally granted in 1851. It was renewed in 1867. The building of the southern portion of the road, between Palmer and Gilbertville, began in May, 1869. Passenger trains commenced running July, 1870. In January, 1870, surveys began on the extension from Gilbertville to Winchendon, by three different routes between Coldbrook and Baldwinsville, through Hubbardston. The first line passed through the Canesto Valley, crossing the turnpike at the Browning Monument, thence to East Templeton via the copperas mine. This line was found to be of so high grades that it was abandoned. The second line passed farther east, through Natty-Pond-brook Valley, via Lamb's mills and the Warren tannery to East Templeton and Baldwinsville. This route would probably have been adopted had there been the interest manifested in its vicinity that the corporation desired. The people of Hubbardston Centre already having the Boston, Barre and Gardner Railroad a mile to the eastward, and having contributed to that project all that they felt like giving to railroads, allowed the matter to drag, thereby giving the Burnshirt Valley people time to fully show their claims; which was done by the prompt action of J. Otis Hale and John D. Williams, who authorized costly surveys to be made at their own expense and created so great an interest that the Burnshirt Valley line was adopted. Construction was begun on this road in Hubbardston in November, 1870, and passenger trains commenced running upon the whole road in November, 1873.

CHAPTER XV.

MILITIA.

IN the early days of these New England towns, the militia was as much an institution as the church or the school. The numerous wars with the French and Indians compelled men to be constantly organized, armed and equipped for their own defence and the safety of their families. The War of the Revolution confirmed them in the conviction that a thorough military organization was essential to the welfare of a free state.

For forty or fifty years the military spirit ran high. Every able-bodied man, under a certain age, was required by law, to do duty in some organization, and was fined for neglect; but such was the state of public sentiment that the odium incurred by any attempt to shirk was more to be feared than the law. Promotion in the ranks was more coveted than civil office. To be permitted always to wear the appendage of " Lieut." or " Capt." or " Col." was almost equivalent to immortal honor. From the number of captains that survived till within the re-membrance of the present generation, we judge that these honors were freely distributed.

The spring and fall trainings and the annual musters, were long kept up with great enthusiasm. They were the gala days of those times, especially to the boys, who would stand, on muster days, with arms akimbo, or with hands down deep in their pockets, and gaze at the imposing pageant, wondering if they should ever come to the high honor of carrying a sword and marching in such self-conscious dignity at the head of a

hundred men, or still higher, of riding some stiff-jointed steed
and giving pompous orders to a whole brigade! As these
youngsters listened to "the ear-piercing fife and spirit-stirring
drum," to the firing of platoons and battalions—which sounded
like handfuls of stones thrown against the side of a barn—as
they witnessed the exciting scenes of a sham fight and inhaled
the fumes of burning gunpowder, how they aspired to be
military heroes!

The uniforms of the first companies were anything but
uniform and their guns were of all sorts and sizes. Yet these
organizations were looked upon as the right arm of the civil
power, the safe-guard of American liberty. To be always prepared for war was thought to be the surest way to preserve
peace.

Before 1791, there was but one military company in this town.
It then numbered one hundred and forty men, and was rapidly
increasing, and the town voted to divide it into two companies,
to be called the East Company and the West Company, and to
choose officers for the two, which shows that military officers at
that time were elected in town meeting. The officers of the
West Company were: Ebenezer Mann, captain; Daniel Parkis,
(afterwards spelled Parkhurst) lieutenant; John Browning, ensign. Of the East Company, Moses Greenwood, captain; Asa
Church, lieutenant; Paul Matthews ensign.

Rifle Company. — In 1816, an independent company was
chartered, called the Hubbardston Rifle Company. The first
officers were: James H. Wheeler, captain; Ephraim Mason,
lieutenant; Brigham Davis, ensign.

In 1829, after the active militia was so reduced as to include
only able-bodied men between the ages of eighteen and thirty,
the West Company was disbanded. The officers—Asa Underwood, captain; Makepeace Clark, lieutenant, and Samuel A.
Knox, ensign—were discharged, and the non-commissioned
officers and privates were enrolled in the East Company.

After this the military spirit rapidly declined. The Rifle
company, which had been very spirited, became so regardless

of duty that in the fall of 1833, Capt. Israel Davis, Jr., neglected
to warn them out for the regimental review, and he was court-
martialed.   Lieut. William Hobbs was ordered to call them out,
but the order was not obeyed, and the company was soon disbanded, the commissioned officers being dismissed and the privates enrolled in the East Company, which now had but one
officer, Lieut. Jonas G. Clark.   A meeting was called to elect
officers, but no one could be found who would accept the office
of captain.   Soon after, the old militia law was abolished and a
new law enacted, which authorized a volunteer militia.

Light Infantry.—In 1843, another independent company was
chartered, called the Hubbardston Light Infantry.   This company had its origin in a temperance organization called the
Washingtonian Guards which existed a year or two, of which
Chas F. Barrows was first captain.   Their uniform was a dress
coat, white pants with blue stripes, blue sash, and cap with gilt
lace band.   Their arms were wooden spears adorned with small
blue flags.   No ammunition was required.   Their colors were
presented by the ladies of the town.   They went to muster one
year, and the novelty of the affair attracted considerable attention.   The first officers of the Infantry Company which followed were: George Williams, Jr., captain; Henry Chase, 1st
lieut.; Daniel Witt, 2d lieut.; Joseph Russell, 3d lieut.; and
Harvey Brown, 4th lieut.   The members of the company provided themselves with a good uniform, the state furnished the
arms, and the town provided an armory.   For a time this company was kept up with much spirit, but at length showed signs
of going the way of its illustrious predecessors.   When Capt.
Williams was discharged, Lieut. Chase was promoted to his
place, and labored hard to keep up the same interest.   He was
soon discharged, and Harvey Brown took his place; after serv-
ing one year he was discharged, and no one could be found to
accept the office of captain.   The command came upon Lieut.
William D. Cheever, who discharged this duty for one year.   In
1850, Moses Brown was chosen to the office, but the next
spring, in his absence, orders were sent to Lieut. John B. Flynn

to warn out the company for the May training. Less than half responded to the call. The company soon surrendered its charter, the arms were returned to the adjutant-general, and thus ended military reviews, inspections and drills in this town, and no great calamity or peril followed. Indeed it was found, when the War of the Rebellion broke out, that our citizens could defend their country without all this holiday training.

FIRE COMPANIES.

The first arrangement made by the town for extinguishing fires was in 1829, when the town voted to raise one-half the money for a fire engine if the other half should be raised by private subscription, and the whole cost should not exceed $200. The next year an engine was purchased, and soon after, a company was organized to man it. This engine was a small one, but did good service in one or two instances.

After a few years another company was formed, called the Hook and Ladder Company, whose object was to be prepared to tear down buildings in case of necessity.

After a few years, the engine being out of repair, and the interest of the company having abated, it was found that the town had no reliable means for protection against fire. In 1847, the old engine was repaired and a new one purchased, which was afterward exchanged for the present one. New companies were formed and for a time much interest was manifested. The annual supper for the engine-men, with speeches, poems and toasts, was for many years an entertainment of considerable interest.

Until 1878, the engine-men were allowed their poll tax only; since that time their annual compensation has been about $5.00 each.

The present efficient company is under the lead of Herbert W. Howe.

TEMPERANCE.

The tone of moral sentiment in Hubbardston has probably been as high as in most other places. The people have entered heartily into all true reforms. Few crimes have been committed. Still, here as elsewhere, the use of intoxicating drinks has been the cause of much mischief, wretchedness and pauperism. The church records show that most cases of discipline and excommunication were for intemperance, and at some periods these were frequent.

For sixty or seventy years after the incorporation of the town, the people indulged in free rum. The best men sold it. Almost everybody drank it. Public sentiment was so universal in favor of its use that the few who abstained were considered mean and niggardly. It was brought forward on all occasions : at raisings, huskings, trainings, and parties, it was freely used : people could neither be married, nor bury their dead without the great tumbler of toddy; ministers preached on its inspiration; the military customs of the day helped to make these drinking habits more universal. There was no organized effort to suppress the evil, and little said against it : yet drunkenness was regarded with as much abhorrence as in later times. There was a class given to tippling and tavern-haunting, but the proportion was not large.

During all this time there were those who clearly saw and deplored the state of things, and when the temperance movement began, about fifty years ago, they were ready to engage in it. The first temperance pledge did not include abstinence from ale, beer, wine, or cider, and it was regarded as a great act of moral courage to sign a pledge against distilled spirits. It was soon found by experience, that either the reform must be abandoned, or the pledge must include all that could intoxicate, for men would not only keep their appetites alive, but would become intoxicated upon fermented beverages. Then began the second great stage of temperance reform, upon the principle of total abstinence.

It was about this time that the people here began to be in earnest in the matter. Ministers preached in favor of abstinence. Leading men talked with their neighbors. Lecturers came from abroad. When the Washingtonian movement began, Mr. Gough, Mr. Hawkins, and other reformed men, held meetings here, and much enthusiasm was awakened. A large portion of the people signed the pledge and united in an organization for efficient work. The children were gathered into a Cold Water Army, and later, in a Band of Hope. Much was accomplished towards the suppression of intemperance, and the general sentiment of the town was against the use of ardent spirits.

The first efforts made to check the sale of liquors was under the old license law. No one was allowed to sell without a license, and they who were licensed must be "approbated" by the selectmen. The hotel-keepers and the traders were usually approbated. In 1838, the question came up whether the town would instruct the selectmen not to approbate any retailers of liquor. The vote stood, negative 113; affirmative, 110; showing that public sentiment was about equally divided upon the subject. Soon after, boards of selectmen were chosen who refused to approbate most of the applicants, which caused some excitement, but helped on the reform.

Several temperance organizations have flourished for a time, among them were: The Washingtonian Guards, Sons of Temperance, Good Templars, and the Temperance Refuge Society. At one time a Ladies' Temperance Social Circle was sustained with much enthusiasm. After the passage of the prohibitory law, a league was formed to enforce it. The result was that all the grog-shops were closed, and for several years the sale of liquor appeared to be entirely suppressed. Probably the majority of the people have been in favor of prohibition ever since, though they have relaxed their efforts at times.

In April, 1872, the question was submitted to the towns of the state whether they would allow the sale of beer and ale. The vote in this town was about three to one, in the negative.

In April, 1879, it was voted, "yeas forty-three, nays forty-eight, not to license any one to sell intoxicating liquors." "Also, Voted to instruct the selectmen to prosecute all violations of the law the present year."

At present, though there is no temperance organization in working order, monthly union meetings are held alternately in the Congregational and Methodist Churches, Sabbath evenings.

LIBRARIES.

Until the opening of the present century, there were comparatively few books in town, but as the people began to have more leisure, they sought to supply themselves with reading matter.

Sometime before 1825, an organization was formed known as the Hubbardston Library Association. It was composed of individuals who paid a certain amount annually, and were entitled to the reading of the books, which numbered two or three hundred. After a few years the interest in it was so diminished that the books were sold at auction.

About 1840, by the aid of the state, libraries were placed in all the school-districts, and for many years were read with interest; but after a time these books became scattered or were laid aside unread. Remnants of some of these libraries are still in existence.

For twenty or twenty-five years before 1870, a Library Association was kept up in the village. The annual fee varied from fifty cents to one dollar. There was no fund for the purchase of books except the amount of these fees. In 1870, a new constitution and by-laws were adopted; the library was largely increased and gained many readers. In 1871, the Farmers' Library, which had existed eight or ten years, was embodied in it, adding 110 volumes. One of the old district-libraries of thirty volumes was also added. Jonas G. Clark, then of New York city, gave a full set of Appleton's Encyclopedia, and several other volumes. Valuable donations were also received from other sources making the whole number of volumes added during the year, 400. In January, 1872, Mr. Clark sent another donation of 450 volumes. The library then numbered 1159 volumes.

In 1872, the association offered the library to the town on condition that it be made free to all the inhabitants. The proposition was accepted and the town appointed a committee to take charge of the matter. Miss Sarah E. Marean was chosen librarian, and the library was then opened to the public, under. certain regulations. A library committee of three is appointed by the town in the same manner as the school committee, one member being elected annually for three years. An annual appropriation is made, which for eight years averaged $220.

Mr. Clark has donated more than 1500 volumes since the library passed into the hands of the town, and it now contains 3800 volumes.

It was kept in Mechanics Hall till September, 1875, when, by the munificence of Mr. Clark, it was removed to its present excellent accommodations in the Library Building.

THE FARMERS' CLUB.

This club was organized in 1860. The constitution thus states its object: "To increase the interest in and knowledge of agriculture and horticulture in this town."

For several years animated meetings were held during the winter, once in two weeks, in which practical questions were discussed, with an occasional address or poem. Their "Farmers' Library," now a part of the town library, numbered over a hundred volumes.

The annual Cattle Show and Fair, arranged for by the club, is a gala day for the town, attended by crowds of people. There is usually a good display of stock, farm products, flowers and fancy articles. By a festival and private contributions, funds were raised for cattle pens and other articles for use at these cattle shows, and for the Agricultural Building which stands on the east side of the common.

CHAPTER XVI

UNUSUAL SEASONS.—The summer of 1816 was extremely cold. Snow fell in June, and there was more or less frost every month. No corn ripened that year; even the hoeing had not been finished at the beginning of " dog-days."

The year 1826 is spoken of as the great " grasshopper year." The season was extremely dry and the grasshoppers became almost like the locusts of Egypt, for number and destructiveness. So great was the scarcity of fodder the next spring that some farmers, in order to keep their cattle alive, drove them to the woods to browse upon the bare branches of the trees.

On the 11th of June, 1839, snow fell nearly all day, though it melted as it came. The night following, there was a frost that cut down most of the corn, and did great damage to other crops.

In the spring of 1841, the snow lingered very late, and was increased by a heavy fall on the 2d of May. The next day people went to town meeting in sleighs, and the drifts had not all disappeared from the roads a week later. On " Old Election Day," the last Wednesday in May, the writer found in the woods on the hill above Natty Pond, a snow drift which was then eight feet deep by measurement.

The spring of 1867 was very backward and cold. Appleblossoms were still on the trees on the day of the centennial celebration, June 13.

The great freshet of October, 1869, occasioned much damage to roads and bridges. The dam and mills, with valuable machinery, owned by A. & H. W. Howe, were all swept away.

The next year was unprecedented for drought. Little rain fell from June till winter. The hay crop was good, but all the later crops were nearly ruined. Corn, partly grown, perished in the field. Nearly all the wells in the village were dry, and many families were supplied with water brought from a distance.* In many cases stock was driven a long distance to find drink.

FIRES.

Probably few towns have suffered less from fires, yet we have the following instances of destruction of life and property to record:—

In May, 1781. the house of Joseph Parmenter; two of his children perished in the flames. "Gates Mills" in 1830. The Willard shop, about 1836. The Rhode Island Mill in 1841. A shop for pressing hats on the site of the mill now owned by Howe and Gleason, in 1842. The Mason shop, nearly opposite the Crystal House, March, 1848. The Mansion House and all the outbuildings on the farm of Hon. E. A. Greenwood, July, 1849. House at the copperas mine, 1855. House of Samuel H. Hastings, April, 1858. House of Joseph Falis, 1862. House of Lyman Greenwood, January, 1863. All the buildings, with stock and tools, on the farm of Ebenezer Tilton, March, 1864. Mills of Increase S. Waite, January, 1868; his house in 1871. Saw-mill of John S. Lovewell, December, 1872. Mill in Heald Village, April, 1875. Mechanics Hall, February, 1877. House of George W. Ballou, November, 1878. House of Mr. Bullard, 1879. Crystal House, January, 1880. Saw-mill and box factory in Williamsville, February 10, 1881. Also the Mundell house, and mills known as the Samuel Warren, the Horace Whitney, the Perez Coleman and Frank Pierce's.

By Lightning.—Barns belonging to the following individuals: David Merriam, in 1828; Sylvanus Dunton, August, 1838; Israel Davis, August, 1841; John Adams, October, 1854; Levi Conant, May, 1856.

---

*See Natty-Pond Brook, Chapter I.

DEATHS BY DROWNING AND OTHER CASUALTIES.

Drowned.—On the Sabbath, May 15, 1808, Joel Matthews, nineteen years old, Dorcas Wright, fourteen, and Cynthia Greenwood, thirteen and a half, went to the mill-pond of Major Greenwood, built an insecure raft, and started for a trip upon the water. The raft parted, and they were all drowned.

July 16, 1820, Bildad Wright attempted to swim across the pond at Oliver Brown's saw-mill, in his usual clothing. When part way over, he alarmed his companions by a cry of distress. Hastening to his relief they found him standing erect in the water, which was not deep enough to cover his hat; but life was extinct.

In June, 1828, a son of Artemas Mann, four and a half years old, was drowned in a well near the house.

December 18, 1830, Abel Thompson started to go from the village to the house of John W. Bellows (the Tenney place) in the evening. As the water was over the road on the causeway at Natty Pond, and the ice was broken up by teams, he left the road to walk on the ice the other side of the railing. Just below the bridge, the brook was open. Not observing this in the darkness, he walked into the open water and was carried under the ice. The next morning his tracks were discovered in the snow, and his body recovered.

April 19, 1844, a son of John F. Woodward, three years old, was drowned in a tan vat.

On the 2d of June the same year, Charles Reid, son of Micajah Reid, went to the pond near his father's house, to bathe, and to experiment with a new life-preserver which had been given him. While divesting himself of his clothing, the wind blew the inflated life-preserver out upon the water. He plunged after it, but the motion of the water carried it farther and farther on. Becoming exhausted he sank, and it was several hours before his body was recovered. He was borne to his father's residence as the people of the community were assembling for Sabbath morning service.

In August, 1870, a son of Alanson Allen was drowned in the pond at Sumner Waite's mill. He was about ten years old.

April 21, 1880, a child of H. A. Farwell, seventeen months old, fell into a tub of water and was drowned.

Other Casualties.—In June, 1777, Esek, son of Joshua Phillips, was killed at the raising of a frame. The work was never resumed and after a time the frame was taken down and put up in another part of the town.

July 14, 1787, a child of Asa Hoyt, eighteen months old, was at play with other children in the saw-mill where Parker's mills afterwards stood. Falling into the basement he was instantly killed.

At the raising of the house of Ephraim Mason, on the west side of the common, Amasa Bellows was killed by the falling of a portion of the frame, June 22, 1795.

On the 24th of June the next year, Bezaleel Lyon was killed by the falling of a limb of a tree, while cutting lumber in the woods.

June, 1806, at the raising of the house now occupied by Albert Bennett, Benjamin Church was so injured by being thrown from the frame that he died in a short time.

Charles Ellinwood, son of Justus, aged six years, fell from an ox wagon in which he was riding, was run over and killed, October 23, 1820.

On the evening of July 24, 1821, Ezra Peram, with two yoke of oxen and a wagon load of lumber, started down the hill east of the common. The load of lumber was found the same evening in the road at the foot of the hill, the tongue of the wagon broken, and the oxen missing. As no apprehension was felt for the driver, no search was made till the next morning, when his body was found beside the road, near the present residence of James Browning. Though no external injuries were found upon his body, it was supposed that he was thrown down by the oxen, and that the load passed over him.

In September of the same year, Darius Mann was injured by the kick of a horse, and survived but a few hours.

On the Sabbath, September 7, 1828, Mrs. Betsey, wife of James Browning, in returning from meeting was descending the hill west of the almshouse, when the harness broke and the horse took fright. Mrs. Browning was thrown from the wagon and instantly killed. A monument marks the spot.

On the 27th of June, 1836, William Smith of Plymouth, N. H., was instantly killed by the premature discharge of a blast at the copperas mine, where he was at work.

Oliver Johnson was killed by the falling of a tree March 8, 1837.

January 29, 1838, Jesse Lovewell was thrown from his wagon and killed.

On the 25th of August, 1841, Moses Phelps, Jr. was instantly killed, on the steps of his father's house, by the accidental discharge of a gun in the hands of his brother. He was in business in Boston, but was at home for a visit.

August 16, 1843, Foster W. Haskell of New Salem, fell from a staging in front of Mechanics Hall, and lived but a short time.

Isaac Clark Thompson, son of John, was thrown from an ox-cart and killed, September 27, 1845.

Benjamin Slocomb and his wife were riding, August 17, 1852; his horse ran, and he was caught by the driving lines and dragged, receiving fatal injuries.

Lowell Leland was killed by the falling of a timber while repairing the house at the Clark Gates place, April 14, 1855.

February 1, 1861, Alonzo Damon, with his wife and child were crossing the Cheshire Railroad in Fitzwilliam, N. H., in a sleigh, when they were overtaken unawares by a passing freight train; Mrs. Damon and the child were instantly killed. Mr. Damon escaped unharmed though the sleigh was dashed in pieces, and the horse was killed.

June, 1865, a child of William J. Eveleth was scalded and died from the effects, on the 22d.

January 17, 1867, in the absence of others from the room, the clothes of a daughter of William Stowe took fire, and she was past consciousness when found but a few minutes afterward.

Nellie, a daughter of S. B. Beaman was scalded and died December 26, 1869.

April 11, 1871, Levi Hartwell, while sawing lumber at the steam-mill of William Bennett, was so severely injured by a board thrown from the saw that he died in a few hours.

April 19, 1872, Mrs. Barnes of Westminster was killed near the house of Elisha Woodward, by being thrown from a wagon.

October 23, 1876, John Davis while at work in the mills of Howe & Gleason, in adjusting a belt, was caught by it and carried over a revolving shaft, receiving such injuries that he survived but about four hours.

December 14 of the same year, Abraham Wilson, while descending the hill from the schoolhouse in District No. 2, was thrown from his wagon and dragged. He died in a few hours.

May 9, 1877, Rev. John M. Stowe was thrown from a wagon, and survived, in an unconscious state, less than three hours.

October 28, 1879, as John D. Williams was descending the hill west of the almshouse, his horse ran and he was thrown from his wagon and instantly killed.

Instant Deaths.—Daniel Parkhurst; Windsor Hapgood, December 24, 1829; Shubael Russell, July 1, 1832; Leonard Clark, August 8, 1839; Rev. Samuel Gay, October 16, 1848; Alpheus Earle, January 24, 1849; Mrs. Oliver Brown, December 10, 1849; Thomas Hubbard Parker, April 25, 1851; Rev. Freeman Q. Barrows, December 5, 1854; Mrs. Asa Clark, December 22, 1858; Quincy Baker, January 9, 1877.

We have no murder to record, though in 1838, a strange affair occurred, which caused great excitement. About ten o'clock one forenoon a peddler's horse and cart, without a driver was seen coming from "the thicket." Soon after, a man was found lying by the roadside about half-way through the woods, with wounds upon his head and insensible; a club was lying near him. He was brought to the house of Otis Parker. After being restored to consciousness he stated that the day before, a stranger rode with him for a considerable distance. That morning, as he was coming through "the thicket," the same man came out of the bushes with a club in his hand, which he used for a cane; they entered into conversation; suddenly the man struck him and knocked him from his seat; this was the last he knew, till after he was found. He claimed to have been robbed of sixty dollars, but he had fifteen dollars clenched in his hand when discovered. A reward was at once offered for the assassin, by the selectmen, and hundreds of men turned out in search of him. Two or three different men were arrested on suspicion, but their guilt not being proved, they were released. No further clew to the affair was ever gained. By some the peddler was believed to be an impostor, claiming to be robbed when he had not been, though there was strong circumstantial evidence that he had been assaulted. Probably the whole matter will always be involved in mystery.

LONGEVITY.

The average age of thirty of the first men who settled here, all whose ages we find, is seventy-six years, and that of the wives of twenty-five of them is eighty years.

Daniel Mundell died in 1845 at the reported age of 106, but the following statement, copied from Vol. 2, p. 57 of the (copied) town records, would make him but ninety-three: "Daniel Mundell, a state pauper aged eighty, May, 1832, was born at a place called Britport, Eng., came to this country and state at the age of fifteen, became chargeable in 1820, and has continued so to this day, January 1, 1835. Has ten children. (The above was handed in by Capt. Silas Greenwood, one of the overseers, to be recorded.)"

Mrs. Issacher Adams, whose known age exceeds that of any other person who has died in town, lacked but four days of being 100 years old.

William Muzzy, who died at the age of ninety-seven, was the oldest man.

From the following list it appears that the whole number of residents who were eighty, or more, at the time of death, reckoning from the nearest birthday, is 206; ninety or more, 38.

22

Other aged people have gone to spend their last days with their children, and died elsewhere. Some have died here who could not properly be called residents. Neither of these classes are included in the list.

Elisha Adams,	81	Mrs. Anthony Clark (Jenny)	82
Mrs. Elijah Adams (Lizzie)	80	Mrs. Jona. Clifford (Mary)	80
Mrs. Issachar Adams, 99y. 11m. 26d		Josephus Clifford,	86
John Adams,	81	Israel Davis,	82
Mrs. Reuben Alden (Isabella)	84	Mrs. Israel Davis (Sally)	95
Ephraim Allen,	85	Mrs. Oliver Davis,	86
Mrs. Ephraim Allen (Elizabeth)	84	Mrs. Benjamin Dean (Grace)	86
Mr. —— Allen,	85	Mrs. Jona. Dexter (Roxanna)	83
Asa Allen.	83	Mrs. Willard Earle (Rhoda)	83
Mrs. Elihu Allen (Electa)	86	Mrs. Lois Fisher,	84
Mrs. Andrews,	88	Mrs. Metcalf Follett (Mary)	86
Isaac Bellows,	84	Mrs. Stephen Frost (Mary)	82
Mrs. Isaac Bellows (Eunice)	90	Benjamin C. Frost,	81
Asaph Bellows,	80	Henry Gates,	81
Mrs. Asaph Bellows (Elizabeth)	86	Mrs. Henry Gates (Anna)	83
Isaac Bellows.	80	Abner Gay,	81
Mrs. David Bennett (Martha)	83	Mrs. Abner Gay (Caty)	87
William Bennett,	80	Mrs. Isaac Goodspeed (Ann)	95
David Bennett,	84	Mrs. Isaac Goodspeed (Sarah)	83
Mrs. David Bennett (Hannah)	88	Mrs. Heman Goodspeed (Betsey)	83
Ebenezer Brown,	82	Joseph Green,	93
Oliver Brown.	82	Mrs. Moses Greenwood (Polly)	80
Ebenezer Brown,	85	Mrs. Joseph Grimes (Sarah)	80
Asa Brown,	81	Bill Grimes,	86
Mrs. Jona. Caryl (Anna)	82	Joseph Grimes,	90
Mrs. Asa Church (Rachel)	91	Mrs. Joseph Grimes (Huldah)	84
Luther Clark.	85	Aaron Grimes,	90
Mrs. William Clark (Hannah)	95	Mrs. Aaron Grimes (Sally)	86
Ferdinand N. Clark,	82	Ephraim Grimes,	88
Mrs. Ezra Clark (Jemima)	90	Davis Guild,	83
Samuel Clark,	87	Mrs. Davis Guild (Rebecca)	83
Mrs. Abijah Clark (Betsey)	86	Mrs. Luther Hale (Phebe)	82
Mrs. Eli Clark (Lois)	84	Mrs. Thomas Hapgood,	89
Asa Clark,	83	Mrs. Ama Harrington,	88

Simon B. Hartwell,	80
Mrs. Simon B. Hartwell (Roxa)	84
Jesse Harwood,	82
Mrs. (Robinson) (Parker) Haskell,	90
Daniel Haywood,	84
Stephen Heald,	84
Calvin Heald,	81
Mrs. Calvin Hinds (Betsey)	89
Mrs. William Hobbs (Nancy)	82
Mrs. Roxanna Hodge,	83
Ephraim Holt,	81
Mrs. Ephraim Holt (Jerusha)	88
Daniel Howe,	80
Asa Hoyt,	83
Lucinda Hoyt,	84
Stephen Hunting,	97
Mrs. Stephen Hunting (Hannah)	81
Stephen Hunting,	85
Mrs. Stephen Hunting (Eunice)	89
Converse Hunting,	91
Mrs. Converse Hunting (Mary)	90
William Hyde,	80
Mrs. William Hyde (Eunice)	86
David Jenks,	93
Mrs. Dolly Jennison,	83
Mrs. Silas Joslin (Betsey)	83
Elihu Kelton,	87
James Lamb,	82
Mrs. —— Lane,	84
Mrs. Rebecca Lincoln,	81
Mrs. Joseph Lovewell (Sarah)	80
Ruth Lyon,	80
Amos Mann,	82
Mrs. Amos Mann (Betsey)	84
William Marean,	83
Mrs. William Marean (Sybil)	96
David Merriam,	80
Lydia Merriam,	85
Samuel Morse,	94

Sally Morse,	97
Mrs. Persis Mullett,	94
Daniel Mundell,	93
Mrs. Daniel Mundell (Rebecca)	85
Daniel Mundell,	82
Mrs. Daniel Mundell (Mary)	80
Robert Murdock,	80
Mrs. Rob't Murdock (Margaret)	84
Abiel Murdock,	90
William Muzzy,	97
Mrs. William Muzzy (Mary)	84
Timothy Newton,	81
Mrs. Timothy Newton (Lydia)	86
Mercy Newton,	82
Jonathan Nichols,	86
Joseph Norcross,	80
Dana R. Parker,	82
Mrs. Dana R. Parker (Sally)	89
Mrs. Nehemiah Parker (Mary)	85
Otis Parker,	82
Thomas Hubbard Parker,	81
Charles Parmenter,	81
Mrs. Levi Parmenter (Hannah)	97
Calvin Peabody,	87
Thomas Peirce,	82
Mrs. Thomas Peirce (Mary)	83
Mrs. Jehu Perry,	91
Mrs. Moses Phelps (Deborah)	81
Moses Phelps,	87
Ezra Pond,	83
Mrs. Ezra Pond (Mercy)	81
Levi Pond,	84
James Potter,	95
Mrs. James Potter (Lucy)	84
Mrs. Henry Prentiss (Elizabeth)	80
Mrs. Edward Rice (Mary)	88
Mrs. Edmond Rice (Abigail)	81
Mrs. William Rice (Rebecca)	88
Thomas Rice,	83

Job Richardson,	85	Mrs. Josiah Underwood (Betsey)	83
Mrs. Job Richardson (Eunice)	86	Mrs. Israel Underwood (Rhoda)	91
Peter Richardson,	80	Nancy Underwood,	84
Solomon Rolph,	83	Nathaniel Upham,	88
Mrs. Solomon Rolph (Anna)	83	Mrs. Nathaniel Waite (Anna)	93
Thomas Russell,	90	Mrs. Joseph Waite (Hepzibah)	89
Mrs. Shubael Russell (Sally)	92	Moses Waite,	91
Mrs. W. A. Ryder,	85	Mrs. Naomi Ward,	82
John Sanford,	88	Luke Warren,	82
Mrs. Thomas Sargent (Tabitha)	80	Mrs. Asa Wheeler (Nancy)	84
John Sargent,	82	Joseph Whitney,	81
Mrs. John Sargent (Huldah)	80	Mrs. Abel Wilder (Mary)	81
Ebenezer Sargent,	87	Joshua Willard,	80
Solomon Sawyer,	81	Mrs. Joshua Willard (Phebe)	85
Samuel Slocomb,	91	Ephraim Willard,	90
Mrs. Samuel Slocomb (Miriam)	84	Mrs. Ephraim Willard (Abigail)	89
Jona. Warren Smith,	85	Mrs. Luke Williams (Betsey)	82
Mrs. Jona. W. Smith (Catherine)	97	Oliver Witt,	87
Mrs. Clara Browning (Smith)	88	Mrs. Ivory Witt (Eunice)	81
Mrs. Sally Smith,	89	Mrs. Clark Witt (Catherine)	81
Nathan Stone,	81	John Woods,	84
Ebenezer Stowe,	88	Mrs. John Woods (Lydia)	89
Mrs. Ebenezer Stowe (Mary)	85	Jonathan Woodward,	82
Ebenezer Stowe,	94	Daniel Woodward,	93
Mrs. Ephraim Stowe (Sally)	82	Mrs. Daniel Woodward (Keziah)	92
Sarah Sweetser,	98	Rowland Woodward,	80
Mrs. Thomas Temple (Nancy)	91	Nathan Wright,	80
James Thompson,	83	Mrs. Charles Wright (Betsey)	89
Asa Underwood,	84	Levi Wyman,	83
Mrs. Asa Underwood (Anna)	84	Mrs. Levi Wyman (Polly)	85

The average ratio of deaths from 1842 to 1850, was one in 59 of the population, or 16.9 per 1000; from 1850 to 1860, one in 58.2 or 17.1 per 1000; from 1860 to 1870, one in 59.9 or 16.6 per 1000; from 1870 to 1880, one in 58.2 or 17.1 per 1000; for the whole period, one in 58.8 or 17.2 per 1000.

Of those now living in town, two are over ninety; Mrs. Hager, mother of the late Charles Hager, was ninety-two in September, 1880; Mrs. Isaac Follett will be ninety-two in May, 1881. The oldest man in town is Williams Wilbur, who will be ninety November 25, 1881.

CHAPTER XVII.

BIOGRAPHICAL.

OLD GRIMES. Perhaps no person in town ever gained greater notoriety than Ephraim Grimes, known everywhere by the sobriquet of "Old Eph Grimes." He was a son of Joseph and Sarah Grimes, born in Tewksbury about 1756, and was five years old when he came to this town with his parents. His father and mother were good people, but very superstitious, and often excited the fears of their children with stories of bears, wolves, Indians, ghosts and evil spirits, which had an injurious effect upon this son, whose mind was always weak; had he lived in these days he would probably be considered as a fit subject for a school for idiots.

From early childhood he was, at times, exceedingly timid, afraid of the dark, low-spirited and taciturn; at other times he was wide-awake, very loquacious and full of mischievous pranks. In the latter mood he roamed about the country, indulging freely in ardent spirits, exempt from all fear of man or spirit. The stocks, pillory, and prison had no terrors for him, though when the reaction came, he was terrified by shadows, and remained quietly at home for weeks or months. This quiet side of his character was little understood, and he had the reputation all through New England of being bright and witty, but vicious and immoral, utterly regardless of law. He frequently attended the sittings of the courts in Worcester and Keene, and was often imprisoned for contempt of court and for disturbing the peace. Stories enough to fill a volume have been told of his tricks and crimes, some of them true, but many of them probably without foundation in fact. We insert here only a few of those which seem to be well authenticated.

He had a horse which partook of the perversity of his master, and had been so trained that when the reins were tightly held with apparent effort to stop him, he would plunge furiously forward.   At one time Old Grimes was galloping about the streets of Keene when the court was is session.   Riding up to the open door of the court-room he reined up his horse and began to cry "whoa!" "whoa!" when the horse rushed up the steps and through the door, to the great consternation of the court.   He made a very humble apology to the judge, said his horse was uncontrollable, that he held on with all his might to prevent his coming in, and if he could ever get the old villain out of that court-room he would see that *justice* was done him!

At one time he was arrested for creating disturbance in a small village in Vermont.   The magistrate was a bald-headed man.   The people from all quarters came to see Old Grimes and listen to the trial.   Before proceedings began, he looked wildly around the room and asked in a whisper, "Are there any bears about here?"   The bystander addressed replying in the negative, he quickly left his seat, went up to the magistrate and with a flourish of the hand called out, "Go up! thou bald head!"

He had had one ear cropped for passing counterfeit money. While traveling afterward in the region of Canada, he entered a store and asked what would be charged for a piece of ribbon long enough to reach from one of his ears to the other.   When told "a few cents," he said, "Begin to measure off!   I have one ear here and they have the other in Worcester!"

One Sabbath morning he was conducting himself in a very indecent manner at the hotel in Hubbardston, when a stranger present sharply rebuked him.   Assuming the air of injured innocence he told the stranger he guessed he did not know to whom he was talking; that he was one of the most highly respected citizens of the town, associated with the best society, and that even the minister would come and drink there with him that morning.   This was in the days when drinking at a public bar was a common custom.   A bet was made.   Mr.   ·

Grimes mounted his horse, went to the house of the minister, and with a sad face and mournful tone, told him his mother was lying at the point of death and desired to see him. The minister said he would go as soon as he had taken his breakfast. Grimes urged his going without delay, as his mother was failing fast and her reason might not long continue; and as to breakfast, they would find it waiting on their arrival. So the faithful and kind-hearted pastor was persuaded to mount the horse behind him, to go, as he supposed, to the dying mother. As they came near the hotel, Mr. Grimes said it was a cold morning, they were faint, and he proposed to stop and have a drink of sling before going on. The minister consented. They went together to the bar; Mr. Grimes called for a half mug of sling, sipped a little from it and passed it to the minister, who did the same and returned it. Thus the mug was passed back and forth between them till drained of its contents, when Mr. Grimes very coolly said, " I guess we will not go any farther. Mother is better by this time."

Thus about half the time for many years, he was wild, lawless, and regardless of all proprieties; the rest of the time, quiet, timid, and harmless. At about the age of forty-two he left town and was gone till he was eighty. On his return he was cared for at the almshouse for six years. Even at this age he manifested the same characteristics which had marked his earlier years. His sons were respectable and respected. One of them came for his father about a year before his death, took him from the almshouse and provided for him while he lived. The song about Old Grimes of which the first four lines are :—

> "Old Grimes is dead, that good old man,
> We ne'er shall see him more ;
> He used to wear an old blue coat
> All buttoned down before,"

and which has been supposed to refer to Ephraim Grimes, was probably written with reference to some other person. Long years after that song began to be sung we had ocular demonstration that

"Old Grimes yet lived, that deaf old man,
    We all could see him more ;
    He always wore an old gray coat
    All open down before."

Hon. Ethan A. Greenwood graduated at Dartmouth College and studied law with Hon. Solomon Strong, but did not long continue the practice. For a few years he was a successful portrait-painter, after which he became the proprietor of the New England Museum in Boston, where he acquired a large property. After the death of his parents he returned to Hubbardston and built a large house on the old homestead. He rebuilt the old Clark Tavern and gave it the name of the Star Hotel. He also erected Mechanics Hall and many other buildings in the village.

He inherited much of the military spirit of his father, and during the war of 1812 began to paint a silk banner for the military companies in this town. Owing to ill-health it was not completed till after the war closed. When finished it was forwarded with the following letter :—

BOSTON, Sept. 30, 1815.

To the Officers and Soldiers of the Militia of the Town of Hubbardston.

Gentlemen : You will receive herewith a stand of colors painted expressly for your use. Be pleased to accept it as a small token of my respect and affection for the inhabitants of my native town. It was begun and nearly finished a year ago, at a time when this metropolis and our whole coast was threatened with invasion ; at a time when it was not only necessary for every man to do his own duty, but to strengthen and encourage the hearts of his brethren. (Circumstances then, and ill-health afterward, prevented its being finished and forwarded to you more seasonably.) I hope by this small testimony to be instrumental, in some degree, of keeping up that military ardor and disposition to good order and correct discipline which so happily prevailed when I resided among you. The mottoes, " FOR GOD AND OUR COUNTRY," and " WE DEFEND OUR RIGHTS AND OUR SOIL," which are painted on the two sides of the standard, I chose to designate the duty of militia, which is to defend their religious and political rights to the last drop of their blood.

I congratulate you, gentlemen, that we now enjoy the blessings of peace; but I charge you to remember that to enjoy permanent peace it is necessary to be always prepared for war. You will therefore not suffer your military ardor to abate, but like true freemen, show your patriotism to consist not in words, but in actions, in the correctness of your discipline, in your promptness to serve your country when danger calls.

I wish the standard to be used by both companies on all occasions, when forming together or otherwise. If circumstances render it necessary for one company to have it more than the other, I should say that the East Company should have the greater right, as being the company to which I once belonged. But you will no doubt always live in mutual good understanding with each other, remembering that harmony renders all the duties of life pleasant.

Accept, gentlemen, my warmest wishes for your prosperity. With sentiments of respect,

Your most obedient, humble servant,

ETHAN A. GREENWOOD.

To which the following response was sent:—

HUBBARDSTON, Nov. 20, 1815.

Dear Sir: The undersigned received your letter the 18th inst., having previously been presented with a stand of colors from you as a token of your affection and respect for the inhabitants of your native town. We, with the militia of Hubbardston, accept your act of generosity as proceeding from the purest motives, and be assured, sir, we feel grateful towards you for the donation.

The mottoes, "FOR GOD AND OUR COUNTRY" and "WE DEFEND OUR RIGHTS AND OUR SOIL," deserve a place in the minds and hearts of every American, especially the militia, who are the defenders of the religious and political rights of the people, and their own.

With such sentiments, we hope and trust the militia of your native town will ever be inspired; and should the course of events require it, will unfurl the banner under which they march, and meet danger with manly courage.

The style of your colors is much approved. The use of the standard shall be appropriated according to your directions, sensible that harmony renders all the duties of life pleasant.

23

Accept, sir, our best wishes for your health, happiness and prosperity.
With gratitude and respect,
Your obedient, humble servants,

EBENEZER STOW, JR.,	MOSES GREENWOOD, JR.
JAMES H. WHEELER,	SEWELL MIRICK,
WILLARD EARL,	SILAS GREENWOOD.

This banner was used till the old military organizations were given up, and was regarded with much pride by the citizens of the town.

Mr. Greenwood took an active part in public. He was for many years justice of the peace, and was twice elected representative of the town, and twice senator for the county.

William Bennett, the projector of this history, who spent much time and labor in collecting materials for it, was in some respects the most remarkable man ever reared in town. He was born March 4, 1809. When seventeen years old he went to Phillipston to teach; at the end of the term he became clerk in the store of Mr. Goulding in Phillipston. He was afterwards successively employed, in the same capacity, by Justus Ellinwood and David Bennett in this town, and by a Mr. Cole in Watertown. In 1835, he returned to Hubbardston and began business for himself, having purchased the store of the heirs of John Church, now occupied by Charles Davis. From there he removed in 1849, to the store at present occupied by the Wheeler Brothers. In 1857, he purchased the Hubbardston Chair Works, and carried on that business till 1874. His health, already impaired, continued gradually to decline from that time till his death January 28, 1881.

His education, except that acquired by himself, was received in the old schoolhouse which stood until quite lately near the house of Charles Hinds, the present residence of George E. Morse. In solving difficult problems in mathematics he has had few equals. He was possessed of such a memory, until his last days, that "what he once knew he always knew," and was thus able to carry most of the affairs of the town in his own mind. Probably no other man was ever so long and so inti-

Jonas G. Clark

mately connected with town affairs as he; no one was ever more trusted, or proved more efficient and faithful in those trusts; he was town treasurer three years; assessor seven years; member of the school committee twenty years; town clerk twenty-nine years; postmaster from 1854 to 1861; representative in the Legislature eight years, and member of the State Constitutional Convention in 1853.

Probably no other man in town ever wrote so many deeds and other legal documents, or settled so many estates. His sound judgment and accurate legal knowledge could always be relied upon. On common points of law his opinion was regarded of as much weight as that of most lawyers, especially in probate affairs. His correctness in these matters was so well known that the judge seldom examined papers that bore his name.

At the first town meeting after his death the following resolution was passed:—

That in the death of our venerable townsman, William Bennett, we recognize the loss of an upright citizen, for many years a wise and faithful town officer, ever kind and considerate towards the poor, of deep convictions of public and private duty and fearless in their discharge; that his good name has largely contributed to give character and respectability to the town, and that his memory deserves to be held in grateful remembrance.

Jonas G. Clark, whose wealth is now counted by hundreds of thousands of dollars, if not by millions, began the business of carriage-making in the shop now used for black-smithing by Gordon P. Thompson. After building the house now occupied by James Savage, he resumed carriage-making, and was also engaged for a time in finishing and selling chairs. Subsequently he entered the tin business, erecting the buildings which continued to be used for that purpose till 1872; he seemed to possess the skill, which the old alchemists failed to acquire, of transmuting the baser metals into gold; copper, tin, old iron, and even old rags turned into gold in his hands. He soon increased his business by opening also a tin shop and hardware store in Lowell, and another in Milford. All these he afterwards sold, and with George B. Wilbur of this town, engaged in the California trade, in which they acquired a fortune. After giving up this business Mr. Clark traveled extensively and repeatedly in the old world, when in this country residing on Fifth Avenue, New York. In 1880, he built the fine residence he now occupies in Worcester.

He has not forgotten his native town. Many of the changes on Main Street, and on the road leading to Barre, which have so greatly improved the appearance of our village within the last few years, are due to his hand, and were made in connection with the building of the edifice which bears his name and which is the finest structure within our limits. For thoroughness of construction and beauty of finish it will compare favorably with any building in the county. It is of brick with granite trimmings, sixty by thirty-six feet in size, and contains the following apartments: library, thirty-six by twenty-two, and twenty-seven feet high; post-office, thirty-six by twenty-two, and fifteen feet high; a room over the post-office of the same size and twelve feet high; on the first floor, a room under the library of the same size; under the post-office a real estate office and a room used by town officers. The use of the room last named and of the library is free to the town. In addition to this gratuity Mr. Clark has given the library more than 2000 volumes within ten years.

The town records of the meeting in March, 1873, contain the following minute :—

Resolved, That the citizens of Hubbardston hereby gratefully acknowledge the large and valuable donations to the public library received from J. G. Clark, Esq. of New York, and would assure him that the books have been a source of interest and profit to their many readers.

That this resolution be entered upon the records of the town, and a copy of the same be transmitted to Mr. Clark.

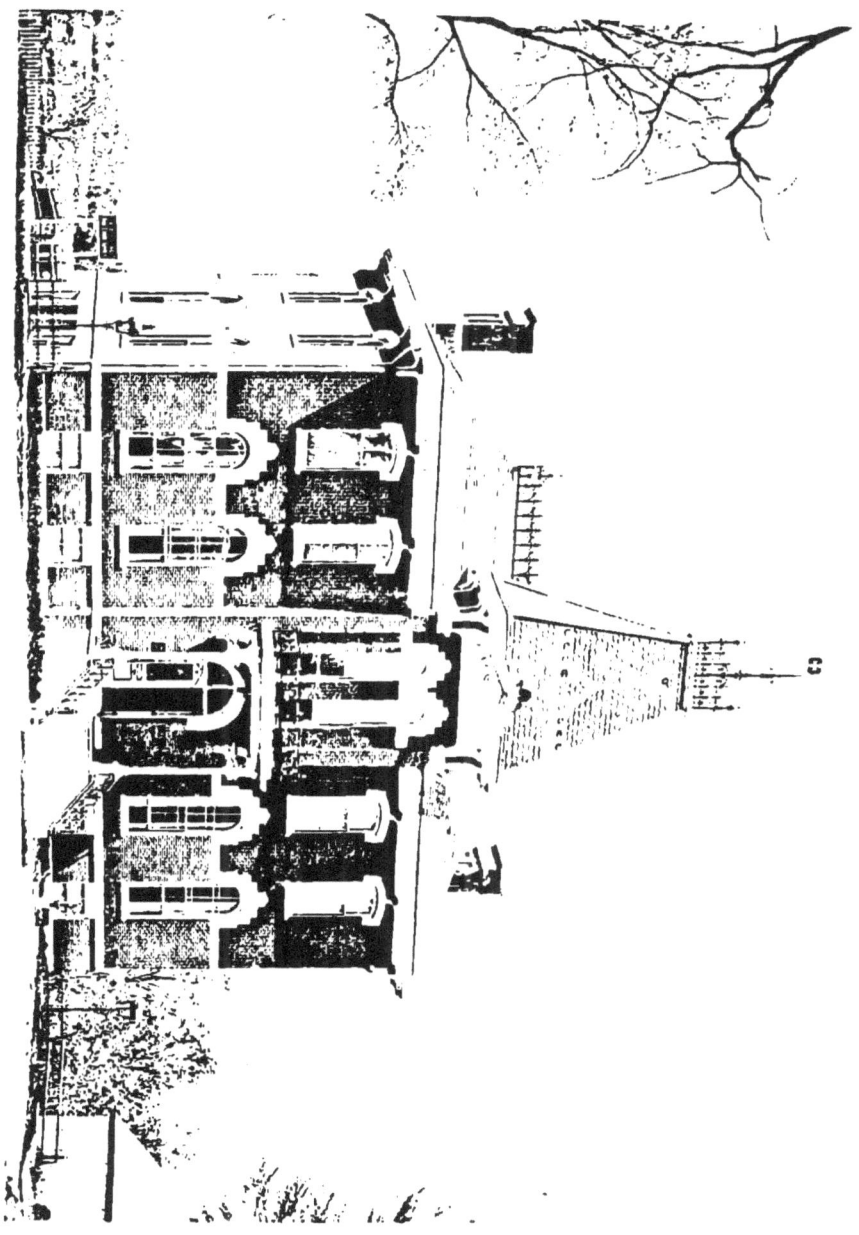

REPRESENTATIVES OF THE PROFESSIONS—PHYSICIANS.

Royalston began its second century with its fourth minister and fourth physician in the centre of the town. We have had scores to preach and almost as many to practice.

The first practicing physician in town was Dr. Moses Phelps, who came here in 1776, and for more than half a century visited his patients on horseback with his huge saddle-bags of medicine. His son, Moses Phelps, studied and practiced with him, except for four years spent in Barre; after more than fifty years of active service, he continued to be consulted till his death in 1873, the father and son thus covering almost a century of practice.

Of the many who have succeeded them, for longer or shorter periods, we shall mention little beside their names.

Dr. Goodnow came in 1803 and was succeeded by Dr. Howe in 1808. The diploma of Dr. George Hoyt we find recorded in Latin in the town records for the year 1826. Drs. Brown, Holmes, Taylor, Alexander, Billings, Bemis, Pillsbury, Scribner, Freeland, Lincoln, Sylvester, Ruggles and Ames, have come and gone. Dr. Joseph M. Tenney, a native of the town, was for several years the only physician here, till near the close of 1872, when Dr. H. O. Palmer came. Dr. Amory Jewett came soon after the death of Dr. Tenney, in 1877.

The following were Hubbardston men:—

William Parkhurst was educated at Dartmouth Medical School. He subsequently studied with Dr. Whiton of Winchendon, practicing there at the same time, and afterwards in New Salem. In 1815, he went to Petersham, where he practiced till his death in 1861.

John Browning, early in the century, went to Mendon, N. Y., where he died May 31, 1866.

" A practicing physician for forty years in the immediate vicinity where he died, his faithfulness, integrity and skill drew around him a large circle of acquaintances who mourn his loss. He fell like a shock of corn fully ripe, at the advanced age of four-score years, and has left behind him an example of un-

swerving confidence in revealed truth, which it would be well
for his survivors to imitate."[*]

Shepherd Clark received the degree of M. D. in 1820, and
began the practice of his profession in Hubbardston. He was
a member of the Massachusetts Medical Society.

Joseph M. Tenney began the study of medicine with Dr.
Benjamin Joslin in Pascoag, R. I. He subsequently entered the
office of Dr. J. Virgil Wilson in Norwich, Conn., where he
practiced under Dr. Wilson's supervision. He also spent some
time as a student in the office of Dr. H. H. Brigham of Fitchburg, before entering the Eclectic Medical College in Worcester,
from which he graduated. From 1865 till his death, twelve
years later, he practiced in Hubbardston. He was a member of
the Worcester Eclectic Medical Society.

Nelson P. Clark studied medicine with Dr. Parker and anato-
my with Dr. Haynes, in Concord, N. H. After practicing successfully from 1850 to 1856 in Andover, N. H., he returned to
Concord and studied Homœopathy with Dr. Morrill. From
September, 1857 till his death, June 25, 1880, he practiced in
New Boston, N. H., combining both modes of practice, Allop-
athy and Homœopathy.

Jubal C. Gleason, a graduate of Amherst College in 1863,
and of the medical department at Harvard in 1867, practiced in
Gilbertville three years, and since 1870 in Rockland. He is
medical examiner for the Second Plymouth District. In 1870,
he was a member of the Massachusetts House of Representatives. For the last seven years he has been chairman of the
school board in Rockland.

S. Elliot Greenwood graduated from Wilbraham Academy in
1873, and from Harvard, medical department, in 1877. For a
few months he practiced in New England Village, and since the
spring of 1878 in Templeton.

LAWYERS.

But few representatives of the bar have ever lived here, and
the town has furnished but little business in that line.

---

*E. B. V. in Obituary Notice

Samuel Swan spent most of his life here. He took a leading part in town affairs, and had considerable probate business, besides occasional suits in the courts.

George Swan, son of Samuel, after a course at Amherst College, studied law with his father and with Hon. B. F. Thomas; was admitted to practice in 1848; built an office and commenced business here, but soon removed to Worcester, where he has met with success in his profession.

No others have practiced law in town as a profession.

Hon. Ethan A. Greenwood, a graduate of Dartmouth College, studied law with Hon. Solomon Strong, but did not long continue the practice.

Thomas O. Selfridge became a distinguished lawyer in Boston early in the present century.

William A. Williams studied at academies in Ashby, New London and Leicester. Prevented by poor health from entering the academical department at Harvard, he afterwards entered the law department there and graduated in 1847. He was admitted to the bar in 1848, since which time he has practiced in Worcester. In 1872, he was admitted to practice in the United States Circuit Court, at Boston.

Edward B. Savage studied law in the office of Bacon and Aldrich, Worcester; was admitted to the bar in November, 1872; practiced about a year in the office of Judge Hartly Williams, Worcester. In February, 1874, he opened an office in Grafton and remained there two years. At present he is practicing in Blackstone.

CLERGYMEN.

The names of those who have had charge of churches here, appear in connection with the church history. The following paragraphs refer to natives of this town:—

John Hubbard Church, D. D., a graduate of Harvard University in 1797, studied theology with Dr. Backus of Somers, Conn., and was ordained at Pelham, N. H. in 1798, where his pastorate continued for nearly forty years. Rev. Mr. Berry of

Pelham, says of him: "Dr. Church was a man of culture, fervent piety, and power as a preacher. He was known, revered and loved, very widely, ir the churches of the state. His ability and theological attainments called him to the counsel of the Theological Seminary at Andover and the life-long friendship of its professors. In missions and all the aggressive work of the church in his day, he bore a prominent part; was sought as preacher and counselor, and often promoted to positions of responsibility in their management."

He was a member of the American Board of Commissioners for Foreign Missions from its beginning; for thirty-one years, secretary of the N. H. General Association; president, and for thirty-five years a trustee of the N. H. Home Missionary Society; a trustee of Andover Theological Seminary, and for thirty-one years, of Dartmouth College. He died June 12, 1840, at the age of sixty-eight.

Rev. Silas Stearns Hyde graduated from the Theological Seminary, Gilmanton, N. H., June, 1845. For thirty three years he was connected, as pastor, with Congregational or Presbyterian churches in New Hampshire, Massachusetts, Rhode Island, Michigan, and Ohio, and for more than half of that time, with small home missionary churches in southeastern Michigan and northwestern Ohio. Since his retirement from active ministry in 1878, his residence has been in Hicksville, Ohio. His only son is in the Presbyterian ministry in western Pennsylvania.

Rev. Clarendon Waite, a graduate of Brown University in 1852, and of Andover Theological Seminary in 1856, studied six months in the University of Halle, Prussia; he was ordained and installed in Rutland, February 25, 1858. During the winter of 1864–5, he did good service in the Freedmen's Bureau, N. C. On his return north he was settled over the Crombie Street Church, Salem. The winter of 1866–7 was spent in Cuba in search of health. He had accepted a professorship in Beloit College and was on his way thither when he was seized with the attack from which he died December 16, 1867.

" During his ministry of eight years in Rutland, eighty-four persons joined the church there, and this statement is not even an indication of his success, though in some measure a tribute to his faithfulness. There was a large work of love in the church, and many happy results secured that can be recorded only in men's hearts, and will not be fully known till the final day. In Salem, he won quickly the strong love of his people, which was shown in their thoughtful and generous deeds toward him and his. It were hard to tell whether by thoughtfully studied and carefully written sermons, or by warm-hearted pastoral work he accomplished most for the Lord he loved."*

Rev. George Whitefield Phillips graduated from Amherst College in 1861 ; studied theology at Andover Seminary, and was licensed to preach in 1864. He was ordained and installed in Haydenville, October, 1864, where he remained about three years, and was then settled over the First Congregational Church in Columbus, Ohio. In 1871, he became pastor of the Plymouth Church, Worcester, which position he still holds.

Rev. John M. Stowe graduated at Bangor Theological Seminary, August 30, 1854, and was ordained and installed in Walpole, N. H., January 31, 1855. After a pastorate there of nearly nine years he supplied the church in Sullivan, N. H., for about seven years. September 14, 1870, he was installed over the Evangelical Congregational Church of Hubbardston; this relation continued till his sudden death, May 9, 1877.

" The churches and the ministry in Worcester North Association sustain a great bereavement in the sudden death of Mr. Stowe. He was a man of solid, substantial qualities. His sermons were wrought out carefully. He put prayer, and study and heart into their composition. He loved the word of God, and honored that word in his ministry. In the association with his ministerial brethren, Mr. Stowe was loved and honored. They looked upon him as a man wholly unselfish, whose only desire was the peace, the purity, and the prosperity of the

---

*Congregational Quarterly, July, 1868.

24

churches. His piety was deep and unquestioned. Those who have known him in his different fields of labor, invariably speak of him in terms of warmest personal friendship. After eighteen years of absence from his early home, he was recalled by the unanimous vote of the church and parish to the pastorate of the Congregational Church in his native town. He had grown up amid the clashing of theological opinions. He was a man of positive opinions himself. In his early boyhood, the church in Hubbardston had been rent asunder. Yet such was the wisdom and catholicity of Mr. Stowe that he was received with the most cordial kindness in all the families on either side of the line of disruption.

At his funeral the entire town was represented. All classes united in paying a tribute to his great worth. All felt that a good man, a useful citizen, and a faithful gospel minister had been taken away. In these days when so much is made of surface brilliancy, it is refreshing to see how deeply sterling good sense and unaffected goodness had made themselves felt in the community that had known his entire life."*

To these words of a ministerial associate, a fellow-townsman adds the following tribute:—

"As a young man, Mr. Stowe took an active part in the Lyceum; was connected with our schools as teacher, and for a short period before leaving town, as a member of the superintending committee; and gave a ready hand to every project for the mental, moral or outward improvement of the place. That he possessed the confidence of his townsmen in subsequent years, is indicated by their calling him home to deliver the centennial address in 1867; and later, by his call to the pastorate of the church where he was best known. Again a resident in town, he was active in the school district, on the school committee, and in the town library. Nor did a cemetery association or the Farmers' Club appeal in vain for a share of his time and consideration. He consented also to write the history of the

---

*Congregational Quarterly, July, 1878.

town, and had mainly completed this work before his death.

He was a man of public spirit and thoroughly identified with the best interests of the community. Free from partisan prejudice, seeking no distinction or emolument, he was regarded as prudent and wise in counsel, and was honored and loved by all. Perhaps no man, at the time of his death, had more influence in the affairs of the town than he. But it was in the pastoral relation that he was best appreciated and most warmly loved. His people remember his solicitous care for souls and his self-forgetful ministrations, even when his own soul was pierced with sorrow.

Distrustful of himself he had firm confidence in God, and therefore was always hopeful. He believed—let us hope the same—that better days were in store for his people and for Hubbardston than he was spared to see."

CHAPTER XVIII.

The following account of the Centennial Celebration is abridged from the pamphlet published at the time, containing the "Address and poem, with other proceedings and exercises connected with the occasion:"—

At a legal meeting of the inhabitants of the town of Hubbardston, held on the 2d day of April, 1866, a committee consisting of William Bennett, Elisha Woodward, Levi Peirce, Henry Prentiss, and Aaron Greenwood was chosen to take into consideration the propriety of holding a centennial celebration, when the one hundredth anniversary of the incorporation of the town should arrive.

At a subsequent meeting, held November 6, the committee made their report, recommending that a day, on or about the 13th of June, 1867, be set apart and observed by a centennial celebration in accordance with the customs of the times in the vicinity. And also recommended that a committee of arrangements, and other necessary committees be appointed, and an appropriation of three hundred dollars be made to defray the expenses of procuring a historical address to be delivered on that occasion, and the publication of that address, and other statistics and historical information connected therewith.

The town voted to accept and adopt the report, and chose Levi Peirce, Elisha Woodward, William Bennett, Lyman Woodward and T. Sibley Heald, as the committee of arrangements. Wm. G. Clark, Abel Howe, Horace Underwood, Spencer Prentiss, Luke Williams, Jr. and Moses C. Wheeler, were afterwards added to the number.

The committee took measures to secure an address and poem, and having engaged a caterer, and made such other arrangements as they deemed necessary, selected the following gentlemen as officers of the day :—

President, LEVI PEIRCE.

Vice-Presidents :

COL. MOSES WAITE,*	MOSES C. WHEELER,
DR. MOSES PHELPS,†	OREN MAREAN, } §
CAPT. EBENEZER STOWE,‡	ABEL HOWE.

To which were afterwards added nearly all the aged gentlemen in the town.

Chief Marshal, LYMAN WOODWARD.

Assistant Marshals :

WM. H. WHITTEMORE, F. P. MORSE, ROCKWELL H. WAITE, ASA H. CHURCH.

The school children to be marshaled by the school committee.

Toast Master, J. C. GLEASON.   Chaplain, REV. I. B. BIGELOW.

The day preceding the celebration was remarkably fine, and life and animation pervaded our village. Two spacious tents had been erected on our common. under one of which the exercises before dinner were to be performed, and under the other, the dinner, poems, sentiments, responses and other exercises were to come off. A broad arch spanned the street midway, bearing a hearty welcome to all the returning sons and daughters of Old Hubbardston, supported by a smaller arch on each side, spanning the sidewalks, crowned with appropriate devices and mottoes. All the dwellings upon Main Street were tastefully decorated, and the preparations for the coming day seemed complete. As the sun descended to the west that afternoon it was obscured by clouds and the evening betokened an approaching storm, so that many of our citizens retired that

---

*One of the selectmen first in 1814, representative in 1830, and now in the eighty-eighth year of his age.
†One of the selectmen in 1818, representative in 1828, and now in the eighty-second year of his age.
‡One of the selectmen in 1821, and now in the eighty-seventh year of his age.
§The present board of selectmen.

night with feelings of despondency, lest the festivities of the coming day should be interrupted by the state of the weather; a slight sprinkle of rain during the evening had the effect of laying the dust, and rendering the air more salubrious. But as morning dawned the clouds departed, and the sun rose in splendor upon green fields and meadows, and the full foliage of our woodlands and beautiful shade trees. And at his appearance above the horizon, he was greeted with one hundred reports from the open mouth of the cannon, and the chiming music of our village bells. The town was resplendent with flags and evergreens as if it had put on its holiday attire to extend the right hand of fellowship, and welcome all to the paternal mansion. At an early hour groups of children were seen upon all the roads entering the village, in vehicles and on foot, hurrying towards the centre of attraction. And the little children were not alone in their glee, but children of a larger growth joined in the general throng. And the hoary headed upon whose brows the snows of more than fourscore years had fallen and bleached their thin locks to the hue of the drifted snow, and who were now leaning on crutches and staves, were also making haste to join in the gathering, and persons of all ages and conditions met on one common level and extended the hand of welcome to their relatives and friends, who were now pouring in from the surrounding towns.

At about nine o'clock, the children, under the lead of Horace Underwood, formed in procession near the Star Hotel, and preceded by the Hubbardston Brass Band, marched to the Unitarian Church where they were addressed by Rev. C. W. Allen, Rev. J. M. Stowe, Rev. G. W. Phillips and others. After the addresses, the procession was again formed and marched to Mechanics Hall, where a bountiful supply of refreshments had been provided, and they were then left to enjoy themselves to the best of their ability.

At about eleven o'clock the grand procession formed on the common under the lead of the chief marshal, in the following order :—

The Asnaconcomic Lodge of Good Templars,

Hubbardston Brass Band,

The President of the Day, Orator and Chaplain,

Vice-Presidents,

The Committee of Arrangements,

The Rev. Clergy, Invited Guests and Representatives of the Press,

Citizens of Rutland, Barre, Princeton and Oakham,

Citizens of other Towns,

Citizens of Hubbardston.

The procession passed through the village beneath the beautiful shade trees on the easterly side of Main Street, and returned on the westerly side of the street, and entered the Grand Pavilion on the westerly side of the common, where as many of the audience as could be accommodated with seats, were thus provided for, while the remainder stood.

The exercises were: Music by the band; reading of the scriptures by Rev. S. Saltmarsh, of Dorchester; the song. "Home Again," by the choir; prayer by the chaplain; an original hymn by Dea. Ephraim Stowe, was sung by the choir, after which Rev. J. M. Stowe, the orator of the day, was introduced by the president, and for two hours received the undivided attention of the entire audience.

The benediction was pronounced by Rev. G. W. Phillips of Haydenville.

The assembly now immediately repaired to the other tent, where the dinner was waiting. After that had been despatched, the poem, by Dea. Ephraim Stowe, was read by Horace Underwood. Among the responses to the toasts that followed, there were poems also by Sampson Mason of Concord, George Swan of Worcester, and William E. Richardson of Boston.

Letters were read from Governor Bullock and others who could not be present.

After the sentiments and responses at the table were concluded, the band gave the closing benediction in some well chosen and fitting strains, and as the sun was sinking below the western horizon, the vast concourse abdicated the tent, parting greetings were hastily given and received, and many visitors left for their homes.

Thus passed the thirteenth day of June, 1867; a day long to be remembered in the annals of Hubbardston; a day which was closing without the happening of any accident to mar the pleasure of the occasion; a day that had brought together more people than had ever before been assembled in the town on any occasion; a day rendered pleasant by all its surroundings—a clear sky, a bright sun, pure air and gentle zephyrs; pleasant by the friendly greetings of old friends and associates, the returned sons and daughters of Old Hubbardston, returned to the old homestead for an affectionate embrace. Many had returned to meet aged parents or other relatives, others to meet no kindred or relative, but nevertheless to meet friends, warm friends, and revisit and review, and revive the scenes, the haunts and the memories of former years, the homes which they had once left without, possibly, at the time, "casting one longing, lingering look behind," but to which they now turned with fond delight.

It may be of interest to some readers now, and to others hereafter, to obtain such glimpses of the town and its individual inhabitants at the end of its first century, as will be afforded by the subjoined list of manufactures and productions in 1865, and the tax list of 1867, which, with most of the statistics that follow, are copied from the appendix of the pamphlet above quoted.

MANUFACTURES AND PRODUCTIONS IN 1865.

Establishments for the manufacture of chairs, 5 ; value manufactured $35,004 ; capital $11,700 ; employ 41 males, 50 females.

Tin ware, 1 ; value of ware $3,000 ; capital $1,000 ; employs 4 males.

Tannery, 1 ; hides tanned 1,200 ; value of leather $9,000 ; capital $3,000 ; employs 3 males.

Box establishments, 2 ; value of wooden boxes manufactured $3,100 ; capital $1,700 ; employ 4 males.

Lumber prepared, 1,669,000 ft. ; value $24,784. Shingles 143,000 ; value $550 ; capital $16,100 ; employ 19 males.

Firewood and bark prepared, 1,306 cords ; value $3,688.

Shoe tools, 1 ; value $3,000 ; capital $2,500 ; 4 males employed.

Boots 22,328 pairs ; shoes 300 pairs ; value of boots and shoes $69,-717 ; capital $16,000 ; employ 32 males and 3 females.

Toy wheelbarrows and hand sleds, value $2,000.

Card board establishments, 3 ; boards manufactured 7100 dozen pairs ; value $4,450 ; capital $1,700 ; employ 9 males.

Sheep 307, value,	$1,768 00
Wool produced, 1303 lbs., value,	652 00
Horses, 246, value,	19,935 00
Oxen, 106, } Steers, 80, } value,	12,322 00
Milch cows, 508, } Heifers, 39, } value,	23,810 00
Neat stock not enumerated above, 241, value,	5,669 00
Butter, 18,286 lbs., value,	7,314 40
Cheese, 8,068 lbs., value,	1,613 60
Milk, 1,855 gals., value,	480 10
Indian corn, 124¾ acres, 3,918 bushels, value,	7,836 00
Wheat, 10¾ acres, 144½ bushels, value,	433 50
Rye, 5¾ acres, 83 bushels, value,	207 50
Barley, 60 acres, 1,517 bushels, value,	1,517 00
Oats, 94 acres, 2,755 bushels, value,	2,755 00
Potatoes, 146½ acres, 17,368 bushels, value,	8,684 00
Turnips, carrots, etc., 1,599 bushels, value,	799 50
English hay, 2,222 acres, 1,811 tons, value,	36,220 00
Swale and meadow hay, 448 tons, value,	4,480 00
Apples, value,	3,099 00
Pears, value,	80 00
Other cultivated fruit, value,	30 00

VALUATION OF, AND TAX UPON THE PROPERTY OF THE TOWN OF HUB-BARDSTON, AS TAKEN MAY 1, 1867.

Valuation of real estate,	$544,110	
personal estate,	199,506	
		$743,616 00

Number of polls, 409.

Amount of money raised to defray town charges, $4,000 00

for support of schools, 2,000 00

to repair highways, 2,000 00

25

Amount of state tax,	$4,050 00
county tax,	730 55
Overlayings,	483 11
	——— $13,263 66

Scale, $16.30 on $1,000.

NAME.	TAX.	NAME.	TAX.
Adams, Amos T.	$3 08	Bigelow, Increase B.	$10 24
Adams, Darius	2 91	Bigelow, Joseph	17 58
Adams, Henry M.	2 91	Bigelow, Sullivan	6 17
Adams, Homer M.	20 20	Bigelow, Warren N.	2 91
Adams, John	65 34	Blake, Ella	2 91
Adams, John, Jr.	25 45	Blake, John	3 73
Allen, Apollos A.	3 89	Blood, Charles W.	44 63
Allen, Asa	19 97	Blood, Joseph W.	7 80
Allen, George	8 06	Blood & Jackson,	3 26
Allen, John G.	69 50	Blood, Theodore F.	3 89
Allen, Mary	6 52	Bowker & Balcom,	97 80
Allen, Sally	6 52	Bowker, George L.	5 36
Ashley, Charles W.	15 54	Boyd, Hiram C.	2 91
Austin, Charles	19 38	Brant, William	10 25
Bacon, Elbridge G.	2 91	Brigham, Orlando S.	90 60
Baker, Quincy	18 96	Brigham & Potter,	9 78
Baker, Sally	22 01	Brooks, Henry D.	3 97
Balcom, Joseph G.	4 54	Brown & Bacon,	47 98
Barnes, Francis	12 61	Brown, Austin	24 10
Barnes, Myra	6 52	Brown, Clinton	4 54
Barnes, Myra and Lucy	2 77	Brown, Dana	191 89
Bates, George S.	12 53	Brown, Emeline	8 15
Beaty, William T.	8 86	Brown, Gilbert	31 35
Bellows, Isaac	20 84	Brown, Harvey	3 57
Bennett, Addison	70 33	Brown, Moses	162 20
Bennett, Albert	29 34	Brown, Sewell	5 84
Bennett, Albert and Edwin	228 81	Brown, Shepherd	19 01
Bennett, David	123 39	Brown, Thomas H. heirs of,	49 71
Bennett, Hannah	29 34	Brown, Walter R.	2 91
Bennett, Henry	25 61	Brown, Welcome	2 91
Bennett, Loring	16 35	Browning, Abby D.	9 78
Bennett, Martha	7 82	Browning, James	16 93
Bennett, Moses	5 43	Browning, Joshua	18 54
Bennett, William	136 97	Browning, Lyman W.	2 91

NAME.	TAX.	NAME.	TAX.
Bruce, Charles R.	$2 91	Cleaveland, Joseph A.	$4 21
Burroughs, George H.	7 97	Cleaveland, Joseph A., Jr.	2 91
Butler, Eli H.	5 36	Codding, Zenas	12 04
Campbell, Vincent	4 79	Cole, John T. A.	2 91
Chase, George A.	4 21	Cole, Stephen T.	18 64
Cheney, Lovering A.	18 72	Coleman, Almond	6 34
Church, Asa H.	2 91	Coleman, Benjamin F.	18 23
Church, Eliza	6 52	Coleman, Frederick	2 91
Church, Sophia	6 52	Coleman, Hervey	9 84
Church, Stephen D.	2 91	Coleman, Oliver B.	2 91
Clark, A. B. & E. H.	82	Coleman, Reuben	12 53
Clark, Amos F.	20 03	Colon, Warren	2 91
Clark, Anson B.	28 51	Conant, Benjamin P.	11 55
Clark, Asa	5 36	Conant, Levi	62 82
Clark, Asa G.	23 94	Conant, Levi W.	15 62
Clark, Betsey	29 34	Cummings, Frederick A.	2 91
Clark, Betsey and Maria	27 71	Cushman, David Q.	2 91
Clark, Charlotte	12 22	Damon, Alonzo	12 69
Clark, Danford	61 75	Daniels, Augustus	2 91
Clark, Edwin H.	33 67	Davis, Ann C.	7 33
Clark, Ferdinand N.	62 41	Davis, Amasa G.	81 42
Clark & Goodnow,	13 04	Davis, Carlo B.	16 76
Clark, Hervey	38 77	Davis, Charles	40 73
Clark, James W.	7 48	Davis, Fred E.	2 91
Clark, John C.	2 91	Davis, Isaac	28 18
Clark, John F. heirs of,	3 26	Davis, Israel	73 65
Clark, Martin & Myrick, Wal-		,Davis, John	19 21
ton	30 37	Davis, John S.	7 80
Clark, Mary Ann	17 93	Davis, Moses	2 91
Clark, Merrifield	11 06	Davis, Waite & Co.	70 09
Clark, Noah A.	14 71	Day, Charles M.	2 91
Clark, Peter F.	20 35	Day, Nabby T.	9 13
Clark, Washburn	11 06	Day, William B.	2 91
Clark, Warren	52 63	Delano, C. O.	10 16
Clark, William G.	15 62	Dewey, Francis H.	7 80
Clark, William S.	44 99	Dexter, Benjamin	24 45
Clark, William S., Jr.	45 05	Downey, Michael	2 91
Clark & Wilson,	8 15	Dunton, Newton	15 39
Cleaveland, Henry L.	15 26	Dunton, Sylvanus, heirs of,	54 75

NAME.	TAX.	NAME.	TAX.
Dyer, Otis	\$2 91	Gleason, Andrew	\$126 92
Eames, Ambrose	4 21	Gleason, Freeland S.	2 91
Earle, James	31 60	Gleason, Samuel S.	4 95
Earle, Jonathan P.	18 48	Goddard, S. W. E.	50 18
Earle, Silas	10 49	Goodspeed, John	27 11
Earle, Tyler	2 91	Gregg, Frank	2 91
Earle, William H.	6 52	Green, John C.	20 51
Eaton, John H.	2 91	Green, John C., Jr.	2 91
Eveleth, William J.	28 26	Green, Joseph	14 32
Falis, Henry, heirs of,	19 56	Green, William M.	33 23
Falis, Jarvis	3 56	Greenwood, Aaron	42 27
Falis, Joseph S.	2 91	Greenwood, Alson J.	48 30
Falis, Mrs. Joseph S.	25 26	Greenwood, Caroline	13 04
Farrington, Manson	2 91	Greenwood, Ethan A., heirs	
Felton, George W.	5 36	of,	130 40
Felton, Nathan H.	54 28	Greenwood, Horace, heirs of	39 73
Felton & Morse,	15 24	Greenwood, Joseph E.	26 06
Fisher, Charles D.	2 91	Greenwood, Lyman	70 39
Flagg, Joel S.	4 46	Greenwood, Morrill A.	2 91
Flagg, John F.	8 45	Greenwood, Silas N.	25 73
Flagg, Joshua	22 06	Greenwood, Thomas E.	3 11
Flagg, Joshua, Jr.	9 43	Greenwood, William S.	9 92
Flagg, Josiah	7 80	Grimes, Aaron	53 79
Flynn, James S.	2 91	Grimes, Edwin	15 79
Flynn, John B.	46 11	Grimes, Harrison	85 63
Follett, Jonas	18 29	Grimes, H. & Pollard, A.	9 78
Follett, Lucy W.	13 04	Grimes, Hiram	33 23
Forbush, David G.	2 91	Grimes, Joseph	20 02
Fowler, Oscar A.	2 91	Grimes, Sewell	4 54
French, Perez	5 36	Hager, Charles	17 51
Frost, Benjamin C.	98	Hale, Irving T.	15 95
Gardner, Volney	2 91	Hale J. Otis	75 89
Gates, Jonathan	26 46	Hale, Merrill	25 63
Gates, Jonathan D.	19 54	Hale, Seth P.	2 91
Gay, Almer	43 01	Hale, Thomas, heirs of,	39 28
Gay, Elbridge A.	1 30	Hale & Williams,	110 02
Gaut, Samuel H.	2 91	Hallock, Isaac	43 88
Gibbs, Amasa	12 12	Hallock & Pollard,	25 57
Gilson, Nathaniel	2 91	Hallock, William A.	2 91

NAME.	TAX.	NAME.	TAX.
Hamilton, George W.	$38 48	Joslin, Levi G.	$2 91
Harrington & Howard.	90 99	Joslin, Silas	25 57
Harris, Calvin P.	5 83	Joslin, Silas 2d.	6 17
Harris, Joseph H.	14 32	Joslin, William	67 70
Hartwell, Alonzo	21 13	Joslin, Wm. as Guardian for	
Hartwell, James H.	40 73	Dana Lyon,	18 41
Hartwell, Edson	2 91	Kelton, Elihu	73 62
Harwood, Sumner	42 03	Kendall, Chester B.	20 03
Hastings, Dorinda C.	19 97	Kendall, Esther J.	5 54
Heald, Abigail	16 30	King, Amos F.	2 91
Heald, Calvin	2 93	King, Francis F.	2 91
Heald & Goodspeed.	66 13	Lamb, Harrison W.	2 91
Heard, Catherine	40 75	Lamb, James	2 91
Hemenway, Albert	21 26	Lamb, Larkin	2 91
Hinds, Charles E.	41 63	Lanphear, S. H.	49 52
Hobbs, Charles	69 50	Laughna, Terrence	7 48
Hobbs, Charles E.	2 91	Leamy, William	15 47
Hobbs, Moses G.	6 66	Leland, Moses	15 38
Hodge, Asa S.	68 97	Leonard, Richard	20 35
Holt, Dennis	12 04	Lester, Anthony	6 17
Holt, Elias O.	2 91	Lewis, Albert S.	2 91
Holt, Jonas	20 03	Lewis, Fanny S.	14 26
Horton, Andrew	5 92	Lovewell, John	27 37
Hosmer, Amos	14 12	Lovewell, Joseph	25 97
Hosmer, D. & A.	18 91	Lovewell, Leander	23 24
Howe, Abel	59 51	Lucius, Andrew	2 91
Howe, Herbert W.	2 91	Lyon, Aaron	10 41
Hunting, Daniel	4 87	Magrath, Roxana, heirs of,	4 89
Hunting, Henry	3 21	Maney, Edward	17 99
Hunting, Julianna	29 91	Mann, Ebenezer	22 89
Hyde, William	6 69	Marean, Cecelia	7 33
Hyde, William, heirs of,	8 15	Marean, Clark W.	17 58
Jackson, Augustine	38 69	Marean, Dumont	3 24
Jacobs, Charles	3 73	Marean, Joseph P.	53 45
Jennison, Edward H.	2 91	Marean, Oren	79 36
Jennison, Flint	19 21	Marean, William	12 20
Johnson, D. L.	32 66	Marean, William C.	2 91
Joslin, Hollis	58 67	Martin, George W.	2 91
Joslin, Levi	67 18	May, Patrick C.	4 38

NAME.	TAX.	NAME.	TAX.
May, Mrs. Patrick C.	$6 52	Murdock, Leander L.	$2 91
Maynard, Fred	2 91	Murdock, Sumner	27 93
Maynard, Samuel J.	4 21	Myrick, Walter	1 75
McClenathan, Whiting	14 32	Nelson, Oliver	2 91
McCormack, Michael	7 72	Newton, Timothy	3 73
McCormack, Timothy	2 91	Nichols, Joseph C.	2 91
McFarland, Elijah	8 64	Nichols, Moses	28 75
McFarland, Elijah W.	18 56	Nichols, Samuel G.	3 09
Merriam, Asa	64 03	Olmstead, Israel J.	2 91
Merriam, Willard	2 91	Orr, Thomas	2 91
Miller, Addison	2 91	Osgood, Henry W.	4 70
Miller, Fidelia	6 52	Osgood, Isaac	15 95
Minns, James	2 91	Parker, Otis	49 19
Minns, John	2 91	Parker, Stephen S.	2 91
Minns, Thomas	19 36	Parker, William J.	13 89
Moore, Rufus D.	2 91	Parkhurst, A. H.	14 65
Moore, Joseph W.	3 89	Parsons, Willard	10 65
Moore, Luke S.	60 46	Partridge, Abijah, heirs of,	49
Moore, Thomas L., heirs of,	3 75	Peirce, Levi	32 60
Morrissey, John	6 17	Peirce, Watson I.	2 91
Morrissey, Patrick	2 91	Perry, Charles M.	4 54
Morse, Adeline B.	8 15	Phelps, Benjamin D.	95 41
Morse, Augusta	26 08	Phelps, Dexter	14 67
Morse, Augustus	26 08	Phelps, Henry B.	2 91
Morse, Fred P.	7 07	Phelps, Moses	16 05
Morse, Horace	31 44	Phillips, Benjamin F.	3 26
Morse, John	77 43	Phillips, James	2 91
Morse, John Q.	59 56	Pierce, Benjamin F.	79 09
Morse, Joel	4 38	Pike, Amos	15 46
Morse, J. & F. P.	12 22	Pollard, Alden	28 19
Morse, Lyman	15 95	Pollard A. & Greenwood, J. L.	9 78
Morse, William H.	83 60	Pollard, Charles A.	2 91
Morse & Pollard,	97 80	Pollard, Charles E.	2 91
Moulton, Sewell	180 33	Pollard, David	146 24
Mulstay, Owen	14 38	Pollard, Edmond A.	39 59
Mundell, Isaac	17 91	Pond, Ezra P.	48 26
Murdock, E. & Stowe, W.	12 43	Pond, George H.	2 91
Murdock, Elisha	41 13	Pond, Hollis	44 31
Murdock, Joseph C.	26 58	Pond, Horace G.	48 63

NAME.	TAX.	NAME.	TAX.
Pond, Levi T.	$2 91	Smith, John A.	$7 80
Potter, Bennett	27 85	Smith, Loring	2 91
Potter, James H.	29 15	Stone, Andrew	12 23
Prentiss, George	43 66	Stone, A. & Conant, B. P.	11 41
Prentiss, Henry	207 47	Stone, Jotham	21 17
Prentiss, Spencer	77 22	Stone, Milton	31 19
Prouty, Norman F.	3 26	Stowe, Charles E.	2 91
Putnam, Rufus	2 91	Stowe, Ephraim	18 96
Rand, William C.	2 91	Stowe, George W.	4 54
Raymond, Nathan	2 91	Stowe, Reuben	15 54
Reid, Joseph B.	50 26	Stowe, Sumner M.	2 91
Reid, Sophia P.	32 60	Stowe, William	51 89
Reid, George W.	152 75	Taft, Alonzo J., heirs of.	1 30
Reid, George W., as Trustee		Taylor, Edward T.	3 61
for Amasa Clark,	48 90	Taylor, Lemuel F.	6 74
Rice, David	3 40	Taylor, Nathaniel	6 99
Rice, Francis	21 33	Temple, Rhoda	28 53
Rice, George W.	2 91	Tenney, Charles F.	2 91
Richardson, Peter	79 60	Tenney, Daniel W.	3 89
Robbins, Albert	2 91	Tenney, Joseph M.	13 67
Roper, Samuel	24 26	Thatcher, Elbridge G.	2 91
Russell, Joseph	29 52	Thomas, Herbert G.	2 91
Russell, Silas	2 91	Thompson, Charles J.	10 25
Sanford, Richard	3 56	Thompson, Henry C.	3 85
Sargent, Ellwell	2 91	Thompson, John	72 70
Sargent, E. M.	5 36	Tilton, Ebenezer	68 80
Sargent, Mrs. E. M.	2 45	Tilton, E. & Co.	44 82
Sargent, William H.	2 91	Tilton, Joseph	7 23
Savage, Edward B.	2 91	Titus, William C., heirs of,	9 78
Savage, James	24 73	Tolman, Henry J.	2 91
Savage, Samuel K.	22 01	Tracy, Richard	2 91
Savage, Seth	27 90	Tyler, Nathan	7 15
Sawyer, Luke	71 95	Underwood, Amos G.	20 12
Shaffer, Jacob	2 91	Underwood, Asa	61 10
Sheedy, William	2 91	Underwood, Caleb	33 07
Sheron, John	3 64	Underwood, Horace	98 18
Simonds, Willard A.	2 91	Underwood, John	8 13
Smith, Emmons	16 11	Underwood, Josiah	106 42
Smith, Ira W.	2 91	Upham, James P.	6 17

NAME.	TAX.	NAME.	TAX.
Waite, Aaron	$47 90	Williams, David R.	$4 95
Waite, Albert H.	2 91	Williams, John D.	143 79
Waite, George A.	2 91	Williams, Luke	22 95
Waite, Increase S.	55 89	Williams, Luke, Jr.	86 25
Waite, Joseph	27 86	Williams, William C.	23 05
Waite, Luke	75 67	Willis, George	18 40
Waite, Moses	9 13	Wilson, Abram H.	20 35
Waite, Rockwell H.	26 06	Witt, Daniel	14 32
Ward, Hiram	11 72	Woods, Edward	2 91
Ward, James	12 69	Woods, Edwin	22 56
Ware, Albert	2 91	Woodward, Elisha	22 55
Warren, Betsey	27 71	Woodward, John F.	128 66
Warren, Harriet	9 78	Woodward, John F., as Trus-	
Warren, Walter	60 45	tee for P. Grimes,	97 80
Wheeler, Albert	23 49	Woodward, Lyman	71 08
Wheeler, Jennison	26 06	Woodward, Rowland	33 39
Wheeler, Moses C.	26 87	Woodward & Warren,	60 31
Wheeler, Sewell	64 44	Wright, Benjamin	3 56
Whitney, George W.	12 73	Wright, Benjamin F.	7 23
Whitney, Jonathan W.	15 95	Wright, Elizabeth	40 10
Whitney, Rebecca G.	4 89	Wright, John R.	26 22
Whittemore, William H.	10 25	Wright, Joab C.	80 34
Wilbur, Priest, heirs of.	11 90	Wright, Nathan, heirs of,	19 56
Wilbur, Williams	43 67	Wyman, Harrison	26 59
Wilder, Henry A.	34 37	Young, Allen	4 94
Willard, Ephraim	41 89	Young, Sumner C.	30 31

There are about 3968 acres of non-resident lands; valuation thereof, $62,830.00; tax on the same, $1,024.13.

In addition to the foregoing, there were school district taxes raised in the following districts :—

District No. 2,	Grant $50.00,	Overlayings $1.75,	Scale 0.60
" " 3,	" 25.00,	" 1.91,	" .40
" " 7,	" 25.00,	" 1.68,	" .40
" " 9,	" 75.00,	" 1.90,	" 2.00

The money granted by the town for the support of common schools is [was at that time] divided among the several districts in the following manner, viz: one-third part thereof is divided equally among the districts, and the remainder is allotted to the districts in proportion to the children therein, between the ages of four and twenty-one years.

POPULATION AT DIFFERENT PERIODS.

1767, about	-	-	150	1850,	- - -	1,825
1776,	- · -	-	488	1855,	- - -	1,744
1790,	- -	·	933	1860,	- - -	1,621
1800,	- -	-	1,113	1865,	- - -	1,546
1810,*	- -	-	1,127	1870,	- - -	1,654
1820,	- -	-	1,367	1875,	- - -	1,440
1830,	- -	-	1,674	1880,	- - -	1,385
1840,	- -	-	1,784			

The whole number of families in 1782 was 107 ; in 1794, 131 ; in 1800, 146 ; in 1810, 182 ; in 1820, 213 ; in 1830, 261 ; in 1840, 291 ; in 1850, 325 ; in 1860, 365 ; in 1865, 373 ; in 1875, 385.

The valuation of the town as prepared by the state at the several different dates has been as follows, viz :—

	Polls.			Polls.	
1831,	346,	$314,467	1865,	361,	$741,433
1841,	423,	411,458	1870,	431,	904,457
1851,	473,	643,503	1875,	414,	903,176
1861,	454,	609,054	1880,	367,	789,238

---

*The southeast corner of Hubbardston, containing about 500 acres of land, with five families and about forty inhabitants, was set off and annexed to Princeton, February 26, 1810.

26

CHAPTER XIX.

RETROSPECTIVE.

" SUCH was the town of Hubbardston
When this last century begun.
There were no stages, good or poor,
To take us up at our own door ;
No carriages,—at least, but few.
To meeting and to weddings, too,
E'en ladies rode on Dobbin's back,
Jog-trot along the narrow track ;
And very often you would find
The lady mounted on behind
The man, with each a lesser chap
All snug and warm within the lap.

*   *   *   *   *   *

No railroad tracks have here been laid
To give an impetus to trade ;
No telegraphic wires put down
To bring their messages to town.

*   *   *   *   *   *

'Tis said improvements will go on,
And more and greater things be done
Before the next half century's past
Than those we witnessed in the last.
If so, then we shall fly through space,
Like morning sunbeams on a race,
For cars now carry us so fast
We hardly know where we were last ;
And Europe and America
Can talk together any day ;
And words across the ocean find

MAIN STREET LOOKING NORTHWESTERLY, 1839.

Their way almost as quick as mind.
'Tis doubtful whether man e'er will,
With all his deep artistic skill
And great inventive powers, be able
To run before the Atlantic cable,
If he outruns the iron horse
By any new propelling force."

So wrote the "Hubbardston poet" at the time of the centennial celebration, looking backward, at the time then present, and looking forward. The changes that have taken place within the fourteen years since he wrote, promise the fulfilment of his vision. No longer ago than then, instead of our present telegraphic and mail accommodations, we had but one mail daily from Gardner, and one from Worcester, both by stage. If one wished to take public conveyance to Boston or New York, he had these two stage routes between which to choose, to reach any line of railway. If he would visit New Hampshire, he must either go from Gardner toward Greenfield and Brattleboro and thence northward, or to Ashburnham or Groton Junction and wait for northern connections. By either route, nearly a whole day must be consumed in getting from here to Keene, a journey now accomplished in an hour and a half by either morning or afternoon trains.

"No parks or Broadways here are seen,
Yet we've a pretty village green.
*　　*　　*　　*　　*　　*　　*

Some few within this audience know
How this street looked long years ago.
A tavern stood at either end,
Where those who had some cash to spend,
Or idle hours to pass away,
Might wet their whistles any day;
And it was said, we know not why,
That whistles then were often dry.
One single dwelling house, between
These two old taverns, could be seen;
A schoolhouse, shop, and old *potash*

For turning ashes into cash,
Were all the buildings on the way
Through what we call the street, to-day ;
While on the common, some horse-sheds
'T would hardly cover horses' heads,
A meeting-house then pretty good,
And one or two old dwellings stood.
There was one little business spot
That is not easily forgot ;
At one end of the street were found
A tavern, shop, schoolhouse and pound.
Between the shop for shoeing horses,
For long years known as Mr. Morse's,
And that one where the idle fool,
As he deserved, got whipped at school,
A pound with walls 't would stand one battle,
Stood to shut up the unruly cattle.
Here, the poor horses' tender feet
Were fitted for the rocky street,
And made in winter not to slip,
While owners, waiting, took their flip.
Here boys were taught their A, B, C,
And naughty cattle made to be
Content on their own fields to graze,
And not be found on the highways ;
And 'twixt the cattle and the boys
At noon you'd hear a frightful noise."

Those who heard these words read on the occasion for which
they were written, will remember, in contrast, the village main
street as it was in 1867. It is the same shady street still; and
until the burning in 1880, of the Crystal House, known formerly as the Central Hotel, there were the church, hotel, and
store, at either end; but in place of the old hotel barn, the tin
shop and its buildings, we have now the fine edifice occupied
by the library and post-office. A new schoolhouse, standing
well back from the street, on what was once the engine lot, has
taken the place of the old carriage-shop, a part of which was
moved to the north side of the common some years ago and

fitted up for a workshop. Nearly opposite the schoolhouse stands the new residence designed for the declining years of Dr. Phelps, but which he did not live to see completed. The house and grounds then owned by Horace Morse have been greatly improved. But without enumerating the many improvements in different residences it must suffice to mention those erected by Joseph Falis, near the Star Hotel, Albert Goodspeed, Harrison Grimes, and farther on toward Gardner, by Capt. Norcross and E. M. Coffin.

Turning from the common toward Barre, we see the boot-shop towering high above the new buildings of William S. Clark, Ebenezer Mann, Homer Peabody and Hervey Clark. The schoolhouse, then known as "No. 1," is now a tenement house with two flats, and near it is the Mason house, moved from its old site and finished off in tenements.

We miss Mechanics Hall, burned in 1877, and the steam-mill, taken down and removed to Gardner in the same year.

Of the men who took an active part in commemorating the completion of the town's first century, a large number are seen no more among us. The president of the day, five of the six vice-presidents, the orator, the poet and William Bennett, have "gone over to the great majority." And to their number has been added the following from the ranks of men then seventy years of age, or over :—

David Bennett,	Asa Allen,	Sewell Wheeler,
Simon Hartwell,	William S. Clark,	Davis Guild,
Amos Mann,	Luke Williams,	John Adams,
Perez French,	Ebenezer Brown,	Josephus Clifford,
Aaron Grimes,	Asa Clark,	Elihu Kelton,
Calvin Heald,	Josiah Underwood,	Isaac Bellows,
John Morse,	Benjamin C. Frost,	Asa Underwood.
Daniel Hayward,	Ephraim Willard,	Calvin Peabody,

But it must be admitted that death is not the only agent in lessening our numbers; our old men die, our young men go to Worcester, or Gardner, or other places larger than this, which absorb our enterprise and feed upon our life. Alluding to this feature, in response to a toast on centennial day, Dr. J. C. Gleason said :—

"We have often heard the regret expressed that so many of the young men, and especially those of energy and talent, leave their native town, elsewhere to seek their fortunes and make their homes. To this we need only reply, it is but natural. Just as in obedience to the law of gravity, water will run down hill, so to-day, the direction of business energy and capital is toward those places most accessible and best adapted by nature to become the centres of trade and industrial interests. Let then, your young men go where they can best display their energies and develop their talents. In this way, will they most honor the place of their birth. Your pride shall be that your town has sent so many away to win laurels for her. Like the old New Hampshire farmer who, when asked, 'What do you raise up here among these rocks and hills?' replied, '*Men*, sir! men who are known all over the land for their character and influence;' so you, if need be, may remember that men are the noblest product of any soil, and that the lessons of thrift and industry and virtue which the youth in these hilly, quiet towns are getting will not be in vain."

Concerning the people who remain the following lines from the poem already quoted are probably as true to-day as in 1867 :—

> "There is one pleasant feature about our old place,
> That e'en to be proud of would be no disgrace—
> If we travel New England all through, up or down,
> We find but few places, perhaps not a town,
> Where less aristocracy is to be found,
> Or more democratic feelings abound.
> There's little of *caste*; the rich and the poor,
> Have access alike to every man's door.
> If we look at the present or past, we shall find
> That Hubbardston people are friendly and kind.
> As a general thing, for the last hundred years,
> They've regarded and treated their neighbors as peers.
> If any grew haughty, if rich, young or old,

They soon found themselves 'left out in the cold.'
If they took a position above their true place,
They met with no favor, but rather disgrace.
We have no religious dissensions of note ;
The ladies don't grumble because they can't vote.
And at all the social gatherings, we find
All classes can mingle with one heart and mind.
We hope it will be so for long years to come,
When we are forgotten at this, our old home."

In conclusion we adopt the closing paragraphs of the centennial address : —

" We have partially surveyed the history of the town and the characters and achievements of its citizens. We have seen how wisely the proprietors planned for us. We have followed the first settlers through some of their toils and sacrifices. We have witnessed their patriotic struggles, their patient endurance and christian faith in those days which tried men's souls. We have traced their influence in politics, in religion, and in industrial pursuits. If time would permit, we might also show how they have helped forward almost every cause of benevolence and philanthropy. They have shown a liberal spirit. The poor outcast, the manacled slave, and the besotted drunkard have always found friends in Hubbardston. But their indignation has burned like an oven against the oppressor and the rumseller. No high reputation nor saintly garb has shielded a man when they thought him corrupt. Thus their benevolence and mercy has been tempered with a high sense of justice.

But if it were possible to lift the veil and show how they have lived in their own homes, how they have discharged the kindly offices of friends and neighbors, it is there we believe their characters would shine most brightly.

Now these fathers sleep all around us in these sacred enclosures of the dead, but 'out of the silence of their graves comes a voice which repeats the lessons of their lives.'

It is for us to take up and carry forward what they so faithfully began. In this age of progress we ought to improve upon what they did, and leave to our children a richer legacy than was bequeathed to us. If they have transmitted to us schools and churches, it is for us to make them more efficient means of good. If they gave up their lives in their efforts to pass over into our hands the Union, the Constitution, and the laws, then it is for us not only to guard the sacred treasure, but following the light of that banner which waves so proudly over us, and on every one of whose ample folds is inscribed in letters of living light, 'Liberty and Union, now and forever, one and inseparable;' it is for us to promulgate the principles of liberty till all men are free indeed.

When time's ceaseless pendulum has measured the hours of another hundred years, our dust will mingle with theirs, and our deeds will have passed, a few into history, but most into oblivion. And if, on the 13th day of June, 1967, our descendants shall be pleased to observe their centennial day, may the records of this coming century show as little to censure and more to admire than we find in that just closed."

CHAPTER XX

MUNICIPAL OFFICERS.

THE following lists contain the names of those who have served in the town offices designated, with the year or years of service; a – between two dates indicates that the years intervening are included with those dates:—

SELECTMEN.

Israel Green,	1767	Elisha Woodward,	1778, 9, 1802
Benjamin Nurse,	1767	William Stone,	1778
Benjamin Hoyt,	1767–9	Joseph Shattuck,	1780, 6
Stephen Heald, 1768, 70, 1, 3, 5,		Nathaniel Waite,	1780, 92–4
9, 86.		Abijah Greenwood, 1780, 3, 7, 92–4	
Adam Wheeler,	1768, 9, 83	Samuel Slocomb,	1781–3
William Pain,	1769	Joel Pollard,	1781
Ezekiel Newton,	1770, 2–4	Reuben Totman,	1783
William Marean, 1770, 1, 5. 82,		James Thompson,	1784, 92, 3
92–1800, 1, 2, 6, 9.		Eli Clark,	1784
Joseph Eveleth,	1771, 3, 85	Joseph Wright,	1784, 6, 92–4
Joseph Slarrow,	1772	Hollis Parker,	1785
John Woods, 1772, 6, 87, 1807, 8		Nathan Stone,	1785
Ezra Pond,	1774, 80, 1, 7	John McClenathan,	1785, 94, 7,
William Muzzy, 1774, 5, 9, 82, 95, 6		1807, 8.	
Jonathan Gates, 1776, 80, 4, 6, 8, 9		Edward Selfridge,	1788, 9
Robert Murdock, 1776, 85, 6, 90		Buckley Howe,	1788, 9
1, 8, 9, 1800, 1.		Moses Greenwood,	1790, 1, 5–7
John Clark,	1777, 9	Moses Clark,	1790, 1, 5, 6
*Isaac Bellows,	1777, 83	Joshua Murdock, 1790, 1, 1807, 8	
George Metcalf,	1777	Samuel Follett,	1790, 1
Thomas Caryl,	1778	Thomas Hapgood,	1795–7

*Resigned to enlist in the army, and Ebenezer Joslin was elected May 22, 1777, to serve for the remainder of that year.

27

John Browning,   1797, 1803–5
Daniel Parkhurst, 1798, 9, 1800, 1
Ephraim Allen, 1798–1800, 9, 10,
    12, 13.
Ebenezer Warren, 1798–1800, 1, 3–
    5, 16, 17.
Israel Davis, 1801, 2, 6, 9, 12–15,
    21, 22.
Ebenezer Stowe,   1802
Abraham Cutting,   1802
Levi Greenwood,   1803–5, 16
Jonathan Cutting,   1803–5
William Morse, 1804, 5, 10–12, 20
Asa Wheeler,   1806, 10–12, 15
Daniel Woodward, 1806, 9, 14, 15,
    18, 19, 21–3.
Samuel Morse,   1806, 13
Otis Parker, 1807, 8, 12, 15, 19, 22
Aaron Gates, 1807, 8, 18–20, 4, 5,
    31, 2.
Luke Warren,   1809, 20
Asa Lyon,   1810
Delphos Gates,   1810, 11
Moses Phelps,   1811
Levi Conant,   1811
Robert Murdock, Jr.   1813
Daniel Barnes,   1813
Moses Waite, 1814, 15, 19, 20, 4,
    6–9, 30, 4, 6–9, 42.
Aaron Wright,   1814, 17
Joel Pollard, Jr.   1814
Ebenezer Mann,   1816
Timothy P. Marean, 1816, 17, 21
Ephraim Mason,   1816
Nathan Wright,   1817
James H. Wheeler,   1817, 18
Moses Phelps, Jr.   1818
Jotham Stone,   1818, 19
Isaac Follett,   1820

James Browning,   1821, 4
Ebenezer Stowe, Jr.   1821
Silas Greenwood, 1822, 3, 6–9, 30–
    2, 4, 6, 9, 40.
Sewell Mirick,   1822, 3, 6
Warner Hinds,   1823, 4, 6
John Church,   1823
Samuel Swan,   1824–7
Henry Prentiss,   1825
George Williams,   1825
Abijah Clark,   1825, 7–9, 31, 2
Jonas Heald,   1827, 8, 43
Nathan Warren,   1828
Asa Marean, 1829, 30, 1, 3, 5, 40,
    1, 3–5.
Rowland Woodward,   1829, 33–5
Justus Ellinwood,   1830
David Bennett,   1830
Elisha Woodward,   1831–3
Ethan A. Greenwood,   1833
Dana Brown,   1833, 5–8, 44, 5
Stillman Morse,   1834
Lyman Greenwood, 1834, 6–8, 46–
    9, 52–4, 9, 60, 2, 4.
William S. Clark,   1835
William Joslin, 1835, 41, 3, 59, 70
Levi Allery,   1836, 7
Sewell Wheeler,   1837, 8, 44, 5
Crusoe Kendall,   1838–40, 2, 3
Henry Prentiss, Jr. 1839, 40, 52–4
    61.
Levi Joslin, 1839, 42, 4–6, 50, 1, 60
Ephraim Stowe,   1840, 1, 3–8
Aaron Greenwood, 1841, 2, 6, 55–8
James A. Waite,   1841
Luke Williams,   1842
John F. Woodward, 1846–9, 50, 1,
    7–9, 60, 2–4.
Caleb Underwood,   1849–51

Sylvanus Dunton,	1852–4, 7, 8	Spencer Prentiss,	1869
Levi Miles,	1855, 6	Ebenezer Tilton,	1870, 1
Augustus Morse,	1855, 6	David Pollard,	1870
*T. Sibley Heald,	1861	Lyman Woodward,	1871, 2
Horace Underwood,	1861, 5, 6	William J. Eveleth,	1872, 3
Moses C. Wheeler,	1862–5, 7, 8	Alson J. Greenwood, 1872, 3, 6–80	
Andrew Gleason,	1863, 5, 6, 71	Danford Clark,	1873
John G. Allen,	1866	Samuel S. Gleason,	1874–81
Isaac Hallock,	1866	Silas Wheeler,	1874–81
Oren Marean,	1867, 8	Anson B. Clark,	1874, 5
Abel Howe,	1867–9	Warren Clark,	1881

ASSESSORS.

Israel Green,	1767	Ebenezer Joslin,	1785
Benjamin Nurse,	1767	Philemon Woodward, 1786, 8–98,	
Benjamin Hoyt,	1767–9, 72	1800, 4–6, 9, 12–15.	
Stephen Heald,	1768, 70	†Samuel Morse,	1787.
Adam Wheeler,	1768, 9, 71	Moses Greenwood,	1787, 90
William Pain,	1769	John McClenathan,	1791, 3–6
Ezekiel Newton,	1770	Asa Church,	1791, 3–7
William Marean,	1770, 1, 92	Daniel Woodward, 1798–1801, 17	
Joseph Eveleth,	1771–3, 5, 7	Abijah Greenwood,	1799
Nathaniel Waite,	1772	James Thompson,	1799
John Woods,	1773–6, 8, 9	Edward Selfridge,	1800
George Metcalf,	1773	Jacob Waite, 1801, 3–8, 10, 11	
Isaac Bellows, 1774, 5, 7, 9, 81, 7		Abner Gay, 1802, 3, 13, 16	
William Muzzy, 1774, 7, 9, 86,		Abraham Cutting,	1802
92, 8.		Israel Davis,	1804, 5
Jonathan Gates, 1776, 80, 3, 4,		Levi Greenwood,	1806, 18
8–90, 1802, 3		Asa Wheeler,	1807, 8
Robert Murdock,	1776	Luke Warren, 1807–9, 12, 14, 15,	
Joel Pollard,	1779–82	20.	
Elisha Woodward,	1780, 2–4	Timothy P. Marean,	1809
Joseph Shattuck,	1780, 2, 5, 6	Aaron Gates, 1810, 11, 16–22,	
Ebenezer Mann,	1780, 97	5–30.	
Alpheus Morse,	1781, 5	Nathaniel Waite, Jr.	1810
Moses Phelps,	1783, 4	Luther Hale, 1811–15, 21	

---

*Resigned to enlist in the army, and John F. Woodward was elected to serve the rest of the year.
†Died April 20, 1787, and John Woods was elected to fill the vacancy.

William Rice,   1816
Nathan Wright,   1817
Joel Pollard, Jr.   1818, 19, 22–4,
    30, 39, 40.
William Hobbs,   1819
Sewell Mirick, 1820, 2–4, 6, 7, 30
James H. Wheeler,   1821
Justus Ellinwood,   1823, 4
George Williams,   1825
Abijah Clark,   1825
Russell Brown, 1826, 8, 9, 31, 3–5
Ephraim Stowe,   1827
Silas Davis,   1828, 9, 31. 2
John Church,   1831. 2,
William Young,   1832, 3
Shepherd Clark.   1833
John D. Pierce,   1834, 5
Elisha Woodward,   1834–42, 4–9,
    51, 8–60, 3, 4.
William Bennett,   1836–40
James H. Peirce,   1836, 7
Henry Prentiss, Jr.   1838, 41, 2,
    4–9, 51.
Lyman Greenwood.   1841–3
Dana Brown,   1843, 54
Rowland Woodward,   1843
William Bennett, Jr. 1844–8, 50, 1

Sylvanus Dunton,   1849, 59
Levi Miles,   1852, 3
Simpson C. Heald,   1850
Joseph Raymond,   1852–4
Israel Davis,   1852–4
Almer Gay, 1855--7, 9, 60–3, 5–8,
    70, 4–7.
Horace Underwood,   1855
Leonard Clark,   1855, 68
William Joslin,   1856, 7, 61–9
Abijah H. Greenwood,   1856, 7
Levi Joslin,   1858
Albert Bennett, 1858. 60, 73, 4, 80
Lyman Woodward, 1861, 2, 4, 9,
    70, 1.
Oren Marean,   1865, 6, 73
Nathan H. Felton,   1867
Danford Clark,   1869–73
Samuel S. Gleason, 1871, 2, 8, 80, 1
Albert H. Waite,   1872
Asa Bennett,   1874, 6, 9, 80, 1
Warren Clark,   1875
Alson J. Greenwood, 1875, 8, 81
Luke S. Moore,   1876, 7
Edwin Bennett,   1877, 8
George H. Davis,   1879
Joseph Jewett,   1879

TOWN CLERKS.

John LeBourveau,   1767–9
William Marean,   1770
Joseph Eveleth,   1771
John Woods,   1772–84, 95, 6
*Stephen Church,   1785, 6
Elisha Woodward,   1786–94
Abner Gay,   1797–1802, 16–18

Jonathan Cutting,   1803–6
Jacob Waite,   1807. 10, 11
Daniel Woodward, 1808, 9, 12, 13
Samuel Swan.   1814, 15, 20–35
William Bennett, Jr.   1836–64
Lyman Woodward,   1865–81

*Died July 11, 1786, and Elisha Woodward served the rest of the year.

TOWN TREASURERS.

Ezekiel Newton,	1767, 8, 72, 5, 6	Samuel Swan,	1822, 3
Adam Wheeler,	1769–71 ·	Clark Witt,	1824–7
William Marean,	1773, 4	John Church,	1827–30
John Woods,	1778–81	Levi Peirce,	1831–4, 46, 8, 9, 56–8.
Joel Pollard,	1782–4		
Elisha Woodward,	1785–90, 99	Shepherd Clark,	1835–7, 40, 1
Jonathan Gates,	1791–8	Moses Phelps,	1838
Abijah Greenwood,	1800–3, 9	Appleton Clark,	1842–5
Daniel Woodward,	1804–6	Luther A. May,	1850–3
Ebenezer Warren,	1807, 8	John Phelps,	1849
Otis Parker,	1810, 11	William Bennett, Jr.	1854, 63, 4
Ebenezer Stowe,	1812	Benjamin D. Phelps,	1855, 9–62
Levi Greenwood,	1813–16	Moses Greenwood,	1865
Israel Davis,	1817–19	Lyman Woodward,	1866–81
Justus Ellinwood,	1820, 1		

SCHOOL COMMITTEE.

The first allusion to a supervision of schools by the town, is found in the records of 1805, in the article, "To see if the town will choose a committee to visit the schools in said town." "Voted in the negative."

The action upon the same article in 1806, was to choose Rev. David Kendall, Jonathan Cutting, Abner Gay and Elisha Woodward for the purpose named.

In 1807, "Chose the selectmen with the addition of Rev. David Kendall."

In 1808, the same article was voted in the negative.

In 1809, "Voted to choose one man in each school plot [eight in number] to visit and inspect schools."

From 1810 to 1820, there was annually chosen a committee of three, four or five, for the same purpose.

In 1821, three were chosen to visit the schools and three to examine teachers.

In 1825, "Voted and chose three, a committee to examine schoolmasters and mistresses the present year, and that each district choose their own man to visit the schools with the minister." Similar action was taken annually for the next ten years.

The services of all these officials were evidently without remuneration until about 1838, when the law pertaining to the duties of the school committee became more explicit.

The list below begins with 1810.   That part of it which falls between 1838 and 1880, is copied from the school report of 1880:

Samuel Swan, 1810, 12–15, 20, 1, 3–8, 31. 2. 4.	George T. Hill, 1848–52
Abner Gay, 1810, 12–14	D. B. Bradford, 1849–51
Reuben Wheeler. 1810, 11	George Swan, 1851
Asa Howe, 1811, 12	Burtis Judd, 1852
Jacob Johnson. 1811–14	John M. Stowe, 1852, 73–7
Justus Ellinwood, 1812–16, 20, 21, 3–6, 31.	*George B. Wilbur, 1852
Sewell Mirick, 1813 17, 19, 21	Horace Underwood, 1852–5, 9, 60, 2–70, 3–6, 80, 1.
William Rice, 1816–18	Cyrus W. Allen, 1853–5, 7–9
Clark Witt, 1817, 18	E. H. Pillsbury, 1855–7
Asa Wheeler, 1817	William H. Earle, 1856
John Browning. 1817, 18	*Leonard Clark, 1856
William Hobbs, 1818, 19, 23. 6	Abijah Eddy, 1857
Ephraim Stowe, 1819, 21–3, 6, 39–41, 5–8, 58. 60, 1.	George P. Richardson. 1859
Moses Phelps, Jr. 1820–2, 4–30, 2, 3. 5, 8.	William S. Greenwood, 1860, 4–7
	J. Gilman Waite, 1860
Shepherd Clark, 1821, 2, 34	George P. Earle, 1860
Nathan Wright, 1823	Abel Howe, 1861–6
George Hoyt, 1827, 8, 31	James H. Gleason, 1861–3
Abner D. Jones, 1829–32	*Charles H. Vinton, 1865
Samuel Gay, 1829–31, 8–40, 2–4, 6–8.	Increase B. Bigelow, 1867
	Porter M. Vinton, 1868–70
E. Robinson, 1833–5	Edward B. Savage, 1868–72
John A. Thompson, 1833	Sarah E. Marean, 1870–80
William Bennett, 1835–41, 4–51, 3–6. 8.	Henry A. Wilder, 1871, 2
	Addison A. Parker, 1877–81
John D. Peirce, 1836, 7	*Joseph J. Woodbury, 1877
James H. Peirce, 1836, 7	John F. Norton, 1878, 9
Claudius Bradford, 1841–5	Wm. H. Wheeler, 1880
Oliver B. Bidwell, 1842, 3	Harris O. Palmer, 1880, 1
George W. Bates, 1844	Henry A. Farwell, 1879–81
S. H. Lloyd, 1846	*Arthur D. Greenwood, 1880
	Sumner H. Marean, 1881

*Elected by selectmen and school committee to fill vacancies caused by death or resignation.

REPRESENTATIVES TO THE GENERAL COURT.

William Muzzy,	1786, 7, 96, 8
John Woods,	1788
William Marean.	1791, 2, 4, 1800, 1
Jonathan Gates,	1803
John McClenathan,	1804–7
Jacob Waite,	1809, 10
Ephraim Allen,	1812, 13
Levi Greenwood.	1814, 16
Daniel Woodward,	1818, 21
Samuel Swan,	1824
Henry Prentiss,	1827, 9, 31, 2, 6
Moses Phelps,	1828
Moses Waite,	1830–4, 7
Ethan A. Greenwood,	1833. 4
Silas Greenwood,	1835
Asa Marean,	1835–8, 41, 2
Micajah Reed,	1839, 40
George Williams,	1839. 40
Sylvanus Dunton,	1843
William Bennett, Jr.	1846, 8–52.
the District, 1861, 4.	
Leonard Clark,	1855
Levi Miles,	1856
Henry Prentiss,	1857
Aaron Greenwood,	the District,
1859	
Horace Underwood,	the District.
1863, 78.	
Lyman Woodward,	the District.
1865, 7, 72, 3.	
Otis Hale,	the District, 1868
Samuel S. Gleason,	the District.
1876.	

From 1831 to 1837, and in 1839 and 1840 the town sent two representatives.

For the years not mentioned above, prior to 1858, the town was not represented.

From 1858 to 1866, Templeton and Hubbardston comprised one district.

From 1866 to 1877, Barre, Dana, Hardwick, Hubbardston, Petersham Phillipston and New Braintree made one district.

Since 1877, Petersham, Phillipston, Templeton and Hubbardston compose this district.

SENATORS

Who have represented the county, in part, in the Legislature :—

Henry Prentiss,   1835   Ethan A. Greenwood.   1836, 7

DELEGATES TO THE SEVERAL CONVENTIONS HELD IN MASSACHUSETTS.

John Clark, delegate to convention held at Concord,   -   -   1774
William Muzzy, representative to Provisional Congress, Watertown, 1775

William Muzzy, representative to General Court held at Watertown, 1775

John Woods, delegate to Constitutional Convention held at Cambridge, - - - - - - - - - 1779

William Marean, delegate to convention held at Concord, - 1779

John Woods, delegate to convention held at Boston to adopt the United States Constitution, - - - - - 1787

Ephraim Allen, delegate to convention held at Boston to revise the Constitution, - - - - - - - - 1820

William Bennett, Jr., delegate to convention held at Boston to revise the Constitution, - - - - - - 1853

GENEALOGICAL RECORDS.

INTRODUCTION.

IN tabulating the genealogical history begun by William Bennett, the present arrangement is adopted because the most compact.

Not all who have at any time lived in town are represented in these lists. Many of the early families became extinct by removal or death, and the space their records would occupy is reserved for others. The names of some of these appear in one or more of these four lists, viz: Revolutionary soldiers, Chapter V; families here before 1800, Chapter III; school squadrons, Chapter IX; municipal officers, Chapter XX. Records of early families not inserted, have been collated from the town books and preserved by themselves.

Many later families are omitted because their transient residence here prevented their becoming identified with the history of the town.

In September, 1880, a notice was publicly posted requesting all present residents desirous of having their records appear in these tables, to furnish for that purpose certain specified items. Those who responded will find their names inserted.

The records close with 1880.

The record of families previous to their residence in town has not been attempted, nor that of families or individuals removed, except for the purpose, in some cases, of completing the record of a family which would otherwise be broken off in the midst.

28

Thanks are tendered to the many who have aided by prompt responses in furnishing the necessary items.

In cases of intermarriage between resident families, the dates of marriage and death, or present residence if living elsewhere, are generally given in connection with the husband's name only.

Towns whose location is not indicated, are understood to be in Massachusetts.

To collect the following dates concerning so many individuals—here are nearly 7000 names with one, two, or three dates each—involves many perplexities. Frequent disagreement between family, monumental, and town records renders absolute accuracy impossible; nor is any claim laid to entire freedom from error in transcribing, notwithstanding the exertion of great care.

EXPLANATION.

Members of the same generation follow the same perpendicular line.

The figures used, designate the number of the generation from the first name in the family; for instance, in the family of ISSACHAR ADAMS, the figure 3 against the name of Henry H., indicates that he is in the third generation from ISSACHAR, who stands first in the family; the figure 2 against the name of Homer M. (father of Henry H.), indicates that he is in the second generation from ISSACHAR; the figure 1 against the name of John (grandfather of Henry H.), shows him to be the son of ISSACHAR.

Abbreviations; b., born; m., married; d., died; a. aged; c. f., came from; rem., removed; res., resides, or resided.

The * is used to designate a Revolutionary soldier; a † to designate a Revolutionary pensioner.

ADAMS.

ELIJAH ADAMS* c. f. Medway, 1774; m. Lizzie Morse of Holliston; d.
Dec. 17, 1817, a. 65; she d. Dec. 31, 1833, a. 80.

1. Abner,b. Dec.29, 1774; m. Molly Underwood,Apr. 17, 1797; rem.Vt.
1. Lizzie, b. Mar. 12. 1777; d. Oct. 12, 1785.
1. Lydia, b. Mar. 31, 1779; m. Thomas Lazell, Oct. 24, 1805; d.
June 25, 1823.
1. Elijah, b. Mar. 27, 1781; d. Oct. 22, 1785.
1. David, b. Apr. 1, 1783; d. Oct. 28, 1785.
1. Azubah, b. June 16, 1785; d. Oct. 22, 1798.
1. Elisha, b. Aug. 16, 1787; m. Betsey Dean. Oct. 12, 1808, who d.
May 26, 1859, a 70; he d. July 14, 1868.
   2. Abner Sumner, b. Oct. 4. 1809; rem. Va.
   2. Elisha Edson, b. July 18, 1812; d. Ill., 1871.
   2. Mary, b. Sept. 7, 1814; m. A. Gardner Thomas of Rutland, June
   16, 1842.
   2. Elijah, b. May 14, 1818; d. Mar. 18, 1842.
   2. Silas, b. Aug. 31, 1820; m. Roxa Hunting, Apr. 18, 1845, who
   d. June 21, 1861; m. 2d. Pamelia Temple of Gardner; res.
   Gardner.
   2. Rhoda, b. June 12, 1823; m. Geo. W. Plummer, Nov. 20, 1849;
   d. Fitchburg.
   2. Nelson, b. May 6, 1831; res. New Haven, Ct.
1. Isabel, b. Dec. 23, 1789; m. Josephus Clifford.
1. Rhoda, b. Mar. 22, 1792; m. Willard Earle.
1. Rebecca, b. Feb. 13, 1795; d. Oct. 1, 1798.
ISSACHAR,* bro. of ELIJAH, c. f. Medway. 1778; m. Melicent Alden in
1777; d. June 18, 1829, a. 75; she d. Sept. 9, 1855, a. 99y.
11m. 26d.
1. Huldah, b. June 1, 1778; m. Esek Phillips of Peru, Vt.

ADAMS.

1. Olive, b. Apr. 16, 1781 ; m. D. Elliot ; res. Vt.

1. Issachar, b. June 24. 1783 ; rem. Vt.

1. Sally, b. Mar. 31. 1785 ; m. Jonathan Elliot, Jan. 16, 1804 ; res. N. H.

1. Melicent, b. June 17, 1787 ; d. June 6. 1798.

1. Clara, b. Apr. 6, 1789 ; d. Aug. 20, 1807.

1. Moses, b. Aug. 10, 1791 ; rem. Vt.

1. Sybil, b. July 13, 1793 ; m. Asa Phillips of Peru, Vt.

1. John. b. Aug. 27, 1795 ; m. Lucy Mirick, Dec. 24, 1818, who d. Jan. 30, 1872, a. 71 ; he d. July 29, 1876.

  2. Homer M., b. July 28, 1820 ; m. Olive A. Houghton of Petersham, Apr. 20, 1842 ; d. Aug. 16, 1879.

    3. Henry H., b. Dec. 11, 1843 ; m. Josephine E. Barnes, Oct. 3, 1866 ; res. Gardner.

    3. Horace M., b. Apr. 28, 1845 ; m. Almira D. Gleason of Hillsboro', N. H., Dec. 25, 1869 ; res. Baldwinsville.

    3. Homer Augustus, b. July 27. 1852 ; m. Catherine A. Smith, May 28, 1879.

      4. Harry L., b. June 14, 1880.

    3. Olive Augusta, b. July 27, 1852 ; m. Herbert E. Brigham of Rutland, Nov. 30, 1876.

    3. Herbert T., b. Jan. 11, 1856.

    3. John W., b. Oct. 24, 1859.

  2. Darius, b. Feb. 14, 1823 : d. Feb. 15, 1879.

  2. Abigail G., b. Apr. 29, 1826 ; m. William Henry Clark.

  2. John, b. Jan. 16, 1830 ; m. Catherine Houghton of Petersham. Apr. 3, 1850.

    3. Eveline R., b. Aug. 2, 1852 ; m. John E. Snow of Woodstock, Conn., Dec. 31, 1871, who d. Aug. 10, 1875 ; m. 2d, Oliver Osgood of Princeton, Nov. 1, 1878.

    3. Charles Frederick, b. Dec. 19, 1855 ; m. Grace A. Blake of Framingham, May 8, 1880.

    3. Alice M., b. June 2, 1861.

  2. Amos T., b. June 7, 1843 ; m. Lucy Ware of Barre, Feb. 10, 1862.

    3. Sarah Elsie, b. Feb. 27, 1863.

    3. Winnifred Abigail, b. Oct. 15, 1872.

1. Obed, b. Dec. 6, 1797 ; m. Nancy Stoddard, Dec. 1827 ; rem. Vt.

RALPH ADAMS (colored) came to Hubbardston about 1780 ; m. Anna Clark, (daughter of Anthony Clark the celebrated colored doctor)

ADAMS.

who, for many years after her husband's death, continued her father's practice, by the use of roots and herbs, and became the celebrated doctress "Granny Adams ;" she d. Nov. 4, 1835, a. 73.

ALLEN.

Ephraim Allen c. f. Rutland ; m. Anna Rogers ; rem. Rutland.
1. Ephraim, b. 1804 ; m. Mary Ann Hill, Nov. 17, 1830 ; d. Apr. 12, 1857 ; she d. Nov. 5, 1875, a. 64.
   2. George, b. Aug. 28, 1831 ; m. Rebecca Marsh.
     3. Barzillai H., b. Jan. 8, 1859 ; d. Dec. 7, 1864.
     3. Daniel W., b. Nov. 27, 1860 ; d. Nov. 28, 1864.
   2. Stephen P., b. Oct. 20, 1833 ; m. Hannah Gleason, Apr. 8. 1855 ; res. North Rutland.
     3. Walter Frank, b. Jan. 17, 1856.
     3. Sydney E., b. Feb. 20, 1860 ; d. Sept. 30, 1860.
     3. Flora Lillia, b. Feb. 20, 1860.
   2. Mary P., b. Apr. 20, 1835 ; m. Thomas Elvyn Greenwood.
   2. Moses B., b. Feb. 6, 1837 ; res. Rutland ; m. Lucy Patch of Worcester.
   2. Clarissa P., b. May 18, 1839 ; m. George F. Greenwood.
   2. Eveline D., b. Jan. 3, 1842 ; m. Aaron S. Bolton of Westminster.
   2. Charles W., b. Mar. 11, 1844 ; m. Addie Allen of Rutland.
   2. Ephraim, b. Mar. 4, 1847.
   2. John R., b. Dec. 2, 1852 ; d. June 5, 1872.
1. Lucinda, b. Nov. 9, 1810 ; m. Zebulon Winn of Holden, Sept. 1, 1830.
1. Eunice, b. Apr. 9, 1813 ; m. Otis Parker.
1. Abner, b. May 19, 1815 ; m. Susan Merrill ; d. Aug. 31, 1841.

Ephraim Allen c. f. Rutland ; m. Lydia Warren, who d. Feb. 7, 1827. a. 59 ; m. 2d, Mrs. Elizabeth Nichols, who d. Dec. 8, 1845, a. 84 ; he d. Oct. 28, 1848, a. 85.
1. Asa, b. Apr. 18, 1788 ; m. Lydia Adams, Dec. 1, 1814, who d. Apr. 26, 1871, a. 75 ; he d. Dec. 8, 1870.
   2. Adaline, b. May 22, 1816 ; m. John Davis ; res. Gardner.
   2. Sumner, b. Nov. 16, 1817 ; d. Apr. 20, 1846.
   2. Martha, b. July 3, 1819 ; m. Learned Rice of Barre, Jan. 31, 1839.

ALLEN.

2. Mary, b. July 31, 1821 ; m. Hiram Johnson.

2. John, b. Jan. 23, 1824.

2. Harriet, b. June 28, 1826 ; m. Josiah Hunting.

1. Rebecca, b. Jan. 11, 1790 ; m. William Rice.

1. Levi, b. Nov. 27, 1791 ; m. Isabella Mann, Mar. 1818 ; rem. Westminster.

    2. Roxa, b. June 27, 1818 ; m. Solon Raymond of Westminster.

    2. Darius M., b. May 14, 1822 ; m. Ruth Pollard, Oct. 25, 1849, who d. in Westminster ; m. 2d, Sophia Ober ; res. Ohio.

    2. Lyman, b. Jan. 15, 1826 ; rem. Westminster.

    2. Addison, b. Sept. 20, 1833 ; d. Mar. 20, 1834.

1. John, b. Sept. 14, 1793 ; d. Nov. 14, 1863.

1. Roxa, b. Oct. 30, 1795 ; d. Jan. 15, 1818.

1. Breck, b. Apr. 9, 1798 ; m. Sally Derby, Dec. 15, 1824 ; d. June 28, 1857.

    2. Lucy, b. Oct. 6, 1825 ; d. June 2, 1839.

    2. John Gilman, b. June 19, 1831 ; m. Hannah Greenwood, Dec. 16, 1858.

       3. Abby G., b. Aug. 17, 1860.

       3. J. Harry, b. May 27, 1865.

    2. Calvin, b. Jan. 16, 1834 ; m. Sarah T. Walton, Jan. 7, 1857 ; d. army, Aug. 14, 1863. [See p. 138.]

       3. Arthur Willie, b. July 28, 1858.

       3. Mary Lizzie, b. May 2, 1860.

    2. Sarah, b. Feb. 28, 1836 ; m. O. A. Fowler of Whitingham, Vt., Jan. 22, 1859.

    2. Mary, b. Aug. 8, 1838 ; res. Chelmsford.

    2. Lydia W., b. Dec. 18, 1841 ; d. Feb. 15, 1846.

1. Lucy, b. June 23, 1800 ; d. Feb. 22, 1823.

1. Lydia b. Sept. 14, 1802 ; m. John Whitney of Westminster, Nov. 1, 1821.

1. Harriet, b. Oct. 23, 1804 ; d. Jan. 13, 1827.

1. Willard, b. Dec. 25, 1806 ; m. Alona B. Hubbard of Holden, Jan. 30, 1828, who d. May 20, 1830 ; m. 2d, Sarah S. Savage, Sept. 4, 1832 ; res. Worcester.

    2. Sarah Alona, b. June 15, 1833 ; m. Horace A. Smith, May 1, 1855 ; d. Feb. 18, 1856.

    2. Mary A., b. Feb. 16, 1835 ; m. Jeremiah Winn of Worcester, Dec. 14, 1856.

ALLEN.

2. Dwight D., b. May 9, 1837 ; m. Helen M. Aldrich of Worcester, June 4, 1861 ; fell in battle at Petersburg, Va., July 30, 1864.

2. Joseph S., b. May 11, 1839 ; d. Apr. 12, 1840.

2. Lucy Hubbard, b. July 8, 1841 ; m. Daniel D. Winn of Webster, Sept. 1, 1863.

2. Delia Sophronia, b. Nov. 20, 1844 ; m. Samuel A. Myrick of Holden, July 30, 1868.

2. Caroline Maria, b. Sept. 20, 1847 ; m. George B. King of Worcester, Jan. 3, 1869.

2. Georgia Ann, b. Jan. 20, 1850 ; m. George S. Peck of Westfield, Oct. 27, 1870.

2. Emma Josephine, b. June 17, 1853 ; m. Louis H. Burr of N. Y., Oct. 13, 1874.

1. Sumner, b. Apr. 17, 1810 ; d. Mar. 7, 1816.

APOLLOS A. ALLEN c. f. Rindge, N. H. ; m. Harriet Coleman, Jan. 12, 1831.

1. David A., b. Jan. 13, 1833 ; d. Oct. 18, 1853.

1. Courtland A., b. May 4, 1835 ; res. Gardner.

1. Susan B., b. July 7, 1837 ; m. M. P. Dillingham, Jan. 30, 1858. who d. 1871.

REV. CYRUS W. ALLEN c. f. Coleraine 1852 ; m. Mary Folger of Nantucket, June 6, 1837 ; rem. 1863 ; res. W. Roxbury.

1. George Otis, b. Oct. 25, 1838, physician W. Roxbury ; graduated medical department Harvard University, 1866.

1. Rowland Hussey, b. Aug. 13, 1840 ; m. Willianna Brooks of Chelsea, Apr. 18, 1866 ; d. Neponset, Sept. 12, 1872 ; graduated Amherst College 1862 ; Andover Theological Seminary, 1865 ; ordained Nov. 1, 1865 ; pastorates in Canton and Neponset.

1. Henry Folger, b. Sept. 2, 1841 ; merchant, Boston.

1. Laban Wheaton, b. Dec. 11, 1843 ; d. Hanover, Aug. 23, 1875 ; graduated Amherst College, 1866 ; Andover Theological Seminary, 1869 ; ordained, 1869 ; pastorates in S. Braintree, and Greeley, Col.

1. Mary Abby, b. June 19, 1845 ; m. Geo. F. Sylvester of Hanover, Jan. 15, 1874.

1. Eliza Catherine, b. Nov. 1, 1850 ; d. Nov. 8, 1853.

ALLEN.

1. William Cyrus, b. Nov. 7, 1852 ; d. July 29, 1854.
1. Fanny Florence. b. Apr. 25, 1855 ; m. John F. Simmons, Esq. of Hanover, Jan. 10, 1877.

AUSTIN.

CHARLES AUSTIN, (name changed from Hunting—son of Alexander and Tryphena Hunting.) m. Miranda Peck, Nov. 12, 1834, who d. Sept. 29, 1852. a. 42 ; m. 2d, Sophina Peck, Apr. 4. 1857.

1. Tryphena. b. Oct. 8. 1835 ; m. John DeForest Williams of Fitchburg. June 11. 1861.
1. Louisa. b. Oct. 20, 1837. m. Daniel G. Harwood of Barre, Mar. 31, 1859.
1. Almina, b. Mar. 17. 1840 ; m. S. E. W. Peck of Hardwick, Apr. 30. 1862.
1. Elvira, b. Mar. 4, 1844 ; m. Oscar C. Rice of Barre, July 26, 1871.
1. Harriet S.. b. Feb. 20. 1847 ; m. Henry Harwood of Barre.

BAKER.

ARTEMAS BAKER c. f. Gardner ; m. Sarah Nichols. who d. Aug. 30, 1844, a. 63 ; he d. Dec. 8, 1854. a. 77.

1. Artemas. b. Mar. 3. 1801 ; m. Phebe Young ; d. E. Templeton.
2. William. b. 1827 ; m. Lucy French, Jan. 11, 1848 ; rem. E. Templeton.
3. Henry, b. Apr. 1, 1852 ; d. Sept. 18, 1852.
3. George L., b. Apr. 27, 1855.
2. Sarah A. J., b. 1830 ; m. Perez French, Apr. 3, 1848.
1. David, b. May 7. 1802 ; m. Sally D. Holt, Nov. 18, 1827 ; d. Sept. 7. 1864 ; she d. Mar. 22, 1880, a. 78.
2. Harriet Augusta. b. Nov. 17, 1829 ; d. Aug. 21, 1864.
2. Mary Elizabeth, b. May 22, 1835 ; d. Mar. 14, 1853.
1. Luther, b. July 31, 1804 ; m. ——— Pierce of Westminster ; both d. Wendell.
1. Sally. b. June 20, 1806 ; d. Dec. 18, 1845.
1. Quincy, b. May 8, 1808 ; m. Roxa Green. May 16, 1839, who d. Oct. 7, 1851 ; m. 2d, Nancy Kendall of Gardner, Nov. 22, 1855 ; d. Jan. 9, 1877.

BAKER.

2. Huldah F., b. Sept. 17, 1847.
2. Roxa Edna, b. July 20, 1850 ; res. Holden.
2. Charles H., b. Aug. 15, 1857.
1. Isaac, b. Jan. 9, 1811 ; res. Ohio.
1. Ibri, b. Sept. 18, 1812 ; res. Warwick.
1. Uri, b. July 23, 1814 ; res. N. H.
1. Persis, b. May 1, 1816 ; m. ———— Whipple of E. Templeton.
1. Amos, b. July 25, 1819 ; m. Fanny S. ———— ; res. N. H.
2. Samuel A., b. Feb. 20, 1853.

BALCOM.

Isaac Balcom, m. Sally Green, who d. Apr. 22, 1869 ; rem. Hague, N. Y.
1. Uriah, b. Apr. 8, 1808 ; m. Lucy Wheeler, Dec. 31, 1835 ; d. Hague, N. Y., June 27, 1864.
   2. William H., b. Sept. 2, 1836 ; m. Clementine Brown of Dana, June 6, 1863 ; res. Athol.
   2. Julia M., b. Oct. 23, 1838 ; d. Feb. 22, 1841.
   2. James Alfred, b. Aug. 21, 1840 ; rem. Hague, N. Y. ; m. Olive Newton of H., N. Y., Nov. 28, 1868.
   2. Myron Burr, b. July 5, 1842.
   2. Julia Roxana, b. Oct. 2, 1846 ; d. Apr. 4, 1861, Hague, N. Y.
   2. Lucy Elizabeth, b. Apr. 13, 1849 ; m. Alvah Albee of Warwick, Oct. 8, 1872.
   2. Harvey Wheeler, b. Feb. 11, 1851 ; d. Winchester, N. H., June 24, 1873.
   2. Owen Willis, b. Apr. 9, 1853 ; res. W. Brookfield.
   2. Eva Clara, b. Nov. 11, 1854 ; m. Frank Grovener of Dana.
   2. John Lane, b. Feb. 13, 1857 ; res. Athol.
1. Joseph, b. June 1, 1820 ; m. Maria L. Holland of Barre, Nov. 16, 1852.
   2. James L., b. Oct. 12, 1865.

BALLOU.

George W. Ballou c. f. Franklin, 1875 ; m. Eliza Daniels, Apr. 27, 1854.
1. Jessie C., b. Aug. 15, 1856.
1. Katie L., b. Apr. 18, 1858 ; m. Herbert E. Snow of Franklin, May 24, 1876.
1. S. Lizzie, b. May 26, 1863.

29

BARNES.

DANIEL BARNES c. f. Marlboro'; m. Louisa Howe. who d. Dec. 6, 1833, a. 58.
m. 2d, Mary Powers, June 12, 1834, who d. Gardner; he
d. Nov. 5, 1844, a. 69.

1. David, b. July 4, 1795; m. Myra Peck, Nov. 29, 1824; d. Nov.
10, 1827.
2. Lucy, b. Mar. 21, 1825; d. Oct. 23, 1871.
2. David, b. Oct. 28, 1827.

DAVID BARNES c. f. Barre; m. Submit T. Willard, Apr. 11, 1826, who d.
Feb. 13, 1873, a. 70; he d. Dec. 6, 1874, a. 74.

1. Lorenzo L., b. Apr. 8, 1827; m. Oella J. Greenwood, Nov. 20,
1850; res. Worcester.
2. Alfred Lorenzo, b. July, 1852.
2. Cora T., b. Feb. 9, 1856.
1. Miranda D., b. May 8, 1828; m. Henry E. Warren.
1. David T., b. Feb. 25, 1830; m. Augusta Hill.
1. Augustus M., b. Sept. 3, 1831.
1. Julia A., b. Apr. 29, 1833; d. Dec. 18, 1864.
1. Phila A., b. Feb. 5. 1835; m. Myron Stone of Rutland; res. Barre.
1. Asenath M., b. Dec. 30, 1836; m. Samuel S. Gleason.
1 Laura Ann, b. Dec. 13, 1838; d. Apr. 12, 1841.
1. George Harrison, b. Aug. 23, 1841: d. army, June 3, 1864. [See
p. 138.]
1. Emoretta Josephine, b. Sept. 3, 1845; m. Henry H. Adams.

FRANCIS BARNES c. f. Stoneham; m. Betsey Nichols, Apr. 2, 1840.

1. Ellen M., b. Apr. 9, 1841; m. Charles S. Newton of Petersham,
Apr. 8, 1869; res. Gardner.
1. Clara E., b. May 20, 1843; d. July 19, 1850.
1. Francis, b. Jan. 8, 1845; m. Melissa M. Sweatland, Nov. 25,
1876; res. Minn.
1. Abby Rosella, b. Apr. 23, 1849; m. Charles W. Murdock.
1. John Robert, b. May 2, 1851.
1. George H., b. May 11, 1853.
1. James B., b. Dec. 12, 1856; m. Laura E. Gocheneour of Wabash,
Ind., Apr. 3, 1879; res. Ind.

BATES.

GEORGE S. BATES c. f. Attleboro', 1850; m. Alice Jane Coleman, June
9, 1856.

BATES.

1. Elnora, b. Feb. 10, 1857; m. Edwin A. Mann.
1. Everett Eugene, b. May 7, 1860.
1. Jennie Augusta, b. July 20, 1862.
1. Lester L , b. Jan. 22, 1865.
1. Rosa Bella, b. June 27, 1868.
1. Warren Elvin, b. Jan. 31, 1870.
1. Ada Mattie, b. Nov. 9, 1872.
1. Clarence A., b. May 2, 1875.

BELLOWS.

ISAAC BELLOWS c. f. Rutland, 1772; became a prominent citizen. He
   was among the first volunteers in the spring of 1775; in
   1777, he re-enlisted at the age of fifty; his son, aged
   seventeen, enlisted at the same time; m. Eunice Stone.
   who d. Mar. 11, 1827, a. 90; he d. May 22, 1811, a 84.
1. Isaac. b. 1760; d. army, near Albany, N. Y., Dec. 29, 1777.
1. Amasa, b. Jan. 31, 1763; m. Elizabeth Woods, Feb. 23, 1790.
   Killed at a raising, June 22, 1795. [See p. 166.]
   2. Asa, b. Feb. 13, 1792; d. Oct. 9, 1802.
   2. Amasa, b. July 19, 1795. Killed by fall of a tree, in Madison,
      N. Y., 1819.
1. Zebina, b. Mar. 14, 1765; d. Aug. 16, 1782.
1. Asaph, b. Nov. 10, 1767; m. Elizabeth (Woods) Bellows, Dec. 25,
   1796; d. Aug. 19, 1847; she d. Dec. 3, 1853.
   2. Isaac, b. Sept. 3, 1797; m. Charlotte Hapgood, Feb. 11, 1838,
      who d. Aug. 6, 1839, a. 34; m. 2d, Eliza Wilder, Oct. 5,
      1852, who d. Nov. 5, 1852; he d. Jan. 21, 1878.
   2. Eliza, b. July 27, 1800; d. Sept. 4, 1803.
   2. Asa, b. Jan. 25, 1804; d. Sept. 28, 1818.
   2. John W., b. Feb. 18, 1806; m. Melissa Ames, Jan. 6, 1828;
      rem N. H. ; d. Ill., Mar. 8, 1860.
      3. William Henry, b. Sept. 29, 1829; m. Seraphina Fisk of Green-
         field, Oct. 11, 1853.
      3. Edward Everett, b. Sept. 17, 1831; d. Feb. 12, 1855.
      3. Ann Elizabeth, b. Jan. 12, 1834; d. Sept. 17, 1838.
      3. Asa Ames, b. May 9, 1835; d. Nov. 11, 1854.
      3. Arvilla Elizabeth, b. Mar. 30, 1837; d. Jan. 12, 1855.
      3. John Adams, b. Apr. 18, 1839; d. Nov. 19, 1854.

BELLOWS.

3. Melissa Ann, b. July 30, 1841 ; m. Dexter R. Jones of Belle-
vue, O., Dec. 28, 1864.

3. Albert Isaac, b. Oct. 31, 1843 ; m. Jennie Dunbar of Ottawa,
Ill., Sept. 21, 1876.

3. Alfred Amasa, b. Mar. 13, 1846 ; d. Sept. 9, 1848.

3. Frederick Augustus, b. Feb. 6, 1848 ; d. Sept. 20, 1848.

2. Elizabeth, b. May 24, 1811 ; m. Austin Brown.

1. John Stone, b. Aug. 20, 1772 ; d. N. Y.

1. Abner, b. Dec. 9, 1774 ; d. N. Y.

1. Deborah, b. Oct. 8, 1779 ; m. John Davis of Princeton.

1. Sally, b. Apr. 18, 1782 ; m. Daniel Abbott of Boston, Oct. 23, 1803.

BENNETT.

David Bennett*, b. Shirley ; m. Martha Smith, May 4, 1774 ; d. Apr.
30, 1825, a. 74 ; she d. Nov. 14, 1839, a. 83.

1. William, b. Feb. 13, 1780 ; m. Caty Follett, Jan. 22, 1805, who
d. Jan. 11, 1844 ; he d. Apr. 16, 1860.

2. Addison, b. Mar. 30, 1805 ; m. Mary Ann Gill, May 24, 1838.

3. Henry, b. Apr. 18, 1839 ; m. Emily Randall, Jan. 3, 1866.

4. Henry E., b. Mar. 15, 1868 ; d. May 22, 1868.

4. George A., b. Jan. 12, 1870 ; d. Jan. 30, 1870.

4. Charles A., b. Nov. 15, 1872.

4. Hannah A., b. May 31, 1874.

3. Miriam, b. Mar. 7, 1841 ; m. Harrison W. Lamb.

3. Moses, b. May 5, 1843 ; m. Savira E. Phillips, May 28, 1872.

4. Albert Ellsworth, b. Nov. 15, 1873.   •

3. Mary, b. Oct. 26, 1844 ; m. Albert M. Stone ; m. 2d, Alvin
A. Cleveland of Barre.

3. Edmond S., b. Sept. 20, 1847.

2. Caroline, b. May 7, 1807 ; m. Caleb Perry of Troy, N. H., Apr.
15, 1830 ; m. 2d, Bacon B. Newbury of Gardner.

2. William, b. Mar. 4, 1809 ; d. Jan. 28, 1881. [See p. 178.]

2. Albert, b. Oct. 2, 1811 ; m. Lucy A. Nourse, May 11, 1848.

3. Abby, b. Apr. 27, 1849 ; m. Seth P. H. Hale.

2. Mary, b. June 21, 1814 ; m. E. Kendall, Nov. 8, 1838 ; m. 2d,
B. F. Kendall of Gardner.

2. Harriet, b. June 8, 1816 ; m. Sumner Warren.

2. Adaline, b. May 11, 1819 ; m. John Quincy Morse.

BENNETT.

2. Loring, b. Nov. 22, 1822; m. Susan Gaut of Princeton.
  3. Blanchard, b. Aug. 9, 1857.
  3. William, b. Feb. 29, 1860.
2. Edwin, b. Mar. 30, 1827; m. Elizabeth Powers of Gardner.
  3. Chester E., b. July 9, 1861.
  3. Ida A., b. June 9, 1864.
  3. Edwin Harlow, b. Apr. 23, 1868.
2. Lucy, b. Apr. 24, 1830; d. Oct. 11, 1851.
1. David, b. Apr. 7, 1783; m. Hannah Marean, July 1, 1807: d. Sept. 21, 1867; she d. Jan. 26, 1872.
2. Maria S., b. Feb. 12, 1810; m. James Madison Waite.
2. Sally M., b. Aug. 9, 1812; m. J. P. Sloane, Nov. 17, 1835; d. May 18, 1861.
2. Joseph M., b. Sept. 2, 1814; rem. Ark.; d. Apr. 1870.
2. David E., b. Feb. 16, 1817; d. June 21, 1838.
2. Asa, b. June 18, 1819; m. Mary R. Brigham, Sept. 30, 1845.
  3. Frederick E., b. Nov. 30, 1846; d. Aug. 12, 1848.
  3. Mary Lizzie, b. Dec. 16, 1849; m. Howard McAllister, Aug. 20, 1872; res. Chicago, Ill.
2. Hannah, b. Jan. 27, 1822; m. M. Sparks: rem. Ark.
2. Louisa, b. Mar. 22, 1824; m. Seallum Gates.
2. Martha E., b. Oct 8, 1826.
1. Asa Smith, b. Mar. 3, 1786; d. Mar. 22, 1795.
1. Polly, b. Jan. 26, 1789: m. Ephraim Mason.
1. Abel, b. Dec. 24, 1791; m. Sally Clark: d. Westminster, 1864.
1. Joseph, b. Sept. 24, 1794; rem. Mo.
1. Patty, b. Mar. 30, 1797; d. July 16, 1816.
1. Hannah, b. July 27, 1800; d. July 23, 1872; missionary among the Choctaws.

BIGELOW.

Sullivan Bigelow c. f. Chester, Vt.: m. Martha H. Clark, Nov. 26, 1840; d. Dec. 5, 1869, a. 60.

BLOOD.

Francis Blood c. f. Pepperell; m. Harriet (McClenathan) Marean, Mar. 28, 1826; rem. Sterling.
1. Charles W., c. f. Pepperell; m. Mary R. Clark, Mar. 19, 1835.

BLOOD.

who d. Mar. 20, 1875 : m. 2d, Lydia S. (Jones) Witt,
    Dec. 10, 1877.

2. Theodore F., b. Jan. 23. 1836; m. Julia A. Murdock, Jan. 12,
        1858, who d. July 18, 1875; he d. Aug. 29, 1875.

3. Charles H., b. Apr. 22, 1858.

3. Fred Emerson. b. Sept. 30, 1860.

3. Lula Bell, b. Mar 9, 1870; d. Mar. 12, 1870.

2. George W., b. June 4, 1839 : d. army, in the hands of the
        enemy. [See p. 138.]

2. Joseph W., b. June 20, 1841 ; m. Minerva Sargent, Aug. 3, 1862,
        who d. Oct. 13, 1871 ; m. 2d, Mary Ann Risley of
        Holyoke, Apr. 19. 1873 ; rem. Worcester.

3. Mabel Louisa, b. Oct. 10. 1865.

2. Mary Ann, b. Sept. 5, 1849 : m. Seymour E. Dibble of Chester,
        Nov. 24, 1870.

BOWKER.

SYLVANDER BOWKER c. f. Phillipston ; m. Eliza Marsh ; d. May 8, 1860,
    a. 57 : she d. July 10, 1880.

1. George L., b. Oct. 3. 1828 ; m. Hannah Witt, Oct. 10, 1850 ; rem.
        Worcester.

1. Eliza Jane. b. Nov., 1831 ; m. Sewell Underwood of Barre, Nov.
        21, 1849.

BRIGHAM.

HOSEA BRIGHAM, an early settler, m. Catherine Davis of Holden ; d. Dec.
    17, 1817, a. 67 ; she d. Oct. 19, 1823, a. 74.

1. Peter, b. Oct. 2, 1781 ; rem. Boston ; m. Mary Shirley, Oct. 27,
        1808 ; d. Roxbury.

1. Joseph, b. Aug. 9, 1785 ; m. Rebecca (Brown) Lamb, Feb. 26,
        1823, who d. Mar. 23, 1863 ; he d. Oct. 18, 1864.

2. Mary R., b. Jan. 13. 1824 ; m. Asa Bennett.

2. Elizabeth. b. Apr. 27. 1828 ; m. Alden Pollard.

1. Samuel, b. May 12, 1787 ; rem. N. Y.

1 Betsey, b. Aug. 12, 1792 ; d. Mar. 15, 1851.

ORLANDO S. BRIGHAM c. f. Barre ; m. Lucy A. Rice, Dec. 31, 1840 ; res.
    Springfield.

BRIGHAM.

1. Louisa A., b. June 12, 1842 ; m. Edward Bigelow of Rutland, May 3, 1864.
1. Lucy Agnes, b. Sep. 4, 1843 ; m. George W. Stowe.
1. Stella J., b. Aug. 7, 1845 ; m. Wm. G. Pond.
1. Ella S., b. Dec. 25, 1848 ; m. Leroy W. Brown.
1. Carrie Maria, b. Mar. 1, 1855 ; m. Frank P. Frost of Springfield, June 6, 1877.

BROWN.

ELEAZER BROWN was the first settler. [See p. 18.]

EBENEZER BROWN,* b. Sutton, Aug. 13, 1752 ; m. Rebecca Witt ; m. 2d, Lydia Coggswell, who d. Dec. 19, 1841, a. 76 ; he d. Apr. 1, 1834.

1. Oliver, b. Dec. 23, 1776 ; m. Azubah Pond, who d. Dec. 10, 1849, a. 73 ; he d. May 18, 1858.
    2. Freeman, b. Aug. 20, 1799 ; m. Arethusa Pond, Dec., 1825 ; d. Sept. 30, 1840.
        3. Sewell, b. May 2, 1826 ; m. Eliza Jane Williams of Barre, Dec., 1852.
            4. Sewell, b. Feb. 26, 1854 ; d. Sept. 19, 1854.
            4. Lizzie Jane, b. Nov. 15, 1855 ; m. Angelo L. Whitcomb of Templeton, May 11, 1878.
            4. Lucius, b. Dec. 28, 1857.
            4. James F., b. Aug. 1, 1861 ; d. Mar. 15, 1863.
            4. James C., b. June 7, 1865.
            4. Nathan Williams, b. Oct. 21, 1867.
            4. Sewell, b. Jan. 12, 1874.
        3. Betsey, b. July 21, 1827 ; m. Lucius Penniman of Millbury.
        3. Lyman, b. June 30, 1834 ; m. Almeda Rice of Princeton ; rem. Fitchburg.
    2. Gardner, b. Apr. 23, 1801 ; m. Abigail Derby of Westminster, Apr. 6, 1824 ; d. Wendell.
        3. Elisha Rockwood, b. Dec. 23, 1824 ; m. Hannah Hunting, Dec. 1, 1846 ; res. Templeton.
        3. John Curtiss, b. Apr. 19, 1827 ; rem. Wendell, d. there.
        3. Gilman, m. Lucy W. (Hunting) Sawin ; res. Gardner.
        3. Asaph, m. and settled in Phillipston.

BROWN.

3. Christopher C., b. May 26, 1835 ; rem. Templeton.
3. George, b. Nov. 27, 1837 ; res. Templeton.
3. Sarah, b. July 20, 1840 ; m. Augustus Dyke of Montague.
3. Marcus M., b. Mar. 28, 1842 ; res. Wendell.
3. Benjamin F., b. Nov. 24, 1845 ; res. Wendell.
2. Dana, b. Mar. 5, 1803 ; m. Mary Wright, Nov. 7, 1827 ; d. Jan. 8, 1875 ; she d. Dec. 8, 1880.
3. Almeda, b. Sept. 16, 1828 ; m. Hugh Nugent.
3. Clinton, b. July 26, 1830 ; d. Jan. 22, 1869.
3. Ellen, b. Dec. 30, 1833 ; d. Feb. 14, 1877.
3. Sarah, b. Sept. 25, 1836 ; d. Apr. 20, 1838.
3. Mary W., b. May 18, 1839 ; d. July 14, 1840.
3. Freeman, b. May 15, 1841 ; d. July 14, 1842.
3. Mary W., b. July 21, 1843 ; m. Herbert W. Howe.
2. Ezra Parker, b. Dec. 13, 1804 ; m. Mary Hobbs, Mar. 19, 1829 ; m. 2d, Adeline Hobbs ; all d. Worcester.
2. John Curtiss, b. Mar. 1, 1807 ; d. Jan. 24, 1826.
2. William, b. May 23, 1809 ; m. Emeline Clapp of R. I., Apr. 12, 1832 ; d. on voyage to Cal., Feb. 16, 1853 ; she d. Feb., 1872.
3. Charles D., b. Dec. 28, 1835 ; rem. Milford.
3. Merrick C., b. May 6, 1837 ; d. Sept. 7, 1856.
3. Frederick L., b. Feb. 7, 1840 ; d. Ashburnham.
3. Eliza Jane, b. Apr. 16, 1842 ; m. Edward W. Weston of Brookline, July 13, 1870 ; res. Holyoke.
3. Azubah Ann, b. Apr. 3, 1844 ; d. Jan. 27, 1865.
3. Herbert, b. June 11, 1846 ; rem. Milford.
3. Lura E., b. July 23, 1848 ; m. Nelson W. Haskell of Montague, Dec. 1., 1869.
3. Irving S., b. Aug. 7, 1850 ; d. Oct. 24, 1852.
3. William Irving, b. May 16, 1853 ; rem. Milford.
2. Oliver Witt, b. May 19, 1811.
2. Harvey, b. Jan. 17, 1813 ; m. Mary Wilder, May 10, 1836.
3. Mary Leuann, b. Aug. 25, 1838 ; m. Joseph H. Harris.
3. Webster H., b. June 10, 1841 ; d. Sept. 23, 1846.
2. Lyman, b. Mar. 24, 1815 ; m. Salome Rich of Athol, May 31, 1836 ; res. Worcester.
3. Henry H., b. Apr. 10, 1840 ; d. May 6, 1855.

BROWN.

3. Laura Ann, b. Mar. 26, 1842 : res. Worcester.
3. Freeman, b. Jan. 31, 1845 ; m. Flora I. Clark of Worcester, Sept. 1, 1868 ; res. Worcester.
3. Leander E., b. Apr. 10, 1847: d. June 1, 1852.
3. Eugene, b. Mar. 26, 1855 ; d. Aug. 9, 1855.
2. Moses, b. Feb. 9, 1821 ; m. Eliza Bixby of Barre, Feb. 25, 1845 : rem. Springfield ; killed by a fall, Jan. 6, 1870.
3. Leroy W., b. July 23, 1846 ; m. Ella S. Brigham, Sept. 8, 1869.
3. Waldron, b. Apr. 17, 1849 ; d. June 4, 1853.
3. Lyford, b. Oct. 6, 1850 ; res. Gardner.
3. Eliza Jennette, b. Feb. 26, 1853 : m. Hamilton Sawin ; rem. Gardner.
3. Lucy Arvilla, b. Jan. 27, 1856 ; m. Arthur Derby of Gardner.
3. Wallace, b. June 15, 1858 ; d. July 9, 1858.
1. John, b. Sutton, Jan. 27, 1778 ; m. Polly Witt, 1800 ; lost at sea, Jan. 20, 1807.
2. Russell, b. Sept. 1, 1802 ; m. Julia Goddard of Athol, June, 1836 ; d. Oct. 5. 1849.
3. Mary E., b. Aug., 1837 : m. Benj. F. Armington of Templeton. Sept. 29, 1859.
3. Walter Russell, b. Apr. 17, 1840 ; d. July 2, 1871.
3. Julia, b. Mar. 17, 1843 ; m. Eri Shepardson of Royalston.
3. Frank A., b. Dec. 20, 1846.
2. Mary, b June 3, 1805 ; m. Emory Johnson of Wallingford, Vt., Oct. 16, 1825.
2. John, b. Aug. 11, 1807 ; m. Maria Taylor of Richmond, N. H., 1833 ; d. Sept 12, 1838.
3. Frances Maria, b. Sept. 8, 1833 ; m. William Palmer of Grafton ; d. 1853.
3. Susan Augusta, b. Apr. 12, 1835 ; m. Alonzo H. Dana of Oxford ; rem. Ohio.
1. Polly, b. May 16, 1780 ; m. Moses Greenwood.
1. Charlotte, b. 1782 ; m. Stephen P. Church.
1. Rebecca, b. July 7, 1784 ; m. Pliny Lamb : m. 2d, Joseph Brigham.
1. Ebenezer, b. 1786 ; m. Lois Metcalf, who d. Apr. 30, 1816 : m. 2d, Lydia Harwood, June, 1817, who d. Dec. 21, 1846, a. 69 : m. 3d, Vida Underwood of Barre, Dec. 27, 1849, who d. May 17, 1869, a. 62 ; he d. Oct. 22, 1871.

30

BROWN.

2. Edwin, b. Nov. 14, 1810; m. Sally Witt, Apr. 10, 1834; rem. Springfield.

3. Lois L., b. June 28, 1838; m. Simpson Clark.

3. George A., b. Oct. 21, 1840; d. June 4, 1859.

3. Charles E., b. Dec. 19, 1842; res. Springfield.

2. Austin, b. June 13, 1813; m. Elizabeth Bellows, May 10, 1836; res. Springfield.

3. John Austin, b. Aug. 27, 1838; d. Oct. 6, 1853.

3. Ebenezer Welcome, b. June 6, 1840; m. Carrie Hill; rem. Springfield.

3. Louisa E., b. May 8, 1842; m. Luke Williams.

3. Asaph B., b. Mar. 12, 1845; rem. Albany, N. Y.

3. Lydia Harwood, b. May 31, 1846; d. Oct. 10, 1846.

3. Lydia Harwood, b. June 14, 1848; m. Estus G. Clark of Northampton, Apr. 26, 1876.

3. Willard M., b. Oct. 17, 1851; res. Albany, N. Y.

2. Louisa, b. June 13, 1815; d. Oct. 4, 1815.

1. Dexter, b. Oct. 9, 1788; rem.

1. Russell, b. Nov. 8, 1791; m. Clarissa Waite, Oct. 5, 1819; rem. Warwick; d. there.

2. Clark, b. July 9, 1820; res. Pa.

2. Russell, b. Mar. 11, 1822; d. Sept. 29, 1823.

2. Clarissa, b. Sept. 15, 1823; m. James Farrar of Warwick, Jan. 1, 1852; res. Adrian, Mich.

2. Stephen, b. July 4, 1825; m. Mana Mayo of N. Y., June 28, 1851; res. N. Y.; judge of court for a time.

2. Gilbert, b. June 27, 1832; m. Abby B. Kilburn of Athol, Jan. 28, 1856.

3. Fred Gilbert, b. May 28, 1857.

3. Frank Herbert, b. Aug. 21, 1858.

2. Gilman, b. June 27, 1832; res. Pa.

1. Sewell, b. Feb. 11, 1793; rem. N. Y.

1. Clarissa, b. June 25, 1795; d. Sept. 15, 1816.

1. Jonas, b. May 8, 1797; m. Abigail Wilbur, Feb. 22, 1821; d. Dec. 20, 1873; she d. Oct., 1870.

2. Jonas, b. July 7, 1822; m. Harriet F. Houghton of Petersham, Jan. 3, 1854; d. Jan. 25, 1879.

2. Abigail J., b. June 9, 1824; m. Elijah White of Phillipston, Dec. 12, 1843.

BROWN.

1. Clark, b. Feb. 16, 1799 ; d. Sept. 20, 1820.
1. Harriet, b. Mar. 23. 1801 ; m. Leonard Clark.
1. Shepherd. b. Jan. 28, 1803 ; d. June 20, 1880.
1. Foster, b. July 1, 1805 ; rem. Lowell.
1. Melinda, b. Oct. 3, 1807 ; d. young.

THOMAS H. BROWN c. f. Sterling ; m. Emily Marean, May 10, 1827, who
    d. Sterling ; m. 2d, Amia (Morse) Harrington, Apr. 8, 1834.
    who d. Aug. 9. 1849 ; m. 3d, Jerusha Wheeler Goss of Bol-
    ton, who d. Feb. 3, 1864 ; he d. Nov. 26, 1866.

1. Ann E., b. Apr. 10, 1828 ; d. Jan. 5, 1877. in Worcester.
1. Amia M., b. Mar. 24. 1836 ; m. William Harrison Whittemore.
1. Eliza. b. Nov. 16, 1843 ; d. St. Louis, Apr. 7, 1874.

REV. ABEL BROWN m. Catherine Swan, May 15, 1843 ; d. Canandaigua,
    N. Y., Nov. 8, 1844.

1. Abel Swan, b. July 3, 1845 ; rem. Brooklyn, N. Y.

BROWNING.

JOHN BROWNING c. f. Rutland ; m. Clara Sherman ; settled on the farm
    now occupied by Joseph H. Harris ; d. Nov. 4, 1809, a.
    51 ; she d. June 10, 1853, a. 88.

1. John, b. July 31, 1785 ; physician, Mendon, N. Y. ; m. Elizabeth
    Stearns, Aug., 1810 ; d. May 31, 1866. [See p. 181.]
    2. John Stearns, b. Oct. 6, 1812.
    2. Elizabeth, b. Oct. 6, 1816.
1. Clara, b. Dec. 31, 1786 ; m. Moses Phelps, M. D.
1. James, b. Nov. 30, 1788, m. Betsey Brigham, July 4, 1811, who d.
    Sept. 7. 1828, a. 35 [see p. 167] ; m. 2d, Eliza Underwood
    Davis, Feb. 11, 1830, who d. Newburg, O. ; he d. Nov. 12, 1837.
    2. Clara S., b. July 7, 1813 ; m. Appleton Clark.
    2. Sally B., b. Mar. 6, 1817 ; d. Aug. 24, 1819.
    2. James, b. Apr. 14, 1820 ; m. Ann W. Whittemore, Apr. 2, 1844.
        3. Elizabeth Ann, b. Dec. 18, 1846 ; m. Eugene D. Shattuck of
            Ohio, Jan. 22, 1872.
        3. Sybil H., b. Mar. 9, 1857 ; m. Silas A. Greenwood.
    2. John, b. Feb. 21, 1822 ; m. Abigail D. Greenwood, Dec. 2, 1847 ;
        d. June 13, 1859.
        3. Henry H., b. Apr. 11, 1856.

BROWNING.

2. Betsey B., b. May 10, 1824; m. James O. Curtis of Medford.

2. Sybil M., b. Apr. 7, 1826; m. Henry J. Hunt of Chelsea, Sept. 9. 1852.

2. George D., b. Feb. 5, 1831; m. Jane Moore of Templeton; d. army.

2. Josiah, b. Aug. 13, 1833; rem. Cleveland, O.

1. Asaph, b. Mar. 3, 1791; m. Lois Hastings of Petersham, Apr., 1816; rem. Petersham.

1. Rebecca, b. Mar. 22, 1793; m. Williams Wilbur.

1. Susan, b. Feb. 5, 1795; m. Silas Wheeler; m. 2d, William Marean.

1. George, b. Jan. 29, 1797: d. July 28, 1817.

1. Joshua, b. Jan. 15, 1799: m. Lavina Morse, Dec. 27, 1821, who d. Nov. 7, 1870; he d. Apr. 11, 1877.

  2. Asa B., b. Sept. 16, 1822: m. Eliza Whittemore, May 20, 1846: d. army, Aug. 8, 1863. [See p. 138.]

    3. Lyman W., b. Feb. 10, 1847; m. Flora Worrick of Athol, Nov. 8, 1873: res. Leominster.

      4. Minnie Bertha, b. Nov. 29, 1879.

    3. Albert H., b. Dec. 2, 1848; res. Portland, Me.

    3. Lucius Herbert, b. Apr. 1, 1851; m. Martha Raymond of Westminster; res. Worcester.

    3. Sarah L., b. Sept. 20, 1853.

    3. Edgar A., b. June 14, 1856; res. Worcester.

    3. Charles G., b. Oct. 4, 1858; res. Worcester.

    3. Susan E., b. Feb. 1, 1862.

  2. Susan, b. Feb. 1, 1825; m. Silas Newell Greenwood.

  2. Lavina, b. Jan. 7, 1828; m. Wheelock A. Cheney of Athol, May 25, 1852; res. Worcester.

  2. Lucretia, b. Jan. 6, 1830; m. Levi Warren.

  2. Lucy, b. June 20, 1832; m. J. Otis Hale.

  2. Joshua Gilman, b. Dec. 3, 1835; rem. Conn.

  2. Esther, b. July 12, 1841; m. Robert H. Chamberlain of Worcester, Jan. 10, 1865.

1. Lucy, b. Dec. 27, 1800; m. Asa Marean.

1. Eliza, b. May 29, 1803; m. Joel Morse.

CAMPBELL.

Vincent Campbell c. f. Hardwick; m. Louisa Shumway, 1853.

1. Anna Eliza, b. Dec. 15, 1853; d. Sept. 17, 1872.

CAMPBELL.

1. Susan L., b. July 5, 1855 ; m. Chester Hinds of South Gardner, Oct., 1877.
1. Mary F., b. Apr. 1, 1859 ; m. Frederick Homan of Worcester, Feb. 5, 1880.
1. George H., b. Aug. 19, 1860.
1. Albert V., b. Mar. 5, 1862 ; d. Oct. 16, 1864.
1. William V., b. Sept. 15, 1870.

CASE.

REV. RUFUS CASE, a retired clergyman, c. f. Jaffrey, N. H., 1875 ; m. Elvira Fish of Hardwick, June 2, 1842.

CHENEY.

LOVERING A. CHENEY c. f. Barre ; m. Mary C. Hemenway, Nov. 27. 1851 : d. Mar. 29, 1879. a. 51.
1. Ella M., b. Sept. 27, 1857 ; d. Dec. 28, 1859.
1. Etta M., b. Jan. 11, 1861.

CHURCH.

STEPHEN CHURCH c. f. Rutland, 1774 ; built on the site afterward occupied by the Crystal House. In the Revolutionary War he was among the first to volunteer as a minute man, and afterward enlisted for the war ; m. Esther Moore ; d. July 11, 1786 ; she d. Pelham, N. H., 1823.
1. John Hubbard, b. Mar. 17, 1772 ; m. Thankful Watson of Rutland ; m. 2d, Hannah Farnham of Newburyport, 1806 ; both d. Pelham, N. H. ; he d. June 12, 1840. [See p. 183.]
1. Mercy, b. June 22, 1774 ; m. Jene Stowel ; d. Lebanon, N. Y., Nov. 13, 1802.
1. Cynthia, b. July 1, 1776 ; m. Enoch Stowel ; d. Lebanon, N. Y., Sept. 24, 1827.
1. Stephen Parker, b. Apr. 10, 1784 : m. Charlotte Brown, Nov. 20. 1806 ; rem. Beverly ; d. there.
1. Hannah, b. Nov. 24, 1786 ; m. Daniel Gage of Hudson, N. H. ; d. July 28, 1839.

ASA, bro. of STEPHEN, c. f. Rutland, 1776. He was in the battle of Bunker Hill, and served through the war ; during his army service he

CHURCH.

kept a carefully written journal. which was sacredly preserved by the family till 1835 or '36, when it was used in confirmation of testimony in reference to the pension of his widow, and was never returned. He m. Rachel Newton: d. Feb. 15, 1809. a. 59; she d. Dec. 2, 1843. a. 91.

1. Benjamin, b. Oct. 4, 1776: m. Elizabeth Heald, Oct. 9. 1803; d. June 23, 1806. [See p. 166.]

2. Mary White, b. Jan. 24, 1804: m. Sampson Mason of Concord: d. Aug. 27. 1876.

2. Eunice Dodd, b. Oct. 1, 1805.

1. Lucy, b. Dec. 5, 1782; m. Salmon Gates.

1. Patty. b. July 9, 1784: d. Oct. 3. 1840.

1. Asa, b. June 6. 1786: rem. Maine: d. June 10, 1844.

1. Ephraim. b. Mar. 18, 1788: d. Oct. 29, 1816.

1. Luke, b. June 15. 1790: d. Oct. 1, 1837.

1. John. b. July 1, 1792: m. Eliza Morse, May 26, 1822; d. Mar. 9, 1833: she d. Feb. 2. 1874.

2. John Blanchard. b June 24, 1823: m. Adelaide Woodward, Aug. 4. 1853. who d. Oct. 10, 1858: m. 2d, Julia Leonard of Ashfield: rem. N. Y.

3. Mary Emma. b. Sept 27. 1853: d. Feb. 14. 1854.

3. Eliza Estelle. b. Dec. 9, 1855: d. Feb. 16, 1866.

2. Adelphia E., b. Sept. 1, 1825.

2. Asa H., b. May 23. 1828; res. Boston.

2. Eunice Almeda, b. Apr. 16, 1832.

1. Stephen, b. Aug. 20. 1794; m. Sophia Marean, Dec. 6, 1821; d. Oct. 24. 1861.

2. Lucy E., b. Nov. 24, 1822; d. July 21, 1825.

2. Lucy E., b. Apr. 18, 1825.

2. Stephen Delavan, b. Feb. 26, 1828; m. Adelaide B. Wheeler, 1852; rem. Gardner.

3. Elizabeth A., b. Jan. 9, 1853; m. Elinus E. Young of Gardner, May 27, 1873.

2. Sophia Francene, b. July 1, 1830.

2. Mary Harriet, b. July 31, 1832; m. Asa Temple of Gardner, Nov. 24. 1853.

CLARK.

The two principal families of CLARKS descended from the brothers JOHN and SAMUEL who came from Hopkinton.

CLARK.

JOHN CLARK in 1774, was delegate from Hubbardston to the first Provincial Congress of Massachusetts; b. July 21, 1730; m. Elizabeth Norcross, June 7, 1750; d. Chester, Vt.

1. John, b. 1751 ; m. Jerusha Andrews ; d. Apr. 21, 1810.
2. Luther, b. Mar. 18, 1771 ; m. Sally Walker, Nov. 9, 1791, who d. Oct. 17, 1855 ; he d. May 3, 1856.
   3. Luther Reed, b. Mar. 19, 1792 ; m. Keziah Gates, June 4, 1821 ; rem. Leominster.
   3. Pamelia, b. July 24, 1794 ; m. Willard Johnson, Apr. 29, 1823 ; rem. Rutland.
   3. William, b. Apr. 16. 1796 ; d. Aug. 18, 1800.
   3. Ira, b. Jan. 28, 1799 ; m. Rebecca Wood, Dec., 1826 ; rem. Leominster.
   3. William A., b. July 1, 1801 ; m. Martha Rice ; m. 2d, Elizabeth Root ; rem. Ludlow.
   3. Sally, b. May 13, 1803 ; m. Gilman Powers of Rindge. N. H., Mar. 10, 1833.
   3. Adolphus, b. June 5, 1805 ; m. Eliza Mundell ; rem. Leominster.
      4. James Warren, b. Dec. 17, 1837 ; m. Sarah L. Morrow of Sheldon, Vt., Oct. 11, 1856.
         5. Nora A., b. Sept. 7, 1867 ; (adopted.)
   3. Arethusa, b. June 15. 1807 ; d. young.
   3. Anson, b. Dec. 2, 1809 ; m. Fanny Clapp, Apr. 8. 1830 ; d. Rutland, May 24, 1854.
2. Martha, b. Apr. 9, 1772 : m. Aaron Rice Clark of Barre ; d. July 22, 1811.
2. Anna, b. July 19, 1773 ; m. John Morse ; rem. Keene, N. H.
2. John, b. Dec. 29, 1774 ; m. Sally Rice of Barre ; rem. Chester, Vt.
2. Oliver, b. June 3, 1776 ; m. Lois Clark, 1798 ; d. Aug. 11, 1835 ; she d. Mar. 1, 1853.
   3. William Smith, b. July 7, 1799 ; d. unmarried.
   3. Dana, b. 1800 ; d. Dec. 3, 1859.
   3. Elizabeth, b. 1804 ; m. Metcalf Wellman of Brimfield.
   3. James Sullivan, b. July 23, 1807 ; m. Elizabeth R. Walker, Aug. 8, 1830 ; res. Grafton.
      4. Appleton, b. Dec. 3, 1832 ; d. Sept. 5, 1835.
      4. James Sullivan, b. Nov. 3, 1836 ; d. Apr. 2, 1859.

CLARK.

4. Edward Sumner, b. Sept. 3, 1839 ; m. Sarah G. Pratt, Nov. 21, 1861 ; res. Grafton.

4. David, b. Oct. 6, 1840 ; d. Oct. 20, 1840.

3. Edward Sumner. b. July 23, 1807 ; rem. Worcester ; m. Martha P. Brigham ; d. Oct. 2, 1859.

3. Emily, b. 1810 : m. James P. Appleton of Athol.

3. Oliver, b. 1813 : m. Lucy Smith, July 15, 1834 : d. Rutland.
   4. Ellen, b. 1838 : m. Charles E. Reed of Rutland, Aug. 30, 1856.

3. Nancy, b. 1815 : m. Benj. Arnold of Worcester : rem. Chicago.

3. William Henry, b. Oct. 6, 1818 : m. Abigail G. Adams, Oct. 2, 1844 : res. Wayland.

3. Louisa Jane, b. 1824 : m. Oliver Wellington of Phillipston, Mar. 1, 1849.

2. Hannah, b. Dec. 23, 1777 : m. Moses Rice, Dec. 21, 1800 ; d. Apr. 4. 1808.

2. William. b. Nov. 18, 1779 : d. May 15, 1780.

2. Betsey, b. Nov. 18. 1781 ; m. James Smith of Brimfield : d. June 30, 1809.

2. William Andrew. b. Oct. 2. 1783 : m. Louisa Jennings of Ludlow : drowned. Ohio. 1820.

2. Jerusha, b. Feb. 27. 1785 : m. Luther Gates of Barre, Feb. 26, 1809 : rem. Chelsea. Vt.

2. Calvin, b. Jan. 1. 1787 ; m. Nancy Norcross, 1808 : rem. Holland Purchase. N. Y.

2. Edmond, b. Aug. 13. 1790 : m. Patty Kelley of Barre, 1810 ; rem. Chelsea, Vt.

2. Mary, b. Nov. 9. 1792 ; m. Asa Tyler Grimes.

1. William*, b. Apr. 1753 : m. Hannah Smith of Rutland, Apr. 21, 1776 : d. Mar. 6. 1812 : she d. Jan. 17, 1853, a. 95.

2. Lois, b. May. 17. 1780 ; m. Oliver Clark.

2. Abigail, b. Apr. 15, 1782 : d. Feb. 8, 1813.

2. William Smith, b. Jan. 22, 1784 ; m. Elizabeth Clark, May 22, 1803, who d. Oct. 21, 1857 : he d. Dec. 21, 1870.

3. Simpson, b. June 19, 1804 : m. Nancy Lamb, May 3, 1827 : d. Apr. 14 : 1833.

4 Adelphia Elizabeth, b. May 24, 1828.

4. George. b. Oct. 2, 1830, m. Theodocia Elmina Thompson, Mar. 16, 1854 ; res. Worcester.

CLARK.

4. Simpson, b. May 28, 1832; m. Lois E. Brown, Oct. 29, 1857, who d. June, 1871 ; rem. Springfield.

4. Jane N., b. May 28, 1832; d. Mar. 31, 1847.

3. William Smith, b. May 3, 1804 ; m. Mary Davis, Mar., 1828. who d. May 11, 1852; m. 2d, Louisa (Stone) Morse, Dec. 25, 1860; d. June 14, 1877.

    4. Charles, b. Sept. 3, 1828; d. Apr. 19, 1850.

    4. John Davis, b. July 14. 1830; d. Aug. 12, 1849.

    4. William Lyman, b. May 19, 1832 ; m. Alecia M. Buxton, May 15, 1861 ; rem. Springfield.

    4. Mary H., b. Mar. 23, 1834 ; m. Fred Parker Morse.

    4. Caroline Elizabeth, b. Jan. 31, 1836 ; d. Oct. 8, 1844.

    4. Albert, b. Aug. 12, 1838 ; m. Jemima McFarland, Aug. 11, 1860 ; d. July 30, 1863.

        5. Alice, b. Dec. 3. 1860.

        5. Frederick Burt, b. Nov. 3, 1862.

    4. Sarah Augusta, b. May 25, 1840 ; m. Julius B. Hubbard, Jan. 26, 1861 ; d. Oct. 3. 1867.

    4. Susan. b. Nov. 6, 1842 ; d. June 21, 1843.

    4. Alson Waite, b. Apr. 25, 1844 ; d. Apr. 18, 1868.[See p. 138.]

    4. Elizabeth Susan. b. May 1, 1849 ; m. Frederick E. Davis.

3. Appleton, b. Aug. 10, 1807 ; m. Clara S. Browning. Apr. 29. 1835, who d. Jan. 22. 1878 ; res. Cambridge.

    4. Mary Harriet, b. Oct. 14, 1839 ; m. John Gilman Waite.

    4. Abby Mason, b. Apr. 2, 1841.

    4. Cecelia Witt, b. Oct. 29, 1843.

    4. Susan R., b. Feb. 9, 1845.

    4. Herbert A., b. Aug. 17, 1847 ; m. Ella Fletcher of Belmont ; res. Haverhill.

    4. Sybil E., b. Dec. 30, 1849 ; m. Ephraim Emerton of Salem.

    4. Alice C., b. Dec. 14, 1856 ; d. Dec. 21, 1859.

3. Elizabeth Caroline, b. May 22, 1811 ; m. James Alson Waite.

3. Jonas Gilman, b. Feb. 1, 1815 ; m. Susan Wright, Oct. 6, 1836 ; res. Worcester. [See p. 179.]

3. Abigail, b. Apr. 4, 1818 ; m. Elijah D. Allen, Apr. 30, 1839 ; res. Springfield.

3. Leonard, b. Nov. 18, 1821 ; m. Althine Woodward, Feb. 10, 1847 ; res. Springfield.

CLARK.

4. George Frederick, b. Dec. 26. 1847; m. Clara Beebe of Longmeadow.

4. Ella Althine. b. May 18, 1849 : d. Aug. 19, 1860.

4. Charles Hobart. b. Apr. 29, 1851; m. Helen M. DeRussy, Apr. 29, 1880.

4. Emma Caroline, b. Sept. 22, 1854; m. Henry J. Whitcomb of Springfield.

4. Addie Louise. b. May 22, 1857.

4. Mary Alice. b. Aug. 22, 1859.

4. Jonas Gilman. b. Mar. 28, 1862; drowned June 22, 1872, picnic excursion to Mt. Tom.

4. Susan. b. Oct. 28, 1865.

3. Sumner. b. Dec. 11. 1823; m. Martha Ann Hartwell, Jan. 4. 1853; res. Agawam.

4. Carrie B., b. Sept. 9, 1854 : m. Almon Jones of Camden, N. Y., Apr. 15. 1880.

4. Nettie Lee. b. May 4. 1856; d. Apr. 16, 1860.

4. Gilbert. b. Dec. 3. 1857; d. May 4, 1859.

4. James H., b. Sept. 28, 1859.

4. Minnie M., b. Jan. 4. 1862 : m. John Schwartz of Philadelphia. Pa., Feb. 17, 1880.

4. Hattie J., b. Nov. 25, 1864.

4. Mary E., b. July 19. 1866.

4. M. Jasmine, b. Sept. 1, 1874 : d. Feb. 17, 1875.

2. Hannah, b. Apr. 3, 1786; m. Joel Smith.

2. David, b. Feb. 18, 1788; m. Betsey Rugg. July 3. 1814 : rem. Worcester; d. Mar. 3. 1828.

2. Leonard. b. Mar 15, 1790; m. Nancy Heard, 1815 : m. 2d, Eunice Gleason, 1819; rem. Worcester.

2. Mary Parker, b. Jan. 15. 1794; m. Samuel Cobb of Groton, Mar. 19, 1811.

2. Isabella, b. Aug. 15, 1796; d. July 31, 1800.

2. Simpson. b. Oct. 14. 1799; d. Aug. 26, 1800.

1. Moses, b. 1755; m. Mary Child of Rutland, Nov. 10, 1778; who d. Mar. 22, 1805; he d. Oct. 17. 1823.

2. Polly, b. Aug. 15. 1779; m. Jason Woodward.

2. Moses. b. June 7, 1781; m. Arethusa Parkhurst. Aug. 4. 1804; d. May 14, 1849; she rem. N. Y.

CLARK.

3. Lysander C., b. Nov. 17, 1805 ; m. Lucy Hastings ; m. 2d, Mary W. Hastings ; res. Worcester.

3. Mary Melissa, b. Oct. 11, 1807 ; m. Levi Peirce.

3. William Chapman, b. Nov. 13, 1809 ; m. Mary Worthington ; m. 2d, Cynthia W. Ball ; both of Springfield ; res. Worcester.

3. Daniel Parkhurst, b. Mar. 8, 1812 ; m. Mary S. Merrick of Royalston, Dec. 11, 1844 ; res N. Y.

3. Moses Parkman, b. June 24, 1814 ; d. N. Y., Sept. 30, 1858.

3. Parker Plympton, b. Jan. 4, 1817 : m. Mary E. Acker of Washington, D. C., Dec. 10, 1844 ; rem. N. J.

3. John Quincy, b. July 31, 1819 ; m. Catherine A. Adams of N. Y., Jan. 22, 1856 ; res. N. Y.

3. Arethusa Elizabeth, b. Nov. 12, 1821 ; res. N. Y.

3. Bainbridge Shepherd, b. Mar. 27, 1824 ; m. Armedia Smyder of Washington, D. C., Dec. 18, 1855 ; res. N. Y.

3. George Homer, b. Feb. 5, 1827 ; m. Phillie A. Beatty of N. Y., May 16. 1855 ; res. N. Y.

3. Elijah Flagg. b. June 9, 1831 ; res. N. Y.

2. Elizabeth, b. Apr 15, 1783 ; d. Sept. 13, 1790.

2. Amiable, b. Nov. 7, 1785 ; m. Daniel Parkhurst.

2. Anna, b. Mar. 29, 1788 ; m. Roland Parkhurst.

2. John Flavel, b. Apr. 24, 1790 ; m. Mary White of Weymouth ; rem. Worcester.

2. Nehemiah Parker, b. May 31, 1792 ; d. Mar. 16, 1827.

2. Shepherd, b. Aug. 17, 1794 ; m. Mary Ann Dickinson of Petersham, Jan. 1825 ; d. Sept. 24, 1852 ; she d. Apr. 16, 1877, a. 70. [See p. 182.]

3. Mary Ann Field, b. Jan. 31, 1826 ; m. Anson B. Clark.

3. Sarah Elizabeth, b. Mar. 10, 1827 ; m. Daniel E. Hastings of Barre, June 5, 1849 ; d. Mar. 13, 1850.

3. John Flavel Warner, b. June 30, 1830 ; d. June 1, 1854.

3. Ellen Augusta, b. May 2, 1832 ; d. June 16, 1857.

3. Maria D., b. July 13, 1834 ; m. Joseph S. Paige ; m. 2d, Henry C. Waite of Minn., Jan. 1, 1860.

3. Nehemiah Parker, b. Apr. 8, 1836 ; m. Caroline E. Field of Roxbury, Sept. 12, 1860 ; res. St. Cloud, Minn.

CLARK.

3. Clara Swan, b. Jan. 27, 1839; m. Thomas C. McClure of St. Cloud. Minn., Dec. 4. 1859.

3. Caroline Louise, b. Feb. 24. 1841 : d. Aug. 3. 1860.

1. Elizabeth, b. 1758: m. Oliver Fairbanks, Nov. 9, 1777; rem. Springfield, Vt.

1. Isaac† b. 1760; m. Martha (Clark) Rangaw of Rutland, June 3. 1784. who d. May 6, 1798; m. 2d, Polly Gates of Barre, June 9, 1804, who d. Aug. 14. 1859: he d. June 11, 1836.

2. Elizabeth, b. Jan. 24. 1785 ; d. Jan. 2, 1795.

2. Persis Rice. b. Aug. 20. 1786 ; m. Moses Whiting of Dedham, Jan., 1809.

2. Roxana Moore, b. June 30. 1788 ; res. Boston.

2. George, b. Mar. 12. 1790 ; m. Charlotte Prentiss of Boston. Nov. 19. 1820 ; rem. Boston.

2. Isaac. b. Feb. 14, 1792 ; m. Hannah E. Wells of Charlestown. Sept. 13. 1818. who d. June 1, 1865. He served in the war of 1812 : rem. Washington, D. C.

2. Noah, b. Oct. 8, 1793 ; m. Ruthy Billings of Sharon, May 29. 1819 ; rem. Boston.

2. Justus, b. Sept. 22, 1795 : d. 1848.

2. Ferdinand Nimrod. b. Apr. 18, 1798 ; d. May 18. 1880.

2. Makepeace Gates. b. Jan. 8, 1805 ; m. Lucy Stone, June 20. 1830 ; d. June 2, 1839 : she d. Oct. 7, 1865.

   3. Ferdinand, b. Feb. 19. 1831 ; res. Barre.

   3. Noel Augustus. b. Oct. 9. 1833; m. Sophronia R. Titus of Sutton, Nov. 15. 1854 ; res. Uxbridge.

   3. Hattie Elizabeth, b. July 12, 1835.

   3. Ellen, b. May 15. 1837 ; m. Isaac Henry Clark of Boston.

   3. Lucy, b. Sept. 10. 1839.

2. Martha Huntington, b. Oct. 29, 1806 ; m. Sullivan Bigelow.

2. Catherine Smith, b. May 17, 1808 ; m. Eli Clark.

2. Sarah Gates, b. Nov. 12, 1811 ; m. Edwin Woods. •

2. William Gates, b. May 3. 1813 ; m. Lois Stone. Sept. 23, 1835.

   3. Mary Ann, b. Mar. 31, 1836; m. Isaac Bryant, Sept. 22, 1857 ; rem. No. Brookfield.

   3. Adelphia, b. May 9, 1839 ; m. Watson I. Peirce.

   3. Eleanor, b. Feb. 6, 1841 ; m. Merrifield Clark.

   3. Sophila. b. Apr. 9, 1844.

CLARK.

3. Sarah Anna, b. Jan. 7, 1850: m. Alden W. Paine of Whitins-
    ville, Oct. 22, 1872.

3. Arabella, b. July 9, 1856: d. June 17, 1864.

2. Mary Harding. b. Jan. 6. 1815; m. John Thompson.

2. Anson Bates, b. Nov. 6, 1817; m. Mary Ann Field Clark, June
    8, 1851.

3. Mary Elizabeth, b. Mar. 24, 1852; m. Dolson B. Searle of
    Minn. Feb. 16, 1875.

3. Abbott Bates, b. May 16, 1854.

3. Frederick Henry, b. Nov. 24, 1861.

2. Abigail Amanda, b. Oct. 27, 1819; m. Hiram Young; m. 2d.
    Elisha Murdock.

2. Edwin Henry, b. Oct. 27, 1821: m. Sarah Young. Apr. 18, 1843.

3. Sarah Olivia. b. Apr. 13, 1844: d. Sept. 1, 1851.

3. Alfred, b. Nov. 21, 1846; d. May 5, 1858.

2. Noah Addison. b. Sept. 14, 1824.

1. Samuel, b. 1763: m. Persis Hinds, Nov. 9, 1786; rem. Chester, Vt.

1. Experience, b. 1765; m. Nathan Holden; d. Oct. 1, 1790; he d.
    June 25, 1806, a. 53.

1. Joseph, b. Apr. 22, 1767; m. Phebe Rice of Marlboro', Nov. 28,
    1784: d. Apr. 17. 1828; she d. Apr. 1, 1829.

2. Susanna, b. May 31, 1785; m. Calvin Hinds.

2. Sally, b. Mar. 24, 1787; d. Dec. 2, 1820.

2. Joseph, b. May 20, 1789; m. Susanna Perkins, May 27, 1810,
    who d. June 20, 1827, a. 37; m. 2d, Lucinda (Clark)
    Claflin of Milford, Nov., 1827; rem. Worcester; d. Oct.
    7, 1839.

2. Stephen. b. Sept. 24, 1791; m. Azubah Irskine of Claremont,
    N. H., d. July 9, 1851.

2. Martin, b. Sept. 7, 1794; m. Harriet Howes Perry of Barre,
    Nov. 20, 1823.

3. Harriet Augusta, b. Aug. 20, 1824; d. Feb. 19, 1825.

3. Freeman Henry, b. Jan. 4, 1826; m. Mary H. Burnett of Hol-
    den, Aug. 26, 1849; res. Holden.

3. Louisa Elizabeth, b. Dec. 31, 1827; m. Clark Burnett of Hol-
    den, Nov. 7, 1850.

3. Charles Perry, b. Nov. 5, 1830; m. Susan Forbush of Hard-
    wick, Nov. 11, 1853; d. Aug. 14, 1863.

CLARK.

4. Dwight Edgar. b. Mar. 14, 1856.

4. Frank H., b. Mar. 28, 1858.

3. Laura Maria, b. Apr. 20, 1833; m. Julius P. Varney of Barre, Jan. 1, 1861.

3. Mary Jane, b. Oct. 10, 1835.

3. Eveline Howes, b. Mar. 6, 1838; m. Walton M. Mirick, Nov, 7, 1865; d. Jan. 6, 1874.

3. Leander Harrison, b. Mar. 22, 1841; m. Ella A. Thayer of Barre, Apr. 20, 1871.

4. Charles Wesley, } b. Jan. 31, 1875.
4. Clarence Leslie, }

4. Effie May, b. Mar. 25, 1877.

4. Minnie Ella. } b. Feb. 15, 1879.
4. Winnie Adella. }

3. Lyman Franklin, b. May 1, 1844; d. Dec. 28, 1863.

3. Dorothy Quincy, b. Oct. 5, 1796; d. Aug. 14, 1864.

3. Freeman. b. Oct. 13. 1799; d. July 28. 1820.

· Ezra, b. May 1, 1768; m. Jemima Nightingale, Sept. 16, 1790: d. May 1. 1827: she d. Apr. 29. 1855. a. 90.

2. Samuel, b. Dec. 28, 1791; m. Sally Johnson, Apr. 20, 1816: rem. Canada.

2. Experience. b. Jan. 1, 1793: m. Nathan Holden, Sept., 1809; d. Feb. 21, 1838; he d. Mar. 7. 1838, a. 52.

2. Elizabeth, b. Sept. 27, 1794: d. Sept. 22, 1796.

2. Ezra, b. June 20, 1796; m. Susan Hinds, Apr.,1816, who d. Sept. 21. 1817, a. 27; m. 2d, Abigail Rice of Barre, Mar. 28, 1820, who d. Sept. 20, 1860, a. 60; m. 3d, Sabrina (Cooper) Bixby of Dover, Vt., Apr. 22, 1861; rem. Barre.

2. Elizabeth. b. May 22, 1798; d. Mar. 17, 1799.

2. Aaron. b. Jan. 23. 1800; m. Achsah Hinds, Oct., 1819; rem. Ohio.

2. Robert. b. Mar. 22, 1802; m. Maria Rice of Barre, Apr. 2, 1828; rem. Barre.

2. Timothy Parker, b. May 26, 1804; m. Emeline Moulton of Spencer, Dec. 29, 1829; rem. N. Brookfield.

2. Jemima, b. Oct. 21, 1807; m. Harrison W. Sherman of Sterling, June 27, 1830.

2. John Stedman, b. May 26, 1809; m. Eliza Ann Newell of Brimfield, Dec. 31, 1845; res. Worcester.

CLARK.

1. Susanna, b. 1770; m. William Nightingale, May 29. 1788; res. Canada.

SAMUEL, bro. of JOHN, b. May 20, 1743; m. Mary Stone of Framingham. Sept. 10, 1772: came to H., 1796: d. May 22,1830; she d. Feb. 8, 1829.

1. Mary, b. Dec. 14, 1773; d. Jan. 10, 1776.
1. Simpson, b. Aug. 25, 1776; d. Jan. 22, 1841.
1. Mary. b. Oct. 3, 1777; d. Nov. 3, 1777.
1. Samuel, b. Sept. 25, 1778; m. Fanny Holden, Apr. 22, 1805; d. May 4, 1854; she d. May 26, 1847, a. 66.
1. Leonard, b. Apr. 6, 1781; m. Harriet Brown, Sept. 12, 1824; d. Aug. 8, 1839: she d. June 25, 1877.
   2. Danford, b. Jan. 5. 1825: m. Harriet E. Johnson of Barre, Dec. 3, 1846.
      3. Ashton D., b. Apr. 5, 1863.
   2. Leonard, b. Oct. 6, 1827: d. May 31, 1877.
   2. Lucius, b. Oct. 25. 1829; d. Oct. 14, 1843.
   2. Clarissa Melinda, b. Apr. 9. 1832: m. John Phelps.
   2. Sewell, b. Feb. 28, 1834; m. Mary N. Gleason, Jan. 12, 1858: res. Springfield.
1. Abijah, b. June 16, 1783; m. Betsey Heald. May 6, 1810: d. Aug. 28, 1859; she d. July 27, 1872.
   2. Maria, b. Sept. 25, 1811.
   2. Elizabeth, b. Dec. 20, 1813; m. Clark S. Bixby of Barre, Nov. 3, 1836, who d. Brookline, June 15, 1867.
   2. Louisa, b. Jan. 24, 1816; m. Rev. John M. Stowe, Sept. 7, 1854.
   2. Abijah Stone, b. Oct. 2, 1818; m. Clara Swan, May 1, 1845, who d. Apr. 5, 1873; m. 2d, Mary Ann (McFarland) Phelps, Mar. 31, 1875; res. Turners Falls.
      3. Elizabeth, b. Feb. 1, 1846.
      3. George Abijah. b. Oct. 11, 1847; res. Holyoke.
      3. Maria Louise, b. Mar. 2, 1850; m. J. Harrison Waterman, M. D., of Westfield, Dec. 28, 1876.
      3. Clara Swan, b. Apr. 7, 1852.
      3. James Samuel, b. July 21, 1854.
      3. Mary Kate, b. Aug. 31, 1856.
      3. Charles Reuben, b. Apr. 11, 1861; d. Aug. 16, 1862.

CLARK.

1. Elizabeth, b. Feb. 19, 1786 ; m. William Smith Clark.
1. Nancy, b. Aug. 10, 1788; m. Almon Stewart of Stafford, Conn., Oct. 31, 1813 ; rem. N. Y.
1. Isaac, b. May 17, 1791 ; m. Betsey Thompson, Nov. 1, 1814, who d. Nov. 24, 1858 ; he d. Dec. 30, 1854.
    2. Valentine, b. July 31, 1815 : d. Sept. 20, 1823.
    2. Samuel. b. Aug. 24, 1817 : d. Aug. 27, 1817.
    2. Hervey, b. Dec. 19, 1818 ; m. Louisa Clark, Sept. 7, 1843.
        3. Louisa Elizabeth, b. Nov. 2, 1844 ; m. Moses Leland.
        3. Eleanor Maria, b. Dec. 24, 1847 : d. Feb. 14, 1879.
        3. Fanny Etta. b. May 31, 1851 ; m. William H. Sargent.
        3. Charles Hervey. b. Dec. 10, 1852.
        3. Frederick Merrifield. b. Apr. 22, 1855 ; m. Addie W. Hartwell, May 30, 1880.
        3. Alfred Stockwell, b. June 4, 1857.
        3. Hobart, b. Dec. 31, 1860.
    2. Fanny. b. Sept. 13, 1821 ; m. Edward Merrick of Sterling. Nov. 7, 1841 : res. Princeton.
    2. Elizabeth, b. July 8, 1825 ; m. Leonard Wilson of Rutland, Jan. 16, 1850.
    2. Isaac. b. June 4. 1828 : d. May 29, 1833.
1. Abigail, b. Sept. 1, 1793 ; m. Jonas Heald.

ELI CLARK c. f. Barre about 1770 ; m. Lois Stone of Rutland, who d. Dec. 12, 1836. a. 84 : he d. Dec. 26, 1817, a. 66.
1. Anna. b. Dec. 9, 1771 ; m. Jonas Merriam of Westminster.
1. Moses, b. May 6, 1773 ; d. Oct. 26, 1819.
1. Eli, b. Nov. 2, 1775 ; m. Patience Stone : rem. Roxbury.
1. Polly, b. Aug. 16, 1779 ; m. Nathan Raymond of Westminster.
1. Nathan, b. Mar. 18, 1783 ; m. Diantha Merritt of Templeton ; d. Aug. 14, 1825.
    2. Eli, b. June 13, 1808 ; m. Catherine S. Clark, Aug. 5, 1834, who d. Oct. 27, 1845 ; m. 2d, Laura Grimes, Feb. 9, 1847 ; d. Jan. 22, 1856.
        3. Almond W., b. Mar. 6, 1841 ; d. army, Sept. 16, 1862. [See p. 138.]
    2. Lois, b. June 21, 1810 ; m. Ira Stearns of Lancaster, who d. Aug. 15, 1879 ; she d. Nov. 3, 1879.

CLARK.

2. Nathan, b. Aug. 8, 1812 ; d. Nov. 21, 1836.

2. Diantha, b. Apr. 25, 1814 ; m. Almond Whittemore of Leominster.

2. Asa, b. Feb. 25, 1818 ; res. Sandwich Islands.

2. Simeon, b. Apr. 30, 1820 ; m. Mary Morse, Dec. 17, 1846 ; rem. Princeton.

2. Hiram, b. July 2, 1822 ; m. Virginia M. Wakefield of Worcester ; rem. Worcester.

2. Sarah, b. Oct. 10, 1825 ; m. Orville James Gibson of Leominster, May 10, 1848.

1. Samuel, b. Oct. 18, 1787 ; m. Nancy Spring, Oct., 1809 ; d. Dec. 24, 1837 ; she d. Nov. 8, 1851.

2. Betsey Cook, b. July 14, 1810 ; m. Joseph Wyatt of Lowell ; d. Dec. 4, 1869.

2. Mary Robbins, b. June 1, 1812 ; m. Charles W. Blood.

2. Nancy, b. June 22, 1815 ; m. J. Emerson Greenwood.

2. Moses, b. July 13, 1818 ; m. Sarah Cunningham of Leicester ; res. Chester.

2. Samuel, b. May 6, 1820 ; m. Georgianna Batchelor of Deerfield, N. H. ; d. Concord.

2. Ann, b. Sept. 5, 1822 ; m. George H. Mann ; m. 2d, Moses Davis.

2. Nelson Parker, b. Mar. 8, 1825 ; m. Susan F. Knowlton of Northwood, N. H., June, 1859 ; d. New Boston, N. H., June 25, 1880. [See p. 182.]

2. Sarah, b. July 6, 1827 ; m. Stratford C. H. Bailey of Hopkinton, N. H. ; res. N. Y. City.

2. Ellen, b. Sept. 27, 1831 ; m. Phinn P. Bixby of Concord, N. H.

2. Elbridge Gerry, b. June 8, 1834 ; d. June 25, 1853.

1. Asa, b. Jan. 6, 1789 ; m. Lois Simonds, Nov. 23, 1815, who d. Dec. 22, 1858 ; he d. Mar. 16, 1872.

2. Mary Maria, b. June 13, 1817 ; d. Sept. 1, 1849.

2. Louisa, b. Sept. 5, 1819 ; m. Hervey Clark.

2. Asa Gardner, b. May 5, 1821 ; m. Miriam L. Newton, Sept. 30, 1845, who d. Nov. 8, 1879 ; he d. Mar. 20, 1870.

3. Mary Ann, b. Sept. 25, 1848 ; d. Sept. 5, 1849.

3. George W., b. June 23, 1850.

3. Etta Maria, b. Mar. 19, 1854.

2. Charlotte, b. Feb. 12, 1823 ; d. Mar. 21, 1873.

32

CLARK.

2. Lura, b. July 30, 1826 ; m. S. A. Whitney ; m. 2d, S. K. Buell of
Worcester.

2. Merrifield, b. Sept. 8, 1828 ; m. Eleanor W. Clark, Mar. 28, 1859.

   3. William Merrifield, b. Dec. 28, 1863.

   3. Mary Isabel, b. Sept. 1, 1869.

   3. Nellie Lois, b. Aug. 28, 1873.

2. Lorinda, b. July 10, 1830 ; m. John V. Stone of Roxbury ; res.
Worcester.

2. Stockwell, b. Mar. 30, 1832.

2. Eli Edward, b. Nov. 28, 1834 ; d. army, Sept. 12, 1864. [See p. 139.]

2. Washburn, b. Dec. 2, 1836 ; m. Ella A. McCoy of Hudson, N. H.,
Jan. 29, 1874.

   3. Lottie, b. 1873.

   3. Sumner, b. Mar. 10, 1876.

   3. Lois Ella, b. Dec. 22, 1877.

   3. Arthur S., b. Aug. 9, 1880.

1. Betsey, b. Jan. 29, 1792 ; m. Charles Wright.

1. Lois, b. Mar. 10, 1794 ; m. Dexter Phelps.

ANTHONY CLARK c. f. Rutland 1768 ; settled where Warren Clark now
lives. He, his sons, his daughter Anna (Mrs. Adams),
and his grandsons, Amos and Benjamin, all had a wide
reputation for skill in curing diseases by the use of roots
and herbs. He d. May 29, 1792 ; his wife Jennie, d.
Feb. 12, 1814, a. 82.

1. Peter, m. Mitty Rhodes, May 10, 1788 ; d. June 22, 1820.

2. Elizabeth, b. July 5, 1788 ; m. Otis Gale ; m. 2d, Wm. Jackson,
who d. Templeton.

2. Anna, b. Feb. 17, 1791 ; rem. Boston.

2. Peter, b. June 5, 1793, m. Elydia (Wiley) Chester, Sept. 23, 1841 ;
d. Feb. 27, 1854.

   3. Arthamiza, b. Dec. 11, 1842 ; d. Feb. 16, 1846.

2. Daniel, b. May 12, 1796 ; m. Betsey P. Bartlett, 1832 ; d. Apr.
19, 1843.

2. Jonas W., b. June 17, 1799 ; res. Boston.

2. Mitty, b. Sept. 15, 1801 ; m. Amos Clark.

2. Jenny, b. Nov. 21, 1804 ; rem. Boston.

2. Amos F., b. Nov. 9, 1808 ; res. Boston.

CLARK.

2. Caleb S., b. July 7, 1810 ; res. Boston.
2. Anthony F., b. July 16, 1813 ; res. Boston.
1. Anna, b. 1762 ; m. Ralph Adams.
1 Amos, b. June 30, 1768 ; m. Jemima Cobb, June 2, 1789, who d. Oct. 15, 1833, a. 70.
2. Patty, b. Dec. 28, 1789.
2. Olive, b. June 9, 1792 ; d. May 26, 1820.
2. Amos, b. June 9, 1798 ; m. Mitty Clark, Mar. 14, 1821 ; who d. Aug. 9, 1846 ; he d. July 5, 1860.
3. Amos F., b. July 20, 1830.
3. Eliza Ann, b. Sept. 12, 1835.
3. Lyman F., b. Oct. 13, 1837 ; m. Nellie M. ———
4. Moses Franklin, b. Nov. 10, 1877.
3. Jonas W., b. Sept. 24, 1840.
3. George W., b. June 25, 1843 ; d. Oct. 23, 1843.
3. Francis J., b. Jan. 5, 1846.
2. Benjamin A., b. Mar. 15, 1803 ; d. June 21, 1826.
2. Peter F., b. Feb. 27, 1807 ; m. Mary Smith ; d. Apr. 27, 1873.
3. Esther, b. Aug. 15, 1838.
3. John C., b. Aug. 1, 1840 ; m. Sarah J. Beede of Gilmanton, N. H. ; rem. Worcester.
4. Eva Marcella, b. May 18, 1868.

WARREN CLARK, b. Apr. 23, 1825 ; m. Eliza Ann Paddon of Nashville, N. H., 1849.

1. Warren, b. Apr. 1, 1850.
1. Ainsworth, b. Nov. 17, 1851.
1. Edward, b. May 19, 1855.
1. Irving, b. June 26, 1858.
1. Arthur Sumner, b. July 18, 1860 ; d. Jan. 6, 1863.
1. Eliza Jane, b. July 8, 1862.
1. Charles, b. Feb. 16, 1865.
1. Helen Myra, b. Dec. 21, 1868 ; d. Dec. 11, 1872.

STILLMAN CLARK c. f. Dorchester ; m. Miranda Newton, Nov. 3, 1840 ; rem. Jamaica, Vt., 1856.

1. Mary M., b. July 12, 1841 ; m. R. Howard of Jamaica, Vt., July 6, 1875.
1. George A., b. July 22, 1842 ; d. Jan. 17, 1843.

CLARK.

1. Emily M., b. Feb. 4, 1845 ; m. H. A. Morse of Leominster, Aug. 8, 1865.
1. Ella L., b. July 31, 1848.
1. John M., b. Dec. 22, 1850 ; m. Abby Prouty of Jamaica, Vt., Dec. 7, 1875.
1. Hiram A., b. July 30, 1852 ; d. Sept. 14, 1852.
1. Warren H., b. May 9, 1854 ; d. Aug. 25, 1854.
1. Charlotte A., b. Oct. 7, 1855 ; m. W. G. Sheffner of Jamaica, Vt., June 6, 1876.

CLEMENCE.

HENRY CLEMENCE, c. f. Brookfield about 1814 ; m. Harriet W. Waite, Nov. 27, 1821, who d. Dec. 11, 1824 ; m. 2d, Betsey Loring of Sturbridge, Dec. 31, 1826, who d. July 16, 1860, a. 64 ; rem. Worcester.

1. Richard H., b. Sept. 28, 1821 ; d. Sept. 17, 1868.
1. Mary, b. Aug. 1, 1823 ; d. Jan. 14, 1825.
1. Mary E., b. Jan. 13, 1828 ; m. Henry C. Willson of Worcester, Sept. 6, 1851.
1. Lucia C., b. Apr. 26, 1830 ; d. Sept. 6, 1836.
1. Nancy A., b. July 20, 1831 ; d. Sept. 6, 1831.
1. Chloe Ann, b. Jan. 17, 1833 ; d. Sept. 13, 1836.
1. Lucia Ann, b. Feb. 9, 1838 ; m. Samuel D. Perry of Coldbrook, Nov. 26, 1859 ; res. Worcester.

CLEVELAND.

HENRY L. CLEVELAND c. f. Hardwick ; m. Amanda Keith, Oct. 23, 1851.
1. Charles Henry, b. Feb. 9, 1855 ; m. Alice Brooks, Oct. 6, 1875.
2. Helen Mabel, b. Mar. 6, 1877.
2. Jessie M., b. July 9, 1879.
1. Horace Fremont, b. Aug. 2, 1856.
1. Simeon Leroy, b. July 25, 1859 ; d. Feb. 23, 1861.

CLIFFORD.

JONATHAN CLIFFORD c. f. Southboro', 1778 ; m. Mary Bridges, who d. Mar. 5, 1839, a. 80 ; he d. Aug. 21, 1803, a. 51.
1. Thankful, b. Oct. 17, 1779 ; m. Daniel Green.
1. Joanna, b. June 16, 1781 ; m. John Murdock of Westminster, July 1, 1804 ; both d. Westminster.

CLIFFORD.

1. Luther. b. Dec. 24, 1782; for many years deputy sheriff of Worcester County; m. Lydia Murdock of Westminster, Sept., 1805; d. Fitchburg, Jan. 25, 1864.

2. Martin, b. Sept. 3, 1806; m. Mary Ann Hancock, Apr., 1832, who d. June 15, 1834, a. 28; m. 2d, Eliza Baker of Prescott; d. Amherst, Dec. 14, 1879.

2. Achsah, b. Jan. 27, 1808; d. Nov. 2, 1819.

2. Warner, b. Feb. 25, 1810; m. Lorinda Hartwell, May 6, 1833; res. Worcester.

2. William J., b. Nov. 29, 1812; m. Sarah P. Spring, Dec. 2, 1834: d. Fitchburg, Aug. 5, 1860.

2. Betsey, b. July 2, 1819; m. Edward Murdock; m. 2d, Samuel W. Hayward of Fitchburg, Sept., 1852, who d. Feb. 27, 1859; m. 3d, Asa R. Trowbridge of Newton, Sept. 6, 1877.

2. Samuel Newell, b. Feb. 20, 1827; res. Fitchburg.

1. Nellie, b. Jan. 24, 1785; m. Gideon Reed; both d. New Salem.

1. Josephus, b. Apr. 20, 1790; m. Isabel Adams, Dec. 21, 1813, who d. Mar. 4, 1865; he d. Oct. 15, 1876.

2. Anson C., b. Apr. 17, 1815; m. Clara Wyman. July 7, 1842: res. Worcester.

2. Betsey, b. Jan. 13, 1817; m. Henry B. Rice of Natick, Nov. 4, 1850; d. Aug. 13, 1868.

2. Celicia, b. Aug. 31, 1818; m. Harrison Wyman.

2. Dorinda, b. Feb. 9, 1820; m. Samuel H. Hastings.

2. Eleanor, b. Nov. 16, 1821; m. John Webster of Southbridge, Nov. 29, 1843; res. So. Royalston.

2. Fidelia, b. Aug. 22, 1823; d. Aug. 27, 1843.

2. Isabel, b. Sept. 5, 1825; m. John A. Smith of Worcester, Nov. 27, 1851.

2. Josephus, b. Mar. 31, 1827; m. Lucy E. Dunn, Nov. 25, 1852; res. Phillipston.

2. Nathan, b. Oct. 27, 1828; d. Nov. 16, 1846.

2. Rebecca, b. Feb. 19, 1831; d. July 31, 1857.

1. Polly, b. Sept. 7, 1795; m. Luther Rice; m. 2d, Luther Kendall; d. Framingham.

CODDING.

ZENAS CODDING c. f. Vt.; m. Mary Ann Mundell, Aug. 9, 1849.

CODDING.

1. Mary Emily, b. Sept. 29, 1851 ; m. Warren Handy of Holden, Sept. 23, 1880.
1. Franklin E., b. Oct. 1, 1853.
1. Adin Everard, b. June 24, 1855 ; d. Aug. 29, 1858.
1. William E., b. Feb. 10, 1857 ; d. Aug. 30, 1858.
1. Julia Ann, b. Mar. 28, 1861.
1. Lizzie Jane, b. Aug. 26, 1863.
1. Freddie Albert, b. July 5, 1868.
1. Arthur Edson, b. Jan. 31, 1873.

COFFIN.

EBEN MOULTON COFFIN c. f. Woburn, 1872 ; m. Mattie E. Corey, Jan. 18, 1866.

1. Mattie E., b. Jan. 26, 1867.
1. Willie, b. Apr. 18, 1869.
1. George Irving, b. June 18, 1871.
1. Arthur Gilman,) b. Dec. 7, 1875 ; d. Sept. 27, 1876.
1. Albert Clark,) d. Sept. 12, 1876.
1. Charles, b. May 15, 1878.

THOMAS T. COFFIN, bro. of Eben Moulton, c. f. Woburn, 1873 ; m. Esther E. Gilman, 1853 ; d. July 16, 1874, a. 41.

1. John Henry, b. Sept. 21, 1857.
1. Frank Benjamin, b. Jan. 26, 1861.
1. Fannie Gilman, b. Mar. 7, 1863 ; d. Feb. 12, 1878.
1. Fred T., b. Jan. 24, 1865.
1. Florence T., b. Jan. 10, 1867.
1. Lizzie, b. Mar. 25, 1869.
1. Josie M., b. Oct. 18, 1872.

COLEMAN.

Six brothers, JOHN, ALMOND, AMHERST, PEREZ, BENJAMIN FRANKLIN and LAFAYETTE COLEMAN c. f. Templeton.

JOHN COLEMAN m. Lucinda Underwood ; d. Jan. 20, 1840, a. 56.

1. George B., b. Apr. 20, 1816 ; m. Mary D. Prentiss, Apr. 30, 1840 ; rem. Worcester ; d. there.
1. John W., b. Feb. 3, 1818 ; d. May 8, 1821.
1. Samuel M., b. Nov. 1, 1819 ; d. Oct. 7, 1822.
1. John W., b. Dec. 28, 1821 ; rem.

COLEMAN.

1. Reuben C., b. Oct. 16, 1823.
1. Samuel M., b. Sept. 24, 1825 ; d. Sept. 17, 1847.
1. Sylvanus, b. Sept. 10, 1827.
1. Horace U., b. Aug. 24, 1829.
1. Washington, b. June 4, 1832.
1. Larkin, b. June 21, 1834.
1. Francis L., b. July 25, 1837 ; d. June 24, 1840.

ALMOND, m. Bethia Homer, who d. Jan. 27, 1828 ; m. 2d, Dorinda Partridge. Oct. 7, 1829, who d. Aug. 17, 1851, a. 47 ; he d. Gardner, July 15, 1864.
1. William, b. Jan. 1, 1809 ; rem. Vt.
1. Harriet, b. Apr. 18, 1811 ; m. Apollos A. Allen.
1. Almond, b. Mar. 11, 1813 ; m. Betsey S. Brown, who d. Dec. 29,
      1864, a. 53 ; m. 2d, Esther (Bullock) Kendall, July 4, 1868.
   2. Oliver B., b. May 15, 1841 ; m. Ellen E. Moore, July 26, 1866,
      who d. Aug. 30, 1870 ; m. 2d, Amy Johnson of Wis. ;
      ˙res. Wis.
   2. Sibbell, b. July 9, 1842 ; m. Elbridge A. Gay.
   2. Abby L.. b. June 15, 1844 ; d. June 8, 1861.
   2. Almond H., b. July 11, 1845 ; d. Aug. 13, 1845.
   2. Persis S., b. June 15, 1846 ; res. Otter River.
   2. William S.. b. Aug. 26, 1847 ; res. Jacksonville, Vt.
   2. Calvin, b. Feb. 2, 1849 ; m. Ruth Matthews of Halifax, Vt. ; res.
      Halifax, Vt.
   2. Charles, b. July 26, 1850 ; m. Cora Day of So. Gardner ; res. So.
      Gardner.
   2. Julia A., b. Oct. 12, 1851 ; m. Leander S. Stone of Fitchburg.
   2. Emerson H., b. Feb. 26, 1853 ; d. June 10, 1861.
   2. Rufus, b. Dec. 2, 1854.
1. Olive G., b. Aug. 28, 1815 ; m. Ebenezer Chapman Warren.
1. Bethia, b. Jan. 28, 1818 ; m. Cyrus Estabrook of Westminster, Oct.
   25, 1838 ; res. Sterling.
1. Hervey, b. Sept. 12, 1820 ; m. Sarah A. French, Mar. 20, 1841.
   2. Sarah Bethia, b. July 25, 1843.
   2. Hervey Perez, b. Dec. 3, 1845 ; m. Clara J. Collins, Sept. 25, 1868.
   2. Henry S., b. 1848 ; m. Ella A. Mann, Aug. 16, 1870.
      3. Grace A., b. Apr. 16, 1873.

COLEMAN.

 3. Elwin H., b. Feb. 10, 1879.

 2. Mary Elizabeth, b. Jan. 12, 1850.

 2. Edrick H., b. 1852 ; m. Nellie J. Cram of Gardner, Feb. 17, 1875.

 2. Frederick, b. Aug. 31, 1861.

 1. Edmond, b. Oct. 8, 1822 ; m. Louisa Pond, Oct. 10, 1844.

  2. Louisa E., b. Dec. 4, 1844 ; d. May 29, 1849.

  2. Stephen Clark, b. Aug. 23, 1846 ; d. Aug. 7, 1849.

  2. Herbert E., b. Oct. 16, 1849.

  2. Willie M., b. Sept. 4, 1857.

 1. Polly, b. Mar. 2, 1825 ; d. May 30, 1831.

 1. Adaline, b. June 15, 1830 ; m. Timothy N. Carroll of Fitzwilliam,
   N. H., Nov. 7, 1850.

 1. Charlotte P., b. Apr. 15, 1832 ; d. Oct. 8, 1851.

 1. Levina, b. Oct. 16, 1833 ; d. Jan. 4, 1849.

 1. Austin, b. May, 1835 ; m. Sarah E. Walker of Winchendon, Jan.
   5, 1860 ; d. Jan. 5, 1861.

  2. Austin Edward, b. Jan. 5, 1861.

 1. Appleton R., b. Dec. 6, 1836 ; m. Minerva A. Bosworth of Royalston, Apr. 5, 1855 ; res. Gardner.

 1. Lucy, b. Jan. 18, 1839 ; m. Frank F. Priest of Gardner.

 1. Darius, b May 7, 1841 ; m. Elmira A. Bosworth of Royalston, Jan.
   28, 1870.

 1. Dorinda, b. Feb. 28, 1843 ; d. Sept. 1, 1863.

 1. Sylvester, b. Feb. 16, 1846 ; rem. Nashua, N. H.

AMHERST, m. Tabitha Pollard, Mar. 30, 1812 ; d. Oct. 8, 1826 ; she d.
   Nov. 15, 1872.

 1. Hannah, b. Sept. 5, 1812 ; m. Ellis Joslin of Leominster.

 1. Mary, b. Mar. 28, 1814 ; m. Hammond Munn of Templeton.

 1. Joel, b. Apr. 8, 1816 ; m. Laura Pratt of New Ipswich, N. H. ; res.
   West Gardner.

 1. Ella Slocomb, b. Aug. 12, 1818 ; m. Mary Ann Pratt of New Ipswich, N. H. ; d. Gardner, 1878.

 1. Eli Amherst, b. Apr. 24, 1823 ; m. Lucy Lufkin ; rem. Barre.

  2. Lucy Emma, b. Aug. 12, 1846.

 1. Philander S., b. Sept. 9, 1825 ; m. Mary Elizabeth Lewis of Westminster ; m. 2d, Catharine Pratt of New Ipswich, N.
   H., who d. 1860 ; he d. Barre.

COLEMAN.

PEREZ, m. Rebecca Clark; d. Oct. 28, 1848, a. 60; she d. Mar. 20. 1854, a. 60.

  1. John M., b. Feb. 17, 1817; m. Hattie Pond, Dec. 24, 1839; rem.

    2. Eliza Anna, b. Apr. 23, 1840.

    2. Mary Rebecca, b. May 15, 1841.

    2. Harriet Adelaide, b. Sept. 11, 1843.

    2. Clara E., b. May 29, 1846; d. Aug. 22, 1849.

  1. Eliza Jane, b. July 1, 1819; d. May 20, 1821.

  1. Stephen C., b. Mar. 7, 1822; d. Apr. 7, 1831.

  1. Perez Gilman, b. June 20, 1823; m. Prudence Murdock, Apr. 26, 1849.

    2. Lemuel E., b. May 16, 1850.

    2. Henry Gilbert, b. May 19, 1851; d. Jan. 10, 1852.

    2. Henry Gilbert, b. Dec. 3, 1852.

    2. Adeline A., b. Aug. 24, 1854; m. Horace Joslin.

    2. Isaac M., b. July 3, 1856.

    2. Mary Ann, b. Sept. 30, 1863.

  1. Eda Ann, b. Oct. 29, 1824; m. Benjamin F. Pierce.

  1. David A., b. Apr. 19, 1828; d. Apr. 18, 1831.

  1. Lemuel F., b. July 13, 1829; d. Sept. 21, 1848.

  1. David C., b. Mar. 18, 1834; d. Oct. 4, 1860.

BENJAMIN FRANKLIN, m. Alice W. Warren, Oct. 27, 1833.

  1. Alice Jane, b. Jan. 9, 1834; m. George S. Bates.

  1. Benjamin Franklin, b. Aug. 7, 1836; d. Oct. 31, 1860.

  1. Christopher Melvin, b. Oct. 29, 1840; d. Jan. 2, 1861.

  1. Delia Ann, b. Dec. 5, 1846; m. Henry H. Lund; d. Aug. 16, 1873.

LAFAYETTE, m. Eunice Green, Apr. 19, 1849; rem. Gardner.

  1. Sarah Augusta, b. July 13, 1851.

CONANT.

LEVI CONANT c. f. Sutton; m. Sarah Foster; d. Dec. 4, 1825, a. 50; she d. Sept. 22, 1849, a. 73.

  1. Levi, b. May 28, 1802; m. Eliza Savage, Feb. 20, 1827; d. Dec. 1, 1878.

    2. Levi W., b. Oct. 3, 1827; m. Mary S. Parkhurst.

    2. Mary Elizabeth, b. Aug. 1, 1830; m. Almander Damon; m. 2d, John B. Flynn.

33

CONANT.

2. Benjamin P., b. May 7, 1832 ; m. Harriet E. Morse, Aug. 10, 1854 ; d. Nov. 22, 1879 ; she d. May 30, 1880.

3. Etta D., b. May 26, 1855 ; m. Elwyn Wheeler.

3. Fred Arthur, b. June 27, 1860 ; d. Oct. 27, 1864.

2. Frances Ann, b. Dec. 13, 1837 ; m. Dumont Marean.

DALRYMPLE.

JONATHAN BRUCE DALRYMPLE c. f. Northboro' ; m. Sylvia Warren of N., 1827, who d. Oct. 14, 1843, a. 42 ; he d. Oct. 28, 1843, a. 39.

1. Charles Henry, b. Sept. 9, 1828 ; m. Rebecca H. Barnes, 1864 : res. Marlboro'.

1. Sarah Sophia, b. Nov. 12, 1829 ; m. Marshall H. Hastings of Shrewsbury, 1848.

1. Hannah Elizabeth, b. Dec. 22, 1830 ; adopted in 1843. by S. D., and Elizabeth Thompson ; name changed to Thompson ; res. Ithaca, N. Y.

1. Samuel Augustine, b. Dec. 5, 1832 ; m. and settled in Ithaca, N. Y.

1. Caleb, b. Sept. 3, 1834 ; name changed to Caleb Warren ; m. a Mrs. Harrington ; res. Washington, Iowa.

1. Wm. Everett, b. Mar. 11, 1836 ; name changed in 1845, to Wm. E. Warren ; m. Lydia Elvira Houghton of Vernon, Vt., 1859, who d. 1872 ; m. 2d, Sarah Houghton of Vernon, Vt., 1873 ; res. Worcester.

DAMON.

ALONZO DAMON c. f. Springfield, Vt. ; m. Harriet E. Osgood, who d. Feb. 1, 1861 ; [see p. 167 ;] m. 2d, Mary (Ball) Grimes, Sept. 4, 1861.

1. Eugene Alonzo, b. May 29, 1846 ; d. Leominster, June 24, 1875.

1. Mary Jane, b. Sept. 12, 1851.

1. George W., b. Oct. 24, 1857 ; d. Feb. 1, 1861. [See p. 167.]

ALMANDER, bro. of ALONZO, c. f. Springfield, Vt. ; m. Mary Elizabeth Conant, June 1, 1854.

1. Herbert, b. Sept. 9, 1855 ; m. Amy A. Parkhurst, May 1, 1878.

1. Alfred Levi, b. Aug. 27, 1857.

1. Alice Eliza, b. Apr. 1, 1860 ; d. Apr. 13, 1860.

DAVIS.

Several families named Davis resided here between 1770 and 1800.

BRIGHAM DAVIS c. f. Holden ; m. Sally Warren, who d. Apr. 27, 1845 ;
   he d. Aug. 22, 1844, a. 59.

1. Caroline, b. July 4, 1810 ; d. May 16, 1816.
1. John Warren, b. Sept. 8, 1813 ; m. Nancy Gray, Oct. 22, 1844 ; d.
   Sept. 10, 1845.
   2. John Warren, b. Aug. 23, 1845 ; d. Dec. 1, 1845.
1. Harriet, b. Feb. 21, 1816 ; d. Dec. 21, 1816.
1. Joseph E., b. Mar. 29, 1820 ; d. Mar. 11, 1831.
1. Sarah Ann, b. Aug. 12, 1823 ; d. Jan. 12, 1844.
1. Carlo B., b. May 3, 1826 ; m. Chloe Broad of Barre, July 20, 1847.
   2. Walter Warren, b. July 22, 1852 ; d. Oct. 1, 1852.
   2. George Henry, b. Sept. 24, 1855.

ISRAEL, bro. of BRIGHAM, c. f. Holden ; m. Sarah Holt, who d. July 27,
   1859, a. 95 ; he d. Aug. 24, 1848, a. 82.

1. Sally, b. Jan. 15, 1794.
1. Israel, b. June 19, 1803 ; m. Chloe W. Waite, Nov. 2, 1824, who
   d. Oct. 21, 1842 ; m. 2d, Lois (Stone) Williams, May 30,
   1848, who d. Sept. 22, 1875 ; he d. Oct. 24, 1872.
   2. Harriet Waite, b. Aug. 5, 1825 ; d. Sept. 21, 1851.
   2. John Sumner, b. July 22, 1827.
   2. Sarah, b. Mar. 9, 1831 ; d. May 18, 1846.
   2. George Hill, b. Mar. 14, 1849 ; m. Rosilla Hager of Athol, June
      1, 1876.
      3. Walter George, b. Aug. 12, 1878.
      3. Warren Horace, b. Jan. 12, 1880.
   2. Horace M., b. Nov. 12, 1850.

ISAAC DAVIS c. f. Princeton, 1829 ; m. Catherine Woodward, May 3, 1842.
1. Myron W., b. July 6, 1844 ; res. Utah.
1. Abby Louisa, b. June 25, 1848 ; m. Edward C. Hamilton.
1. Mary Lizzie, b. Nov. 4, 1857.
1. Ella Althine, b. Nov. 27, 1860 ; d. Oct. 3, 1862.
1. Carrie Rachel, b. Aug. 18, 1863.

SILAS DAVIS c. f. Templeton ; m. Patty Peirce, June 9, 1811, who d. Mar.
   25, 1831 ; m. 2d, Betsey (Rice) Underwood, Dec., 1831 ;
   d. Aug. 17, 1832 ; she res. Spencer.
1. Amasa Gay, b. Oct. 28, 1811 ; m. Polly Goodspeed, Feb. 26, 1835,

DAVIS.

who d. Aug. 8, 1839; m. 2d, Alice Pollard, May 13,
1841, who d. Mar. 18, 1845; m. 3d, Catherine Pierce,
May 9, 1846, who d. Sept. 20, 1851; m. 4th, Maria
D. Lincoln, July 1, 1852.

2. Abby Price, b. Nov. 9, 1835; m. Joseph Arnold of Milwaukee, Wis.

2. Alice Maria, b. Feb. 1, 1854; m. Amos Armsby of Millbury, Oct.
31, 1877.

2. Charles Sumner, b. June 7, 1859; d. July 16, 1860.

1. Silas Sumner, b. Oct. 12, 1812.

1. Alvin, b. Dec. 19, 1817; m. and settled in Elmira, N. Y.

1. Moses, b. Aug. 31, 1820; m. Hattie Sargent, Dec. 30, 1845, who
d. May 4, 1858; m. 2d, Ann (Clark) Mann, Sept. 10, 1861.

1. Charles, b. Nov. 7, 1826.

1. Marvin Augustine, } b. Jan. 29, 1829; res. Princeton.
1. Martha Augusta, } m. John Taylor of R. I.

1. John, b. Mar. 4, 1831; lawyer; res. Lowell; m. Lizzie Stearns of
Lowell, Oct. 6, 1880.

EZEKIEL GARDNER DAVIS c. f. Templeton; m. Lydia S. Kendall; m. 2d,
Julia (Goddard) Brown; m. 3d, Mrs. Harring-
ton of Oakham; rem. Oakham.

1. Ann Susanna, b. Aug. 15, 1828; d. Apr. 18, 1853.

1. Azor Zadoc, b. Sept. 26, 1830.

1. Eliza Rogers, b. Dec. 21, 1832; m. J. S. Turner, who d. June 21, 1875.

1. Ellen Maria, b. Mar. 18, 1835; m. Charles Oliver.

1. Fanny Zebiah, b. Mar. 7, 1837; m. A. F. King.

1. Jennette Josephine, b. Jan. 29, 1841; m. Chas. D. Fisher.

1. Ezekiel Gardner, b. Jan. 16, 1844; m. Eliza (Morrow) Holt, Feb.
6, 1867; rem. Athol.

2. Hattie Mabel, b. July 12, 1868.

1. Frederick Edgar, b. June 1, 1846; m. Elizabeth Susan Clark, Jan.
2, 1868, who d. Feb. 14, 1875.

2. Charles Alson, b. Oct. 16, 1868.

1. Lydia Elsie, b. Aug. 27, 1849; m. Frederick W. Maynard, Sept. 9, 1867.

JOHN DAVIS c. f. Rutland; m. Priscilla Gerry of Leominster, Apr. 14,
1827, who d. Apr. 15, 1832, a 29; m. 2d, Adeline Allen, May
3, 1836; rem.

1. Charles, b. Aug. 29, 1829; d. Sep. 6, 1831.

DAVIS.

1. John, b. Sept. 11, 1831 ; m. Mary A. Lovering of Auburn, Feb. 20, 1857.
1. Adeline Elizabeth, b. Jan. 29, 1837.
1. Lydia Allen, b. Mar. 12, 1839 ; m. Jason W. Whitney of Princeton. Nov. 18, 1857.
1. Sarah Maria, b. Feb. 5, 1841 ; m. Geo. F. Whitney of Princeton. Oct. 18, 1863.
1. Harriet, b. Oct. 30, 1844 ; d. Dec. 6, 1844.
1. Mary Harriet, b. Feb. 27, 1847 ; m. Chas. W. Spring of Boston. Sept. 20, 1870.
1. George Herbert, b. Apr. 22, 1849 ; m. Abbie A. Lincoln of Hingham, June 18, 1873.
1. James Walter, b. June 15, 1851 ; m. Ellen D. Winchester of Gardner, June 14, 1875.
1. Frank Hall, b. Oct. 7, 1856.
1. Alice Josephine, b. Aug. 22, 1859.

JOHN DAVIS c. f. Templeton : m. Dolly H. Warren. Oct. 17, 1842 ; d. Oct. 23, 1876, a. 57. [See p. 168.]
1. Maria E., b. Dec. 27, 1843 ; d. Feb. 27, 1844.
1. George H., b. Nov. 18, 1844 ; d. Nov. 11, 1855.
1. James Alfred, b. May 27, 1850 ; m. Mattie L. Chase of N. H., July 15, 1874.
  2. Alfred Chase, b. Sept. 15, 1875.
  2. Fannie Faith, b. June 13, 1879.
1. Stella Louisa, b. July 31, 1854 ; m. Florus D. Ramsdell of Gardner, June 3, 1873.

DEWEY.

FRANCIS H. DEWEY c. f. Belchertown ; m. Nancy A. Holt, Feb. 13, 1849.
1. Elias Herbert, b. May 11, 1850.
1. Alice Maria, b. Sept. 27, 1852 ; d. May 24, 1857.
1. Abby Ruth, b. June 13, 1855 ; d. June 13, 1857.
1. Francis Arthur, b. Sept. 18, 1857.
1. Merta N., b. Sept. 8, 1859 ; d. Oct. 20, 1859.
1. Henry Gerould, b. Feb. 2, 1861 ; d. Aug. 30, 1861.
1. Vernet Erving, b. Feb. 10, 1863 ; d. June 2, 1864.
1. Charles Erving, b. July 22, 1864.
1. Stella Augusta, b. Jan. 16, 1871.

DEXTER.

JONATHAN DEXTER c. f. Hardwick, Mar., 1837; m. Roxana Dean of
    Raynham, 1812; d. Mar. 14, 1856, a. 70; she d.
    Sept. 5, 1872, a. 83.
1. Cassandra D., b. Sept. 1, 1813; m. Lemuel F. Taylor.
1. Jonathan, b. Oct. 23, 1815; rem. Missouri.
1. Benjamin, b. Dec. 28, 1817.

DUNBAR.

RICHARD DUNBAR c. f. Newton, 1876; m. Mary Galway of Newton, Dec.
    16, 1869.
1. Susan Jane, b. Oct. 24, 1870.
1. Annie Elizabeth, b. Mar. 1, 1872.
1. William Samuel, b. Nov. 3, 1874.
1. Richard, b. Oct. 25, 1878.

DUNTON.

SYLVANUS DUNTON c. f. Barre; m. Susan Newton, Feb. 18, 1830; d. Apr.
    11, 1863; she d. Aug. 11, 1873.
1. Mary Elizabeth, b. Aug. 8, 1831; m. Horace Underwood.
1. Susan Maria, b. Apr. 4, 1834; d. July 30, 1852.
1. Ann Sophia, b. Feb. 7, 1837; res. Worcester.
1. Sarah Jane, b. May 6, 1839; d. Feb. 4, 1853.
1. Lucia Leuann, b. May 2, 1841; m. Lemuel P. Rice of Barre, Mar.
    26, 1863.
1. Sybil Metcalf, b. Aug. 11, 1843; d. Feb. 25, 1844.
1. Sylvanus Newton, b. Apr. 16, 1846; m. Mary A. Laughna, July
    20, 1868; rem.
2. James Newton, b. Aug. 30, 1869.

EARLE.

JOEL EARLE c. f. Leicester; m. Persis Witt, who d. Mar. 3, 1817; m. 2d,
    Phebe (Trask) Spring, Mar. 21, 1819; d. Mt. Holly, Vt.,
    May 2, 1836, a. 77.
1. Willard, b. Nov. 9, 1783; m. Rhoda Adams, Jan. 31, 1815; d.
    June 17, 1851; she d. Oct. 23, 1875.
2. Rebecca, b. Nov. 18, 1815; d. Dec. 7, 1815.
2. William C., b. Apr. 1, 1817; d. Mar. 4, 1831.

EARLE.

2. Lorinda M., b. Dec. 9, 1819; d. May 22, 1820.

2. Sarah E., b. Mar. 24, 1822; m. Amasa Cox of Worcester; res. Ill.

2. Persis, b. Jan. 11, 1824; m. Edwin Chapin of Worcester; d. Mar. 26, 1867.

2. William W., b. Aug. 31, 1830; d. Apr. 26, 1861.

2. Charles N., b. Nov. 23, 1833; m. Charity Price of Ill.; rem. Ill.

2. Louisa, b. Apr. 15, 1836; d. Sept. 1, 1854.

1. Alpheus, b. Dec. 16, 1785; m. Lucretia Murdock, Mar. 31, 1808; d. Jan. 24, 1849; she d. Jan. 16, 1863.

2. Jonathan Parker, b. Feb. 1, 1810; m. Sylvia Hamilton, Apr. 16, 1835, who d. Oct. 3, 1860; m. 2d, Mary Ann Humes, May, 1867.

   3. George P., b. Oct. 1, 1836; m. Charlotte Greenwood, Feb. 9, 1865; rem. Exeter N. H.; d. Mar. 25, 1876.

   3. Harriet Lavinia, b. July 28, 1841; m. Israel Dickinson of Westminster, Jan. 20, 1869.

2. Harriet, b. Feb. 5, 1815; d. Aug. 9, 1819.

2. Lucretia, b. June 1, 1817; d. Sept. 8, 1843.

2. Betsey, b. Dec. 28, 1818; m. George W. Hamilton.

2. James, b. Dec. 7, 1823; m. Mary E. Flint, June 14, 1855.

2. Sumner, b. Mar. 3, 1827; d. Oct. 9, 1843.

2. William Homer, b. May 21, 1831; m. Sarah P. Greenwood, Nov. 25, 1856; res. Worcester.

   3. Alice Mabel, b. July 22, 1860.

   3. Willie Greenwood, b. July 25, 1866.

1. Polly, b. Mar. 2, 1788; rem. Vt.

1. Calvin, b. Feb. 1, 1790; m. Betsey Foster, Sept. 13, 1814; rem. Iowa; both d. Iowa.

2. John W., b. Aug., 1824; m. Sarah Jane Williams, Nov. 10, 1846, who d. Mar. 14, 1850; rem. Iowa.

2. Clark A., b. 1828; m. Lizzie Taylor of Winchendon, 1850; res. E. Templeton.

2. Willard b. 1833; m. and settled in Waukon, Iowa.

2. Ann Maria, b. 1841; d. Mar. 20, 1857.

1. Eli, b. Jan. 30, 1792; rem. Medford.

1. Persis, b. Sept. 8, 1793; m. Daniel Hemenway of Barre; d. Barre.

1. Silas, b. Feb. 25, 1798; m. Mary Willard, who d. Vt.; m. 2d, Lu-

EARLE.

cina Humes, who d. Apr. 13, 1868 ; m. 3d, Mary (Rice) Fisk, Mar. 2, 1869, who d. Gardner.

1. Tyler, b. Feb. 12, 1800 ; m. Annis Morse of Holden, Feb. 2, 1826 ; d. May 15, 1877.
2. Rhoda, b. Jan. 23, 1827 ; m. Nahum Lovewell.
2. Willard, b. Mar. 3, 1830 ; d. Dec. 7, 1831.
2. Fanny, b. Sept. 4, 1833 ; m. William B. Goddard of Royalston.
2. Royal T., b. Oct. 18, 1837 ; d. Oct. 26, 1837.
1. Sophia, b. Nov. 5, 1802 ; m. Loring Goulding ; both d. Oswego, N.Y.
1. Sumner, b. Nov. 5, 1802 ; d. Weston, Vt.
1 Fanny, b. June 17, 1804 ; m. Jonas Pierce of Royalston ; res. Springfield.

ELLINWOOD.

JUSTUS ELLINWOOD c. f. Athol, 1812 ; m. Sophia McClenathan, July 14, 1814 ; d. Sept. 4, 1844, a. 58 ; she d. Sept. 21, 1851.

1. Charles, b. Nov. 18, 1814 ; d. Oct. 23, 1820. [See p. 166.]
1. Phebe, b. July 8, 1817 ; m. Richard Leonard.
1. Addison, b. Aug. 4, 1820 ; m. Phebe Warren, Mar. 8, 1842 ; d. May 25, 1843.
1. Adeline, b. May 28, 1823 ; m. Rufus H. Chase of Worcester, Apr. 20, 1843 ; d. Dec. 3, 1854.
1. Charles A., b. July 21, 1825 ; m. Ann M. Williams, Dec. 30, 1846 ; res. Worcester.
    2. Abby Annette, b. May 7, 1849 ; d. Apr. 19, 1851.
    2. Jennie E., b. Feb. 22, 1852 ; d. Oct. 19, 1861.
    2. Addison Justus, b. Sept. 13, 1853 ; d. Dec. 2, 1855.
    2. Chas. N., b. Sept. 20, 1860 ; d. Oct. 15, 1860.
1. Lucy b. Aug. 31, 1828, m. Manlius May, Mar. 17, 1858, who d. Oct. 31, 1871 ; res. Boston.

EVELETH.

ABISHAI EVELETH c. f. Princeton ; m. Mary Joslin, Feb., 1818 ; both d. Princeton.

1. William J., b. Mar. 10, 1818 ; m. Mary Peirce, Nov. 1, 1842, who d. Dec. 15, 1861 ; m. 2d, Harriet Greenwood, Oct. 17, 1862.

EVELETH.

2. Ella Annette, b. July 30, 1847; m. J. Warren Dunn, Apr. 22, 1869; res. Keene, N. H.
2. Bertha Estelle, b. Aug. 30, 1864; d. June, 22, 1865.[See p. 167.]
2. William Greenwood, b. Jan. 24, 1867; d. May 14, 1871.

FALIS.

JOHN H. FALIS c. f. Germany during the War of the Revolution; m. Phebe
——, of Woburn, who d. Oct. 14, 1839, a. 78; he d.
Feb. 19, 1817, a. 77.
1. James, b. Dec. 5, 1782; m. Martha Smith of Westminster, Aug. 17, 1806, who d. Apr. 30, 1813; m. 2d, Susan Davis of Princeton, Feb., 1814, who d. May 17, 1866, a. 78; he d. Nov. 13, 1841.
2. Freelove, b. Aug. 23, 1808; m. P. W. Lee of Princeton.
2. Joseph S., b. Aug. 10, 1810; m. Lucy D. Whitcomb.
2. Martha, b. July 28, 1814; m. Bainbridge Hayward; res. Milford.
2. Henry, b. Jan. 31, 1817; m. Adelaide Macomber; d. Dec. 26, 1865.
3. Mary Melissa, b. Jan. 15, 1856.
3. Henry. b. Aug. 12, 1858.
3. Harriet Elizabeth, b. Feb. 6, 1863.
2. Jarvis, b. Nov. 4, 1822.
2. Melissa, b. 1828; d. July 9, 1858.
1. Phebe, b. Feb. 13, 1785; m. Daniel Mundell.

FARWELL.

HENRY A. FARWELL c. f. Worcester, 1876; m. Alice A. Benneson of Quincy, Ill., June 27, 1870.
1. Robert Benneson, b. Mar. 25, 1871.
1. Seymour Allston, b. Dec. 8, 1872.
1. Oscar John. b. Jan. 24, 1875.
1. Theodore Channing, b. Jan. 24, 1877.
1. Henry Warren, b. Nov. 29, 1878; d. Apr. 21, 1880. [See p. 166.]
1. Clarence Gilbert, b. Oct. 16, 1880.

FELTON.

NATHAN H. FELTON c. f. Barre; m. Caroline A. Williams, May 2, 1844.

34

FELTON.

1. George W., b. Jan. 31. 1845 ; m. Leonora A. Savage, Mar. 9, 1868 ;
   res. Orange.
   2. Arthur Eugene, b. Sept. 9, 1868.
   2. Marion A., b. Sept. 9, 1870 ; d. Aug. 19, 1871.
   2. Marion Louise, b. May 3, 1880 ; d. July 28, 1880.
1. Susan A., b. June 18, 1850 ; d. Dec. 18, 1870.
1. Carrie R., b. Mar. 25, 1852 ; m. Alexander G. Williams of Barre,
   Sept. 14, 1871.
1. Edward M., b. Jan. 26, 1855 ; d. Nov. 1, 1870.
1. Arthur P., b. July 18, 1860.
1. Mary Bell, b. Jan. 7, 1862.

FISHER.

CHARLES D. FISHER c. f. Athol ; m. Jeanette Josephine Davis.
1. Fred Austin, b. July 11, 1859 ; d. July 10, 1877.
1. Alice Lincoln, b. Sept. 15, 1866.
1. Louise D. Wright, b. Jan. 27, 1879.

FLAGG.

JOSHUA FLAGG c. f. Lunenburg ; m. Almira Smith, Feb., 16, 1826, who
   d. Mar. 9, 1860 ; he d. July 23. 1873. a. 75.
1. Mary Elizabeth, b. Jan. 20, 1827 ; m. William Broad, who d. Jan.
   22, 1873 : she d. Nov. 11, 1861.
1. Almira A., b. Mar. 7, 1829 : m. Hiram K. Davis of New Braintree,
   Oct. 26, 1842 ; m. 2d, William Hill ; d. Jan. 13, 1864.
1. John E., b. Nov. 13, 1830 ; m. Jane Forbush, Oct. 23, 1860.
   2. John Franklin, b. July 22, 1861.
   2. Jennie Izette, b. July 12, 1864.
1. Joel S., b. Apr. 21, 1832 ; m. Minerva R. Spooner from Vt., Sept.
   15, 1850.
   2. Charles F., b. Aug. 23, 1853 ; m. Blanche J. Flynn, Mar. 18, 1874.
      3. Harry John, b. Feb. 22, 1875.
      3. Abby Minerva, b. Dec. 15, 1876.
      3. Gertrude Madge, b. Feb. 2, 1879.
   2. Alfred Clarence, b. July 22, 1856.
   2. Herbert W., b. June 3, 1858.
   2. Gilbert Henry, b. Jan. 8, 1860.
   2. Emma H., b. May 10, 1861.

FLAGG.

1. Amanda. b. Mar. 17, 1834 ; d. Sept. 18, 1843.
1. Martha, b. Feb. 3, 1837 ; m. Freeman Chamberlain of Barre.
1. Silas, b. May 18, 1841 ; d. army, June 16, 1864. [See p. 139.]
1. Joshua, b. Dec. 31, 1842.
1. Levi, b. Jan. 20, 1845 ; d. army, Sept. 9, 1863. [See p. 137.]
1. Lucy, b. Nov. 14, 1846 ; d. Nov. 14, 1847.
1. George W., b. May 5, 1849.
1. Elijah, b. Feb. 27, 1852 ; d. Mar. 16, 1852.
1. Lucy A., b. May 8, 1853 ; m. Charles L. Cleveland, Apr. 4, 1869.

JOSIAH. bro. of JOSHUA, c. f. Lunenburg ; d. Dec. 21, 1867, a. 64.

FLETCHER.

JOSEPH FLETCHER c. f. Sterling (?) m. Eliza Marean, Aug. 25, 1825, who d. Townsend, Mar. 6, 1878.
1. Walter Dana, b. Nov. 14, 1825 ; res. Townsend.
1. Frances Elizabeth, b. May 13, 1828 ; m. Wm. M. Bennett ; rem.
1. Aaron Varnum, b. Feb. 8, 1831 ; rem. : d. Worcester.

FLINT.

SAMUEL FLINT c. f. Templeton, 1850 ; m. Elvira Raymond of Westminster, Nov. 15, 1832 ; d. Jan. 22, 1866, a 66.
1. Mary Eliza, b. Sept. 22, 1833 ; m. James Earle.
1. William, b. May 11, 1835 ; m. Mary Derby of Ashburnham, Dec., 1860 ; d. army, Mar. 14, 1862.
1. Benjamin, b. Nov. 4, 1836 ; d. Apr. 9. 1840.
1. Daniel Webster, b. Feb. 1, 1839 ; d. Mar. 3, 1840.
1. Melissa, b. Oct. 8, 1841 ; d. Sept. 18, 1849.
1. Harrison. b. July 16, 1843.
1. Almira C., b. June 29, 1845.
1. Abijah Raymond, b. Sept. 29, 1851.

FLYNN.

JOHN B. FLYNN c. f. Maine ; m. Abby Studley, Apr. 11, 1840, who d. Dec. 29, 1867, a. 45 ; m. 2d, Mary Elizabeth (Conant) Damon, Feb. 10, 1869.
1. Alice Jane, b. Aug., 1841 : d. Apr. 10, 1851.
1. James S., b. Oct. 22, 1843 ; m. Louisa M. Williams, Dec. 19, 1872 ; d. Feb. 5, 1875.

FLYNN.

1. Mary Ella. b. Aug. 10, 1845 ; m. Moses G. Hobbs.
1. John B., b. Aug. 22, 1847.
1. Abby Henrietta, b. Apr. 8, 1849 ; m. Henry B. Phelps.
1. Blanche Jane. b. May 24, 1851 ; m. Charles F. Flagg.
1. Edward Estes, b. Mar. 9, 1853; m. Helen Giles of Worcester,
    Sept. 30, 1877.
1. Frank Pierce, b. May 10, 1856; d. Mar. 28, 1857.
1. Helen Eliza, b. Dec. 12, 1869.

FOLLETT.

SAMUEL FOLLETT c. f. Attleboro' ; a soldier in the French and Indian
    War, he was taken captive and carried to Martinique ; m.
    Sarah Metcalf. 1775. who d. Mar. 22, 1783. a. 28 ; m.
    2d, Tamar Smith of Dedham, Nov., 1783, who d. Dec.
    19. 1803. a. 48 : he d. Nov. 13, 1803. a. 58.

1. Sally. b. Nov. 14. 1775 ; m. Thomas Howe of Templeton : rem.
    Rindge. N. H.
1. Samuel. b. Oct. 7. 1777 ; m. Sally Phelps ; rem. Jamaica, Vt.
1. Isaac, b. July 25. 1779 ; m. Lucy W. Rice of Templeton, Feb. 18.
    1809 ; d. Mar. 25, 1844.
    2. Eliza. b. Nov. 22, 1809 ; m. Pliny Lamb.
    2. Lucy W., b. Sept. 12, 1811 ; m. Horace Waite.
    2. Rusha R., b. Aug. 1, 1813 ; m. John F. Woodward.
    2. Sarah, b. Sept. 24, 1815 ; m. Wm. E. Leland of Templeton, Jan.
        26, 1839.
    2. Charlotte N., b. Aug. 14, 1817.
    2. Jonas, b. Apr. 7. 1820 ; d. Feb. 12, 1869.
    2. Isaac, b. July 25, 1822 ; m. Susan B. Goulding of Millbury, May
        18, 1861, who d. Dec. 31, 1862.
    2. Mary Ann S., b. Feb. 3, 1825 ; m. Moses C. Wheeler.
    2. John. b. Apr. 24, 1833 ; d. Mo.
1. John, b. Feb. 26, 1781 ; d. Sept. 20, 1803.
1. Caty, b. Feb. 26, 1783 ; m. William Bennett.
1. Otis, b. Sept. 11, 1784 ; d. Nov. 11, 1803.
1. Jonathan Metcalf, b. Feb. 26, 1789 ; m. Mary Wheat of Putney,
    Vt., June, 1816, who d. Apr. 1, 1871, a. 86 ;
    he d. Aug. 14, 1864.
    2. Mary Abigail, b. Apr. 3, 1817 ; d. Sept. 20, 1821.

FOLLETT.

2. Aaron, b. Apr. 5, 1819 ; d. Oct. 22, 1849.

2. 'Samuel, b. May 26, 1823 ; res. Barre.

2. James, b. Apr. 21, 1825 ; d. July 9, 1827.

2. Lyman, b. Aug. 25, 1827.

2. Cynthia, b. Sept. 8, 1830 ; m. Luke S. Moore.

1. Rhoda, b. Dec. 28, 1790 ; m. Joseph Stone of Winchendon.

1. Aaron, b. 1794 ; d. July 28, 1800.

FORBUSH.

AARON FORBUSH c. f. Orange, 1852 ; m. Sarah Fisher of Warwick, Jan. 5, 1841, who d. Mar. 21, 1851 ; m. 2d, Elizabeth M. Holt, Nov. 30, 1854.

1. Sarah J., b Dec. 6, 1841 ; m. John E. Flagg.

1. Alice I., b. Oct. 31, 1848 ; m. Albert Williams of Montague.

1. Ethel, b. Apr. 20, 1863 ; d. Apr. 21, 1863.

1. Freddie E., b. Sept. 24, 1864.

1. Franklin L., b. Mar. 15, 1871.

FROST.

STEPHEN FROST c. f. Rutland ; m. Mary Warren of Brighton ; d. June 18, 1828 ; she d. Mar. 31, 1851, a. 82.

1. Stephen, b. Aug. 15, 1789 ; m. Pamelia Powers, who d. Apr. 18, 1860, a. 77 ; rem. Shutesbury.

2. Milton, b. Aug. 21, 1815 ; rem. ; d. Ashby .

2. Pamelia, b. Jan. 2, 1817 ; m. Horatio Wheeler of Gardner ; res. Ashby.

2. John, b. Sept. 24, 1818 ; d. Sept. 11, 1825.

1. Benjamin C., b. Mar. 19, 1792 ; m. Lydia B. Rice of Wendell, Apr. 17, 1817, who d. July 29, 1864, a. 65 ; he d. July 13, 1873.

2. Lucy, b. Feb. 5, 1818 ; m. L. McGlaflin of Worcester ; d. Middleton, Mar. 31, 1873.

2. Sumner, b. Nov. 23, 1819 ; m. Lura Stone, Nov. 8, 1848 ; d. army, Dec. 28, 1864. [See p. 139.]

3. Roswell Leroy, b. Dec. 4, 1849 ; res. Brattleboro', Vt.

3. Myron Ashley, b. June 25, 1851 ; res. Brattleboro', Vt.

3. Ida Etta, b. Jan. 1, 1855 ; m. George Winter of Barre.

FROST.

2. William. b. June 23. 1823 ; rem.Worcester ; d. army, Mar.11,1862.
2. Jane G., b. May 1, 1825 ; d. Worcester, Dec. 18, 1874. ·
2. Benjamin. b. Nov. 29, 1827 ; m. Louisa Cowden of Rutland ; d. Rutland, July 6, 1853.
2. Mary, b. July 1, 1830 ; m. Charles Blanchard of N. H., Oct. 24, 1852, who d. Sept. 20, 1863.
2. Lydia Elvira, b. Mar. 2, 1834 ; m. Lloyd Manning of Templeton.
2. Hannah S., b. Nov. 13, 1836 ; m. Francis Rice.
1. Sally, b. Aug. 8, 1794 ; m. Joseph Bartlett of Rutland, July 1, 1810, who d. Mar. 27, 1838, a. 46.
1. Ruth. b. May 1, 1796 ; m. Elias Holt.
1. Polly, b. Mar. 18, 1798 ; m. John Phelps ; m. 2d, Joseph Wright.
1. William W., b. Oct. 4. 1800 ; rem. Hardwick.
1. Ebenezer, b. Aug. 18. 1802 ; rem. Ashburnham.
1. Hannah, b. Dec. 19. 1805 : m. Greenleaf Lamb.
1. Hitty, b. June 6, 1808 ; m. Charles Wesson ; rem.
1. Hermon. b. Sept. 18. 1812 : m. Abigail Green ; rem. Ill. ; d. there.
2. Hervey, b. June 16. 1847.
2. Sybil W., b. Aug. 25. 1850.
2. Hermon, b. Oct. 29. 1852.

GATES.

JONATHAN GATES c. f. Rutland, 1770 ; m. Hepzibah Stone, Apr. 26, 1770 ; d. Sept. 30, 1808, a. 62 : she d. Dec. 25, 1818, a. 72.
1. Hepzibah. b. Mar. 14. 1771 ; m. Reuben Clapp, Dec. 29, 1791 ; rem. Montgomery, Vt.
1. Stephen, b. Sept. 21. 1772 ; rem. Vt.
1. David, b. July 11, 1774 ; d. June 2. 1775.
1. Aaron. b. Apr. 26, 1776 ; m. Mehitable Woodward, Mar. 30, 1802, who d. Oct. 19, 1849 ; he d. Dec. 5, 1849.
2. Belinda. b. Mar. 16. 1803 ; m. Moses Kendall, July 2, 1833 ; d. Jan. 20. 1846.
2. Thomas Jefferson, b. Feb. 18, 1806 ; d. Apr. 2, 1806.
2. Jonathan. b. Apr. 27, 1810 ; m. Freelove Stone, Oct. 6, 1842.
3. Roswell Catline. b. Apr. 8, 1844 ; d. Feb. 22, 1846.
3. Aaron. b. Aug. 9. 1845 ; d. Aug. 17, 1845.
3. Mornilra, b. July 24, 1846.
3. Alice Freelove, b. Nov. 15, 1848.

GATES.

3. Charlotte Hill, b. Feb. 8, 1851 ; m. Oliver M. Davis of Brookline, N. H., Mar. 2, 1874 ; m. 2d, George L. Esty of Worcester.
3. Emma Melissa, b. Mar. 27, 1853 ; m. Sumner Young.
3. Clara Hall, b. Sept. 1, 1855.
3. Horatio, b. Aug. 4, 1857.
3. Ann E., b. Sept. 4, 1859 ; d. Nov. 17, 1859.
2. Elbridge Gerry, b. Apr. 12, 1812 ; d. Dec. 8, 1812.
2. Hepzibah, b. Mar. 21, 1816.
2. Stephen, b. July 16, 1817 ; m. Sarah Ann Pinney of Potsdam. N. Y., Apr. 30, 1856 ; rem. Bangor, N. Y. ; d. Feb. 12, 1871.
1 Delphos, b. Dec. 20, 1777 ; m. Sally Howe of Rutland, Apr., 1803, who d. June 20, 1816 ; m. 2d, Hannah Pollard, Mar. 4, 1817, who d. Dec. 4, 1825 ; he d. Sept. 15, 1837.
2. John Nelson, b. May 9, 1808 ; m. Elmira Stone, Jan. 20, 1831 ; d. Apr. 2, 1837.
3. Horatio N., b. June 11, 1834 ; d. army, Oct. 12, 1862.
2. Minerva, b. Mar. 27, 1811 ; m. Crusoe Kendall, Apr. 9, 1833, who d. May 26, 1843 ; m. 2d, Silas Joslin.
2. Francis, b. Dec. 22, 1814 ; m. Lucy Wright, Oct. 11, 1838 : d. Aug. 30, 1846.
3. Irving Chester, b. June 10, 1839 ; rem. Groton, Vt.
2. Horace, b. June 28, 1818 ; m. Jane Gordon of Boston ; rem. San Francisco, Cal.
2. Sylvia, b. Dec. 20, 1820 ; m. Dexter How, Apr. 24, 1843 ; d. N. Y. City, July 7, 1854.
1. Thaddeus, b. Aug. 19, 1779 ; m. Sally Case of Conn., 1800 ; d. Feb. 22, 1810 ; she d. N. Y.
2. Horatio, b. Feb. 23, 1801 ; m. Hannah Head of N. Y. ; rem. Buffalo, N. Y. ; d. Feb. 14, 1852.
2. Betsey, b. Jan. 19, 1803 ; m. Peter Vunk of N. Y.
2. Urbin, b. Aug. 2, 1804 ; d. young.
1. Elizabeth, b. Dec. 8, 1781 ; m. John Davis of Princeton, Apr. 5, 1804 ; d. Mar. 5, 1805.
1. Salmon, b. Aug. 30, 1783 ; m. Lucy Church, May 28, 1804, who d. Aug. 10, 1844 ; rem. Calais, Me. ; d. Apr. 9, 1845.
2. Emeline, b. Aug. 4, 1804 ; m. Gorham Kimball of Maine.

GATES.

2. Caroline, b. Dec. 25, 1805 ; d. Sept. 30, 1808.
2. Harriet I., b. Nov. 5, 1807.
2. Martha. b. Aug. 11, 1813.
2. Asa Church, b. Aug. 17, 1815 ; m. ——— Wentworth.
2. Ephraim C., b. Mar. 28, 1817.
2. Lucy, b. Oct. 21, 1819 ; m. Giles M. Wentworth of Maine.
2. Salmon Stephen, b. Calais, Maine.
1. Jonathan, b. Jan. 15, 1787 ; m. Roxa Green, Jan. 1, 1809 ; rem. Vt. ; d. Jan., 1851.
2. Maria, b. Mar. 17, 1816 ; m. Edmund A. Pollard.

CLARK GATES c. f. Barre ; m. Margaret Fessenden, who d. July 26, 1851, a. 64 ; he d. Dec. 6, 1854, a. 68.

1. Amphion ; m. Charlotte Jones of Dorchester, who d. Aug. 7, 1879 ; res. Dorchester.
1. Corydon ; m. Marianna Ballou ; d. Cal., Feb., 1878.
1. Seromus ; m. Lemira Heywood of Ashby ; res. Waverly.
1. Seallum, b. 1822 ; m. Emily Bullard of Princeton, Aug. 21, 1844, who d. Oct. 9, 1846 ; m. 2d. Louisa Bennett, Feb. 1, 1848 ; rem. Minn.
2. Seallum. b. Aug. 12, 1846 : d. Sept. 15, 1846.
2. Sarah J.. b. Sept. 4, 1851.
2. Emma Elizabeth, b. Apr. 9, 1854.
1. Clesrow, b. Oct. 9, 1823 ; m. Nancy Elvira Pond, Nov. 24, 1846, who d. Dec. 12, 1860 ; m. 2d, Mary P. (Chickering) Rice, July 3, 1861 ; rem. Princeton.
2. Ada L., b. July 22, 1851.
2. Ardelie Louisa. b. Aug. 6, 1854 ; d. Aug. 10, 1855.
2. Montore. b. Aug. 8, 1856.
2. Vertland, b. Jan. 8, 1859.

EBENEZER GATES c. f. Worcester , m. Hannah W. Hinds, Feb. 12, 1829 ; d. Feb. 19, 1854. a. 66.

1. John D., b. Nov. 3, 1829.
1. Sarah E.,b.Sept. 2, 1831 ; m. Samuel M. Brown of Vt. ; res. Gardner.
1. Persis A., b. Mar. 17, 1834 ; m. Samuel White of Lunenburg.
1. Hannah H., b. Dec. 30, 1837 ; m. Henry F. Russell of Petersham, who d. army, Jan. 9, 1863. [See p. 142.]
1. William. b. May 8, 1843 ; d. Apr. 18, 1863. [See p. 139.]

GAY.

Abner Gay c. f. Dedham ; m. Caty Marean, Apr. 27, 1797 ; d. Apr. 11,
1851, a. 81 ; she d. Apr. 13, 1862.

1. Charles Pinkney, b. Aug. 8, 1799 ; m. Dolly Hinds, Mar. 9, 1826 ;
d. Oct. 2, 1849.

 2. Charles Jarvis, b. Dec. 27, 1827 ; served in the army.

 2. Mary Elizabeth, b. Mar. 8, 1830 ; m. Edward Maynard of Oakham.

1. Jarvis, b. Feb. 19, 1801 ; d. Aug. 15, 1814.

1. Moses, b. Mar. 21, 1804 ; m. Lucretia Davis, Dec. 2, 1830 ; rem.
Salt Lake City, Utah ; d. May 27, 1854.

 2. Albert, b. Feb. 19, 1833.

 2. James Davis, b. Nov. 5, 1835.

 2. John Flavel, b. May 7, 1838.

 2. William Henry, b. Sept. 12, 1840.

 2. Maria Henrietta, b. Dec. 12, 1842.

1. Catherine, b. May 6, 1806 ; m. Wm. E. Brigham, Nov. 30, 1826 ;
rem. Worcester.

1. Almer, b. Mar. 14, 1808 ; m. Sophia Rice, Sept. 17, 1839.

 2. Elbridge Almer, b. Sept. 29, 1841 ; m. Sibbell Coleman, Dec.
23, 1869 ; res. So. Gardner.

1. Nancy, b. Oct. 17, 1809 ; m. Joseph P. Whitcomb of Boylston,
Apr. 25, 1833 ; d. Sudbury.

1. Elizabeth, b. Dec. 11, 1811 ; m. David Wright of Gardner, Sept.
6, 1836.

1. Sally, b. Jan. 28, 1814 ; m. A. M. Greenwood ; m. 2d, Lorenzo
Cheney, both of Gardner.

1. William, b. Mar. 7, 1816 ; res. Gardner.

Rev. Samuel Gay [see chap. X,] m. Elizabeth Chickering of Dedham,
Nov., 1812, who d. July 9, 1863, a. 78 ; he d. suddenly, Oct. 16, 1848, a. 64.

1. Samuel, b. Sept. 15, 1813 ; d. June 7, 1831.

1. Hannah, b. Aug. 1, 1815 ; d. May 8, 1832.

1. Lucy Elizabeth, b. May 22, 1817 ; m. Thomas Taylor, M. D., Mar.
16, 1837.

1. Rebecca, b. May 19, 1819 ; m. Jonathan W. Whitney, Sept. 21,
1845 ; res. Holden.

1. Alfred, b. Aug. 14, 1821 ; d. Aug. 7, 1838.

35

GAY.

1. Charles, b. Apr. 21, 1824 ; d. Apr. 10, 1835.
1. Edward, b. Aug. 2, 1827 ; d. Mar. 8, 1836.
1. George, b. Oct. 3. 1829 ; m. Elizabeth Morse, Feb. 8. 1852 ; rem.
    2. Clara Elizabeth. b. Sept. 18, 1860 ; d. Aug. 4, 1861.

GLEASON.

ANDREW GLEASON c. f. Worcester, 1838 : m. Celia Harwood, Dec. 1, 1836.
1. Jubal C., b. Nov. 9. 1837 ; m. Harriet A. Pierce of N. Abington.
    July 31, 1867 ; res. Rockland. [See p. 182.]
1. James H., b. Apr. 22. 1839 ; m. Helen A. Greenwood, Aug. 16,
    1866 ; rem. N. Abington ; d. Feb. 4, 1876.
1. Judson M., b. Aug. 20. 1840 ; d. Dec. 1, 1841.
1. Samuel S., b. May 1. 1842 ; m. Asenath M. Barnes, Apr. 11, 1861.
    2. Celia Eldora. b. Nov. 25. 1861 : m. Wm. A. Jewett. Nov. 28, 1878.
1. Freeland S., b. July 18, 1844 : m. Eliza J. Brigham of Barre, Nov.
    30. 1869.
    2. Mabel F., b. June 3. 1871.
    2. Alice E., b. Feb. 7. 1873.
1. Willard F., b. Dec. 24. 1846 ; m. Hattie A. Reynolds of Barre, Aug.
    28. 1873 ; res. Holbrook.

GODDARD.

SAMUEL W. E. GODDARD c. f. Malden ; m. Sophia D. Lawrence of Belch-
    ertown, Nov. 3, 1853.

GOODNOW.

ASA GOODNOW c. f. Princeton ; m. Cynthia W. Hamilton, Dec. 31, 1845,
    who d. Nov. 1, 1856 ; res. Boston.

GOODSPEED.

ISAAC GOODSPEED c. f. Barnstable : m. Ann Jenkins ; d. Mar. 20, 1800 :
    she d. Apr. 5. 1826, a 95.
1. Isaac, b. Apr. 29. 1758 ; m. Sarah McClenathan, Mar., 1782 ; d.
    Dec. 24, 1818, a. 61 ; she d. Oct. 22, 1841, a. 83.
    2. James Rivers. b. Mar. 30. 1784 ; d. Boston, Mar. 25. 1863.
    2. Betsey, b. May 6. 1786 ; d. Boston, Nov. 16, 1827.

GOODSPEED.

2. Isaac, b. Sept. 27, 1788 ; m. Lucy Nutting ; rem. Winchendon ; d. Oct. 13, 1851.

2. Lot, b. Oct. 6, 1790 ; d. Haydenville, Mar. 25, 1872.

2. Martha, b. Jan. 17, 1793 ; d. Jan. 5, 1822.

2. Tabitha, b. Aug 10, 1795 ; d. Feb. 16, 1813.

2. John, b. Mar. 17, 1798 ; m. Louisa Wheeler. Oct. 19. 1826.

   3. Charles, b. Mar. 15, 1828 ; m. Ann Sophila Peirce, May 5, 1852, who d. Worcester ; he d. Worcester, Sept. 14, 1866.

   3. John, b. May 11, 1829 ; d. New Orleans, Aug. 16, 1853.

   3. Elizabeth, b. Sept. 25, 1830 ; m. Samuel T. Gates of Templeton, Dec. 28. 1853 ; d. Oct. 1, 1856.

   3. Albert. b. June 20, 1840 ; m. Dorcas C. Prentiss, June 29, 1865.

      4. Charles Albert, b. Apr. 6, 1868.

      4. Eugene Frederick, b. May 17. 1870.

      4. Leon Prentiss. b. July 12, 1875.

   3. Frederick, b. June 6, 1847 ; d. Sept. 10, 1851.

1. Luther, b 1762 : m. Margaret Murdock, Oct. 13, 1794, who d. Jan. 1, 1802 ; m. 2d, Betsey Rugg of Lancaster. Sept. 20. 1802, who d. Dec. 18, 1830 ; he d. Sept. 19, 1832.

2 Sophia, b. Mar. 29, 1795 ; d. Aug. 28, 1798.

2. Anna, b. Aug. 13, 1796 ; m. Asa Underwood.

2. Sally M., b. Apr. 15, 1798 ; m. Ephraim Stowe.

2. Thomas H., b. Nov. 8, 1803 ; m. Mary Goulding of Phillipston ; d. Aug. 30, 1839.

   3. Harriet, b. May 16, 1831 ; m. Theodore Miller of Phillipston ; d. in Phillipston.

   3. Thomas H., b. Nov. 15, 1833 ; m. Elvira Richardson of Phillipston ; res. Athol.

   3. Philander, b. May 23, 1836 ; m. Susan Vinton ; res. Laconia, N.H.

   3. Mary Abby, b. Aug. 20, 1838 ; m. Sydney O. Little ; res. Keene, N. H.

2. Amelia, b. Feb. 16, 1805 ; d. Mar. 14, 1867.

2. Maria, b. July 14, 1806 ; d. Jan. 21, 1815.

2. Sophia, b. Oct. 16, 1808 ; d. Feb. 22, 1815.

2. Eliza Ann, b. Aug. 14, 1810 ; m. Timothy Brooks ; res. Painesville, Ohio.

2. Daniel J., b. Aug. 8, 1812 ; m. Mary Baker, who d. Apr. 24, 1863 ; he d. Mar. 30, 1863.

GOODSPEED.

1. Heman, b. 1766; m. Betsey Parker; d. Aug. 30, 1844; she d. Feb. 16, 1851.
2. Melinda, b. Oct. 4. 1794; m. Luther Hale.
2. Polly, b. Oct. 27, 1798; m. Amasa G. Davis.
2. Benj. Franklin, b. Mar. 12, 1800; rem. N. Y.
2. Maria, b. Jan. 29, 1802; m. John McClenathan.
2. Fidelia, b. Jan. 8, 1804; m. Wm. M. Wheeler; m. 2d, Addison Miller; d. Nov. 29, 1872.
2. Philander P., b. Feb. 22, 1806; d. N. Y.
2. William C., b. Mar. 24, 1808; m. Martha Wright, Apr. 9, 1832; res. Brooklyn, N. Y.
    3. Helen. b. Jan. 31, 1835; m.——Prentiss of Brooklyn, N. Y.
    3. Isabella, b. Apr. 4. 1837; m. Wm. Thornton of Grafton; res. Brooklyn, N. Y.
    3. Mary Davis. b. Feb. 28, 1839; m. George Swan.
    3. Harriet, b. May 6, 1842; m. Philip Cooty of Brooklyn, N. Y.
    3. Martha E., b. Dec. 22, 1843; m. Simon Cooty of Brooklyn, N. Y.
2. Sophronia, b. May 29, 1809; m. Willard Pratt of New Ipswich, N. H., Feb. 16, 1829, who d. Jan., 1860.
2. Betsey, b. Oct. 21, 1812; m. Hollis Pond.
1. Elijah; m. Anna Goodnow, Mar. 7, 1793; rem. Mich.

GOULDING.

JOEL GOULDING c. f. Phillipston; m. Anna Howe, June 24, 1807, who d. July 3, 1837, a 59; he rem.
1. Joel Rice, b. Apr. 13, 1808; d. Sterling.
1. Mary Ann, b. Feb. 25, 1811; m. James Burrell, July 3, 1834; m. 2d, Sawyer Houghton.
1. Louisa, b. June 5, 1813; d. Sept. 28, 1818.
1. Harriet, b. May 4. 1816; d. Apr. 14, 1857. Missionary among the Choctaws.
1. Louisa, b. Nov. 19, 1819; d. Feb. 26, 1820.
1. Loanza, b. Feb. 15, 1822; m. Rev. Wm. A. Benton, May 18, 1847. Missionaries in Syria; he d. suddenly, Barre, Aug. 23, 1874; she res. Cambridge.

GREEN.

JOSEPH GREEN c. f. Lexington, 1773; m. Hepzibah Heald, Sept. 21, 1771, who d. Aug. 10, 1798; m. 2d, Mrs. Eunice Foster

GREEN.

of Holden. who d. Nov. 2, 1834. a. 79 : he d. June 6, 1844. a 93.

1. Daniel, b. Oct. 28, 1775 ; m. Thankful Clifford, Dec. 11, 1800, who d. June, 1854 : he rem. and d. Barre.

2. Melissa, b. June 21, 1804 ; m. Reuben Partridge, Apr. 21, 1824 : d. Templeton.

2 Mary, b. Mar. 28, 1806 ; m. Harvey Sibley of Worcester, Apr. 13, 1828.

2. Sally, b. Mar. 20, 1808 ; m. Amos Jones Rice.

2. Lucetta, b. Apr. 4. 1810 ; m. Isaac Fisk of Natick.

2. Eleanor, b. July 3, 1812 ; m John Sanders of Barre, who d. Oct. 6, 1867 ; m. 2d, Isaac Fisk of Natick ; d. Dec., 1879.

2. Caroline, b. Aug. 2, 1814 ; m. Pennuel Carpenter of Penn., who d. 1879.

2. Thankful, b. Dec. 6. 1816 ; m. Dexter Sibley of Penn., who d. Penn.

1. Sally, b. Dec. 25, 1777 : m. Isaac Palcom.

1. Hepzibah, b. June 25, 1779 ; m. Josiah Dana Hinds.

1. Joseph, b. Dec. 27, 1782 ; m. Huldah Allen, Mar. 21, 1809, who d. Oct. 26, 1814 : m. 2d, Sally Foster, Mar. 7. 1816, who d. Oct. 24, 1845, a. 60 ; he d. Apr. 25, 1853.

2. Harriet A., b. Dec. 1, 1810 ; m. James Lamb.

2. Roxa, b. Jan. 12, 1814 ; m. Quincy Baker.

2. William M., b. Dec. 21, 1817 ; d. Aug. 9, 1819.

2. William M., b. Sept. 9, 1820 ; m. Sophronia Homer of Rutland, Apr. 13, 1847.

3. Charila A., ⎫ b. Dec. 22, 1847 ; m. William A. Hallock.
3. Charles A., ⎭ m. Mary Ann Truax, May 17, '71.

4. Lillian Estelle, b. Aug. 8, 1872 ; d. Aug. 24, 1872.

4. William Homer, b. May 17, 1875.

4. Joseph Ernest, b. Nov. 8, 1876.

3. Mary, b. Sept. 11, 1861.

2. Charles King, b. Feb. 13, 1823 ; d. Oct. 18, 1845.

2. Eunice, b. Nov. 10, 1825 ; m. Lafayette Coleman.

2. Addison R., b. Jan. 26, 1828 ; m. Mary Homer of Rutland ; res. Gardner.

2. Joseph, b. Feb. 12, 1832 ; rem. Gardner ; m. Elmira Bent, Nov. 15, 1859.

1. Roxa, b. Sept. 4, 1786 ; d. Oct. 15, 1789.

GREEN.

1. Stephen, b. May 6, 1789; d. Feb. 4, 1799. Fell into a kettle of hot soap.
1. Roxa. b. Nov. 1, 1791; m. Jonathan Gates.
1 Hannah, b. Apr. 4, 1794; m. Charles King of Rutland, Dec. 29, 1814; d. Mar. 9, 1833.
1. Lucy, b. June 2, 1797; d. Mar. 6, 1798.
1. Rebecca Dana. b. Dec. 27. 1802; m. John Parmenter, June 5, 1823; rem. Chester, Vt.
1. John C., b. Feb. 14, 1804; m. Sophia Brown of Bristol, R. I.; d. Mar. 10, 1872.
2. Elizabeth, b. Aug. 21, 1833; m. Alden Pollard.
2. John C., b. Oct. 19, 1841; m. Mary V. Grimes, Jan. 4, 1868; res. Leominster.

GREENWOOD.

Three brothers. Abijah, Moses and Levi Greenwood c. f. Holden about 1770.

Abijah enlisted and was called into active service before the battle of Bunker Hill: m. Rhoda Pond. July 14. 1774. who d. July 16, 1782; m. 2d Elizabeth Marean, Oct. 3, 1783. who d. Feb. 15, 1814, a. 65: he d. Jan. 9. 1814, a. 65.

1. Ethan, b. Jan. 8, 1775; d. Oct. 2, 1777.
1. Ethan, b. Jan. 26. 1780; m. Sally Allen, May 16, 1802, who d. West Boylston; left town.
2. William A., b. Sept. 1, 1802; rem. Albany, N. Y.
2. Fidelia, b. June 15, 1804; rem. Boylston.
2. Simeon. b. June 4. 1806; rem. Worcester; for ten years in the Fla. Indian War.
2. Abijah, b. Aug. 28, 1808; d. Oct. 3, 1811.
2. Sophronia, b. June 11, 1810; rem. Boylston.
2. Jane Maria, b. May 9, 1813; rem. Boylston.
2. Charles C., b. May 31. 1815; rem. Boylston.
2. Abigail, b. Nov. 27, 1817; rem. Boylston.
1. Otis, b. Dec. 4. 1781; m. Sophia Rice, Nov. 27, 1806; d. Oct. 6, 1814; she d. May 7, 1816.
2. Edmund R., b. Dec. 1, 1807; m. Susan H. Slocomb, Sept. 4, 1828; res. Ashburnham.
3. Otis, b. Mar. 4, 1829; d. California, 1863.

GREENWOOD.

3. John Q., b. Sept. 28, 1830 ; m. Ellen M. Joslin, Sept. 28, 1852 : d. Newton, Oct. 17, 1858.

3. Mary Sophia, b. Dec. 20, 1833 ; m. George H. Barrett of Ashburnham.

3. Theodore, b. July 27, 1835 ; m. Ellen M. (Joslin) Greenwood. Apr. 9, 1860 ; rem. Ashburnham.

3. Edmund R., b. Dec. 18, 1837 ; res. Tenn.

3. Abigail Susan, b. Apr. 14, 1840 ; d. Apr. 13, 1841.

3. James Broad, b. Sept. 10, 1842 ; d. Feb. 10, 1846.

3. Moses Phelps, b. Dec. 22, 1845 ; rem. Ashburnham ; m. Georgiana Whitney.

2. Horace. b. Dec. 30, 1809 ; m. Almira Hartwell, Aug., 1831 ; d. Oct. 21, 1863.

3. George F., b. Mar. 14, 1832 ; m. Clarissa Allen ; rem. Templeton.

4. Horace A., b. June 6, 1855.

3. Thomas Elvin, b. Oct. 23, 1833 : m. Mary P. Allen.

4. Elsie M., b. June 2, 1858.

4. Harry E., b. Sept. 14, 1865.

4. Alice Albertina, b. June 1, 1877.

3. William Solon, b. Aug. 25, 1835 ; m. Susan M. Covell, Apr. 28, 1867 ; res. Springfield.

3. Levi Augustine, b. Sept 19, 1837 ; d. Oct. 21, 1854.

3. Edson Alonzo, b. Oct. 22, 1840 ; d. Sept. 27, 1863. [See p. 139.]

3. Elmira E., b. Oct. 10, 1842 ; m. Baruch Whitney, Feb. 10, 1871, who d. July 26, 1877, a. 65 ; m. 2d, Charles F. Doe, Nov. 26, 1879.

3. Emeline A., b. Jan. 7, 1848 ; m. Frederick A. Cummings. Nov. 29, 1866.

2. Augusta, b. Dec. 11, 1811 ; m. Lyman Learned, Apr. 18, 1835. who d. Aug. 14, 1865, a. 63.

1. Rhoda, b. June 20, 1785 ; m. Isaac Thompson of Princeton.

1. Silas, b. Nov. 19, 1786 ; m. Julia Daniels, Dec. 8, 1811, who d. Jan. 9, 1864 ; he d. Mar. 12, 1857.

2. Joseph Emerson, b. Mar. 14, 1813 ; m. Nancy Clark, Dec. 8, 1840 ; d. Aug. 31, 1872.

3. Emma C., b. Nov. 6, 1843 ; m. Daniel Hutchinson.

2. Abijah Harrison, b. Dec. 28, 1814 ; d. Jan. 3, 1864.

GREENWOOD.

2. Silas Newell, b. Oct. 21, 1817; m. Calista Heald, Dec. 8, 1841, who d. Jan. 23, 1843; m. 2d, Susan Browning, June 2, 1846.

3. Abby Calista, b. May 27, 1849; d. Sept. 19, 1852.

3. Eva Lucy, b. July 12, 1853; m. Walter W. White of Petersham, Dec. 23, 1876.

2. Harriet, b. Aug. 12, 1819; d. Aug. 18, 1819.

2. Julia, b. Oct. 27, 1820; m. Joseph Cheney Murdock.

2. Abigail D., b. June 12, 1823; m. John Browning.

2. Harriet, b. Apr. 15, 1825; m. William J. Eveleth.

2. Hannah, b. Aug. 2, 1827; m. John G. Allen.

2. Alson J., b. Sept. 27, 1829; m. Martha G. Moulton, Mar. 16, 1853.

3. S. Elliot, b. Sept. 15, 1853; res. Templeton. [See p. 182.]

3. Silas A., b. Dec. 6, 1854; m. Sibyl H. Browning, Nov. 25, 1879; res. Winchendon.

3. Arthur D., b. Apr. 23, 1858.

3. Grace, b. Feb. 3, 1862.

3. Harrison, b. Aug. 31, 1863.

1. Mary, b. Mar. 24, 1789; m. Elisha Woodward.

1. Hannah, b. May 28, 1791; m. Aaron Thompson of Princeton, Apr. 29, 1817.

Moses; m. Betsey Dunlap, Mar. 22, 1779, who was born Cherry Valley, N. Y., where at the age of four, she was rescued from the Indians, who murdered her parents, and burned their dwelling; she d. Dec. 9, 1826, a. 70; he d. Mar. 8, 1827, a. 75.

1. Ethan A., b. May 27, 1779; m. Mrs. Caroline Warren of Roxbury, who d. Jan. 20, 1875; he d. May 3, 1856. [See p. 176.]

1. Aaron, b. Mar. 22, 1781; m. Eliza Thatcher, Dec., 1807; rem. Penn.; d. there.

1. Sally, b. May 6, 1783; m. Abel Warren of Northboro', June 4, 1805; both d. Northboro'.

1. Moses, b. Nov. 4, 1785; m. Polly Brown, Jan. 9, 1806; d. Sept. 26, 1828; she d. Jan. 14, 1859.

2. Lyman, b. June 13, 1806; m. Augusta Marean, Nov. 19, 1829; d. Oct. 5, 1880.

3. Milo, b. Mar. 4, 1831; rem. south; d. in the War of Rebellion.

3. Moses, b. Oct. 9, 1832; m. Adelaide Wright, Jan. 1, 1857; res. Cambridge.

GREENWOOD.

4. Helen Mabel, b. July 9, 1862.

3. Ann Elizabeth, b. Sept. 16, 1834 ; m. Lyman Woodward.

3. Joseph L., b. June 10, 1836 ; rem. Abington.

3 Asa Morrill, b. Dec. 22, 1839 ; m. Mary E. Nichols, Apr. 12, 1865 ; res. Leominster.

3. Helen A., b. May 29, 1843 ; m. James H. Gleason.

3. Mary Alice, b. Mar. 21, 1847 ; m. Thomas B. Grimes.

3. Frank, b. Nov. 25, 1851.

2. Moses, b. May 23, 1808 ; m. Adeline Ayres of No. Brookfield ; res. Louisiana.

2. Aaron, b. May 23, 1808 ; m. Adeline Rice, Apr. 14, 1831 ; rem. Worcester ; d. Aug. 3, 1878.

   3. Oella Jane, b. Feb. 28, 1832 ; m. Lorenzo Barnes.

   3. Sarah Rebecca, b. Jan. 5, 1834 ; m. Wm. Homer Earle.

   3. Lucy Agnes, b. Jan. 31, 1836 ; d. Apr. 17, 1843.

   3. Charlotte, b. May 15, 1838 ; m. George P. Earle.

   3. Aaron Hobart, b. Jan. 21, 1841 ; d. army, Feb. 10, 1863. [See p. 139.]

   3. George, b. May 11, 1843 ; d. army, May 10, 1864. [See p. 140.]

   3. Lucy Addie, b. Apr. 3, 1845.

   3. Chester, b. June 22, 1847.

   3. Charles, b. Nov. 21, 1849 ; m. Ella E. Grimes ; res. Worcester.

2. Cynthia, b. Feb. 20, 1812 ; m. William Joslin.

1. Betsey, b. Dec. 12, 1787 ; d. Apr. 24, 1797.

1. James, b. Sept. 4, 1792 ; m. Sally Hunting, Mar. 3, 1814, who d. Oct. 17, 1818 ; m. 2d, Betsey Rice, May 1, 1819 ; rem. Penn. ; both d there.

2. Lucy, b. Dec. 1, 1814 ; d. Harford, Penn.

2. Stephen, b. Aug. 23, 1817 ; d. Apr. 22, 1818.

2. Asa Willard, b. Nov. 4, 1819.

1. Cynthia, b. Oct. 1, 1794 ; drowned May 15, 1808. [See p. 165.]

1. Betsey, b. May 20, 1799 ; m. Elisha Whittemore.

LEVI ; m. Anna Shattuck, Nov. 30, 1785, who d. Feb 17, 1823, a. 64 ; he d. Mar. 27, 1826, a. 68.

1. Lucy, b. Sept. 12, 1789 ; m. Edward Partridge of Oakham, Dec. 1, 1808 ; d. Sept. 23, 1814.

1. Anna, b. May 1, 1794 ; d. Aug. 29, 1796.

1. Nancy, b. May 1, 1794 ; m. Thomas Temple.

36

GRIMES.

JOSEPH GRIMES c. f. Tewksbury in 1761 ; he was the first man who came here with the intention of making a permanent settlement, all before him having come for hunting or other temporary purposes. Such were his expectations of the rapid growth of the place, that he is said to have made the prediction to his sons, that if they lived to be old men, they would see roads built in the region, over which wheeled carriages could pass. The house lot on which he settled remained in the family till sold to E. M. Coffin in 1879. It had then been for many years the only lot in town which had not been transferred since the original deed. He d. Aug. 4, 1794 ; his wife, Sarah, d. Aug. 4, 1798, a. 80.

1. Bill, b. 1742 ; m. Rebecca Reed, 1767, who d. May 5, 1794 ; he d. June 19, 1817, a. 75.

2. Betsey, b. Feb. 10. 1768 ; m. Seth Savage of Princeton, Aug. 30, 1789.

2. Bill, b. Feb. 7, 1770 ; m. Dorcas Murdock, who d. Dec. 7, 1844 ; he d. Aug. 16, 1855.

   3. Hiram, b. June 9, 1809 ; m. Mary Ann Murphy, June 6, 1859 : d. June 15, 1879.

   3. Almira, b. June 28, 1812 ; m. William Hobbs ; res. Baldwinsville.

   3. Sumner, b. Aug. 10, 1814 ; d. Ark., June, 1844.

   3. Harrison, b. Jan. 21, 1817 ; m. Rosanna Nugent, Dec. 27, 1847.

      4. Alvah E., b. June 17, 1849 ; m. Emma R. Lyon, Aug. 16, 1875 ; res. Worcester.

      4. Walter A., b. Apr. 7, 1851 ; d. June 1, 1852.

      4. Fred H., b. Dec. 2, 1853.

      4. Charley, b. Nov. 30. 1860.

      4. Carrie, b. July 28, 1869.

   3. Porter, b. Jan. 23, 1819 ; d. Jan. 18, 1876.

   3. Lucy, b. May 12, 1821 : m. Benjamin Stoddard, Nov. 30, 1843, who d. Mar. 10, 1851 ; m. 2d, Charles Foster of Petersham, Sept. 18, 1855.

   3. Laura, b. June 28, 1824 ; m. Eli Clark ; m. 2d, George Gates of Gardner, Jan. 3, 1866.

2. Sally, b. Apr. 17, 1778 ; m. John Grimes of Marlboro', N. H., Jan. 8, 1804.

2. Waldo, b. Nov. 2, 1783 ; m. Nancy Hunting, Feb. 5, 1816 ; rem. Ohio.

GRIMES.

3. Luke, b. Sept. 13, 1824 ; d. May 18, 1825.

3. Luke, b. Dec. 28, 1825.

2. Lucy, b. Mar. 22, 1786 ; m. George Smith of Rutland, Mar. 22, 1808.

2. Asa, b. Aug. 5, 1788 ; d. Calais, Maine.

2. Hannah, b. Dec. 3, 1790 ; m. Joel Smith of Rutland, June 2, 1811.

1. Joseph, b. Aug. 9, 1744 ; m. Huldah Wheelock, who d. Apr. 22, 1833, a. 84 ; he d. Nov. 19, 1834.

2. Susanna, b. May 23, 1772 ; m. Asa Sawin of Ashburnham.

2. Zephaniah, b. Mar. 31, 1774 ; d. Sutton, Lower Canada.

2. Attarah, b. Mar. 18, 1776 ; m. Asa Lyon.

2. Aaron, b. Jan. 14, 1778 ; m. Sally Stowe, Aug. 26, 1804 ; d. July 5, 1868 ; she d. Oct. 28, 1868.

3. Aaron, b. Nov. 27, 1804 ; m. Louisa Marean, Apr. 4, 1830, who d. Gardner, Dec. 4, 1856 ; he d. May 11, 1872.

4. Joseph Marean, b. Dec. 16, 1830 ; res. Cal.

4. Lucy Adelia, b. Mar. 4, 1832 ; m. Aaron O. Wilder of Leominster.

4. George Clayton, b. Jan. 4, 1834 ; res. Cal.

4. Martin Van Buren, b. Mar. 4, 1837 ; res. Templeton.

4. Harriet Elizabeth, b. Feb. 22, 1841 ; d. Aug. 20, 1844.

4. Sybil Parker, b. Mar. 12, 1843 ; m. Charles Hall of N. Y.

4. Lucius Blood, b. Feb. 4, 1846 ; res. Leominster.

4. William A., b. Sept. 13, 1849 ; d. Sept. 2, 1851.

3. Sophia, b. Jan. 23, 1806 ; m. Simon Reed ; res. Boston.

3. Otis, b. Sept. 14, 1808 ; m. Elizabeth Lawton ; res. N. Y.

3. Charles, b. Nov. 11, 1810 ; m. Mary Ball ; d. Jan. 26, 1845.

4. Charles O., b. May 31, 1838 ; d. Nov. 10, 1846.

4. Mary V., b. Sept. 18, 1841 ; m. John C. Green.

4. Thomas Ball, b. Apr. 22, 1844 ; m. Mary Alice Greenwood, Nov. 18, 1869 ; res. Leominster.

3. Silas, b. July 27, 1815 ; d. Feb. 21, 1872.

3. Jarvis, b. July 5, 1817 ; d. Oct. 19, 1835.

3. Joseph., b. Apr. 18, 1820 ; m. Harriet A. Maynard, Oct. 12, 1843 ; res. Gardner.

4. Mary A., b. May 21, 1844 ; m. Frederick H. Minot of Westminster, May 21, 1863 ; d. Westminster.

4. Sarah Jane, b. June 11, 1847 ; m. Joseph B. Drury of Gardner.

GRIMES.

4. Ella E., b. Feb. 10, 1849 ; m. Charles Greenwood.

4. Frederick W., b. May 20, 1851 ; m. Ella Gibbs of Westminster.

4. Nellie, b. Jan. 21, 1857.

4. Angie A., } b. Aug. 23, 1860.
4. Alice A., }

4. Stella Mabel, b. Feb. 6, 1865.

3. Sarah, b. Oct. 21, 1821 ; d. Oct. 11, 1846.

3. Sewell, b. Aug. 24, 1824 ; m. Harriet W. Peirce, May, 23, 1854, who d. Jan. 11, 1867 ; m. 2d, Abby Davidson of Belfast, Me., Apr. 6, 1869.

4. Vernet, b. Nov. 27, 1854.

4. Abby Oradel, b. June 21, 1872.

4. Lucy Harriet, b. Aug. 30, 1873.

3. Edwin, b. Jan. 25, 1826 ; m. Hannah E. Ferguson of Belfast, Me., Oct. 3, 1858 ; res. Princeton.

4. Albert Byron, b. June 30, 1859.

4. Edwin Lincoln, b. Nov. 8, 1864.

4. Thaddeus Stowe, b. Oct. 13, 1866.

4. Maurice Wasson, b. Mar. 20, 1871.

2. Ruth, b. Apr. 29, 1780 ; m. Nathaniel Flagg of Worcester, Dec. 12, 1802 ; d. Worcester.

2. Asenath, b. Apr. 4, 1782 ; m. Joel Constantine of Ashburnham, Jan. 17, 1811 ; d. Wallingford, Vt.

2. Betsey, b. Oct. 28, 1784 ; d. Sept. 26, 1863.

2. Amiable, b. Mar. 12, 1787 ; d. Dec. 27, 1803.

2. Lucretia, b. Feb. 17, 1789 ; d. Oct. 25, 1796.

2. Clarissa, b. Jan. 28, 1794 ; m. Joseph Waite.

1. John, b. 1750, d. July 20, 1828.

1. Molly, b. June 17, 1754 ; m. Asa Hoyt, July 3, 1776, who d. Jan. 4, 1832, a. 83 ; she d. Dec. 27, 1789.

1. Ephraim, b. 1756 ; m. Mary Gibson, who d. July 18, 1825 ; he d. Feb. 2, 1844. [See p. 173.]

2. Asa Tyler, b. Mar. 20, 1792 ; m. Polly Clark, 1813 ; rem. Chelsea, Vermont.

2. Ephraim, b. Mar. 12, 1796 ; served in the war of 1812 ; d. Sept. 11, 1814.

2. William Cargill, b. Sept. 30, 1798 ; rem.

2. Dennison, b. Aug. 27, 1802 ; d. Sept. 15, 1819.

HAGER.

CHARLES HAGER c. f. Grafton. 1851 ; m. Lydia P. Whipple, May 6, 1838 ;
d. Nov. 30, 1880, a. 67.

1. Ellen, b. Sept. 11, 1838 ; m. Lucius A. Murdock.
1. Ann, b. May 22, 1840.
1. Mary, b. Sept. 4, 1842 ; m. George D. Boyden of Worcester ; d.
June 30, 1869.
1. Sarah Jane, b. July 1, 1845 ; m. Ruel K. Whitcomb of Lowell, Apr.
16, 1868.
1. Charles W., b. May 26, 1849 ; m. Mary E. Lund of Templeton,
Mar. 11, 1871.
1. Emma L., b. Mar. 23, 1852.

HALE.

LUTHER HALE c. f. Leominster about 1788 ; m. Joanna Carter, Jan. 16,
1787, who d. July 30, 1803, a. 33 ; m. 2d, Phebe Wyman,
Apr. 8, 1804, who d. July 23, 1826, a. 47 ; m. 3d, Phebe
(Kimball) Upham, Oct. 23, 1834, who d. Mar. 8, 1846,
a. 82 ; he d. Feb. 7, 1845, a. 78.

1. John, b. June 24, 1787 ; d. Jan. 7, 1850.
1. Lucy, b. Aug. 23, 1789 ; d. May 3, 1805.
1. Clara, b. June 12, 1791 ; m. Samuel Swan.
1. Otis, b. Mar. 16, 1793 ; d. Apr. 13, 1822.
1. Luther, b. Jan. 19, 1795 ; m. Melinda Goodspeed, Jan. 1823 ;
rem. Vt.
1. Roland, b. Dec. 28, 1796 ; m. Clarissa Rice of Templeton, June 13,
1833 ; d. July 29, 1861.
  2. Clara Swan, b. Dec. 27, 1835 ; m. John A. Bryant of Rutland,
Aug. 26, 1862.
  2. William Carter, b. Sept., 1843 ; d. Templeton, 1867.
1. Esther, b. Feb. 17, 1799 ; m. James Newton.
1. Laura, b. Jan. 1, 1801 ; d. June 1, 1815.
1. Oliver, b. Sept. 28, 1804 ; m. Sarah D. Parker, Mar. 18, 1830 ;
drowned on voyage to Cal., Feb. 16, 1853.
  2. John Otis, b. Apr. 2, 1831 ; m. Lucy Browning, Nov. 7, 1860 ;
d. Dec. 8, 1873 ; she d. Jan. 28, 1878.
    3. Abby Calista, b. July 21, 1862.
    3. Oliver, b. Dec. 12, 1863.
    3. Joshua B., b. June 14, 1865.

HALE.

3. John Otis, b. Dec. 1, 1866.
3. Lucy Dorrit, b. Aug. 18, 1868.
2. Sarah Maria, b. Aug. 3, 1833; m. Luke Davis of Boston, Aug. 31, 1862; res. Newton.
2. Minerva Florilla, b. June 27, 1837; res. Boston.
2. Catherine Swan, }
2. Clara Swan, } b. June 8, 1841; res. Boston.
2. Seth P. H., b. Feb. 12, 1846; m. Abby Bennett, Dec. 2, 1867.
    3. William B., b. May 14, 1871.
1. Thomas, b. July 6, 1808; m. Mary Pond, Mar. 20, 1831; d. Apr. 2, 1861.
2. Louisa Minerva, b. Sept. 30, 1832; d. Feb. 13, 1854.
2. Thomas Irving, b. Oct. 9, 1838; m. Martha A. (Thompson) Hale, Nov. 29, 1865; m. 2d, Helen D. Pond, Jan. 16, 1878.
    3. Irving Lee Winn, b. Apr. 21, 1878.
    3. Lucy S., b. Apr. 16, 1880.
2. Luther Hobart, b. Feb. 11, 1841; m. Martha A. Thompson, Mar. 28, 1862; d. Sept. 12, 1863. [See p. 140.]
2. Merrill, b. Nov. 25, 1845.
2. Luke, b. July 15, 1850; d. Oct. 3, 1862.
1. Lucy, b. Feb. 13, 1810; m. Daniel Wilkinson of Templeton, July, 11, 1833.
1. Joanna, b. Mar. 11, 1812; m. Benjamin W. Fletcher of Worcester.
1. Susan, b. Apr. 2, 1814; m. Amasa Hyde.
1. Charles, b. Sept. 5, 1816; d. Dec. 30, 1818.
1. Luke, b. Aug. 21, 1818; m. Sophronia Wyman of Winchendon; res. Winchendon.

HALLOCK.

Isaac Hallock c. f. Vt., m. Nancy (Lamb) Clark, Mar. 3, 1836.
1. William A., b. Apr. 27, 1837; m. Charilla A. Green, Mar. 21, 1866.
    2. Henry Herbert, b. Aug. 1, 1869.
    2. Charles, b. Sept. 19, 1870.
    2. Leroy Eugene, b. Dec. 30, 1875.
1. Eleanor W., b. Nov. 1, 1840; d. Nov. 12, 1842.
1. Charles H., b. Nov. 11, 1843; rem. Springfield.

HAMILTON.

MRS. ELIZABETH HAMILTON c. f. Westminster; d. Apr. 3. 1842, a. 62.

  1. George W., b. Apr. 4, 1816: m. Betsey Earle, Sep. 16, 1841, who
        d. Dec. 4, 1843; m. 2d, Julia Wheeler, Apr. 16, 1846,
        who d. June 13, 1873; m. 3d, Mrs. Susan Claflin of
        Framingham, Sept. 29, 1874.

    2. George Willis, b. Dec. 17, 1842; m. Camilla Ensign; res. Hart-
        ford, Conn.

    2. Edward Clinton, b. Dec. 28, 1847; m. Abby Louisa Davis, Dec.
        5, 1871; res. Springfield.

    2. Lucy Elizabeth, b. Jan. 4, 1853; m. Charles O. Stone.

    2. Zoilla Cynthia, b. Oct. 24, 1855; d. Dec. 21, 1875.

  1. Sylvia, b. Sept. 2, 1810; m. Jonathan P. Earle.

  1. Cynthia W., b. Nov. 9, 1819, m. Asa Goodnow.

HENRY HAMILTON, b. Springfield, c. f. Minn., 1874: m. Elizabeth T.
        Arper of Worcester, Jan. 22, 1846, who d. Aug 23.
        1869; m. 2d, Frances E. Underwood of Me., Oct.
        31, 1870.

  1. Lilla B., b. Nov. 23, 1860.

  1. Gracie M., b. Apr. 5, 1865.

  1. Lizzie E., b. Sept. 2, 1868.

  1. Sewell L., b. May 19, 1872.

  1. Eddie A., b. May 12, 1875.

  1. Willie A., b. June 26, 1876; d. Aug. 12, 1877.

  1. E. Everett, b. Apr. 18, 1878.

HARRIS.

JOSEPH H. HARRIS c. f. Richmond, N. H.; m. Mary Leuann Brown,
        Apr. 27, 1861.

  1. George Herbert, b. Mar. 25, 1863.

  1. Ella Mabel, b. June 8, 1864.

  1. Hattie Gertrude, b. May 23, 1869.

  1. Jennie Edith, b. July 7, 1870.

HARTWELL.

AMOS HARTWELL c. f. Concord, m. Betsey Pond, Aug., 1808, who d. July
        5, 1821; m. 2d, Esther F. Dibble of Elbridge, N. Y.,
        1838; d. May 24, 1855.

HARTWELL.

1. Reuben P., b. Nov. 2, 1809; m. Almeda Merritt of Templeton, May 26, 1832; d. Ia., Jan. 1, 1864.
1. Emeline, b. Mar. 1, 1812; m. Thomas Jefferson Coleman of Templeton, Sept. 11, 1832.
1. Almira, b. Mar. 1, 1814; m. Horace Greenwood.
1. Edson, b. Feb. 18, 1816.
1. Levi, b. Apr. 16, 1818; m. Dolly Noteman of N. Y., Oct , 1847; d. Apr. 9, 1871. [See p. 168.]
  2. Larkin, b. Mar. 30, 1850; rem.
1. Betsey, b. Apr. 22, 1821; m. Nelson Witt.
1. Cyrus W., b. Dec. 24, 1843; m. Ella A. Lord of N. Y., Jan. 1, 1867.

SIMON B., bro. of AMOS; m. Roxa Sargent, Apr. 16, 1809; d. Jan. 24, 1868, a. 80; she d. Jan. 27, 1875.
1. James Harvey, b. June 17, 1809; m. Charlotte Wyman, Nov. 30, 1831.
  2. Mary Jane, b. Jan. 27, 1833; m. Emory Rice of Barre, May 8, 1851.
  2. Martha Ann, b. Mar. 29, 1834; m. Sumner Clark.
  2. Alonzo, b. May 24, 1835; m. Josephine B. Tilton, Apr. 16, 1856.
    3. Ebenezer Tilton, b. Sept. 24, 1856.
    3. Edward Alonzo, b. Oct. 27, 1858.
    3. Addie W., b. Mar. 30, 1863; m. Fred M. Clark.
    3. Rollin E., b. June 9, 1866.
    3. Phebe, b. Sept. 12, 1868.
    3. Lottie Gould, b. July 4, 1871; d. Feb. 27, 1872.
    3. Josie G., b. June 13, 1873; d. Aug. 26, 1874.
    3. Walter Eugene, b. Nov. 12, 1875.
    3. Ralph Wilcox, b. Mar. 26, 1880.
  2. George, b. Nov. 27, 1836; m. Mary Ann Brown of Holden, Dec. 3, 1859; rem. Worcester.
  2. Clara M., b. Jan. 15, 1838; m. William C. Titus; m. 2d, Luther A. Bolles of Worcester, Aug. 13, 1874.
  2. Angeline, b. Sept. 9, 1839; m. Joseph Merriam of Peterboro', N. H., Nov. 3, 1857; m. 2d, John Wesby of Trenton, N. J., Sept. 13, 1868.
  2. Rollin E., b. Nov. 24, 1840; d. army, May 5, 1863.
  2. Henry H., b. June 17, 1842; d. Dec. 27, 1842.
  2. Harriet A., b. Feb. 1, 1844; d. Sept. 7, 1846.

HARTWELL.

2. James H., b. Sept. 13, 1847 ; m. Lucy F. Waite, May 28, 1874 : res. Worcester.
2. Charles H., b. Mar. 29, 1849 ; d. Aug. 11, 1870.
2. Charlotte E., b. June 15, 1850.
1. Lorinda, b. Oct. 14, 1811 ; m. Warner Clifford.
1. Mary Parker, b. Dec. 31, 1813 ; m. Wesson Bixby, Dec. 3, 1829 ; d. Jan. 26, 1830.
1. William Stedman, b. Aug. 21, 1817 ; m. Mary Prescott ; rem. Fitz-william, N. H.; d. Aug. 1, 1865.
1. Harriet Newell, b. Mar. 22, 1820 ; m. George Rugg ; d. May 9, 1843.
1. Phebe S., b. Apr. 14, 1822 ; m. Daniel Brown of Claremont, N. H., Oct. 10, 1842 ; m. 2d, Moses Pollard.
1. Sarah, b. June 22, 1826 ; m. Benjamin F. Wright.
1. Samuel Willard, b. Feb. 14, 1829 ; m. Mary Bigelow of Fitzwilliam, N H.; res. Eldora, Iowa.
1. Mary R., b. Nov. 28, 1835 ; m. Willard Parsons.

HARWOOD.

JESSE HARWOOD c. f. Barre ; m. Mary Sibley, who d. July 24, 1849. a. 76 ; he d May 8, 1847, a. 82.
1. Sumner, b. Jan. 9, 1806 ; d. Apr. 16, 1876, a. 70.
1. Sylvia, } b. Mar. 1, 1808; d. Aug. 12, 1839.
1. Celia, } m. Andrew Gleason.

HASTINGS.

SAMUEL H. HASTINGS c. f. Worcester: m. Dorinda Clifford, Aug. 8, 1844 ; d. army, July 21, 1863; [see p. 140.] She d. Oct. 23, 1875.
1. Lilla Maria (adopted), b. Aug. 2, 1853 ; m. Alvin W. Monroe.

HAYDEN.

JAMES F. HAYDEN c. f. Boston ; m. Adeline Prentiss, Dec. 17, 1872.
1. James F., b. Apr. 30, 1879 ; d. May 1, 1879.

HEALD.

STEPHEN HEALD* c f. Rutland, 1762 ; m. Hazadiah Howe of Rutland, who d. Mar. 22, 1812, a. 79 ; he d. Oct. 3, 1814, a. 84.

HEALD.

1. Hepzibah, b. Oct. 11, 1753; m. Joseph Green.
1. Timothy, b. Feb 19, 1756: m. Lois Smith of Rutland, June 12, 1785. who d. Apr. 29, 1818; he d. May 1, 1814.
    2. Betsey, b. Sept. 1, 1786; m. Abijah Clark.
    2. Calvin, b. Feb. 8, 1788; m Tamar Ward, Jan. 18, 1825; d Feb. 22, 1869; she d. Dec. 28, 1869, a. 77.
        3. Abelena Elizabeth, b. Oct. 28, 1825; d. Sept. 11, 1865.
    2. Jonas, b. Feb. 13, 1790; m. Abigail Clark, Sept. 6, 1815; d. Worcester, Feb. 3, 1866; she d. Feb. 26, 1868.
        3. Mary Stone, b. June 9, 1816; m. George Williams.
        3. Simpson C., b. Jan. 26, 1818; m. Martha Caroline Loring; res. Worcester.
        3. Calista, b. Feb. 2. 1820; m Silas Newell Greenwood.
        3. Lois, b. Feb. 3, 1822; m. Lyman Wheeler; m. 2d, 1. Nelson Keyes of Worcester, Nov. 27, 1856.
        3. Nancy, b. May 27, 1824; m. David D. Keyes of Worcester, Nov. 23, 1849
        3. Jonas, b. Nov. 26, 1826; m. Maria Kettell; res. Worcester.
        3. Timothy Sibley, b. Sept. 29, 1832; m. Lucy R. Prentiss, June 29, 1865, who d. Jan. 31, 1872; m. 2d, Ada Davis of Rutland.
            4. Harriet Prentiss, b. Nov. 26, 1867.
            4. Lucy Daisy, b. Jan. 23, 1872.
        3. Samuel Clark, b. Jan. 22, 1835; res. Chicago, Ill.
    2. John, b. Jan. 2, 1792; m. Mary Wood of Hardwick, Oct. 11, 1821; d. Dec. 21, 1869.
        3. Philena, b. Nov. 11, 1822; m. Lewis F. Ball of Worcester, Nov. 12, 1844; d. 1847.
        3. Hannah, b. June 29, 1824; d. Dec. 10, 1838.
        3. William, b. July 22, 1826; m. Lizzie Stubbs; res. Worcester.
        3. Sarah, b. July 24, 1828; m. Albert Witt.
        3. Carmi, b. July 4, 1830; m. Lizzie Gibson of Woburn; m. 2d, Sarah Gleason; res. Worcester.
        3. Mary, b. Nov. 21, 1838; m. W. O. Watson; res. Spencer.
        3. Clara, b. Oct. 17, 1840; m. Hiram B. Oliver of Worcester.
    2. Hannah, b. June 10, 1794; m. Joseph Stone.
    2. Sally, b. June 2, 1796; m. Samuel Thompson.
    2. Stephen, b. Sept. 17, 1799; m. Mary Newton, May 17, 1827; res. Barre.

HEALD.

2. William, b. Jan. 1, 1803 ; d. Mar. 11, 1804.
1. Josiah, b. May 29, 1758 ; rem. Chester, Vt.
1. Sarah, b. May 19, 1760 ; m. Ebenezer Heald ; d. Rutland.
1. Eliphalet, b. Feb. 9, 1763 ; d. Dec. 7, 1770.
1. Hannah, b. Mar. 3, 1765 ; d. Dec. 13, 1770.
1. Lucy, b. Apr. 30, 1767 ; d. Dec. 29, 1770.
1. Lois, b. May 22, 1769 ; d. Dec. 12, 1770.
1. Hannah, b. Nov. 11, 1771 ; m. Calvin Upham, Feb. 12, 1797, who
    d. Nov. 22, 1827 ; m. 2d, Moses H. Peirce.
1. Lucy, m. Jeremiah Thompson.

HINDS.

CORNELIUS HINDS c. f. Barre ; his wife, Martha, d. May 15, 1802, a. 59 ;
    he d. Aug. 23, 1812, a. 70.
1. Eli, m. Polly Stone, Mar. 12, 1789 ; rem. Eden, Vt. ; both d. there.
1. Abner, m. Sally Woodward, June 16, 1800, who d. June 2, 1810 ;
    m. 2d, Betsey (Blood) Marean, Jan., 1812 ; rem. Temple-
    ton ; d. Apr. 19, 1835.
    2. Woodward, b. Jan. 10, 1813 ; rem. Walpole, N. H.
    2. Sally, b. Aug. 1, 1814 ; m. Artemas Hancock of Templeton ; d.
        Mar. 25, 1876.
    2. Jarvis, b. Oct. 14, 1816 ; m. and settled in Walpole, N. H.
    2. Harriet, m. Charles Laselle of Worcester.
1. Josiah Dana, m. Hepzibah Green, Aug. 1, 1802 ; rem. Belfast,
    Me. ; d. there.
    2. Lucy, b. Nov. 7, 1802 ; res. Maine.
1. Cornelius, b. Dec. 3, 1775 ; m. Hannah Waite, Apr. 9, 1801 ; d.
    Apr. 3, 1848 ; she d. Dec. 27, 1859.
    2. Hannah Waite, b. Aug. 13, 1805 ; m. Ebenezer Gates.
    2. Hiram D., b. Feb. 13, 1807 ; m. Elemander Woodward of So.
        Reading ; d. Oct. 3, 1879.
    2. Elizabeth, b. Feb. 16, 1809 ; m. Jonathan G. Day of Worcester,
        Dec. 2, 1834 ; d. Feb. 17, 1880.
    2. Cornelius, b. Sept. 12, 1811 ; m. Augusta Witt, Apr. 17, 1834 ;
        res. Athol Center.
        3. Sarah Augusta, b. Jan. 27, 1836 ; m. Albert Dow of Ashburnham.
        3. George Augustus, b. July 17, 1838.

HINDS.

2. William, b. Oct. 9, 1813; m. Nancy Goulding; drowned in Erving, July 15, 1835.

2. Mary Ann, b. Mar. 13, 1816; m. George W. Davis.

2. Charles E., b. Nov. 2, 1819.

2. Anna, b. May 7, 1822; m. William H. Hubbard, July 4, 1850; res. Amherst.

1. Abijah, b. Sept. 27, 1787; m. Susanna Coleman of Templeton, Dec. 30, 1810, who d. Sept. 27, 1839, a. 59; m. 2d, Persis (Pollard) Slocomb, June 8, 1841, who d. Jan. 15, 1862; rem. Gardner; d. Mar. 5, 1868.

HOWARD, bro. of CORNELIUS, m. Anna Peirce, Apr. 8, 1778, who d. Nov. 19, 1821, a. 62; he d. Worcester.

1. Molly, b. July 1, 1778; d. Aug. 22, 1782.

1. Anna, b. Sept. 12, 1780; m. Sanford Bullard of Vt., Oct. 2, 1803.

1. Calvin, b. June 30, 1783; m. Susanna Clark, Dec. 1, 1805, who d. Sept. 1, 1820; m. 2d, Betsey (Lyon) Woodward, Dec. 8, 1826, who d. Oct. 19, 1871; rem. Holden; d. Oct. 21, 1857.

2. Lucretia, b. Apr. 29, 1806; m. Parker Webber of Troy, N. Y.; d. 1833.

2. Dorothy Q., b. Feb. 3, 1808; m. Minot French of Goffstown. N. H., Apr. 22, 1833; res. Newport, R. I.

2. Lowell L., b. Jan. 5, 1810; m. Polly Wright, Apr 5, 1832; rem. Chelsea.

2. Alanson G., b. Feb. 26, 1812; m. Dianthia R. McKnight of Grafton; res. Worcester.

2. Eliza, b. Jan. 15, 1814; m. Nathaniel Richardson of Chester, Vt.; d. Chester, Vt., Feb. 1, 1848.

2. Martin, b. Sept. 24, 1815; d. Sept. 23, 1820.

2. Calvin P., b. Sept. 1, 1817; m. Mary Covell of Boston; res. Boston.

2. William A., b. Apr. 2, 1819; m. Rebecca Lougue of Boston; d. Jan. 18, 1876.

1. John Haven, b. Jan. 23, 1786; d. Aug. 20, 1811.

1. Polly, b. July 17, 1788; m. Lewis Pond.

1. Warner, b. Aug. 10, 1790; m. Achsah Woodward, June 30, 1811; rem. Worcester; both d. there; he d. Jan. 15, 1873.

2. Nancy, b. Sept. 29, 1811; m. Josiah W. Allen of Worcester,

HINDS.

June 10, 1839, who d. Worcester; she res. Newton Highlands.

2. Warner, b. June 19, 1818; m. Sarah Ryder of Southbridge, June 24, 1841; d. Apr. 5, 1855.

2. Elisha W., b. Nov. 22, 1819; m Martha Goddard of Grafton, Aug. 29, 1844; res. Ill.

2. Chauncy, b. Apr. 24, 1822; m. Ruth Shurtliff of Worcester; Nov 28, 1844; res. Brooklyn, N. Y.

1. Lydia, b. May 22, 1793; m. William Rice of Barre; d. Barre.

1. Chenery, b. June 29, 1796; m. Melinda Underwood of Barre; rem. Ohio; d. Mar. 1847; she d. June 4, 1833.

1. Zenas, b. Feb. 11, 1799; d. Feb. 20, 1800.

1. Achsah, b. May, 15, 1801; m. Aaron Clark.

HOBBS.

WILLIAM HOBBS c. f. Princeton; m. Nancy B. Gill; d. June 17, 1830. a. 48; she d. May 21, 1868. a. 82.

1. William, m. Elmira Grimes. Jan. 21, 1830; rem. Templeton; d. May, 1868.

2. Ann Maria, b. June 30, 1831.

2. Sarah Avaline, b. May 15, 1833; m. Washington Whitney of Templeton.

2. Theodore S., b. Oct. 9, 1837; m. Clara Merritt of Templeton; res. Worcester.

1. Mary, b. Jan. 12, 1809; m. Ezra Parker Brown.

1. Charles, m. Sophia H. Murdock.

2. Moses G., b. Aug. 16, 1837; m. Mary Ella Flynn, Mar. 19, 1863.

3. Frank W., b. Oct. 7, 1863.

3. Eugene B., b. Apr. 5, 1866; d. Aug. 22, 1876.

3. Alice Mary, } b. Oct. 30, 1868; d. Aug. 24, 1876.
3. Alfred Moses, }

3. Jerry, b. Apr. 2, 1871; d. Feb. 11, 1874.

3. Blanche Lunette, b. Jan. 27, 1877.

2. Sophia E., b. Aug. 1, 1840; m. R. Stickney of Templeton.

2. Nancy B., b. Apr. 21, 1843; m. John Merritt.

2. Lucy A., b. Dec. 4, 1844; m. Charles F. Tenney.

2. Charles E., b. Feb. 25, 1846.

2. Thomas J., b. Feb. 28, 1847.

2. William H., b. Apr. 26, 1850.

HOBBS.

2. Friendy A., b. Aug. 25, 1851 ; d. Dec. 18, 1866.

2. George, b. Aug. 29, 1857.

1. Thomas J., b. Apr. 13, 1814 ; d. July 16, 1844.

1. Adeline, b. Apr. 16, 1819 ; m. Ezra Parker Brown.

1. Louisa, b. 1822 ; d. Sept. 10, 1871.

HODGE.

Asa S. Hodge c. f. Athol ; m. Lucy Parker, May 8, 1845, who d. Feb.
4, 1874.

HOLT.

Ephraim Holt* c. f. Holden : m. Jerusha Kenney, who d. Nov. 2, 1857,
a. 88 ; he d. June 3. 1844, a. 81.

1. Simeon K., b. Aug. 3. 1797 ; m. Sophia Mundell, Jan. 7, 1824 ; d.
Feb. 28, 1833 ; she d. June 10, 1868.

2. Davis, b. May, 19 1824 ; m. Mary Welch of Rutland ; m. 2d,
Lucy Moore. Oct. 1. 1849, who d. Nov. 3, 1854 ; m. 3d,
Mary Amanda Moore, Feb. 7, 1856 ; d. July 11, 1865.

3 Fred Ashley, b. July 2, 1852.

3. Henry Hilton, b. Oct. 23, 1854 ; name changed. [See Mundell.]

3. Lucy F., b. Apr. 16, 1856 ; d. Feb. 17, 1872.

3. Joseph, b. July 27, 1862 ; d. Sept. 4, 1875.

2. Dennis, b. Jan. 10, 1826 ; m. Frances M. Moore, Jan. 24, 1856.

3. Cora B., b. July 28, 1859 ; d. Dec. 14, 1878.

2. Jonas, b. Dec. 19, 1827 ; m. Delia Simonds, May 13, 1859.

3. George Edwin, b. June 18, 1860.

3. Charles M., b. Sept. 1862, d. Feb. 13, 1864.

3. Willie Merritt, b. Dec. 16, 1867.

2. Silas, b. Mar. 7, 1830 ; res. Gardner.

2. Julia S., b. Nov. 21, 1832 ; m. James W. Herrick, Sept. 4, 1853.

1. Sally D., b. 1802 ; m. David Baker.

1. Betsey, b. 1805 ; d. Oct. 10, 1857, a. 52.

Elias Holt, m. Ruth Frost, Dec. 2, 1824 ; d. Feb. 6, 1851, a. 54 ; she d.
Aug. 9, 1873.

1. Nancy Azubah, b. Oct. 16, 1826 ; m. Francis H. Dewey.

1. Alexis Brooks, b. Apr. 5, 1828 ; d. Aug. 28, 1870.

1. Stedman W., b. Nov. 5, 1829 ; d. June 13, 1836.

1. Washington Irving, b. July, 17, 1831 ; m. Eliza Morrow of Barre ;
d. army, June 3, 1864. [See p. 140.]

HOLT.

2. Eliza Eva., b. Aug. 22, 1856; m. Henry C. Folsom of Athol;
   res. Turners Falls.
2. Willie Clifton, b. Jan. 2, 1859.
1. Elizabeth Malvina, b. Nov. 1, 1833; m. Aaron Forbush.
1. Oscar Elias, b. Oct. 11, 1835; m. Lucy Underwood, Oct. 6, 1858.
2. Jennie, b. Jan. 12, 1859; d. June 1, 1878.
2. Carrie Delia, b. Oct. 1, 1860.
2. Lizzie Estelle, b. June 29, 1862.
2. George Leroy, b. Feb. 21, 1866.
2. Mary Abby, b. May 17, 1867; d. Feb. 6, 1868.
2. Horace Irving, b. Aug. 30, 1869.
2. Daisy F., b. Sept, 3, 1871; d. Aug. 10, 1872.
2. Nellie B., b. Sept. 29, 1872.
2. Harry, b. Feb. 5, 1874; d. Feb. 27, 1874.
2. Lucy Mabel, b. July, 1875; d. Sept. 30, 1875.
2. Ella Louise, b. Jan. 27, 1877; d. Apr. 15, 1877.
2. Charles Oscar, b. Oct. 11, 1879.
1. Ellen A., b. Nov. 12, 1842; m. George A. Sawyer of Leominster.

HOWARD.

JOHN F. HOWARD c. f. Princeton; m. Sarah Harrington, Apr. 10, 1851.
1. Mary L., b. Apr. 1851; m. John S. Roper.
1. George L., b Oct. 28, 1859.
1. Benj. F., b. Mar. 14, 1862.
1. Myra Miller, b. Apr. 18, 1865.

HOWE.

ASA HOWE, M. D. c. f. Wendell, 1809; m. Relief Woodward, Feb. 4.
            1812, who d. Oct. 9, 1845; he d. New Salem, Aug.
            24, 1863, a. 79.
1. Charlotte W., b. Oct. 16, 1812; m. Sumner Murdock.
1. Hannah N., b. Oct. 11, 1813; m. Prescott Walker; d. New Salem,
            Jan. 9, 1838.
1. Abel, b. Sept. 11, 1815; m. Martha Williams, May 6, 1841.
2. Herbert W., b. Dec. 17, 1842; m. Mary W. Brown, Dec. 17, 1868.
2. Walter E., b. Jan. 6, 1848; m. Abby L. Aldrich of Petersham,
            Apr. 16, 1872.
3. Florence Maude, b. June 2, 1874.

HOWE.

3. Fred Herbert, b. Jan. 4. 1877.
2. Alice S., b. Dec. 22, 1848 ; d. Sept. 3. 1862.
2. Mary A., b. Dec. 8, 1859.

HUCKINS.

AARON S. HUCKINS c. f. Grafton, 1868 ; m. Abby A. Sweeny, Sept. 28, 1861.

1. Fannie E., b. Mar. 6, 1863 ; d. Aug. 1, 1864.
1. Lizzie L., b. Sept. 10, 1865.
1. Arthur Sherman, b. Oct. 31, 1871.

HUNTING.

STEPHEN HUNTING c. f. Needham ; m. Hannah ———, who d. Nov. 19, 1811, a. 80 ; he d. Dec. 11, 1815, a. 96 y., 9 m.

1. Stephen, b. Dec. 23. 1750 ; m. Polly Newton. Dec. 23, 1790, who d. Apr. 1, 1808, a. 36 ; m. 2d, Eunice Dupee, July 1810, who d. May 30, 1855, a. 89 ; he d. Nov. 16, 1835.
   2. Sally. b. June 3, 1791 ; m. James Greenwood.
   2. Leonard, b. July 8, 1794 ; d. Aug. 4. 1800.
   2. Caty, b. May 28, 1796 ; d. Aug. 8, 1800.
   2. Polly, b. Oct. 1, 1799 ; m. Sewell Moulton.
   2. Jarvis, b. Mar. 30, 1804 ; m. Rebecca H. Sawin, Feb. 28, 1830, who d. Apr. 9, 1836 ; his name was changed to Wm. J. Parker ; m. 2d, Lucinda Russell. [See Parker.]
   2. Clarissa, b. Oct. 7, 1806 ; d. Dec 25, 1806.
1. Moses†, b. Sept. 8, 1758 ; m. Elizabeth W. Newton, Jan. 12, 1792, who d. May 1, 1814 ; rem. Westminster ; d. there.
   2. Moses, b. Oct. 23, 1792.
   2. Polly, b. Nov. 24. 1794 ; d. July 25, 1800.
   2. Jonas N., b. Feb. 3. 1797.
   2. Sydney F., b. Sept. 6, 1799.
   2. Catherine, b. Feb. 15, 1802.
   2. Thomas S., b. Mar. 12, 1804 ; d. Sept. 25, 1804.
   2. Sarepta W., b. Apr. 7, 1805 ; m. ——— Graves.
   2. Relief Eliza, b. Mar. 2, 1809 ; m. George Mundell, Aug. 15, 1833.
1. Converse*, b. May 5, 1760 ; m. Mary Parker, who d. Oct. 4, 1849, a. 90 ; he d. July 4, 1851.
   2. Nancy, b. Apr. 18, 1783 ; m. Waldo Grimes.

HUNTING.

2. Josiah, b. Sept. 16, 1784 ; m. Elizabeth Green, who d. Sept. 5. 1842, a. 57 ; he d. Oct. 10, 1853.

3. Eliza, b. Oct. 16, 1814 ; d. Jan. 28, 1837.

3. Parker, b. Apr. 6, 1817 ; d. Jan., 1867.

3. Mary, b. Sept. 20, 1819 ; m. Charles Hodgman of Ashby, Nov. 26, 1857.

3. Josiah, b. Mar. 8, 1823 ; m. Harriet Allen, May 16, 1850, who d. July 23, 1851 ; m. 2d, Elizabeth Struthers of Canada East, Dec. 27, 1860 ; rem. Templeton.

   4. William E., b. June 10, 1851.

3. Sewell, b. Sept., 1825 ; d. Aug. 9, 1827.

3. Horace, b. June 17, 1828 ; m. Harriet A. Kile of N. Y., Apr. 28, 1858 ; rem. N. Y.

3. William, b. July 16, 1831 ; m. Mary Day of Templeton, Apr. 4, 1855 ; res. E. Templeton.

   4. Fred S., b. Sept. 30, 1868.

2. George, b. Apr. 11, 1786 ; d. Dec. 17, 1826.

2. Lemuel, b. May 17, 1788 ; m. Polly Baker of Westminster, Sept. 28, 1820 ; rem. Templeton ; d. July 3, 1868.

3. Stephen, b. Feb. 14, 1821 ; d. Aug. 15, 1833.

3. Anna, b. Mar. 22, 1823 ; m. Jacob Chamberlain, Aug. 25. 1847 ; he d. army.

3. Lucy, b. Oct. 4, 1824 ; d. Oct. 31, 1825.

3. Leonard, b. Mar. 19, 1826 ; m. Sophia Gray ; res. Templeton.

3. Hannah, b. July 7, 1829 ; m. Elisha Rockwood Brown.

3. Lucy W., b. May 11, 1834 ; m. George V. Sawin of Westminster, Aug. 2, 1851 ; m. 2d, Gilman Brown.

3. Sarah V., b. Nov. 26, 1838 ; m. Alphonso B. Rayner, Sept. 26, 1867.

2. Abijah, b. Sept. 10, 1790 ; d. Jan. 10, 1793.

2. Parker, b. July 31, 1792 ; d. Jan. 31, 1817.

2. Aaron, b. Oct. 27, 1797 ; m. Julianna Rice, Sept. 30, 1824 ; d. Dec. 16, 1863.

3. Roxa, b. Sept. 12, 1825 ; m. Silas Adams.

3. George, b. Nov. 12, 1826 ; d. Dec. 20, 1846.

3. Cynthia, b. Nov. 7, 1830 ; m. Henry Perley of Gardner, Mar. 19, 1850.

3. Daniel, b. Oct. 26, 1832 ; m. Charlotte M. Forbush of Brooklyn, N. Y., Nov. 22, 1859 ; d. Feb. 15, 1872.

38

HUNTING.

4. Charles Aaron, b. June 14, 1860.
4. Willie George, b. Aug. 31, 1861.
4. Kate Julianna, b. Nov. 4, 1864.
4. Henry Roderick, b. Sept. 30, 1865.
4. Minnie Lottie. b. Oct. 12, 1868.
4. Gilson Whitson. b. July 6, 1871.
3. Charles, b. May 17, 1834 ; m. Hannah Peirce, Dec. 1, 1854.
.   who d. May 9. 1858 ; m. 2d, Ellen J. Mann, Jan. 18,
1859 ; d. Nov. 15, 1860.
4. Willett L., b. July 15, 1855 ; d. Feb. 3, 1858.
4. George C., b. June 27, 1857.
4. Lilla C., b. Jan. 5. 1860.
3. Eli, b. Mar. 27. 1836 ; m. Ellen J. (Mann) Hunting, Nov. 14.
1864 : res. Gardner.
3. Nancy, b. May 3. 1839 : m. Elwell P. Sargent.
3. John W., b. June 17, 1841 ; m. Mary A. Sargent, Aug. 3. 1862 ;
d. July 29. 1864. [See p. 140.]
3. Henry. b. Nov. 30, 1845 : m. Mary Elizabeth Leeman, Mar.
20. 1867 : d. Gardner. Aug. 10, 1870.
4. John Willard. b. Apr. 19, 1868.
4. Henry Nelson, b. Sept. 24, 1870.
1. William. b. Apr. 17. 1753 : m. Lydia Wheelock, June 9, 1779 ; rem.
2. Luther, b. July 24, 1780.
2. William, b. May 22, 1783.
2. Hannah, b. Aug. 2. 1785.
2. Seth, b. Mar. 1, 1787.
2. Betsey, b. Apr. 18, 1790.

ALEXANDER HUNTING c. f. Marlboro' ; m. Tryphena Eager, 1774. who d.
Dec. 23. 1839, a. 69 ; he d. Sept. 30, 1823, a. 55.
1. Betsey, b. Apr. 23. 1775 ; m. George Felton, Nov. 2, 1828 ; d. Dec.
11, 1828.
1. Tryphena, b. May 7, 1779 ; m. Jason Smith of Barre, June 14, 1820 ;
d. Gardner, Mar. 19. 1873.
1. Alexander, b. Aug. 23, 1793 : m. Mrs. Mary Johnson, who d. Dec.
5. 1866 : he d. Barre.
2. Daniel A., b. Nov. 7. 1835 : rem. Athol.
1. Mary, b. Jan. 14. 1805 : m. Uriah Eager of Marlboro', Jan. 1, 1826 ;
d. Sept. 11, 1870.

HUNTING.

1. Lucy, b. Nov. 17, 1807; d. Feb. 6, 1862.*
1. Charles Austin, b. Oct. 16, 1809; name changed to Charles Austin. [See Austin.]

HUTCHINSON.

DANIEL HUTCHINSON c. f. Worcester; m. Emma C. Greenwood, Apr. 17. 1873.
1. Ralph Emerson, b. Aug. 8, 1877.

HYDE.

WILLIAM HYDE c. f. Newton; m. Eunice Stearns, Nov. 2, 1795, who d. May 27, 1860, a. 86; he d. May 28, 1850, a. 80.
1. Roxanna, m. Silas Lampson of Sterling.
1. Eunice, m. James Sawin of Westminster.
1. Lydia, m. John Stratton of Leominster.
1. William, b. June 3, 1805; d. Oct. 2, 1879.
1. Keziah, b. July 12, 1807; m. James Dean of Shrewsbury.
1. Amasa, b. Nov. 3, 1809; m. Susan Hale, June 5, 1834; rem. Shrewsbury.
1. Elizabeth, b. Jan. 30, 1813; m. Peter L. Spaulding of Lunenburg.
1. Silas Stearns, b. Jan. 18, 1817; m. Nancy Fletcher of New Ipswich. N. H., Oct. 7, 1841; res. Ohio. [See p. 184.]
1. Charles, b. 1820; m. Elizabeth (Sawin) Sweetland of Rockland. Me., Sept. 16, 1849; res. Worcester.

JACKSON.

AUGUSTINE JACKSON c. f. Newton, 1858; m. Abby T. Lamkin of Jay, Me., Jan. 22, 1853.
1. Eva A., b. Dec. 26, 1853; m. William S. Prentiss.
1. Herbert A., b. May 11, 1857.
1. Lorenzo J., b. Aug. 6, 1859.

JENNISON.

MRS. DOLLY JENNISON c. f. Phillipston; d. Sept. 23, 1852, a 83.
1. Flint, m. Mary Stowe, Dec. 1, 1836; rem. Worcester.
2. Sarah Almira, b. July 23, 1840.
2. John Flint, b. Oct. 24, 1843; d. army.
2. Henry Edward, b. Nov. 9, 1846; res. Omaha, Neb.
2. Ella M., b. Dec. 31, 1850.

JEWETT.

JOSEPH JEWETT c. f. Worcester, 1869 ; m. Susan B. (Jenks) Jenks, Nov. 26, 1864.

JOHNSON.

DAVID L. JOHNSON c. f. Barre ; m. Lois Wilbur, Jan. 1, 1846.
1. Lucy Minerva, b. Aug. 16, 1847 ; m. J. Wesley Watson of Kansas.
1. Frank W., b. Aug. 3, 1852.
1. Moses Perry, b. Mar. 2, 1854 ; m. Mary Pettigrew of St. Louis, Mo., res. Mo.
  2. Edith Browning. b. June 21, 1880.

JOSLIN.

EBENEZER JOSLIN c. f. Marlboro', 1770 ; m. Lydia Church of Rutland, who d. Dec. 9, 1805. a. 66 ; he d. Sept. 11, 1806, a. 73.
1. Silas. b. Sept. 22, 1764 ; m. Betsey Greenwood, Oct. 28, 1789 ; d. Aug. 8, 1828 ; she d. Oct. 13, 1849, a. 83.
2. Lydia, b. Jan. 18, 1790 ; d. July 20, 1791.
2. Lydia, b. Feb. 4, 1793 ; d. Oct. 15. 1794.
2. Sally, b. Mar. 17, 1796 ; d. Sept. 18, 1798.
2. Silas, b. Jan. 30, 1800 ; d. Sept. 14, 1803.
2. Hollis, b. July 28, 1803 ; m. Linda Underwood, Apr. 25, 1826.
  3. Jonas, b. Sept. 2, 1826 ; m. Alvina Morse, Apr. 27, 1854 ; rem. Gardner.
  3. Eliza, b. Mar. 26, 1829 ; m. L. T. Whitcomb of Templeton, July 8, 1851 ; res. Brooklyn, N. Y.
  3. Emily, b. Oct. 3, 1831 ; m. Addison Waite.
  3. Clara, b. Dec. 8, 1833 ; m. Amos Hemenway ; res. Gardner.
  3. Silas, b. Dec. 3, 1839 ; m. Mary A. Williams, Sept. 4, 1860 ; res. Gardner.
    4. Frank S., b. Sept. 14, 1861.
    4. Everett D., b. July 24, 1864.
    4. Lewis A., b. Oct. 11, 1867.
2. Levi, b. Apr. 16, 1806 ; m. Dorcas Wright, Apr. 22, 1827.
  3. Adelphia, b. Feb. 10, 1828 ; m. Hiram Wadsworth of Barre, Apr. 30, 1863.
  3. Mary Jane, b. June 18, 1830 ; m. Henry J. Kendall of Barre, Apr. 22, 1852.
  3. Ellen Maria. b. Apr. 7, 1833 ; m. John Q. Greenwood ; m. 2d, Theodore Greenwood.

JOSLIN.

3. Dorcas Elizabeth, b. May 13, 1837 ; m. George Prentiss.

3. Abby Louisa, b. Sept. 12, 1841.

3. Levi G., b. Aug. 21, 1846 ; m. Katie E. Gates of Worcester. Nov. 15, 1877 ; res. Worcester.

2. Silas, b. July 7, 1811 ; m. Minerva (Gates) Kendall, Nov. 26, 1846.

3. Horace, b. May 12, 1849 ; m. Adeline A. Coleman, Apr. 6, 1875, who d. July 8, 1876.

1. Lucy, b. 1766 ; d. Oct. 8, 1806.

1. William, b. 1769 ; m. Rhoda Wheeler, Feb. 19, 1797 : d. Nov. 14, 1807.

2. John, b. May 20, 1797 ; d. Sept. 2, 1799.

2. Mary, b. July 1, 1799 ; m. Abishai Eveleth.

2. Eliza, b. May 19, 1801 ; res. Boston.

2. William, b. Nov. 30, 1803 : m. Cynthia Greenwood, Apr. 15, 1830, d. Jan. 10, 1873.

3. Mary M., b. July 16, 1831 ; d. July, 19, 1858.

3. Elmira A., b. Sept. 15, 1835.

3. Cynthia M., b. Nov. 19, 1836.

3 William H., b. May 14, 1841 ; m. Lydia V. Stratton of Charlestown ; res. Ind.

3. Frederick W., b. May 25, 1845 ; m. Etta K. Beckley of Ind., Feb. 15, 1871 ; res. Mich.

2. Lucy, b. May 28, 1806 ; m. Warren Hubbard of Princeton, Nov. 12, 1828 : d. Princeton.

1. Ephraim, b. 1776 ; d. Apr. 23, 1820.

1. Peter, b. 1780 ; m. Rhoda (Wheeler) Joslin, Dec. 23, 1810, who d. June 19, 1819 ; m. 2d, Betsey Woodis of Barre, Mar., 1821, who d. Dec. 4, 1856 ; he d. Mar. 24, 1847.

2. Susan, b. June 4, 1823 ; m. Rufus Howard, Dec. 21, 1848 ; d. Stoneham, Feb., 1867.

2. Julia Ann., b. Apr. 6, 1827 ; m. Henry A. Smith, Nov. 16, 1848 ; res. Templeton.

1. Moses, b. 1785 ; d. May 18, 1848.

1. Sally, b. 1789 ; d. Aug. 5, 1811.

KELTON.

ELIHU KELTON c. f. Dorchester, 1870 ; m. Ann Blackman, Dec. 13. 1818, who d. Dec. 11, 1875, a. 79 ; he d. Jan. 14, 1878, a. 87.

KELTON.

1. Elihu, b. May 2, 1831; m. Susan J. Hathorne of Bangor, Me.,
   June 10, 1856.
   2. Addie E., b. Nov. 2, 1857.
   2. Harriet L., b. Nov. 26, 1858; d. Dec. 25, 1872.
   2. Annie J., b. May 17, 1860; d. Dec. 1, 1872.
   2. George H., b. Sept. 20. 1861.
   2. Mary R., b. May 6, 1863.
   2. Susie H., b. May 29, 1868.
   2. E. Frank, b. May 7, 1872.

LAMB.

JAMES LAMB,* c. f. Spencer before 1800; m. ———— Knapp who d. Mar.
   3, 1825, a. 73: he d. Dec. 26, 1834, a. 82.
   1. James, b. Spencer; m. Dolly Waite, Nov. 7, 1805; d. Penn.
   2. Dolly Waite, b. May 16, 1808; m. Asa Wheeler, Nov. 6, 1828;
      rem. Warwick; d. there.
   2. James, b. Oct. 19. 1809; m. Harriet A. Green, Sept. 27, 1832,
      who d. May 5, 1864; he d. Feb. 28, 1876.
      3. James W., b. Apr. 6, 1834; sea captain; d. San Francisco.
         June 6, 1870.
      3. Harriet A., b. Apr. 15. 1836: m. Calvin Underwood.
      3. Milton, b. Jan. 8, 1838; res. Cal.
      3. Joseph A., b. May 7, 1840; res. N. J.
      3. Harrison W., b. Dec. 9, 1842; m. Miriam Bennett, Oct. 4,
         1865; res. Gardner.
      3. Larkin, b. Dec., 1844; res. Gardner.
      3. Lewis C., b. Apr. 26. 1848; d. Nov. 21, 1857.
      3. Arabella D., b. Sept. 16, 1853; d. Jan. 29, 1856.
   1. Pliny, b. Spencer; m. Rebecca Brown, Apr. 12, 1804; d. Jan. 7,
      1821.
   2. Greanleaf, b. Jan. 25, 1805; m. Hannah Frost, Apr. 12, 1827;
      rem. Westminster; both d. there.
   2. Nancy, b. June 9. 1807; m. Simpson Clark; m. 2d, Isaac Hallock.
   2. Pliny, b. Sept. 10, 1809: m. Eliza Follett, Apr. 11, 1830; rem.
      Ind.; d. 1855.
   2. Augustus, b. Sept. 30, 1811; m. Amanda Coleman of Westmins-
      ter; d. W., May 2, 1863.
   2. John, b. Mar. 5, 1815; d. Jan. 25, 1816.
   2. William, b. Jan. 1, 1817; rem. Ind.

LAMB.

1. Sally, b. Spencer; m. Daniel Wheeler; m. 2d, Nathan Wright.
1. Amy, b. Spencer; m. Aaron Phelps.
1. Nancy, b. Spencer; d. Aug. 8, 1800.
1. Lucinda, b. Spencer; d. Sept. 4, 1803.

DANIEL LAMB c. f. Oxford, 1813; m. Mary Carter, who d. Nov. 8, 1856,
      a. 72; he d. May 28, 1862, a. 75.
1. Albert, b. Oct. 26, 1807; res. Leominster.
1. Carter, b. Feb. 27, 1809; d. Chicago, Oct. 10, 1866.
1. Mary, b. Dec. 31, 1810; d. Jan. 11, 1816.
1. Adeline, b. June 15, 1815.
1. Charles, b. Aug. 29, 1818; d. Mar. 4, 1880.

LANPHEAR.

SALMON H. LANPHEAR c. f. Princeton, 1860; m. Mary A. Watson of
      Princeton, Feb. 7, 1854, who d. Sept. 22, 1870. a.
      33; m. 2d, Tryphena Udall of Wolcott. Vt., Dec.
      1872.
1. Charles H., b. Mar 25, 1856; d. July 5, 1872.
1. Walter H., b. Oct. 25, 1857.
1. William A., b. Sept. 7, 1859.
1. Elmer E., b. Feb. 25, 1862.
1. Alice L., b. Apr. 15, 1864.
1. George W., b. Nov. 12, 1866.
1. Mary L., b. June 6, 1875.
1. Arthur S., b. Feb. 7, 1877.

LAUGHNA.

TERRENCE LAUGHNA c. f. Ireland; m. Catherine Malone, Feb. 23, 1847.
1. Mary, b. Nov. 27, 1849; m. S. Newton Dunton.
1. James, b. May 8, 1852; d. July 18, 1864.
1. Lawrence, b. July 17, 1853; d. July 6, 1864.
1. William O., b. Jan. 14, 1855; m. Rose Ikirt of Cal., Nov. 6, 1878;
      res. California.
1. Peter L., b. June 8, 1856; d. July 7, 1864.
1. Catherine, b. Oct. 27, 1858; d. July 6, 1864.
1. Jackson H., b. Mar. 26, 1860.

LEARNED.

ALONZO K. LEARNED c. f. Westminster, 1873. Teacher.

LELAND.

LOWELL LELAND c. f. Sherborn, 1803 ; m. Betsey Clark of Gardner, who
     d. Dec. 8, 1829 ; m. 2d, Elizabeth (Wright) Spring,
     June 20, 1830, who d. Fitchburg, Aug. 3, 1865 ; he d.
     Apr. 14. 1855, a. 65. [See p. 167.]

1. Leander, b. Mar. 7, 1815 ; m. Mary Poland of Winchendon ; res.
     Winchendon.
1. Esther M., b. Dec. 27, 1816 ; m. Joel Fairbanks of Gardner ; res.
     Templeton.
1. Elizabeth, b. Apr. 29, 1818 ; d. Mar. 10, 1819.
1. Martha, b. Feb. 28, 1820 ; m. C. M. Leland ; res. Wyoming, Mass.
1. Sarah. b. Mar. 5, 1822 ; d. Apr. 17, 1822.
1. Elizabeth, b. Mar. 5, 1823 ; m. Asher Moore of Ashburnham, Apr.
     26, 1841.
1. Henry. b. Oct. 9, 1825 ; m. Lucy Hubbard of Ashby ; d. Temple-
     ton, 1869.
1. Joseph Willard, b. Sept. 24, 1827 ; m. Eliza A. Hubbard of Ashby ;
     res. Winchendon.
1. Lucy K., b. July 19, 1831 ; m. Ephraim F. Adams of Enosburg,
     Vt., Jan. 2, 1859.
1. Delia Ann, b. Aug. 2, 1833 ; d. Sept., 1841.
1. Mary B., b. Apr. 16, 1835 ; d. June 3, 1846.
1. Moses, b. Oct. 15, 1837 ; m. Louisa E. Clark, Apr. 25, 1862, who
     d. Sept. 9, 1872 ; m. 2d, Elizabeth Merriam of Templeton,
     June 25, 1873 ; rem. Gardner.
   2. Fred. W., b. Aug. 27, 1869.
   2. Walter W., b. Feb. 25, 1875.
   2. Arthur, b. May 26, 1878.

LEONARD.

RICHARD LEONARD c. f. Fitzwilliam, N. H. ; m. Phebe Ellinwood, Jan.
     7, 1836, who d. Jan. 18, 1846 ; m. 2d, Sarah Murdock,
     May 24, 1848.

1. Lucy Jane, b. Nov. 4. 1841 ; m. Sumner C. Young.
1. Elwyn Clayton, b. Apr. 9, 1849 ; d. Sept. 5, 1850.
1. Frank Leslie, b. Oct. 16, 1851.
1. Mary Etta, b. June 28, 1853.
1. Edward Abbott, b. Mar. 27, 1856 ; d. June 17, 1864.

LESTER.

ANTHONY LESTER c. f. Ireland ; m. Bridget Morris, Nov. 23, 1860.

1. Thomas B., b. Jan. 24, 1863 ; d. Aug. 24, 1864.
1. Mary Elizabeth, b. Mar. 4, 1866.
1. Jane, b. July 21, 1870.

LOVEWELL.

JOSEPH LOVEWELL c. f. Needham ; m. Sarah Wilkinson, who d. Aug. 30, 1847, a. 80 ; he d. Nov. 21, 1814, a. 50.

1. Jesse, b. Sept. 25, 1798 ; m. Betsey Comee of Gardner ; thrown from wagon and killed, Jan. 29, 1838.
  2. Nahum Keyes, b. Nov. 6, 1827 ; m. Rhoda Earle, Mar. 3, 1853 ; rem. Phillipston ; d. Phillipston.
  2. David N., b. Jan. 17, 1830 ; res. Boston.
  2. Leander, b. June 14, 1832 ; m. Aurilla P. Gates, Aug. 22, 1867.
    3. Freddie Austin Eugene, b. Nov. 17, 1873.
  2. Sarah, b. Mar. 11, 1835 ; m. Thomas S. Eaton of Westminster, Nov. 28, 1858.
  2. Christiana, b. July 22, 1837 ; m. Norman Seaver of Westminster.
1. Joseph, b. Nov. 10, 1799 ; m. Jerusha Smith, Nov. 28, 1820, who d. Jan. 15, 1871, a. 77 ; he d. Sept. 7, 1876.
  2. Martha, b. May 6, 1821.
  2. Jerusha, b. May 17, 1823.
  2. John, b. Oct. 1, 1826 ; m. Mary V. Hodge of Stowe, Vt., May 6, 1868.
    3. Willis Levi, b. Mar. 8, 1869.
  2. Rebecca, b. Oct. 20, 1832.
1. Isaac, b. July 18, 1803 ; m. Eliza Moulton, Sept. 18, 1825 ; d. Gardner, Jan. 16, 1871.
1. Tryphena, b. Dec. 19, 1805 ; m. Elijah W. Foster of Gardner, Sept. 1, 1830 ; d. Gardner.
1. Asa, b. Sept. 4, 1807 ; d. Sept. 8, 1807.
1. Leonard, b. Nov. 20, 1808 ; m. Louisa Comee of Gardner ; d. G.
1. Rebecca, b. Nov. 4, 1811 ; m. James Phillips.

LYON.

BEZALEEL LYON* c. f. Barre, 1771 ; m. Mary Davenport, who d. Apr. 1, 1803, a. 61 ; he d. June 24, 1796, a. 57. [See p. 166.]

1. Sarah, b. 1767 ; m. Paul Matthews, Jan., 1787, who d. July 20, 1794 ; m. 2d, Luke Warren.

39

LYON.

1. Miriam, b. 1768 ; m. Nathan Newton.
1. Samuel, b. Nov. 25, 1771 ; d. young. .
1. Asa, b. Jan. 4, 1774 ; m. Attarah Grimes, Dec. 5, 1799 ; who d. May 2, 1846 ; he d. Malden.
  2. Dana, b. June 11, 1801 ; m. Harriet Locke, Aug., 1834.
    3. Edward, b. June 10, 1835 ; res. Sacramento, Cal.
    3. John, b. Oct. 20, 1837 ; res. Franklin, N. H.
    3. Mary, b. Feb. 11, 1840 ; m.———— Hancock of Franklin, N. H.
  2. Pliny, b. Mar. 10, 1803 ; d. May 17, 1803.
  2. Asa, b. Nov. 24, 1806 ; d. May 25, 1838.
  2. Aaron, b. Aug. 24, 1808 ; m. Elizabeth C. Lane, June 6, 1841.
    3. Sarah E., b. Apr. 26, 1842 ; d. Sept. 6, 1862.
    3. George, b. Sept. 4, 1843 ; d. Sept. 27, 1844.
    3. Martha Ann, b. Feb. 26, 1845 ; m. John McClenathan of Hague, N. Y., Dec. 23, 1872.
    3. George A., b. June 12, 1847.
    3. Andrew J., b. June 27, 1849 ; rem. Boston.
    3. Emma R., b. Mar. 22, 1852 ; m. Alvah E. Grimes.
    3. John F., b. Aug. 5, 1855 ; d. Jan. 19, 1863.
  2. Amiable, b. July 29, 1810 ; d. Aug. 22, 1813.
  2. Amiable, b. Sept. 12, 1813.
  2. Joseph, b. Mar. 20, 1817 ; d. Boston, Sept. 15, 1870.
  2. Lucy, b. July 28, 1823 ; d. Shirley, June 18, 1851.
1. Martha, b. Feb. 29, 1776 ; m. Joel Wheeler.
1. Ruth, b. Apr. 5, 1778 ; d. May 11, 1858.
1. Lucy, ⎱ b. Apr. 24, 1780 ; m. Jotham Stone.
1. Lois, ⎰   m. Aaron Wright.
1. Betsey, b. 1782 ; m. John F. Woodward ; m. 2d, Calvin Hinds.
1. Anna, b. 1784 ; m. J. Pollock ; d. Dec. 25, 1851.

MANN.

EBENEZER MANN*, b. Wrentham, 1750 ; m. Mary Bullard, Nov. 20, 1777, who d. Nov. 25, 1847, a. 93 ; he d. July 30, 1844 ; both d. Westminster.
  1. John, b. Aug. 20, 1778 ; m. Polly Anderson, who d. July 17, 1816 ; m. 2d, Narcissa Earle of Leicester, May, 1829 ; rem. Leicester ; d. 1848.
    2. Marcena, b. Feb. 7, 1802 ; d. Oct. 2, 1803.

MANN.

2. Seraph, b. Sept. 27, 1803 ; res. Worcester ; d Apr. 14, 1881.

2. Candace, b. Dec. 1, 1804 ; m. Jonathan P. Haynes of Temple-
    ton, Dec. 23, 1823 ; d. Apr. 23, 1878.

2. Augusta Elvira, b. Nov. 22, 1806 ; m. John Brown of Winchen-
            don, who d. 1831 ; she res. Valley Falls, R. I.

2. Louisa, b. Mar. 3, 1809 ; m. J. M. Bryant of Baldwinsville, who
        d. 1839 ; m. 2d, Dr. Albigence Pierce of Stratford, N. H. ;
        d. Oct. 7, 1850.

2. Lurinda, b. Apr. 10, 1811 ; d. July 23, 1811.

2. Parmenus Anderson, b. Aug. 11, 1812 ; d. Rochester, Ind., May
            12, 1856.

2. Sophronia, b. June 27, 1814 ; d. Mar. 1, 1816.

2. George Earle, b. Mar. 21, 1830 ; res. N. Y.

1. Lemuel, b. Sept. 29, 1783 ; m. Lucy Howe of Templeton ; rem.
        Templeton ; d. there.

1. Amos, b. Sept. 10, 1786 ; m. Betsey Rice, Dec. 31, 1810 ; d. Apr.
        5, 1868 ; she d. Aug. 12, 1874.

2. Ebenezer, b. Sept. 6, 1812 ; m. Polly P. Bowers of Royalston,
        who d. Jan. 7, 1869, a. 52 ; m. 2d, Hattie A. Haynes
        of Hinsdale, N. H., Jan. 24, 1872 ; d. Oct. 4, 1877.

    3. Ellen J., b. Apr., 1839 ; m. Charles Hunting ; m. 2d, Eli Hunting.

2. Edmund, b. Sept. 6, 1812 ; d. Dec. 2, 1820.

2. Otis Greenwood, b. Sept. 26, 1814 ; d. Jan. 1, 1815.

2. Otis Greenwood, b. Jan. 1, 1816 ; d. Aug. 26, 1821.

2. Alonzo, b. Oct. 5, 1819 ; m. D. Lavinia Hill of Royalston, Apr.
        26, 1842.

    3. Aurilla M., b. Jan. 6, 1844 ; m. G. L. Thayer of Templeton,
            Dec. 8, 1866.

    3. Mary A., b. Feb. 27, 1846 ; m. J. W. Lord of Winchendon,
            Nov. 16, 1867.

    3. F. Janette, b. Feb. 2, 1848 ; m. George Sibley of Winchen-
            don, Mar. 17, 1865.

    3. Oscar A., b. Aug. 16, 1850 ; m. Martha D. Sawtelle of Win-
            chendon, May 10, 1874 ; res. Winchendon.

    3. Edgar A., b. Oct. 2, 1852.

    3. Edwin A., b. Oct. 2, 1852 ; d. Apr. 16, 1853.

    3. Ella A., b. Oct. 2, 1852 ; m. Henry S. Coleman.

    3. Flora A , b. Jan. 30, 1854 ; d. Oct. 6, 1874.

MANN.

3. Edwin A., b. Oct. 11, 1856; m. Elnora L. Bates, Apr. 17, 1877; rem. Townsend.
3. Cora A., b. Jan. 8, 1860.
3. Eugene C., b. Sept. 27, 1862; d. Sept. 12, 1863.
1. Betsey, b. Jan. 19, 1788; d. Feb. 7, 1831.
1. George, b. Mar. 12, 1790; d. June 12, 1793.
1. Artemas, b. July 27, 1792; m. Polly Knowlton of Phillipston; rem. Phillipston; d. there.
2. George Harrison, b. June 12, 1817; m. Ann Clark, Apr. 11, 1843; d. Sept. 28, 1854.
3. Georgianna, b. Aug. 27, 1850; d. Aug. 29, 1855.
2. Rosanna, b. Mar. 12, 1820; m. Crawford Titus of Westminster; m. 2d, Wilson Bragg of Royalston.
2. Joseph K., b. Dec. 22, 1823; drowned, June 20, 1828. [See p. 165.]
2. Alzina, b. Mar. 14, 1828; m. Rev. D. C. O'Daniels of N. Y., who d. Feb., 1867,; she d. Athol, May 8, 1880.
2. Henry, b. June 12, 1832; d. Phillipston.
2. Joseph; adopted by James Jackson of Petersham; name changed to Jackson; d. army.
1. Isabella, b. Nov. 18, 1794; m. Levi Allen.
1. Darius, b. June 22, 1797: d. Sept. 8, 1821. [See p. 166.]
1. Lucretia, b. Mar. 4, 1800; m. Williams Wilbur.

MAREAN.

WILLIAM MAREAN, formerly of Newton, c. f. Barre, 1768; served in the Revolutionary War; m. Sybil Parker; d. May 10, 1826, a. 83; his widow received a pension from 1832 till she d.. Mar. 22, 1843, a. 96.
1. Catherine, b. Feb. 16, 1768; d. Aug. 25, 1770.
1. Elizabeth, b. Aug. 26, 1770; m. Asa Brigham, May 23, 1791; rem.
1. Timothy Parker, b. Feb. 17, 1773; m. Alice Smith, July 6, 1797, who d. Aug. 28, 1852; he d. Sept. 12, 1826.
2. Asa, b. May 5, 1798; m. Lucy Browning, Apr. 17, 1823, who d. June 8, 1863; he d. May 25, 1866.
3. Clark Witt, b. May 27, 1824; m. Sarah W. Whittemore, Nov. 6. 1850, who d. Sept. 5, 1861; m. 2d, Cynthia Whittemore, Oct. 17, 1862.
4. Frank B., b. Oct. 24, 1863.

MAREAN.

4. Robert Lincoln, b. Jan. 9, 1865 ; d. Sept. 18, 1865.
4. Lucy, b. Aug. 18, 1869.
4. Clara E., b. Nov. 30, 1870.
3. William P., b. May 12, 1826 ; d. Nov. 19, 1827.
3. Asa, b. May 12, 1828 ; d. July 3, 1845.
3. Joseph P., b. Sept. 21, 1831.
3. Sarah E., b. Oct. 12, 1833.
3. John P., b. July 8, 1836 : d. Clarksville, Ark., Mar., 1862.
3. Clara Sophia, b. Oct. 1, 1839.
3. Mary P., b. May 8, 1842 : d. May 9, 1844.
2. Sophia, b. Nov. 28, 1799 ; m. Stephen Church.
2. Moses, b. June 14, 1802 ; d. Sept. 26, 1803.
2. Elmira, b. June 28, 1804 ; d. Nov. 2, 1805.
2. Sumner, b. May 5, 1806 ; m. Sally Wright, Dec. 25, 1825 ; d.
    Apr. 5, 1834 ; she d. Nov. 9, 1872.
   3. Oren Maynard, b. Jan. 13, 1826 ; m. Maria Wheeler of Rut-
          land, Apr. 13, 1854 : d. Oct. 27, 1879.
    4. Valetta C., b. Feb. 14, 1855.
    4. Hubert Sumner, b. Jan. 12, 1857.
    4. Rowland Granville, b. Feb. 2, 1859.
   3. Augusta, b. June 6, 1829 ; m. Charles A. Colby of San Francisco.
   3. Alice, b. Oct. 10, 1831 ; m. Rufus Warren.
2. Augusta, b. July 12, 1808 ; m. Lyman Greenwood.
2. Stedman, b. July 14, 1810 ; m. Mary C. Wheeler, Nov. 11, 1832 :
    res. Washington, D. C.
2. Moses, b. Nov., 1812 ; m. Nancy Wilbur, June 2, 1834 ; d. July
    27, 1860.
   3. George Gilbert, b. Jan. 17, 1835 ; m. Mary Brownlee, Sept. 1,
          1863 : d. Sept. 23, 1872.
   3. Joseph H., b. June 22, 1837 ; m. Mary Ann Warren ; res.
    Boston.
   3. Mary E., b. Jan. 3, 1845 ; m. Edward Morse.
2. Joseph P., b. Apr. 14, 1815 : m. Abigail Mason, Sept. 10, 1839 :
    res. Chicago.
2. Elizabeth, b. June, 1817 ; d. June 7, 1839.
1. Katy, b. Jan. 1, 1775 ; m. Abner Gay.
1. Sally, b. Oct. 20, 1778 ; d. Mar. 20, 1820.
1. William, b. July 20, 1780 ; m. Betsey Blood, Mar. 2, 1801 ; d. Jan.
    22, 1809.

MAREAN.

2. William, b. Jan. 30, 1801 ; m. Susan (Browning) Wheeler, Oct. 4, 1825 ; d. Jan. 23, 1870 ; she d. Cambridge, Jan. 5, 1877.

3. William Henry, b. Mar. 10, 1826 ; m. Polly B. Pond, Aug. 22, 1847, who d. Oxford ; m. 2d, Isabella ——— ; rem. Illinois.

4. Emma Rebecca, b. Dec 8, 1848 ; d. July 24, 1858.

4. Frederick Cooper Starr, b. July 2, 1869.

3. Rebecca, b. Feb. 9, 1828 ; d. Sept. 1, 1844.

3. David Bennett, b. Aug. 5, 1831 ; d. Dec. 22, 1844.

3. Susan E., b. June 15, 1834 ; m. George M. Glazier of Rutland, Aug. 22, 1859.

3. Hannah, b. Nov. 2, 1836 ; d. June 5, 1861

2. Eliza, b. Aug. 12, 1802 ; m. Joseph Fletcher.

2. Emily, b. Dec. 12, 1804 ; m. Thomas Henry Brown

1. Hannah, b. Nov. 3, 1784 ; m. David Bennett.

1. Joseph, b Jan. 6. 1788 ; m Harriet McClenathan, June 21, 1807 ; d. July 28, 1814.

2. Lucy, b. Sept. 28, 1807 ; m. Justin Holden of Keeseville, N. Y., May 15, 1832.

2. Louisa, b. Sept 8, 1809 ; m. Aaron Grimes.

2. Charlotte, b. Nov. 19. 1811 ; m. Justin Holden, Sept. 1, 1835 ; both d. Keeseville, N. Y.

2. William, b. Mar. 28, 1814 ; m. Cecelia Witt, Nov. 12, 1835.

3. Dumont, b. Sept. 10, 1836 ; m. Frances Ann Conant, Oct. 22, 1860.

3. William Clarence, b. Oct. 22, 1839.

MASON.

Ephraim Mason c. f. Medfield ; m. Polly Bennett, June 5, 1811, who d. May 22, 1862 ; he d. Nov. 6, 1866.

1. Harrison, b. Oct. 1, 1813 ; rem South.

1. Martha, b. Apr. 29, 1816 ; m. Cyrus Murdock of West Boylston, Sept. 10, 1839.

1. Abigail, b. Nov. 10, 1818 ; m. Joseph P. Marean.

1. Antoinette, b. Mar. 23, 1821 ; m. Luther Morrill of Sutton, Vt.

1. Hannah, b. Mar. 12, 1824 ; m. Samuel S. Kimball of Concord, N. H.

1. Ann Maria, b. Sept. 12, 1826 ; d. Aug 3, 1843.

1. Narcissa, b. June 6, 1830 ; d. Oct. 12, 1855.

MATTHEWS.

WILLIAM T. MATTHEWS c. f. W. Boylston, 1869 ; m. Amanda Merriam,
Sept. 9, 1851.

1. Hattie A., b. Dec. 30, 1854.
1. Edward W., b. Sept. 16, 1857.

MCCLENATHAN.

JOHN W McCLENATHAN c. f. Rutland about 1774; m. Phebe Bent, Nov.,
1780, who d. Oct. 8, 1799 ; m. 2d, Catherine
Howe of Princeton, Dec. 8, 1800 ; rem.

1. William, b. Apr. 28, 1782 ; m. Betsey Kelley of Barre, Aug. 21,
1808 ; rem. N. Y.
1. John, b. Apr. 15, 1784 ; d. Nov 29, 1784.
1. Patty, b. Dec. 1, 1785 ; m. Increase Warren.
1. Harriet, b. Feb. 25, 1788 ; m. Joseph Marean ; m. 2d, Francis
Blood.
1. Lucy, b. Mar. 8, 1790 ; d. Aug. 10, 1792.
1. Sophia, b. Apr. 5, 1792 ; m. Justus Ellinwood.
1. John, b. May 5, 1794 ; m. Maria Goodspeed, Nov. 6, 1825 ; both
d. New York.
1. Rufus, b. Apr. 9, 1796 ; m. Lucy Pond, May 18, 1820 ; res. Rindge,
New Hampshire.
1. Julia, b. Apr. 13, 1801 ; m. Daniel Thompson : res. Fitchburg.
1. Adeline, b. Aug. 30, 1802 ; d. Dec. 11, 1822.
1. Alvin, b. Aug. 19, 1804 ; d. Hague, New York.
1. Trowbridge, b. Dec. 8, 1806 ; rem Hague, N. Y.; d. Ticonde-
roga, New York.
1. Whiting, b. Mar. 21, 1809; m. Frances (Savage) Lewis, Oct. 9, 1851 :
d. Dec. 3, 1867.
1. Catherine, b. May 8, 1811 ; m. Samuel N. Farnsworth of Concord,
N. H., Nov. 30, 1834.

MCFARLAND.

ELIJAH McFARLAND c. f. Upton, m. Achsah Woods ; d. Aug. 1, 1869,
a. 69.

1. Elijah Walter, b. Mar. 27, 1825 ; m. Nancy M. (Bradish) Derby of
Holden ; rem. Petersham.
2. Jennie, b. 1856: d. Feb. 28, 1862.
2. Sarah Emma, b. Jan. 20, 1859.

MCFARLAND.

2. Ida Adelia, b. May 24, 1861.
2. Carribell Maria, b. Jan. 1, 1868.
2. Walter Henry, b. Mar. 27, 1870.
1. Mary Ann, b. Feb. 21, 1827; m. Benj. D. Phelps; m. 2d, Abijah S. Clark.
1. Joseph Edwin, b. Feb. 19, 1829; res. Cincinnati, Ohio; m. there.
1. John Leonard, b. Dec. 7. 1830; rem. Leicester; m. Lucinda Fessenden of Barre.
1. Daniel Webster, b. Mar. 27, 1834: m. Hattie Kendall; m. 2d, Susan Rawson. both of Gardner; res. Plymouth.
1. Sarah M.. b. Dec. 27, 1837; d. Feb. 3. 1854.
1. Julianna V., b. July 13. 1840: m. Charles E. Skinner of Jamaica, Vt.
1. Jemima A , b. Oct. 7, 1842; m. Albert Clark.

MERRIAM.

Asa MERRIAM c. f. Westminster; m. Sally Warren, May 12, 1825; who d. Sept. 18, 1859.
1. Calvin, b. Mar. 10, 1826; rem. Cohassett: d. 1872.
1. Amanda, b. Aug. 9, 1830; m. William Matthews.
1. Farwell. b. Jan. 14, 1833; res. Council Bluffs, Iowa.
1. John F., b. Jan. 16. 1835; res. Council Bluffs. Iowa.
1. Rufus, b. Nov. 28, 1836: res. Council Bluffs, Iowa.
1. Edward. b. Mar. 8, 1839; res. Texas.
1. Newell, b. Feb. 28, 1841; res. Westminster.
1. Willard, b. Aug. 8, 1843: d. Sept. 29, 1880.
1. Sarah, b. Dec. 2, 1846; m. Henry H. Dexter of Worcester, May 5, 1868; d. Mar., 1878.
1. Emily, b. May 4. 1848.

MILES.

Levi MILES c. f. Lancaster; m. Mary Ann————; rem. Malden.
1. George Henry, b. July 2, 1826; d. July 27, 1851.
1. William Thomas, b. Aug. 16, 1828; m. Isabella S. Reid of Rutland; m. 2d, Mary Woodward, May 4, 1874; res. Worcester.
1. Mary Kate, b. Mar. 19, 1837; m. Daniel Parlin of Petersham, Feb. 12, 1859.
1. Maria B., b. May 2, 1841.
1. Sophronia E., b. Feb. 11, 1846; d. Jan., 1848.

MINNS.

THOMAS MINNS c. f. Ireland ; m. Mary Conlon, who d. Aug. 26, 1880.

1. Frank, b. Mar. 8, 1827 ; m Celia Glancy of Barre ; res. Barre.
1. Ann, b. Apr. 3, 1834 ; d. May 3, 1852.
1. Thomas, b. June 3, 1838 ; res. Fitchburg.
1. James, b. Dec. 21, 1839 ; res. Gardner.
1. John, b. Nov. 1, 1841 ; m. Martha Beatty, July 4, 1866 ; res. Worcester.
    2. Nora, b. Oct. 22, 1867.
    2. Mary Ella, b. July 20, 1869 ; d. Sept. 13, 1869.
    2. Charles, b. Nov. 13, 1870.
    2. George, b. Aug. 29, 1872.
    2. Mary Wilman, b. Mar. 22, 1876.
    2. John N., b. July 12, 1879.
1. Jane, b. Aug. 9, 1843.
1. Maria, b. June 2, 1845 ; m. John W. Clark of Worcester, June 20, 1878.
1. Margaret, b. July 26, 1847.
1. Ellen, b. July 21, 1849.
1. George, b. May 29, 1851 ; res. Barre.
1. Charles, b. Mar. 27, 1855.

MONROE.

ALVIN MONROE c. f. Worcester, 1875 ; m. Lilla M. Hastings, Jan. 3, 1876.

1. Carl Hastings, b. Oct. 1, 1877 ; d. Aug. 30, 1880.

MOORE.

NOAH MERRITT MOORE c. f. Templeton ; m. Mary Young, Nov. 30, 1826 ; d. Feb. 3, 1878, a. 76.

1. Micah, b. May 29, 1827 ; rem. Wisconsin.
1. Lucy, b. Apr. 15, 1829 ; m. Davis Holt.
1. Frances M., b. May 5, 1831 ; m. Dennis Holt.
1. Rufus Dean, b. May 22, 1833 ; m. Fanny Banks of Alstead, N. H. ; rem. Athol.
    2. Jennie B., b. Mar. 12, 1867.
1. Thomas Levi, b. Oct. 27, 1835 ; d. Indiana.
1. Mary Amanda, b. May 3, 1839 ; m. Davis Holt ; m. 2d, John H. Eaton, Aug. 23, 1865 ; d. Sept. 19, 1872.
1. Joseph W., b. Feb. 18, 1841 ; rem. Phillipston.

40

MOORE.

1. Ellen E., b. Sept. 10, 1843; m. Oliver B. Coleman.
1. William Chester, b. Apr. 27, 1847; m. Isabella Richtie, Sept. 17, 1874.
   2. Levi Chester, b. June 5, 1875.
   2. Nellie Frances, b. Sept. 11, 1877.
1. Charles, b. Nov. 9, 1850.

LUKE S. MOORE c. f. Templeton; m. Cynthia Follett, May 28, 1856.

MORSE.

SAMUEL MORSE c. f. Medfield; m. Catherine Clark, Feb. 1, 1759; who
  d. Jan. 17, 1813, a. 76; he d. Apr. 20, 1787, a. 69.
 1. Samuel†, b. Nov. 30, 1759; m. Esther Woodward, Apr. 14, 1785,
   who d. Apr. 1, 1834, a. 72; he d. Aug. 4, 1853.
  2. Russell, b. July 12, 1786; m. Betsey Waite, July 31, 1807, who
    d. Royalston; res. Royalston.
  2. Samuel, b. May 8, 1788; res. Royalston.
  2. James, b. Apr. 4, 1790; rem. Westminster.
  2. John, b. Nov. 14, 1791; m. Electa Nourse, Feb. 2, 1819; who
    d. Sept. 11, 1846; m. 2d, Almira (Stone) Gates, Dec. 22,
    1847; d. May 6, 1869.
   3. Mary, b. Aug. 23, 1820; m. Simeon Clark.
   3. Lucy, b. Dec. 4, 1826; d. Sept. 8, 1846.
   3. Lyman, b. Nov. 27, 1830; m. H. Augusta Stone, May 1, 1851;
    res. Worcester.
    4. Alice Adelia, b. Oct. 30, 1852; m. Anson Perry, Oct. 17,
     1872; d. Oct. 27, 1876.
    4. Edward Ashton, b. Feb. 28, 1856; m. Ella French of Wor-
     cester; res. Worcester.
    4. Jessie Arabel, b. Nov. 7, 1868.
   3. John H., b. Nov. 23, 1850; res. Worcester.
  2. Richard, b. Nov. 12, 1793; m. Hannah Dyke, Apr., 1823; d.
    Feb. 6, 1864; she d. Jan. 18, 1866.
   3. Julia, b. Nov. 23, 1825; m. Newell R. Wheeler of Westmins-
    ter, Mar. 25, 1847.
   3. Alvina, b. Jan. 21, 1828; m. Jonas Joslin.
   3. Joanna, b. Dec. 15, 1829; d. Aug. 30, 1833.
   3. Amos D., b. Dec. 28, 1832; res. Gardner.
  2. Asa, b. May 10, 1796; m. Elizabeth Goulding, May 16, 1822;
   rem. Petersham; both d. Petersham.

MORSE.

3. Edwin, b. Apr. 13, 1824 ; m. Martha J. Worcester of Worcester, May 1, 1850; d. Worcester, June 1, 1879.

3. Lavinia, b. Nov. 13, 1825 ; m. Matthias C. Mayo of Athol, Aug. 21, 1866 ; res. Boston.

3. Elizabeth, b. Feb. 27, 1828 ; m. Azor S. Davis of Athol, Apr. 7, 1853.

3. Esther, b. Mar. 1, 1831 ; m. Silas Gage of Petersham, Apr. 3, 1873.

3. Susan, b. Apr. 13, 1833 ; m. Theron Temple, M. D., of Belchertown, Apr. 14, 1858 ; res. Boston.

3. Franklin Goulding, b. Oct. 10, 1834 ; m. Elvira I. Stockwell of Athol, May 16, 1859 ; res. Holbrook.

3. Nancy, b. Jan. 31, 1836 ; d. Petersham, July 29, 1841.

3. Sarah, b. May 3, 1839 ; m. James Henry Marshall of Athol, Dec. 1, 1869.

3. William Henry, b. Dec. 28, 1840 ; m. Emma L. Hood of Gardner, Dec. 1, 1869 ; res. Gardner.

3. Asa Herbert, b. Jan. 24, 1845 : m. Ella J. Fenno of Gardner, Nov. 16, 1876 ; res. Gardner.

2. Joel, b. July 28, 1798 ; m. Eliza Browning, Dec. 26, 1822, who d. Apr. 5, 1876 ; rem. Lowell.

3. Mary Ann S., b. Oct. 11, 1823 ; d. Aug. 28, 1844.

3. Lucretia, b. May 14, 1825 ; res. Lowell.

3. John B., b. Jan. 13, 1827 ; d. Sept. 10, 1830.

3. Frederick Parker, b. May 30, 1829 ; m. Mary H. Clark, May, 1, 1856, who d. July 30, 1864 ; m. 2d, Betsey A. (Button) Gates, Nov. 3, 1866 ; d. Apr. 29, 1871.

3. Harriet E., b. Oct. 24, 1833 ; m. Benjamin P. Conant.

3. Louisa A., b. Nov. 3, 1836 ; d. Feb. 13, 1837.

3. Lucius N., b. May 8, 1838 ; d. Aug. 19, 1840.

3. Lucy A., b. Sept. 16, 1840 ; d. Oct. 16, 1845.

3. Clarence S., b. Aug. 24, 1846 ; res. Lowell.

2. Lavinia, b. July 7, 1800 ; m. Joshua Browning.

2. Lucretia, b. Apr. 20, 1803 ; m. Sewell Mirick, Mar. 26, 1833 ; rem. Princeton.

1. William, b. Aug. 31, 1761 ; m. Hannah Richardson, May 23, 1791, who d. Nov. 25, 1809, a. 41 ; m. 2d, Hannah Johnson, Oct. 7, 1811, who d. Oct., 1813 ; he d. July 21, 1830.

MORSE.

2. William, b. Aug. 23, 1794 ; m. Louisa Stone, Sept. 29, 1830 ; d May 21, 1851.

3. Arabella, b. Dec. 18, 1831 ; d. Aug. 6, 1833.

3. William L., b. Apr. 10, 1834 ; res. Illinois ; m. Mary Mateer of Kentucky.

3. Samuel, b. Mar. 28, 1836 ; d. army, 1864.

3. Theodore, b. Sept. 16, 1838 ; res. Ill. ; m. Emma Welton of Ill.

3. Gaylord S., b. Sept. 18, 1843 ; m. Kitty Stypes of Ind. ; res. Ind.

2. Hannah, b. June 27, 1796 ; m. Ephraim Spring, Feb. 8. 1816 ; rem. Maine.

2. Stillman, b. Oct. 7, 1798 ; m. Mary Ann Slocomb, Apr. 17, 1822, who d. July 27, 1823 ; m 2d, Sarah M. Warren, Sept. 1, 1825, who d. June 30, 1841, a. 38 ; m. 3d, Augusta (Prentiss) Clark, May 4, 1843 ; d. Oct. 6, 1854 ; she res. Gardner.

3. Lucius S., b. July 25, 1826 ; d. Oct. 13, 1831.

3. Mary Ann, b. Oct. 5, 1827 ; m. William D. Cheever, June 18. 1851.

3. Sarah M., b. May 22, 1829 ; d. Nov. 19, 1841.

3. Lucius S., b. Sept. 16, 1833 ; d. June 4, 1836.

3. Delia F., b. May 20, 1835 ; d. May 13. 1852.

3. Edward A., b. Mar. 23. 1844 ; m. Mary E. Marean ; res. St. Louis, Missouri.

3. Henry S., b. Feb. 27, 1846 ; d. Aug. 2, 1847.

3. Josephine A., b. July 29, 1848 ; m. Chester B. Kendall, Dec. 28, 1870.

3. Stillman, b. Sept. 27, 1850 ; res. St. Louis, Missouri.

2. Eliza, b. Oct. 6, 1800 ; m. John Church.

2. Amia, b. Jan. 21, 1803 ; m. Nehemiah Harrington of North-boro', Sept. 21, 1826, who d. June 1, 1827, a. 34 ; m. 2d, Thomas H. Brown.

2. Horace, b. June 8, 1805 ; m. Harriet E. Williams, Mar. 17, 1831 ; d. Sept. 26, 1869 ; she res. Worcester.

3. Elizabeth, b. Jan. 16, 1832 ; m. George Gay.

3. Harriet A., b. Dec. 25, 1833 ; d. Oct. 15, 1858.

3. William H., b. Dec. 12, 1841 ; m. Mary H. Moore of Con-cord ; rem. Worcester.

4. William H., b. Aug. 10, 1872.

MORSE.

4. Arthur M., b. Nov. 23, 1873.

4. Robert Stearns, b. Mar. 16, 1878 ; d. Mar. 20, 1878.

4. Howard Moore, b. Jan. 16, 1881.

3. Helen E., b. Dec. 1, 1844 ; m. Albert H. Waite.

2. Augustus, b. Feb. 16, 1812 ; m. Lucinda Wright, Apr. 10, 1834 ;
    res. Boston.

3. George H., b. June 15, 1835 ; res. N. Y.

3. Dumont A., b. Mar. 13, 1837 ; res. Boston.

3. Alexander Frederick, b. Sept. 18, 1839 ; d. Nov. 11, 1862.

3. James H., b. Oct. 8, 1841 ; res. N. Y.

3. Clara P., b. May 18, 1844 ; m. Henry N. Sheldon of Boston,
    Dec. 30, 1868.

3. Alice A., b. Apr. 3, 1846.

3. Hannah, } b. Apr. 30, 1848 ; m. Milo Cummings.
3. Eliza, }   d. May 5, 1848.

1. Thaddeus, b. Aug. 31, 1763 ; d. Medfield.

1. Catherine, b. June 15, 1765 ; m. Silas Wheeler.

1. Sally, b. Aug. 14, 1767 ; d. Oct. 10, 1864.

1. Joses, b. Dec. 9, 1770 ; d. Medfield.

1. Nathan, b. Feb. 2, 1779 ; rem. Warwick.

JOHN QUINCY MORSE c f. Gardner ; m. Adaline Bennett.

1. George Edwin, b. May 22, 1854 ; m. Emma L. Arnold, Dec. 5, 1878.

2. Grace E., b. Oct. 19, 1880.

1. Sumner W., b. Dec. 30, 1855 ; m. Ella M. Maley, Jan. 25, 1880.

1. William, b. Sept. 24, 1857 ; d. Dec. 7, 1873.

1. Lucy Isabel, b. Dec. 17, 1859.

1. Albert B., b. Sept. 10, 1862.

MOULTON.

JOHN MOULTON† c. f. Spencer ; m. Martha Gibson, who d. Oct. 13, 1834.
    a. 75 ; he d. July 11, 1839, a. 77.

1. Sewell, b. 1795 ; m. Polly Hunting, Nov. 4, 1823, who d. Aug. 15,
    1837 ; m. 2d, Lurenza (Newton) Taft of Petersham, Dec.
    18, 1838.

2. Jane, b. Jan. 1, 1825 ; m. Isaac F. Thompson of Princeton, Dec.
    19, 1844 ; d. July, 1871.

2. Gardner W., b. Mar 20, 1827 ; m. Jane Thompson of Keene,
    N. H. ; d. May 17, 1864 ; she d. Jan. 26, 1874.

MOULTON.

3. Stella, b. Dec. 27, 1856.

3. Fannie Isabel, b. July 22, 1861.

2. Sarah, b. Apr. 11, 1830; d. Dec. 28, 1837.

2. Martha G., b. July 9, 1833; m. Alson J. Greenwood.

2. Julia, b. July 9, 1835; m. Stillman Whitney of Westminster, Dec. 11, 1856; d. Mar. 2, 1870.

2. Polly, b. June 28, 1837; m. Stillman Whitney of Westminster, Apr. 21, 1871.

1. Lucy, b. 1797; m. Walter Warren; m. 2d, Isaac Whittemore.

1. Eliza, m. Isaac Lovewell.

MUNDELL.

DANIEL MUNDELL c. f. England: m. Rebecca Wheeler of Sudbury, who d. Jan. 19, 1836, a. 85; he d. Feb. 8, 1845, at the reported age of 106. There is probable evidence that he was about 93. [See p. 169.]

1. Hannah, b. Dec., 1773; m. Barzillai Howard; m. 2d, Levi Parmenter.

1. Daniel, b. May 22, 1776; m. Phebe Falis, who d. May 13, 1826; m. 2d, Mary Harrington of Westminster, Oct. 11, 1826, who d. May 4, 1874, a. 80; he d. July 29, 1858.

2. Sophia, b. Aug. 6, 1802; m. Simeon K. Holt.

2. Jarvis, b. Mar. 15, 1804; d. Feb. 25, 1805.

2. Phebe, b. Apr. 18, 1805; d. June 14, 1806.

2. Daniel, b. May 30, 1807; m. Lois Howard, May 12, 1831; d. June 17, 1845.

3. Hannah, b. Mar. 7, 1837.

3. Daniel, b. Mar. 23, 1840.

2. Henry, b. Jan. 31, 1809; rem. Michigan.

2. Betsey, b. Jan. 6, 1811; d. Aug. 21, 1811.

2. Jarvis, b. Mar. 16, 1812; d. Feb. 27, 1816.

2. Phebe, b. Apr. 13, 1814; d. Mar. 7, 1816.

2. Aaron, b. Mar. 10, 1816; d. Nov. 28, 1816.

2. Lucinda, b. Dec. 11, 1817; m. Charles H. Davis of Worcester; res. Barre.

2. Isaac, b. Apr. 26, 1819; m. Eliza Stone of Rutland, July 3, 1851.

3. Henry Hilton, son of Davis Holt; adopted, and name changed to Mundell.

MUNDELL.

2. James, b. Oct. 5, 1820; d. Nov. 1, 1845.
2. Sophronia, b. May 7, 1824 ; d. young.
2. Mary Ann, b. May 1, 1830 ; m. Zenas Codding.
1. James, b. 1784; m. Hannah Blair of Keene, N. H.; d. Mar. 3, 1818.
1. George, m. Hannah (Blair) Mundell ; rem. Rutland ; d.
    2. George, m. Relief Eliza Hunting, Aug. 15, 1833 ; rem. West Brookfield.
1. John, m. Hannah (Blair) (Mundell) ; d. Rutland, a. 82.

MURDOCK.

ROBERT MURDOCK* c. f. Newton ; m. Margaret Cheney ; d. Oct. 1, 1819.
    a. 80 ; she d. Mar. 11, 1826, a. 84.
1. Margaret, b. 1768 ; m. Luther Goodspeed.
1. Ebenezer, b. 1771 ; d.
1. Robert, b. Aug. 31, 1773 ; m. Sally Nichols, Mar. 15, 1804 ; d. Apr. 27, 1852 ; she d. Sept. 5, 1855.
    2. William, b. Jan. 27, 1805 ; m. Sarah Wheelock, Feb., 1833 ; d. Wendell, June 4, 1860 ; she d. Oct. 14, 1863. a. 56.
        3. Lucinda, b. Sept. 9, 1833 ; m. George Gleason of Wendell ; m. 2d, Oscar Bigelow of Wisconsin.
        3. Mary, b. Sept. 6, 1835 ; d. May 2, 1852.
        3. Susan, b. Aug. 24, 1838 ; m. William O. Stuart of Montague : rem. Wisconsin.
        3. Charlotte, b. May 3, 1840 ; m. Riley Watson of Maine.
        3. Chloe, b. Feb. 27, 1844.
        3. Ebenezer, b. Aug. 23, 1845.
        3. Elizabeth, b. Feb. 9, 1847; m. John Gardner, Jan. 1, 1873.
        3. Harriet, b. Apr. 30, 1848; d. Wendell.
        3. William, b. Apr. 22, 1852.
    2. Mary, b. Aug. 10, 1806 ; m. Joshua P. Pillsbury, Mar. 1, 1832 ; res. Washington, D. C.
    2. Ebenezer, b. Sept. 27, 1808 ; m. Betsey Wheeler, Mar. 3. 1836 ; d. July 6, 1845.
        3. Ellen, b. June 3, 1836 ; m. John D. Williams.
    2. Sumner, b. July 28, 1811 ; m. Charlotte W. Howe, Jan. 23, 1833.
        3. Charles W., b. Oct. 15, 1833 ; m. Fanny M. Marshall of Lunenburg ; m. 2d, Abby Rosella Barnes, Dec. 19, 1872 ; res. Gardner.

MURDOCK.

3. Henry L., b. May 26, 1839 ; rem. Gardner ; m. Ellen Wilson of
   Princeton.

3. Clara E., b. Mar. 5, 1849 ; m. Albert Mason of Gardner, Dec.
   31, 1868.

3. Milo Elvin, b. Sept. 19, 1852 ; m. Ella F. Dodge of Littleton.
   4. Edward Herbert. b. Aug. 20, 1876.
   4. Harry Elwin, b. Sept. 11, 1877.
   4. Fanny Maria, b. Feb. 9, 1879.

3. Alvin I., b. Feb. 13. 1855.

2. Joseph Cheney. b. Nov. 30, 1812 ; m. Julia Greenwood, Jan. 5,
   1838.

3. Julia Ann. b. Aug. 27, 1838 ; m. Theodore F. Blood.

3. Leander L.. b. July 5, 1841 ; m. Nettie M. Cummings of Athol.
   4. Minnie Sawin. b. May 21, 1880.

3. Willie C.. b. Aug. 3. 1849 ; rem. Athol.

3. Alfred C., b. June 21, 1854.

3. Abby L.. b. Apr. 19, 1856.

3. John G., b. July 5. 1858.

2. Elisha, b. June 21. 1815 ; m. Nancy Temple, Jan. 17, 1837, who
   d. Sept. 2, 1853 : m. 2d, Abigail A. (Clark) Young, May
   24, 1855, who d. Feb. 17, 1875 ; m. 3d, Mrs. Martha J.
   Evans of Royalston. Apr. 9, 1877.

3. Lucius A., b. Aug. 17, 1837 ; m. Ellen Hager. Nov. 25, 1858 ;
   res. Worcester.

3. George E., b. Aug. 7, 1841 ; rem Worcester.

3. Nancy Ella, b. Mar. 16, 1857.

2. Sarah, b. July 31, 1818 ; m. Richard Leonard.

1. Sarah, b. Nov. 14, 1779 ; d. Sept. 24. 1798.

1. Hannah, b. July 8, 1782 ; m. Ebenezer Stowe.

ABIEL, bro. of ROBERT, c. f. Brookfield ; m. Rebecca Watson, who d.
June 30, 1822, a. 75 ; he d. Jan. 28, 1834. a. 90.

1. Edward, m. Sophia Howard of Winchester. N. H. ; rem. Northfield.

2. Sophia, b. Nov. 5. 1812 ; m. Charles Hobbs.

2. Frindy, b. Apr. 10, 1815 ; m. Paul Bailey of Sterling, May 1, 1834.

2. Edward, b. Nov. 22, 1816 ; m. Betsey Clifford, Aug. 9, 1838 ;
   d. Fitchburg, Feb. 27, 1859.

2. Ephraim, b. Nov. 17, 1818 ; m. Elvira Robbins of Northfield ;
   res. Orange.

MURDOCK.

2. Prudence, b. Mar. 3, 1821 ; m. Perez G. Coleman.
2. Lucina, b. Dec. 9, 1822 ; m. and d. Athol.
2. Isaac, b. May 10, 1826 ; rem. Northfield.
2. Sarah, b. Nov. 27, 1828 ; m. S. Doolittle ; m. 2d, —— Newton.
2. Elizabeth, b. Feb. 18, 1831 ; m. Oliver Brown.
2. Adeline, b. Nov. 28, 1833 ; d. June 20, 1856.
2. Alonzo, b. Oct. 8, 1836.
1. Baxter, b. Nov. 2, 1791 ; m. Emily Gates, Sept. 20, 1815 ; rem. Winchester, N. H.

JOSHUA MURDOCK c. f. Newton ; m. Mindwell Parker, who d. Apr. 21, 1825, a. 69 ; he d. Mar. 20, 1812, a. 58 ; he was in the Revolutionary War and the "Boston Tea Party."
1. Lucretia, b. Apr. 4, 1790 ; m. Alpheus Earle.

MUZZY.

WILLIAM MUZZY* c. f. Lexington, 1773 ; m. Mary Clapp ; m. 2d, Mary Chandler, Sept., 1786, who d. Feb. 17, 1831, a. 84 ; he d. Oct. 10, 1830, a. 97, the oldest man who ever lived in town ; oldest person, Mrs. Issachar Adams.
1. Abigail, b. 1760 ; m. Edmond Rice.
1. Caty, m. —— Monroe of Rutland ; m. 2d, Abram Wheeler of Rutland.
1. Mary, m. Nathan Bryant of Templeton.
1. Sally, m. John E. Newton, Nov. 10, 1789, who d. May 23, 1810, a. 42 ; rem. Templeton.
1. Nancy, b. Aug. 5, 1771 ; m. Asa Wheeler.
1. Relief, m. Jonathan Ames, May 18, 1795 ; d. Apr. 30, 1813 ; a. 40.

NEWTON.

TIMOTHY NEWTON c. f. Shrewsbury, 1766 ; m. Huldah ——, who d. June 13, 1798 ; m. 2d, Mrs. Lydia Martin, Nov. 21, 1799, who d. Aug. 4, 1840, a. 86 ; he d. June 30, 1818, a. 81.
1. Relief, b. Feb., 1764 ; d. Aug. 24, 1788.
1. Joel, b. Sept. 25, 1766 ; m. Nabby —— ; rem. Hague, N. Y. ; d. there.
2. Susan, b. May 28, 1794.
2. Amos, b. Nov. 14, 1795.

NEWTON.

2. Hannah, b. Oct. 12, 1798.

2. Ithamer, }
2. Otis, } b. Mar. 2, 1802.

2. Nabby, b. Mar. 17, 1803.

1. Timothy, b. July 5, 1771 ; rem. Westminster.

1. Huldah, b. July 2, 1774 ; m. John Sargent.

1. Nathan, b. June 21, 1776 ; m. Miriam Lyon, June 26, 1804, who
    d. July 30, 1820 ; m. 2d. Miranda Davis of Princeton, Oct.,
    1821 ; d. Utah. Nov. 13, 1839.

  2. Anna, b. May 5. 1805 ; m. Daniel Woodward.

  2. Nathan, b. May 4. 1807 ; m. Eliza Whittemore ; d. Iowa, 1866.

    3. Eliza Ann, b. Mar. 17, 1835.

    3. Mary Jane, b. Dec. 18, 1836.

    3. Hannah A., b. June 6, 1839.

    3. Sarah P., b. Oct. 19, 1841.

    3. George, b. Dec. 25, 1843 ; d. Apr. 4, 1844.

    3. Caroline, b. Aug. 2, 1845.

  2. Mary, b. Feb. 6, 1810 ; m. Daniel Woodward.

  2. Miranda, b. Sept. 16, 1822 ; m. Stillman Clark.

  2. Miriam L., b. Sept. 12, 1824 ; m. Asa. G. Clark.

  2. Lucy, b. May 9. 1827 : m. Nathan Brick, Feb. 10, 1852.

1. Asa, b. Jan. 26, 1779 : m. Polly Stowe ; rem. Nashua.

  2. Elizabeth, b. June 30, 1801 ; d. Sept. 2, 1803.

  2. Polly, b. Dec. 22, 1803 : m. Luther Robbins of Nashua, N. H.,
    June 8, 1824.

  2. Asa, b. Apr. 14, 1805 ; d. Mar. 4, 1809.

  2. Sally. b. May 2, 1807 ; d. Dunstable, N. H., Oct. 12, 1835.

  2. Asa, b. Feb. 2, 1809 ; m. Lavina Hall of Nashua, N. H., June
    8, 1837 ; d. Feb. 15, 1856.

  2. William P., b. May 11, 1811 ; m. Caroline Huntley, Nov. 26,
    1835 ; d. Sept. 12, 1849.

  2. Ebenezer Stowe, b. Nov. 28, 1813 ; m. Edy Adams, 1837 ; m.
    2d, Julia Tolles, Aug. 28, 1855 ; d. Dec. 25, 1878.

  2. Matilda S., b. Sept. 5. 1816 ; m. Luther Dow of Hollis, N. H.,
    Oct. 18, 1841.

  2. Hannah, b. Dec. 20. 1818 ; m. Daniel M. Smith of Hollis, N. H.,
    May 9, 1843.

  2. Lucy A., b. Jan. 25, 1823 : m. Thomas S. Patch of Hollis, N. H.,
    Apr. 11, 1848.

NEWTON.

1. Ithamer, b. Oct. 24, 1781 ; m. Polly Nichols, Oct. 15, 1807 ; d. July 28, 1838.
2. Eli, b. July 3, 1808 ; d. Sept. 23, 1827.
2. Andrew J., b. Apr. 1, 1815 ; d. June 20, 1854.
2. Sarah, b. June 5, 1818 ; d. Jan. 27, 1840.
2. Isaac, b. Dec. 28, 1820 ; m. Maria Rice, May 4, 1841, who d. Oct. 10, 1843 ; m. 2d, Lydia E. Wiswall, June, 1845 ; res. Lancaster.
 3. Sarah Maria, b. Jan. 22, 1842 ; d. out of town.
 3. Isaac, b. Aug. 5, 1843 ; d. Dec. 1, 1862. [See p. 141.]

JOSEPH NEWTON c. f. Templeton, 1777 ; m. Experience Drury ; d. 1795.
1. Rhoda, b. 1761 ; m. Israel Underwood.
1. Mercy, b. 1766 ; d. Dec. 11, 1848.
1. Ebenezer, b. 1770 ; m. Mary Howe, who d. Oct. 15, 1804, a. 23 ; he. d. Greenfield, Feb. 16, 1844.
2. Keziah, b. July 3, 1799 ; m. Henry Williams.
2. James, b. July 21, 1801 ; m. Esther Hale, Feb. 10, 1824 ; res. Greenfield.
 3. Laura, b. Feb. 15, 1825 ; m. Israel B. Cross of Milwaukee, Wis., June 19, 1855 ; d. Nov. 26, 1865.
 3. Sarah, b. Apr. 2, 1826 ; d. Apr. 26, 1826.
 3. Daniel H., b. June 22, 1827 ; m. Mary A. Coggswell of Essex, Sept. 24, 1862 ; res. Holyoke.
 3. Joseph D., b. Dec. 9, 1828 ; m. Prudence H. Alvard of Shelburne, Nov. 23, 1853 ; res. Holyoke.
 3. Susan, b. May 27, 1830 ; d. July 4, 1863.
 3. James H., b. Jan 13, 1832 ; m. Susan W. Taft of Worcester, Nov. 23, 1863 ; res. Holyoke.
 3. Moses, b. Oct. 27, 1833 ; m. Maria B. Arms of Deerfield, Nov, 3, 1859.
 3. Ebenezer, b. Apr. 6, 1835 ; d. Mar. 4, 1851.
 3. Esther, b. Oct. 24, 1836 ; m. Elias B. McClellan of Greenfield, Mar. 25, 1863 ; res. Whately.
 3. John Carter, b. Apr. 21, 1838 ; m. Lela F. Vulte of N. Y., Nov. 28, 1865 ; res. Holyoke.
 3. Solon Luther, b. Mar. 9, 1841 ; res. Greenfield.
2. Susan, b. Jan 25, 1803 ; m. Sylvanus Dunton.
2. Mary, b. Oct. 2, 1804 ; m. Stephen Heald of Barre.

NICHOLS.

JONATHAN NICHOLS c. f. Athens, Vt.: m. Sarah ——, who d.. May 23,
  1822, a. 68: m. 2d, Mrs. Rachel Nichols of Westminster, Nov. 27, 1823; d. Mar. 3, 1836; a. 86.

1. Sally, b. May 29, 1780; m. Robert Murdock.
1. Polly, b. 1785; m. Ithamer Newton; m. 2d, Luke Warren.
1. John, b. May 5. 1788; m. Mercy Woodward, Nov. 27, 1810; d.
   Oct. 21, 1839; she d. Nov. 27, 1864.
   2. Samuel Gay, b. Oct. 11, 1811; m. Elizabeth Prentiss, Oct. 5,
      1836, who d. Dec. 4, 1876.
      3. Joseph Clark, b. Oct. 21, 1839; m. Sarah A. Shipee of Col-
         eraine. Sept. 18, 1867; res. Winchendon.
      3. Mary Elizabeth, b. Oct. 18, 1841; m. Asa Morrill Greenwood.
      3. Caroline A., b. May 9, 1845.
   2. Polly, b. July 31, 1812; m. Ambrose Chase of Royalston; res.
      Gardner.
   2. Sewell, b. Jan. 2, 1815; m. Philena Newton of Petersham, Dec.
      4, 1845; res. Gardner.
      3. George Franklin, b. Sept. 26, 1847.
   2. Jonathan W., b. Mar. 29, 1816; d. Aug. 14, 1818.
   2. Moses, b. Oct. 1, 1817; m. Lucy Thompson of Princeton, Nov.
      8, 1842.
      3. Susan Elvira, b. Sept. 16, 1843; d. Dec. 9, 1862.
      3. Albert, b. Nov. 16, 1845; rem. California.
      3. Levi H., b. Aug. 22, 1857.
   2. Sally, b. Jan. 14, 1819; m. Ambrose Chase of Gardner, Feb. 5,
      1839; d. Royalston, Oct. 12, 1865.
   2. Betsey, b. Dec. 6, 1821; m. Francis Barnes.
   2. Jason W., b. Jan. 27, 1824; d. Jan. 16, 1879.
   2. Alvin, b. Apr. 8, 1825; m. Mary N. Potter of Leyden, Dec. 25,
      1852.
      3. Julia M., b. Feb. 17, 1856.
      3. Horace A., b. Aug. 26, 1859.
      3. Alice E., b. July 1, 1861.
      3. Hattie E., b. Feb. 28, 1863.
      3. Nellie M., b. Sept. 19, 1865.
   2. John, b. Sept. 27, 1826; rem. Gardner; m. Almira Perley, June
      24, 1847.
   2. Mercy, b. Aug. 23, 1828; m. Nelson Wood of Gardner, May 1,
      1850.

NICHOLS.

2. Susan, b. Apr. 19, 1830; m. George A. Perley of Gardner, Aug. 9, 1853.

NUGENT.

JOHN NUGENT c. f. Ireland; m. Margaret Sweeney: d. June 2, 1853, a. 59.
1. James, b. Jan., 1822.
1. Hugh, b. Sept. 22, 1824; m. Almeda Brown, Nov. 17, 1879; res. Nevada.
1. Eleanor, b. June 7, 1827; m. Lawrence Laughna, Jan. 14, 1843; d. Nov. 15, 1865.
1. Rosanna, b. Nov. 7, 1828; m. Harrison Grimes.
1. Susan, b. Mar. 9, 1831; m. A. L. Wood.
1. Margaret, b. Jan. 7, 1833; m. John Flint.

OSGOOD.

ISAAC OSGOOD c. f. Barre, 1857: m. Mary G. Johnson of Barre, Mar. 25, 1841.
1. Sarah F., b. Jan. 2, 1842; m. Albert M. Burt of Barre, Nov. 16, 1865.
1. Hattie N., b. Nov. 23, 1843; m. Richard M. Johnson of Arlington. Apr. 27, 1869.
1. Henry W., b. Dec. 5, 1845; d. Aug. 13, 1867.
1. Louisa M., b. Mar. 11, 1848; m. Everard Witt.
1. George F., b. Mar. 24, 1850; m. Mary A. Cutter of Gardner, Jan. 12, 1875.
1. Eudora M., b. July 16, 1852; d. Sept. 16, 1855.
1. Carrie E., b. Jan. 10, 1861.

PARKER.

REV. NEHEMIAH PARKER, [see chap. X,] m. Mary Richardson; d. Aug. 20, 1801, a. 59; she d. July 25, 1829, a. 85.
1. Mary, b. July 4, 1766; d. Oct. 1, 1777.
1. Betsey, b. Mar. 1, 1768; m. Heman Goodspeed.
1. Thomas Hubbard, b. May 8, 1770; m. Rhoda Harden, Apr. 19, 1799; d. Apr. 25, 1851.

OTIS PARKER c. f. Westboro', 1804; m. Mary Ann Nourse, who d. Apr. 30, 1850, a. 78; he d. Feb. 27, 1855, a. 82.
1. Isaac, b. 1797; d. May 8, 1829.

PARKER.

1. Daniel, b. Mar. 23, 1799 ; m. Polly White of Phillipston, Jan. 13, 1829 ; res. Greenwich Village.
2. Susan, b. Feb. 18, 1831 ; d. Sept. 5, 1863.
2. Mary, b. Jan. 27, 1833 ; m. Henry Y. Sears of Greenwich, Mar. 5, 1863 ; who d. Oct , 1866 ; m. 2d, Samuel B. Esty of Greenwich, Aug. 12, 1868.
2. Melissa, b. Aug. 7, 1834 ; d. Dec. 8, 1855.
2. Sarah, b. Oct. 15, 1835 ; m. Henry C. Work of Chicago, Ill., Jan. 1, 1857.
2. Daniel W., b. Sept. 26, 1837 ; d. July 24, 1840.
2. Isaac, b. Sept. 23, 1839 : d. July 29, 1840.
2. Daniel Webster, b. June 13, 1841 ; m. Fanny E. Morse of Greenwich Village, Aug. 7, 1865 ; d. Oct. 10, 1875, Greenwich Village.
2. Lucy Augusta, b. Oct. 30, 1843.
2. Hattie Elizabeth, b. May 9, 1845 ; res. Greenwich Village.
2. Abel O., b. Dec. 20, 1847 ; m. Fanny E. (Morse) Parker, June 7, 1880 ; res. Greenwich Village.
1. Lucy, b. 1801 : d. Nov. 19, 1822.
1. Mary N., b. 1803 ; m. Alvin Waite.
1. Otis, b. Aug. 16, 1806 ; m. Eunice Allen, who d. Oct. 14, 1855 ; m. 2d, Mrs. Henrietta M. S. Kendall, who d. Oct. 9, 1868 ; a. 59 ; he d. Sept. 1, 1876.
2. Lucy, b. Nov. 25, 1830 ; m. James Baker of Worcester ; m. 2d, Charles Lester of Wis.
2. Avalina, b. June 21, 1833 : m. Joseph Willard Rice.
2. Elmer, b. Aug. 30, 1836 ; m. Sarah J. Hallock of Conn. ; res. Ashland.
2. Elizabeth L., b. July 23, 1842 ; m. John G. Allen of Pittsfield, Vt., Oct. 8, 1862.
1 Samuel Austin. b. Oct. 2, 1810 ; m. Ruth Ann H. Williams, Nov. 8, 1832 ; d. Hartford, Conn., Apr. 4, 1852.

AMOS PARKER c. f. Shrewsbury ; m. Lucy Robinson, 1771 ; d. Jan. 25, 1801, a. 55 ; she d. Feb. 18, 1845, a. 90.
1. Sylvester, Patty, Joseph and Emory, all older than Dana R., rem. Vt.
1. Dana R., b. Nov. 4, 1781 ; m. Sarah Williams, Nov. 19, 1806 ; d. May 22, 1863 ; she d. May 13, 1877.

PARKER.

2. Lucinda, b. Mar. 9, 1807 ; m. Eli Gray of Templeton, Aug. 28, 1832 ; d. Dec. 31, 1856.
2. Sarah D., b. June 7, 1808 ; m. Oliver Hale.
2. John W., b. Mar. 5, 1810 ; m. Nancy F. Barr of N. Y., who d. July 31, 1847.
2. Elvira, b. Nov. 28, 1811 ; m. Seth P. Hayward of Barre.
2. Jonas, b. Oct. 30, 1813 ; m. Susan Ann Decker of Staten Island, New York.
2. Sophronia, b. Nov. 25, 1815 ; m. Henry Humphrey of Athol, June 26, 1836.
2. Lucy R., b. Nov. 13, 1817 ; m. Asa S. Hodge.
2. Dennison R., b. Aug. 15. 1819 ; m. Mary C. Vroome of Staten Island, N. Y.
2. Mary, b. July 11, 1821 ; m. George Raymond of Westminster, May 5, 1842.
2. Amos, b. Feb. 12, 1823 ; m. Lucy Shepherd of Barre ; d. Nov., 1850.
2. Martha M., b. July 9, 1825 ; m. Lysander Batchelder of Athol, July 2, 1844 ; m. 2d, Seth P. Hayward of Barre.
2. Amory, b. Aug. 2, 1828.
2. George L., b. June 12, 1830 ; d. Aug. 1, 1831.
2. Susan E., b. Apr. 9, 1833 ; m. David Hayward of Barre.
1. Lucy, b. 1788 ; m. Silas Richardson of Sterling, Jan. 12, 1812 ; d. July 4, 1828 ; he d. Jan. 24, 1833. a 51.

WILLIAM J. PARKER, name changed from Jarvis Hunting [see Hunting] ; m. Rebecca H. Sawin, Feb. 28, 1830, who d. Apr. 9, 1836 ; m. 2d, Lucinda Russell, Jan. 25, 1838.
1. Alfred R., b. June 2, 1840 ; d. army, Mar. 16, 1865. [See p. 141.]
1. Stephen S., b. June 29, 1842 ; m. Dora E. Beatty, July 18, 1866.
2. Jenny, b. Aug. 5, 1867.
2. Alfred, b. Dec. 8, 1868.
2. William., b. Apr. 20, 1872 ; d. Mar. 2, 1873.
1. Mary J., b. June 28, 1844 ; m. Albert Ware, Mar. 6, 1867.
1. William J., b. Sept., 1846.
1. Addison A., b. Apr. 29, 1851 ; m. Lucy Ida Green, Dec. 25, 1872.
2. Eva Lucinda, b. Oct. 4, 1873.
2. Ernest Boyden, b. Aug. 24. 1876.
2. Cora Eleda, b. Aug. 30, 1878.

PARKHURST.

DANIEL PARKHURST was here as early as 1782; m. Abigail Estabrook, who d. Apr. 26, 1824; he d. July 17, 1810, a. 54.

1. Daniel, b. Nov. 6, 1779; m. Amiable Clark, Nov. 15, 1803; d. Apr. 14, 1825; she d. Aug. 18, 1826.

2. Alexander Hamilton, b. May 23, 1804; m. Eunice Johnson of Worcester, who d. July 27, 1870, a. 61; he d. Sept. 18, 1879.

   3. William, b. July 3, 1830; d. June 1, 1862.

   3. Sarah Jane, b. May 23, 1832; d. May 17, 1836.

   3. Daniel E., b. Mar. 4, 1836; d. June 4, 1836.

   3. Clara S., b. July 4, 1837: m. Samuel Lang of Fitchburg, Feb. 8, 1864.

   3. Frederick H., b. Jan. 13, 1840; res. E. Somerville.

   3. Mary Stone, b. June 29, 1842: m. Levi W. Conant.

   3. Theodore A., b. Apr. 12, 1844; m. Mary K. Adams of Spencer, May 6, 1865; rem. Spencer.

      4. Emma Lucretia, b. Feb. 21, 1868.

   3. Amy A., b. Apr. 18, 1846; m. Herbert Damon.

   3. Cassius Moses, b. Oct. 5, 1848.

2. William S., b. July 3, 1806; d. Aug. 14, 1808.

2. Clara P., b. June 28, 1809: m. —— Partridge of Barre.

2. William Stedman, b. May 13, 1811: rem. Penn.

2. Arethusa, b. Dec. 10, 1813; m. George Wilson of Petersham; d. Illinois.

2. Amiable, b. Apr. 12, 1816; d. May 10, 1820.

2. John F., b. July 28, 1818; d. Apr. 17, 1819.

1. Roland, b. Mar. 26, 1782; d. Feb. 7, 1785.

1. William, b. Feb. 14, 1784; M. D.; rem. Petersham. [See p. 181.]

1. Arethusa, b. Feb. 7, 1786; m. Moses Clark.

1. Roland, b. Sept. 21, 1788; m. Anna Clark, June 17, 1810; went to Worcester.

   2. Abigail E., d. May 9, 1811; m. Jas. Whittemore of Worcester, July 23, 1829.

   2. Lucretia F., b. Aug. 21, 1813; m William L. Clarke of Worcester, Dec. 21, 1843.

   2. Lorenzo, b. May 23, 1815; d. Oct. 26, 1815.

   2 Mary Anna, b. Sept. 21, 1816; m. Lewis Barnard of Worcester.

   2. Roland A., b. Dec. 15, 1818; d. Apr. 21, 1819.

   2. Harriet B., b. Sept 4, 1820; d. Worcester, Aug. 20, 1866.

PARMENTER.

CHARLES PARMENTER served in the army through the whole of the Revolutionary War; d. Feb. 24, 1802, a. 81.

His son LEVI also served through the war and received a pension from 1818 till his death; m. Bathsheba Parmenter of Holden, Mar. 1, 1792, who d. Oct. 25, 1830, a 63; m. 2d Hannah (Mundell) Howard, Apr. 19, 1832, who d. Mar. 2, 1871, a. 97; she was the last person in town who received a revolutionary pension; he d. July 12, 1837, a 76.

PARSONS.

WILLARD PARSONS c. f. Sutton; m. Mary R. Hartwell, Nov. 30, 1854.
1. Frank Clifton, b. Mar. 9, 1856; d. Sept. 3, 1856.
1. Jenny K., b. Jan. 5, 1867.

DARIUS, brother of WILLARD c. f. Sutton; m. Caroline A. Taylor. Nov. 24, 1877.
1. George Taylor, b. May 4, 1879.

PARTRIDGE.

DANIEL W. PARTRIDGE c. f. Princeton, 1871; m. Elizabeth D. Stowe of Princeton, Sept. 1, 1846.
1. Walter E., b. Apr. 2, 1847; d. July 8, 1871.
1. Ida N., b. Nov. 18, 1848.
1. Lyman F. b. Apr. 30, 1850; m. Mary Wellington of Rutland. Apr. 5, 1872; res. Rutland.
1. Mary E., b. June 26, 1852; m. Henry Thomas of Rutland, Apr. 4, 1871; d. Feb. 25, 1879.
1. Daniel W., b. Aug. 17, 1854; d. July 22, 1864.
1. Levi L., b. Aug. 28, 1856; m. Mary J. Hillery, Dec. 4, 1875.
2. Walter E., b. Nov. 6, 1879.
1. Frank E., b. Oct. 6, 1860.

PEABODY.

CALVIN PEABODY c. f. Princeton, 1862; m. Clarissa E. Knight of Petersham, Apr. 15, 1845; d. Aug. 29, 1880, a. 87.
1. Homer, b. May 10, 1846.

PEIRCE.

THOMAS PEIRCE d. July 27, 1809, a. 82; his wife d. Oct. 22, 1811, a. 83.

42

PEIRCE.

1. Anna, b. 1759; m. Howard Hinds.
1. Lydia, b. 1766; m. John Woods.
1. Moses H., b. 1771; m. Anna Rice, Dec. 6, 1792, who d. Dec. 2,
     1825, a. 53; m. 2d, Hannah (Heald) Upham, who d. Vt. ;
     he d. July 29, 1846.
2. Patty, b. Mar. 15, 1793; m. Silas Davis.
2. John, b. Feb. 15, 1795; d. Oct. 7, 1798.
2. Haven, b. Nov. 12, 1797: m. Hannah Rice, May, 1819, who d.
     Jan. 22, 1869, a. 71.
   3. Mary, b. Nov. 17, 1819; m. William J. Eveleth
   3. Marshall, b. May 3, 1821; m. Elizabeth Jones of Spencer; d.
     Dec. 15, 1859.
   3. Levi, b. Apr. 15, 1823; m. Almira Wilson of Worcester; res.
     Worcester.
   3. Harding, b. Mar. 13, 1825; m. Mary Johnson of Worcester;
     res. Worcester.
   3. Ann Sophila, b. Feb. 27, 1827; m. Charles Goodspeed.
2. Levi, b. Jan. 17, 1799; m. Mary Melissa Clark, Apr. 1, 1830;
     who d. Aug. 25, 1865; he d. Apr. 25, 1875.
   3. Henrietta, b. Mar. 10, 1831; d. Aug. 27, 1831.
   3. Theodore H., b. Aug. 10, 1832; d.
   3. Henrietta M., b. Nov. 4, 1833; d. Worcester.
   3. Frederick L., b. 1837; d. May 7, 1858
   3. Alfred W., b. Jan. 1, 1841; d. Mar. 11, 1871.
2. Asa, b. Sept. 13, 1800: m. Harriet Wheeler, Sept. 4, 1826, who
     d Oct. 20, 1852; he d. Jan. 7, 1875.
   3. Orin, b. Sept. 29, 1826; m. Fidelia Holden of Rutland; res.
     Rutland.
   3. Charlotte, b. Mar. 21, 1828; d. Oct. 20, 1847.
   3. Watson I., b. May 31. 1830; m. Adelphia Clark, Apr. 27, 1861.
   3. Harriet, b. Apr. 21, 1833; m. Sewell Grimes.
   3. Hannah. b. July 2, 1835: m. Charles Hunting.
   3. Moses Dexter, b. June 30, 1839.
   3. Elsie Melissa, b. Dec. 24, 1841; m. Julius Fitts of W. Brookfield.
2. Margaret, b. Oct. 7, 1802; d. Sept. 4. 1823.
2. James Hervey, b. Nov. 23. 1804; m. Eunice Davis of Princeton,
     who d. Nov. 3, 1842; he d. June 25, 1846.
   3. Ellen Maria, b. Dec. 29, 1829: m. James Goodrich of Fitch-
     burg; d. Fitchburg

PEIRCE.

3. Sylvender O., b. Feb. 1, 1832 ; d. July 7, 1866.
3. Herschel Osborne, b. Mar. 31, 1834 ; m. Hattie Rugg of Wil-
   mington, Vt. ; res. Brooklyn, N. Y.
3. Selwyn Adelbert, b. May 10, 1836 ; d. Fitchburg.
3. Wesley H., b. Apr. 2, 1841 ; d. Rutland.
2. John Dexter, b. 1806 ; d. Templeton, Nov., 1850.
2. Melissa, b. Nov. 29, 1811 ; m. John Bryant of Princeton, Mar.
   31, 1842.

PHELPS.

JOHN PHELPS c. f. Rutland ; m. Susanna Gates of Marlboro', who d. Aug.
   26, 1784, a. 70 ; he d. Mar. 23, 1787, a. 78.
1. Catherine, b. Mar. 1, 1737 : d. Nov. 28, 1784, a. 48.
1 Moses, b. May 1, 1750, c. f. Rutland, 1776 : m. Deborah Monroe
   of Bristol, R. I., Mar. 19, 1778 ; d. Jan. 6, 1826 ; she d.
   July 21, 1833, a. 81   [See p. 181.]
2. Polly, b. Mar. 26, 1779 : m. Peleg Slocomb, June 19, 1799 ; m.
   2d, J. Broad of Barre : d. Ashburnham, Sept. 13, 1863.
2. Sally, b. Oct. 8, 1781 ; m. Samuel Follett ; m. 2d, David Witt :
   m. 3d, William Cutting of Athol, Oct., 1829 ; d. Oct. 13,
   1857.
2. Aaron, b. Nov. 23, 1783 ; m. Amy Lamb Nov. 28, 1805 ; d.
   Homer, N. Y., Jan 1, 1817 : she d. 1838.
3. Augustus Stillman, b. Feb. 25, 1806 ; m. Harriet Phelps, Sept.
   7, 1842 ; rem. New Orleans, La.; d. July 3.
   1863.
3. Albert, b. Nov. 22, 1811; d. Donaldsonville, La., 1850.
3. James Hervey, b. Jan. 7, 1816 : d. La., 1844.
2. Moses, b. Feb. 13, 1786 ; m. Clara Browning, June 6, 1810,
   who d. May 11, 1856 ; he d. Aug. 22, 1873.
3. John B., b. Mar. 27, 1811 ; d. Dec. 9, 1812.
3. Harriet, b. Oct. 26, 1813 ; d. Sept. 15, 1816.
3. Moses, b. Jan. 7, 1816 : d. Aug. 25, 1841. [See p. 167.]
3. Harriet, b. July 11, 1818 : name changed to Mary H.
3. John, b. Apr. 7, 1824 ; m. Clara M. Clark, July 3, 1851, who
   d. Aug. 5, 1853 ; m. 2d, Wilhelmina Paulsackel of New
   Orleans, La., Feb. 6, 1858 ; res. La.
4. Ashton, b July 14, 1853.

PHELPS.

2. Sewell, b. Apr. 3, 1788; m. Catherine Wright, Mar. 21, 1811; d. Lambertsville, N. J., Apr. 8, 1830; she d. New York.

2. John, b. Aug. 21, 1790; m. Polly Frost, Apr. 28, 1825; d. June 28, 1841.

   3. George, b. Sept. 17, 1826; rem. Watertown.

   3. Simon B., b. July 17, 1828; rem. Illinois.

   3. Sewell, b. Mar. 15, 1832.

   3. Eliza, b. Feb. 21, 1836; res. Conn.

   3. Benton, b. Apr. 21, 1839.

2. Dexter, b. Dec. 8, 1792; m. Lois Clark, July, 1813; both d. Northfield.

   3. William Harrison, b. Oct. 23, 1813; res. Northfield.

   3. Edward, b. July 9, 1815; rem. Hartford, Conn.

   3. Harriet, b. Mar. 30, 1817; m. Augustus Stillman Phelps.

   3. Aaron, b. Oct. 26, 1820; d. Kansas, 1842.

   3. Eli, b. Apr. 30, 1824; res. Foxboro'.

   3. Susan S., b. May 27, 1827; m. John Maclin of New Orleans, La.

   3. Louisa A., b. Nov. 14, 1835; m. George Prentiss.

BENJAMIN D. PHELPS, name changed from Benj. D. Savage; [see Savage;] m. Elvira Merriam of Westminster, who d. May, 1849, a. 44; m. 2d, Mary Ann McFarland, Mar. 1, 1852; d. Apr. 22, 1870.

1. Henry B., b. Dec. 14, 1841; m. Abby Henrietta Flynn, Apr. 23, 1868; who d. July 5, 1872.

2. George A., b. Mar. 23, 1869.

PHILLIPS.

JOSHUA PHILLIPS, said to be of Scotch descent, c. f. Smithfield, R. I., with his wife Freelove and seven children in 1764; rem. Rutland. Four of his sons, Joshua, Richard, Gideon and Paine served in the Revolutionary War, Richard enlisting from this town, the others from Rutland. Richard accompanied Com. Whipple on his famous expedition to France with despatches from Congress to that government. The daring displayed in running the blockade in Narragansett Bay, and their narrow escape from capture near Newfoundland, on their return are reported as incidents of this expedition.

PHILLIPS.

1. Freelove, b. 1749 : m. Nathan Stone.
1. Joshua, }
1. James, } b. about 1750. m. Sarah Nurse of Rutland, Dec. 4, 1767.
   2. Relief, b. Sept. 6, 1768.
1. Esek, b. about 1752 ; d. June, 1777. [See p. 166.]
1. Richard, b. Sept. 4, 1754 ; m. Olive Evans of Hopkinton, July 11,
      1779 ; rem. Dublin, N. H.
1. Paine, }
1. Gideon, } b. Nov. 7, 1763 ; m. Chloe Shattuck, May 5, 1786 ; rem.
      Roxbury, N. H.
   2. Isabel, b. Feb. 28, 1787 ; m. Reuben Alden, who d. Nov. 24,
      1856, a. 69 ; she d. Feb. 28, 1870.
   2. Reuben, b. Mar. 24, 1788 ; m. and res. Roxbury, N. H.
   2. Barbara, b. Mar. 19, 1793 ; m. and res. Nelson, N. H.
   2. Rufus, b. Nov. 25, 1795 ; d. in the army.
   2. Anna, b. Apr. 13, 1799 ; m. Samuel Warren.
   2. Richard, b. Apr. 13, 1801 ; m. and res. Dublin, N. H.
   2. Joshua, b. Nov. 28, 1802 ; m. Julia Stone of Rutland. Aug. 4,
      1825 ; d. Nov. 25, 1859.
      3. Martha, b. Mar. 26, 1827 ; d. Apr. 7, 1831.
      3. Elizabeth, b. Mar. 3, 1833 ; d. Sept. 2, 1844.
      3. Geo. Whitefield, b. July 5, 1836 ; m. Sarah Ball of Amherst,
            Sept. 14, 1864. [See p. 185.]
      3. David Everett, b. July 26, 1842 ; m. Nellie Armington of Rut-
            land, June 23, 1868 ; res. Columbus, O.
   2. Gideon, b. Mar. 15, 1807.
   2. James, b. Mar. 15, 1809 ; m. Rebecca Lovewell, June 26, 1831,
      wno d. Mar. 28, 1876.
      3. Benjamin Franklin, b. Feb. 28, 1836 ; m. Mary Whitney of
            Gardner, res. Gardner.
      3 Delia Ann, b. Mar., 1837 ; d. Sept. 3, 1851.
      3. Savira E., b. Nov. 13, 1843 ; m. Moses Bennett.
      3. Louisa, b. Oct. 3, 1848 ; m. Jacob Shaffer, May 17, 1866.

PIERCE.

BENJAMIN F. PIERCE c. f. Ashburnham, 1845 ; m. Eda Ann Coleman,
      Nov. 30, 1843, who d. Feb. 19, 1861 ; m. 2d, Mrs.
      Rebecca Adams of Gardner, May, 1863, who d.

PIERCE.

Dec. 30, 1872 ; m. 3d, Almira E. Davidson of Northampton, Jan. 28, 1874.

1. Roxy Ann, b. Sept. 3, 1844 ; d. June 2, 1867.
1. Mary Orcelia, b. June 11, 1848 ; d. Oct. 30, 1849.
1. Charles F., b. Mar. 27, 1852 ; m. Ada M. Haskins of Rochester,
Vt., Mar., 1877 ; res Conn.
1. Nettie A., b. June 17, 1857 ; m. George P. Wood of Westminster,
Aug. 4, 1875 ; d. Apr. 10, 1880.
1. Lucy W., b. July 8, 1864.

POLLARD.

JOEL POLLARD c. f. Rutland, 1770 ; m. Mary Maynard of Rutland, Mar.
8, 1770, who d. Aug. 18, 1789 ; m. 2d, Hannah Goodspeed, Mar. 3, 1791, who d. July 2, 1830, a. 70 ; he. d.
Apr. 26, 1825, a. 76.

1. Dorcas, b. Sept. 5, 1771 ; m. Paul Mirick, Nov. 24, 1790, who d.
July 23, 1814, a. 51 ; she d. Princeton.
1. Molly, b. Jan. 9, 1774 ; d. Apr. 28, 1789.
1. Sally, b. Feb. 21, 1776 ; m. John Teel of Princeton ; d. Princeton.
1. Joel, b. May 14, 1778 ; m. Ruth Fisk, who d. May 30, 1862, a 72 ;
he d. Apr. 24, 1846.
2. David, b. Sept. 2, 1810 : m. Harriet Davis of Shutesbury, Oct.
17, 1838, who d. Apr. 17, 1869, a. 60 ; m. 2d, Emily
Blandin of Norton, May 22, 1873.
3. Naomi E., b. Oct. 16, 1839 ; d. Sept. 19, 1842.
3. Charles E., b. Dec. 7, 1845.
3. George W., b. Dec. 19, 1848 ; d. Aug. 26, 1874.
3. Joel Franklin, b. Sept. 8, 1852 ; m. Ida E. Wright, May 1,
1877, who d. Nov. 25, 1877.
2. Alice, b. Feb. 6, 1813 ; m. Amasa G. Davis.
2. Moses, b. Sept. 8, 1815 ; m. Ann O. Pierce of New Braintree,
who d. Sept. 3, 1875 ; m. 2d, Phebe S. (Hartwell) Brown ;
res. Westboro'.
3. David N., b. Nov. 24, 1846 ; res. Westboro'.
2. Dorcas, b. Feb. 27, 1818 ; d. May 26, 1854.
2. Naomi, b. July 15, 1820 ; d. July 3, 1831.
2. Alden, b. Sept. 29, 1822 ; m. Elizabeth Green, Aug. 2, 1853, who
d. Dec. 2, 1855 ; m. 2d, Elizabeth Brigham, Nov. 10, 1864.

POLLARD.

3. James A., b. Sept. 9, 1854 ; m. Emma F. Albee of Derry, N. H., Apr. 18, 1877 ; res. Leominster.
3. Mabel Alden, b. Dec. 25, 1866.
3. Frederick Eugene, b. Mar. 21, 1871.
2. Ruth, b. Jan. 13, 1827 ; m. Darius M. Allen.
2. Charles, b. Aug. 20, 1829 ; d. Sept. 8, 1831.
1. Lois, b. Aug. 15, 1780 ; d. Feb. 24, 1854.
1. Alice, b. Nov. 17, 1782 ; m. Seth Sumner of Dedham, May 30, 1806 ; d. Dedham.
1. Moses, b. Oct. 16, 1784 ; d. June 19, 1787.
1. Persis, b. Sept. 12, 1786 ; m. Ella Slocomb, Dec. 3, 1810, who d. June 25, 1831 ; m. 2d, Abijah Hinds.
1 John, b. Nov. 29, 1791 ; d. May 21, 1827.
1. Tabitha, b. May 27, 1793 ; m. Amherst Coleman.
1. Hannah, b. Apr. 5, 1795 ; m. Delphos Gates.
1. Isaac, b. Jan. 1, 1797 ; d. Aug. 12, 1828.
1. Anna, b. Mar. 26, 1799 ; rem. Templeton ; d. there.
1. Mary, b. July 7, 1801 ; d. Aug. 23, 1829.

EDMUND A. POLLARD m. Maria Gates, Apr. 28, 1835 ; d. June 19, 1873, a. 63 ; she rem. Gardner.

1. Charles A., b. Apr. 15, 1836.
1. Lois Maria, b. Jan. 23, 1838 ; m. Marshall C. Mower, Nov. 24, 1864.
1. Roxa Caroline, b. Feb. 28, 1840.
1. Henry Gates, b. Aug. 14, 1842.
1. George, b Feb. 4, 1845.
1. Mary Emily, b. Mar. 24, 1849.
1. Hattie J., b. 1852 ; m. Willie D. Piper of Gardner, July 11, 1874.
1. Ella Persis, b. July 20, 1856 ; d. Sept. 14, 1856.
1. Edmund S., b. July 4, 1859.

POND.

EZRA POND c. f. Wrentham, 1768 ; m. Sarah Morse, Mar. 13, 1749, who d. Mar. 19, 1772, a. 42 ; m. 2d, Mercy (Newton) Baker of Bellingham, July, 1774, who d. Apr. 25, 1817, a. 81 ; he d. Dec. 2, 1803, a. 83.

1. Rhoda, b. Oct. 12, 1753 ; m. Abijah Greenwood.
1. Joseph*, b. May 12, 1756 ; m. Margaret Pond, July 20, 1778, who d. Aug. 26, 1828, a. 72 ; he d. Jan. 11, 1823, a. 67.

POND.

2. Preston, b. Jan. 2, 1779; m. Hannah Rice of Princeton, Apr. 7, 1802, who d. July 27, 1855, a. 68; he d. June 30, 1868.

3. Betsey R., b. Feb. 5, 1801; m. Joel Newton of Templeton.

3. Stillman, b. Oct. 26, 1803; m. Elmira Whittemore, Dec. 22, 1825, who d. July 25, 1833; m. 2d, Maria L. Davis, Feb. 4, 1834; res. Utah.

3. Arethusa, b. Dec. 14, 1805; m. Freeman Brown; m. 2d, Peter Newton of Templeton.

3. Hannah, b. Mar. 18, 1807; m. Benjamin Miller of Westminster.

3. Abigail, b. Dec. 18, 1809; m. George Hager of Westminster.

3. Reuben S., b. May 29, 1812; m. in Westminster; went West.

3. Charles S., b. May 6, 1818; went West.

3. Adeline E., b. Dec. 5, 1825; m. —— Hawkes of Templeton.

2. Nancy, b. Jan. 17, 1784; m. Oliver Witt.

2. Joseph, b. Apr. 4, 1788; m. Harriet Rice of Rutland, Mar. 2, 1826. who d. July 9, 1859, a. 61; he d. May 12, 1861.

3. Horace G., b. Sept. 23, 1826; m. Lura Thompson, Apr. 4, '50.

4. Herbert W., b. June ·6, 1851; m. Rhoda Wheeler; rem. Worcester.

4. Helen D., b. Aug. 11, 1856; m. Thomas Irving Hale.

3. Charlotte, b. Dec. 3. 1827; d. Oct. 20, 1843.

3. Susan, b. June 27. 1829; m. Abijah Patridge, Jan 5, 1854, who d. Mar. 14, 1862; rem. Templeton.

3. Joseph Emerson, b. Sept. 26, 1831; res. Sterling.

3. Moses R., b. Nov. 18, 1834; rem. Athol.

3. Lowell, b. Oct. 7, 1836; res. Templeton.

3. Rowland, b. Mar. 27. 1841; d. army, May 16, '64. [See p. 141.]

2. Asa, b. Oct. 22, 1791; m. Emeline Dresser of Charlton, Mar. 9, 1825; rem. Shrewsbury.

2. Caty, b. May 4, 1794; d. Jan. 18, 1871.

2. Rowland, b. May 27, 1798; m. Mary Kimball, Jan. 4, 1821, who d. Oct. 10, 1827, a. 29; he d. May 6, 1865.

3. Harriet, b. June 28, 1821; m. John M. Coleman.

3. Louisa, b. Sept. 10. 1825; m. Edmund Coleman.

3. Lucy, b. July 4, 1827; m. —— Smith of Worcester.

1. Ezra*, b. May 28, 1758; m. Parmelia Hubbell of Vt.; rem. Eden, Vt.

1. Ezekiel*, b. Feb. 21, 1761; rem. Hyde Park, Vt.

1. Levi, b. Nov. 20, 1763; m. Lucy Newton, Apr. 11, 1785, who d. Feb. 5, 1827, a. 59; he d. May 4, 1848.

POND.

2. Lewis, b. Aug. 19, 1785 ; m. Polly Hinds, Mar. 31, 1808, who
   d. Auburn, Feb. 14, 1877 ; he d. Oxford.

   3. Lewis Sumner, b. May 8, 1809 ; res. Illinois.

   3. Lucetta, b. Apr. 20, 1812 ; m. Joab C. Wright.

   3. Emily, b. May 26, 1815 ; m. Constant Davis of Grafton ; res.
      Brighton.

   3. Otis, b. June 3, 1818 ; res. Worcester.

   3. Polly B., b. May 6, 1821 ; m. Wm. Henry Marean.

   3. Julia Ann, b. June 11, 1824 ; d. Apr. 14, 1861.

   3. Philander, b. July 6, 1826 ; res. N. Y. City.

   3. Jane Aurelia, b. Sept. 25, 1829 ; d. Grafton.

2. Rhoda, b. Dec. 3, 1787 ; m. Bildad Wright ; m. 2d, Thomas
   Temple.

2. Betsey, b. Nov. 29, 1789 ; m. Amos Hartwell.

2. Aaron, b. Nov. 28, 1791 ; m. Nancy Waite, who d. Oct. 10, 1857 ;
   he d. Barre.

   3. Hollis, b. Oct. 25, 1812 ; m. Betsey Goodspeed, Oct. 6, 1836.

   4. Ann Eliza, b. July 5, 1837 ; d. May 29, 1859.

   4. Henry D., b. Apr. 13, 1839 ; rem. New York.

   4. William G., b. Aug 25, 1841 ; m. Stella J. Brigham.

   4. George Hollis, b. Sept 4, 1844.

   4. Abby, b. Mar. 9, 1848 ; d. Sept. 12, 1851.

   4. James H., b. Feb. 28, 1852 ; m. Jenny West of Petersham,
      Feb. 5, 1879 ; res. Athol.

   4. Nellie, b. Nov. 28, 1854.

   3. Harrison, b. Mar. 7, 1815 ; d. Sept. 29, 1823.

   3. Louisa, b. Apr. 2, 1818 ; d. July 23, 1820.

   3. Benjamin Franklin, b. Aug. 11, 1820 ; m. Jane H. Warren,
      Dec. 30, 1847 ; res. Sandy Creek, N. Y.

   3. Aaron H., b. May 28, 1823.

   3. Nancy Elvira, b. Mar. 5, 1826 ; m. Clesrow Gates.

   3. Levi Temple, b. Sept. 12, 1828 ; rem. N. Y. City.

   3. Charles Waite, b. Oct. 24, 1831 ; d. South America.

   3. George S., b. July 20, 1834 ; m. Mary F. Crittenden of Con-
      way, Apr. 3, 1861 ; res. Athol.

2. Obadiah, b. Nov. 16, 1793 ; m. Sally Waite, June 23, 1825 ; d.
   Mar. 10, 1835 ; she d. Worcester.

   3. Lucius W., b. Apr. 20, 1826 ; m. Louisa Fisk of Worcester,
      Apr. 20, 1847 ; rem. Worcester.

43

POND.

3. Levi Forrester, b. May 27, 1827; m. Ellen L. Crosby, Feb. 26, 1856; res. Chicopee.

3. Lucy Avaline, b. Dec. 10, 1828; d. Aug. 25, 1829.

3. Sarah Jane, b. June 14, 1830; d. Barre, Sept. 21, 1850.

3. Mercy Waite, b. Apr. 22, 1832; m. Albert M. Smith of Worcester, who d. Cuba; she res. Worcester.

3. Lucy Augusta, b. Feb. 8, 1834; res. Worcester.

2. Levi, b. Mar. 19, 1795; rem. Maine.

2. Rachel, b. June 1, 1798; m. Roland Woodward.

2. Lucy, b. Dec. 29, 1800; m. Rufus McClenathan.

2. Sally, b. Aug 24, 1803; m. Ira Thompson.

2. Mary, b. Jan. 7, 1807; m. Thomas Hale.

2. Ezra Parker, b. Mar. 9, 1811; m. Lucy Temple. Nov. 10, 1836.

3. Frederick William, b. Mar. 5, 1838; m. Susan Hardman of West Cambridge, Aug. 17, 1866.

3. Thomas M., b. Sept. 10, 1839; res. N. Y. City.

3. Ezra Parker, b. Oct. 2, 1842; d. July 16, 1867.

3. Levi Merrill, b. Oct. 18, 1847; rem. Conn.

3. Lucius W., b. June 15, 1855; m. Eliza B. Thompson of Boston, Nov. 25, 1874.

4. Louis Parker, b. June 28, 1876.

1. Tryphena, b. Aug. 12, 1769; m. Jonas Newton, Dec. 15, 1789; rem. probably to Vt.

1. Azubah, b. Dec., 1775; m. Oliver Brown.

1. Moses, b. 1784; m. Elizabeth Ames, May 29, 1800; rem. Rutland; d. Oct. 1, 1827; she d. May 17, 1852.

POTTER.

BENNETT POTTER, b. Walpole, June 13, 1810; m. Louisa Wright, Dec. 28, 1836.

1. Hobert, b. Sept. 15, 1837; d. July 29, 1839.

1. Lucy E., b. Jan. 31, 1840; d. Mar. 6, 1859.

1. Mary A., b. Aug. 11, 1842; d. June 27, 1859.

1. Caroline L., b. Mar. 11, 1845; d. May 22, 1847.

1. Hobert B., b. Nov. 25, 1848; m. Ella L. Phelps of North Adams, Mar. 25, 1880.

1. Charles J., b. Jan. 25, 1854; d. June 25, 1877.

PRENTISS.

HENRY PRENTISS c. f. Princeton; m. Elizabeth Gill, who d. Jan. 7, 1860,
a. 80; he d. Mar. 6, 1843, a. 76.

1. Hitty, b. Apr. 17, 1801 ; m. Peter Richardson.
1. Henry, b. July 18, 1802 ; m. Adeline Wright, Nov. 12, 1829, who
d. Sept. 14, 1872 ; he d. Nov. 2, 1872.
  2. Lois E., b. Aug. 30, 1830 ; d. Oct. 26, 1857.
  2. George, b. Jan. 31, 1832 ; m. Louisa A. Phelps, Oct. 15, 1857, who
d. July 15, 1865 ; m. 2d, Dorcas E. Joslin, Aug. 21, 1867.
    3. Harriet Adelaide, b. June 7, 1865 ; d. Sept. 14, 1865.
    3. Adelaide E , b. Apr. 15, 1870.
    3. Walter Henry, b. July 2, 1874.
    3. George Edward, b. July 30, 1877.
  2. Harriet A., b. Mar. 31, 1834 ; m. Alonzo J. Taft, Jan. 7, 1853 ;
d. Sept. 4, 1873.
  2. Adeline, b. July 30, 1836 ; m. James F. Hayden.
  2. Lucy R., b. July 21, 1838 ; m. T. Sibley Heald.
  2. Dorcas C., b. Dec. 7, 1840 ; m. Albert Goodspeed.
  2. Henrietta, b. Mar. 29, 1844 ; d. June 24, 1854.
  2. Henry, b. Sept. 25, 1846 ; res. Brooklyn, New York.
  2. Aaron, b. Aug. 8, 1852 ; d. New York, Apr., 1880.
1. George, b. May 20, 1808 ; d. June 19, 1830.
1. Elizabeth, b. Mar. 28, 1810 ; m. Samuel G. Nichols.
1. Augusta, b. July 7, 1812 ; m. Joseph Clark ; m. 2d, Stillman Morse.
1. Rebecca, b. May 28, 1814 ; m. Aaron Greenwood of Gardner, Sept.
8, 1841.
1. Spencer, b. Feb. 6, 1818 ; m. Sarah Stone, June 4, 1844.
  2. Sarah Elizabeth, b. Dec. 1, 1846 ; m. James S. Harrington of
Westminster, Mar. 12, 1867.
  2. William S., b. Oct. 22, 1848 ; m. Eva A. Jackson, Jan. 27, 1874.
    3. Mary Abbie, b. June 11, 1877.
  2. Franklin,   ⎫   d. Dec. 2, 1851.
  2. Frederick, ⎬ b. Apr. 16, 185. ; m. Lycera M. Sinclair of West-
         ⎭ minster, May 28, 1877.
  2. Emily, b. Sept. 8, 1853 ; d. Mar. 16, 1878.
  2. Charles Gardner, b. Sept. 12, 1855.
  2. George F., b. Mar. 27, 1859 ; d. July 27, 1859.
  2. Arthur, b. Aug. 23, 1860.
1. Mary Davis, b Mar. 2, 1820 ; m. George B. Coleman.

PRENTISS.

1. Sarah Prince, b. Apr. 24, 1822 ; m. Jacob Farnsworth of Nashua, N. H.
1. Emily, b. Mar. 23, 1824 ; res. Worcester.   .

RAYMOND.

JOSEPH RAYMOND c. f. Westminster ; m. Linda Whitney, Nov. 20, 1823,
      who d. Mar. 23, 1847, a. 45 ; m 2d, Betsey (Wheeler)
      Murdock ; d. Sept. 25, 1857, a. 61 ; she d. Sept. 17, 1872.
1. Alfred Whitney, res. Cedar Rapids, Iowa.
1. Melinda Elizabeth, res. Brookline.
1. Joseph Down, m. Loretta Sheldon ; res. Worcester.
1. Reuben Stearns, d. New London, Conn., 1872.
1. Susan Wood, b. Oct., 1831 ; m. H. Lincoln Chase of Brookline.
1. Henry Chase, b. July 13, 1840 ; res. Council Bluffs, Iowa.

REED.

SIMON REED c. f. Acton ; m. Sophia Grimes, Nov. 21, 1830 ; d. July,
      1872, Nashua, N. H.
1. Charles Theodore, b. Mar. 7, 1831.
1. Henry Clay, b. July 16, 1832.
1. Zelia Ann, b. Aug. 15, 1834 ; m. Barker Marshall of Minneapolis,
      Minn.
1. Sarah Sophia, b. Nov. 30, 1836.
1. Simon Marshall, b. Sept. 3, 1838.
1. Eugene Austinello, b. Dec. 23, 1840.
1. Mary Louisa, b. Nov. 8, 1842.
1. Clarence Meredith, b. Apr. 26, 1844.
1. Herbert Billings, b. July 31, 1846 ; d. Sept. 26, 1846.
1. Edgar Leroy, b. Sept. 3, 1848.

REID.

MICAJAH REID c. f. Sudbury, 1806 ; m. Ruth Gleason, Apr. 27, 1806 ; d.
      Oct. 9, 1860, a. 79 ; she d. Feb. 20, 1864, a. 79.
1. George W., b. Feb. 7, 1807 ; m. Lydia Smith, Dec. 20, 1832, who
      d. May 3, 1868 ; m. 2d, Ann Maria Trow of Hardwick,
      Nov. 11, 1869.
2. George Frederick, b. Nov. 7, 1833 ; d. May 17, 1876.
2. Charles H. F., b. May 3, 1839 ; m. and rem. N. Y.

REID.

2. Joseph B., b. Nov. 12, 1843 ; d. Sept. 4, 1845.
2. Joseph B., b. Dec. 31, 1847 ; res. Texas.
1. Eliza G., b. Nov. 25, 1808 ; m. Benj. Clark ; d. Nov. 23, 1840.
1. Mehitable N., b. Aug. 30, 1811 ; m. William Stowe.
1. Sophia P., b. Mar. 14, 1814.
1. Samuel G., b. Mar. 4, 1816 ; res. Roxbury.
1. Joseph B., b. June 15, 1818 ; d. Apr. 27, 1819.
1. Joseph B., b. Mar. 5, 1820 ; d. May 6, 1873.
1. Hannah, b. Jan. 16, 1822 ; m. George B. Wilbur.
1. Mary, b. July 7, 1824 ; d. Aug. 25, 1825.
1. Charles, b. Mar. 20, 1826 ; drowned June 2, 1844. [See p. 165.]

RICE.

ABEL RICE c. f. Barre ; m. Anna Jones, Aug. 11, 1791 ; both d. Penn.
   1. Amos Jones, b. Mar. 30, 1792 : m. Sally Green, Oct. 12, 1826 ;
       rem. Penn. ; m. 2d, Rebecca Seaver ; d. Apr. 14, 1874.
      2. Harriet Elizabeth, b. Feb. 18, 1827.
   1. Ralph, b. Dec. 19, 1793 ; m. Lavina P. Russell, June 25, 1815 ; d.
       Sept. 17, 1847.
      2. Susan Howe, b. Jan. 3, 1816 ; m. Francis F. Sargent.
      2. David, b. Dec. 1, 1818.
      2. Maria, b. Mar. 7, 1820 ; m. Isaac Newton.
      2. Joseph Willard, b. Apr. 7, 1822 ; m. Harriet Wilder, Dec. 1, 1846,
         who d. Aug. 16, 1852, a. 28 ; m. 2d, Avalina Par-
         ker, Nov. 19, 1854 ; rem. Illinois.
        3. Fred W., b. Sept. 16, 1851 ; d. Jan. 28, 1853.
      2. Francis, b. Aug. 11, 1824 ; m. Hannah S. Frost, May 19, 1873.
      2. Joel, b Dec. 13, 1826 ; d. Mar. 28, 1848.
      2. Samuel Newell, b. Jan. 7, 1829 ; d. Nov. 21, 1846.
      2. George Washington, b. Apr. 6, 1831 ; m. and settled in Gardner.
      2. Hannah, b. Mar. 13, 1833 ; m. Sydney Sargent.
      2. Isaac Newton, b. Aug. 12, 1835 ; m. Mary E. Fisk, Nov. 24,
         1859 ; d. army, May 13, 1863. [See p. 141.]
   1. Betsey, b. Jan. 26, 1797 ; m. James Greenwood ; rem. Penn. ; d.
      May 10, 1840.
   1. Daniel, b. Oct. 29, 1799 ; m. Candace Roper, June 2, 1824 ; rem.
      Penn. ; d. Feb. 22, 1831.
   1. Julianna, b. Mar. 5, 1804 ; m. Aaron Hunting.

RICE.

1. Damaris, b. July 31, 1806 ; d. Penn., Feb. 28, 1824.

1. Abel, b. Aug. 28, 1808 ; rem. Penn ; m. Roxana Green ; m. 2d, Betsey Thatcher ; d. Dec. 9, 1855.

1. Hannah, b. July 7, 1810 ; m. Orton P. Jackson of Penn., Apr. 7, 1837.

1. Willard, b. 1813 ; d. Nov. 11, 1816.

EDMOND RICE c. f. Marlboro' ; m. Abigail Muzzy, Apr. 30, 1782 ; d. Mar. 24, 1790 ; she d. Sept. 4, 1841.

1. Sophia, b. Jan. 23, 1785 ; m. Otis Greenwood.

1. William, b. May 17, 1787 ; m. Rebecca Allen, Dec. 20, 1810 ; d. Nov. 13, 1831 ; she d. July 15, 1878.

    2. Adaline, b. Aug. 8, 1811 ; m. Aaron Greenwood.

    2. Edmond, b. June 4, 1813 ; d. Savannah, Ga., Oct. 14, 1838.

    2. Amanda, b. Dec. 14, 1814 ; d. May, 30, 1815.

    2. Sophia, b June 19, 1816 ; m. Almer Gay.

    2. Lucy A., b. Oct. 23, 1818 ; m. Orlando S. Brigham.

    2. Amanda, b. Nov. 28, 1821 ; m. Silas Wheeler.

1. Betsey, b. Mar. 4, 1790 ; m. Amos Mann.

RICHARDSON.

PETER RICHARDSON c. f. Princeton, 1856 ; m. Hitty Prentiss, Dec. 19, 1820 ; d. Brookline, Mar., 1878, a. 80.

1. Harriet Bullock, b. Sept. 8, 1822 ; m. Russell Hallett of Boston.

1. Henry Prentiss, b. Jan 22, 1824 ; d. California, 1848.

1. William Everett, b. Feb. 21, 1825 ; enlisted from Worcester in 21st Reg. ; promoted lieutenant ; afterwards lieutenant in 35th Reg. ; m. Vesta Hodgdon ; res. Boston.

1. James Myrick, b. Aug. 5, 1826 ; [see p. 142 ;] m. Annie Cartwright ; d. Boston.

1. Thomas Emmet, b. Aug. 21, 1829 ; private in a Missouri regiment.

1. George Prentiss, b. June 15, 1831 ; m. Julia A. Wright, Jan. 1, 1863 ; [see p. 142 ;] res. Auburndale.

1. Spencer Wells, b. Apr. 12, 1834 ; enlisted from Boston as captain in 44th Reg. ; m. Mary Cumston ; res. Boston.

1. Samuel Peter, b. June 12, 1836 ; d. June, 1836.

1. Edward Bangs, b. May 20, 1838 ; enlisted in 45th Reg. ; promoted to lieutenant.

RICHARDSON.

1. Charles Albert, b. Feb. 9, 1840; d. 1846.

Besides six sons, Peter Richardson had, in the army, two grandsons, and two nephews.

ROBERTSON.

RUSSELL ROBERTSON c. f. Framingham, 1876; m. Elvira A. Pratt of Guilford, Vt., Oct. 19, 1842.
1. Lizzie A., b. Jan. 17, 1850.
1. Sereno O., b. Sept. 30, 1856.

ROPER.

SAMUEL ROPER c. f. Holden; m. Adeline Marshall, Apr. 19, 1837.
1. Charles W., b. Jan. 6, 1838; d. Sturbridge.
1. Abel M., b. Nov. 3, 1839; d. Sept. 5, 1846.
1. Lucy E., b. Sept. 10, 1841; m. George Carlyle; rem. Rutland.
1. Mary E., b. Mar. 1, 1844; d. Sept. 24, 1845.
1. Elizabeth E., b. July 7, 1846; d. Holden.
1. William M., b. Aug. 27, 1848; m. Mary Abbie Davis of Worcester, Nov. 18, 1869.
  2. William M., b. Jan. 31, 1871.
  2. Kittie Adeline, b. Sept. 15, 1873; d. Oct. 28, 1875.
  2. Eugene Davis, b. Apr. 25, 1876.
  2. Bertha May, b. June 7, 1878.
  2. Edith Belle, b. Sept. 22, 1880.
1. John S., b. Dec. 11, 1850; m. Mary L. Howard, Sept. 13, 1870, who d. Nov. 16, 1871; m. 2d, Martha Eva Brigham of Rutland, May 5, 1875; res. Barre.
  2. Harry Howard, b. Mar. 26, 1871.
1. Sylvia A. L., b. Mar. 27, 1854; m. George F. Wetherbee of Princeton, May 28, 1873.
1. Charles F., b. Apr. 13, 1857.

RUSSELL.

THOMAS RUSSELL c. f. Sherborn; m. ———— Perry, who d. Jan. 18, 1821, a. 69; he d. Apr. 18, 1834, a. 90.
1. Shubael, b. 1785; m. Sally Merriam, Sept. 22, 1805; d. suddenly, July 1, 1832, a. 47; she d. Jan. 2, 1880, a. 92.
  2. Silas, b. Jan. 20, 1806; m. Susan (Merrill) Allen, Sept. 14, 1842, who d. Nov. 9, 1846, a. 39.

RUSSELL.

3. Susan Maria, b. Nov. 8, 1843 ; d. Sept. 21, 1856.
3. Martha E., b. Jan. 28, 1846 ; m. Wm. F. Osgood ; m. 2d, Lyman F. Partridge.
2. Lucinda, b. Jan. 28, 1808 ; m. William J. Parker.
2. Sally M., b. Dec. 3, 1811 ; m. Geo. W. Phillips of Dublin, N. H., Sept. 20, 1832, who d. Fitchburg ; she d. June 3, '70.
2. Joseph, b. Dec. 13, 1813 ; m. Mary Amanda Bartlett, May 1, '56.
3. Walter, b. June 28, 1857.
3. Edmund, b. Mar. 3, 1859.
3. Agnes, b. May 20, 1861.
3. Jennie Louise, b. Mar. 4, 1865.
3. Austin Lincoln, b. June 12, 1867.
2. Martha, b. May, 1816 ; m. Alfred Russell.
1. Lavina P., b. Aug. 22, 1792 ; m. Ralph Rice.

Isaac S. Russell. c f. Jaffrey, N. H., 1876 ; m. Olive B. Smith of Peterboro', N. H., Nov., 1845.

RYDER.

Rev. Almanza Ryder m. Sophia Thomas ; [see chap. X. ;] rem. Boston ; d.
1. Elliot, b. Jan. 30, 1856.
1. Mary Ella, b Sept. 28, 1857.
1. Howard, b. 1859 ; d. July 28, 1861.

SARGENT.

Thomas Sargent c. f. Leicester as early as 1773 ; m. Tabitha Tuttle, Sept. 27, 1744 ; d. Jan. 25, 1795, a. 74 ; she d. June 10, 1804, a. 80.
1. Samuel, b. Dec. 30, 1748 ; m. Deborah Sylvester, Jan. 13, 1772 ; rem. Marlboro', N. H.
2. Samuel, b. Mar. 5, 1774 ; m. Sarah Gypson, Oct., 1797.
1. John, b. May 24, 1755 ; m. Persis Newton, Oct. 31, 1776, who d. Jan. 3, 1802, a. 43 ; m. 2d, Mrs. Phebe Doyle, Jan., 1804, who d. Dec. 19, 1814 ; m. 3d, Mrs. Esther Dean of Oakham, Sept. 11, 1816, who d. June, 1822 ; m. 4th, Hannah Bond ; he d. Feb. 11, 1837.
2. John, b. Sept. 9, 1777 ; m. Huldah Newton, June 12, 1797 ; d. Jan. 1, 1849 ; she d. Jan. 25, 1854.

SARGENT.

3. John, b. Sept. 8, 1797 ; m. Hannah Dunham, Dec. 4, 1819 ; res. Maine.

3. Relief, b. Nov. 5, 1799 ; d. Aug. 3, 1804.

3. William, b. May 31, 1802 ; m. Abigail Tripp, Sept. 7, 1826 : res. Maine.

3. Isaac, b. Aug. 31, 1804 ; m. Hannah Davenport ; m. 2d, Lucy Jacobs ; res. Maine.

3. Asa, b. June 22, 1810 ; d. Aug. 3, 1818.

3. Salmon, b. May 18, 1812 ; m. Alice Brazier, Nov. 15, 1835 ; res Maine.

2. Asa, b. Sept. 3, 1779 ; m. Polly Ball, Dec. 30, 1801 ; res. Franklin.

3. Betsey, b. Dec. 13, 1802 : m. James Engly : m. 2d, Samuel Alexander.

3. Polly, b. Jan 30, 1805 ; m. George Black.

3. Asa, b. Mar. 8, 1807 ; m. Calista Mason, Aug. 14, 1827 ; res. Connecticut.

3. Persis N., b. Mar. 24, 1809 ; d. Dec. 17, 1827.

3. Charles A., b. Apr. 22, 1812 ; m. Susan L. Brown, Feb. 16, 1834 : res. Oakham.

2. Persis, b. Aug. 2, 1781 ; m. William Perham, Aug., 1802.

2. Thomas, b. Aug. 3, 1784 ; m. Polly Goodnow, Sept. 12, 1804 : rem. Rutland.

3. Sally G., b. Mar. 6, 1807 ; m. Roswell Bemis, Mar. 25, 1835.

3. Persis N., b. Mar. 25, 1809 ; m. Marshall H. Oliver, Oct. 13, 1832.

3. David G., b. Apr. 6, 1812 ; d. Jan. 12, 1814.

3. Hezekiah S., b. May 27, 1814 ; m. Nancy L. Moores, Jan. 9, 1839 ; rem. Spencer.

2. Azubah, b. Jan. 22, 1787 ; m. James Dean of Oakham, Nov. 26, 1807.

2. Martha, b. Sept. 6, 1788 ; m. Silas Gates, May, 1812, who d. Leominster ; she res. Fitchburg.

2. Tabitha, b. Mar. 21, 1790 ; m. Aaron Pease.

2. Edmund, b. Jan. 11, 1793 ; m. Candace Coggswell, Aug. 15, 1815 ; res. Princeton.

3. Mary Emily, b. July 8, 1817 ; m. Aaron Rolph, Jan. 16, 1839.

3. Harriet, b. Nov. 3, 1820 ; m. Moses Davis.

3. Edmund M., b. Aug. 2, 1824 ; m. Anna Rolph, Nov. 15, 1853.

44

SARGENT.

4. Frederick V., b. Nov. 6, 1855.

2. Sally. b. Jan. 10, 1796 ; m. James Luce.

2. Polly, b. June 8, 1798 ; rem. Fitchburg.

2. Susan, b. May 1, 1801 ; d. Nov., 1814.

2. Samuel, b. May 29, 1807 ; d. Mar., 1809.

1. Ebenezer, b. June 5, 1762 ; m. Phebe Shute, Apr. 12, 1785, who
    d. Mar. 5, 1834, a. 70 ; he d. Oct. 12, 1849.

2. Thomas, b. Jan. 28, 1786 ; m. Jane Gray ; rem. Burlington, Vt.

2. Daniel, b. July 23, 1788 ; m. Betsey Rice of Templeton, Dec.
    15, 1810, who d. Mar. 21, 1848 ; rem. Petersham. .

3. Francis F., b. May 7, 1812 ; m. Susan H. Rice, May 21, 1839 ;
    d. Oct. 13, 1850 ; she res. Barre.

4. Mary Angelina, b. Feb. 26, 1840 ; m. John W. Hunting ;
        m. 2d, Nathaniel E. Holland of Barre. Nov.
        29, 1866.

4. William H., b. May 9, 1841 ; m. Fanny Etta Clark, Nov.
        28, 1867, who d. Feb. 24, 1872.

5. Willie Gilmore. b. June 20, 1869.

4. Minerva E., b. Dec. 4, 1842 ; m. Joseph W. Blood.

4. Elwell P., b. Dec. 1, 1844 ; m. Nancy Hunting. Dec. 21,
    1865 ; d. May 27, 1871.

5. Edwin Wallace, b. Apr. 23, 1868.

4. Frederick C.. b. Mar. 20, 1847 ; d. Sept. 12, 1850.

4. Clarissa M.. b. May 25. 1849 ; d. Sept. 20, 1850.

3. Lucy W., b. Feb. 21, 1814 ; m. Lewis Curtis of Petersham,
    May 3. 1836.

3. William P., b. Dec. 21, 1815 ; m. Elizabeth Partridge of Athol,
    June 10, 1840 ; res. Albany, N. Y.

3. Clarissa R., b. Nov. 9, 1819 ; m. Lewis Hardy, Mar. 28, 1843 ;
    d. Oct. 19, 1843.

3. Solomon Brigham, b. Dec. 1, 1821 ; m. Martha A. Kendrick
        of North Brookfield, Dec. 9, 1845 ; d. North
        Brookfield, 1872.

3. Mary E , b. May 7, 1824 ; m. Timothy J. Spooner of Barre,
    Nov. 24, 1851 ; d. Jan. 20, 1868.

3. Henry H., b. Jan. 4, 1827 ; m. Elizabeth Jones of Greenfield,
    Oct., 1854 ; d. Oct. 13, 1867.

3. Sydney H., b. May 10, 1829 ; m. Hannah Rice, June 14. 1851 ;

SARGENT.

d. army Oct. 27, 1862; [see p. 142;] she d. Oct. 3, 1868.

   4. Samuel N., b. Mar. 14, 1852; d. July 9, 1853.

   4. George F., b. May 14, 1854.

   4. Harriet B., b. Oct. 13, 1857.

  3. Charles A., b. Dec. 8, 1831; m. and res. Albany, N. Y.

 2. Roxa, b. Dec. 23, 1790; m. Simon B. Hartwell.

 2. Russell, b. Jan. 28, 1793; res. N. Y.

 2. Parker, b. Apr. 7, 1796; m. Ellen D. Hand, Jan. 19, 1825; res. Albany. N. Y.

 2. Phebe, b. Mar. 12, 1798: m. Isaac Simonds.

 2. Mary, b. June 16, 1802; m. Nathan Wright.

 2. Stillman, b. Apr. 13, 1804; d. July 4, 1874.

SAVAGE.

JOSEPH SAVAGE c. f. Vt., m. Polly Thompson, who d. Feb. 7, 1852; returned to Vt.

 1. Benjamin D., b. June 29, 1799; name changed to Phelps. [See Phelps.]

 1. Mary, b. Sept. 8, 1800; m. Hosea Willard; both d. Wardsboro', Vt.

 1. Eliza, b. Oct. 5, 1802; m. Levi Conant.

 1. Joseph, b. Nov. 6, 1804; d. July 2, 1839.

 1. Frances, b. May 29, 1806; m. George Lewis; m. 2d, Whiting Mc-Clenathan.

 1. Seth, b. June 5, 1808; m. Mary E. Parmenter of Holden, Oct. 2, 1844, who d. Oct. 27, 1858, a. 36.

   2. Hattie F., b. Oct. 9, 1845.

   2. Herbert Leroy, b. May 2, 1848.

   2. Mary E., b. Sept. 14, 1852.

   2. Joseph, b. Mar. 11, 1857.

 1. John, b. Dec., 1810; m. Mary Smith of Rutland; rem. Petersham.

 1. Sarah S., b. Feb. 6, 1813; m. Willard Allen.

 1. Hannah F., b June 1, 1815; m. Wm. C. Metcalf of Holden, Jan. 20, 1839.

 1. Samuel K., b. Mar. 25, 1817; m. Chloe Stone, Apr. 2, 1845.

   2. Edward B., b. Aug. 6, 1846; m. Louise J. Hunton, Nov. 1, 1875; res. Blackstone. [See p. 183.]

SAVAGE.

3. Edward Hunton, b. Sept. 19, 1876.
2. Leonora, b. Feb. 9, 1849 ; m. George W. Felton.
2. Mary Angenette, b. Nov. 17, 1850 ; d. Oct. 8, 1870.
2. Isabel, b. July 3, 1855 ; m. Rev. John A. Day, May 28, 1874.
2. Grace, b. Mar. 8, 1870.
1. Edward, b. May 22, 1819 ; d. Princeton.
1. James, b. Apr. 18, 1821 ; m. Maria F. Guild, who d. Apr. 29, 1858,
    a. 37 ; m. 2d, Roxa (Temple) Wheeler, Nov. 3, 1858.
2. Mary, b. Sept. 22, 1844 ; m. Silas Wright of Dorchester, N. H.,
    Nov. 1, 1868.

SELFRIDGE.

EDWARD SELFRIDGE c. f. Rutland ; m. Hannah Miles, who d. Apr. 19,
    1821, a. 75 : he d. Oct. 26, 1806, a. 71.   Gave his chil-
    dren the best education afforded by the schools of that
    time. Edward d. just after graduating with high honor.
    Lucy and Elizabeth became celebrated teachers.
1. Thomas O., b. Feb. 13, 1775 ; [see p. 183 ;] d. June, 1816 ; two
    of his grandsons are in U. S. Naval service.
1. Lucy, b. Dec. 5, 1776 ; m. Benoni Shurtliff ; d. Middlebury, Vt.
1. Hannah, b. Oct. 6, 1779 ; m. Artemas Goodnow, M. D., Nov. 1,
    1804.
1. Betsey B., b. Apr. 6, 1783 ; d. May 21, 1783.
1. Edward A., b. May 17, 1784 ; d. July 15, 1806.
1. Elizabeth, b. June 17, 1789 ; d. Middlebury, Vt., June, 1871.

SIMONDS.

ISAAC SIMONDS c. f. Princeton ; m. Phebe Sargent, June 13, 1816 ; d.
    Jan. 21, 1862, a. 67 : she d. Watertown, Jan., 1879.
1. Isaac Parker, b. May 23, 1818 ; d. Boston, May 9, 1874.
1. Mary, b. Dec. 20, 1820 ; m. John Lovell of Cambridge ; m. 2d,
    Andrew Cummings ; res. Watertown.
1. Samuel, b. Oct. 2, 1822 ; d. army ; family res. Dunbarton, N. H.
1. Charles, b. June 27, 1826 ; d. Feb. 29, 1832.
1. Willard A., b. Aug. 21, 1830 : m. Sarah E. Heath of Nashua, N. H.,
    Sept. 26, 1856, who d. Aug. 16, 1861 ; m. 2d, Jennie
    Hargrave of Nashua, N. H., Sept. 3, 1862.
2. Parker Sherman, b. Feb. 6, 1865.

SIMONDS.

2. Sarah Etta, b. July 4, 1866.
2. Samuel Lincoln. b. Dec. 8, 1867.
2. Franklin Augustus, b. Sept. 13, 1869.
2. Ann Maria, b. Jan. 25, 1872.
2. Mary Eliza, b. Nov. 16, 1873; d. June 28, 1874.
2. Charles Edward, b. July 3, 1876 ; d. May 25, 1877.
2. Martha Louise, b. Mar. 25, 1878.
1. Adelia, b. Nov. 21, 1833; m. Jonas Holt.
1. Charles H., b. Oct. 1, 1841 ; d. Mar. 19, 1842.

SMART.

HARLAN P. SMART c. f. Portland, Me.. Oct., 1876 ; m. Mary M. Muzzy of Searsmont, Me., Feb. 27, 1866.

SMITH.

JONATHAN WARREN SMITH* c f. Boylston(?)m. Catherine Keyes : d. Aug. 14, 1833. a. 85 ; she d. Mar. 20, 1845, a. 97 y., 5 m.

1. Alice, b. Mar. 14, 1775 ; m. Timothy Parker Marean.
1. Joel, b. Mar. 21, 1777 ; m. Hannah Clark, Sept. 15, 1803 ; d. Feb. 27, 1861 ; she rem. Upton.
    2. Emory, b. Aug. 12, 1804 ; m. Phebe Flagg, Oct. 27, 1825 ; rem. Lunenburg ; both d. there.
    2. Almira, b. June 28, 1806 ; m. Joshua Flagg.
    2. Emmons, b. Apr. 15, 1810 ; m. Catherine Howe, Apr. 15, 1835, who d. Jan. 8, 1839 ; m. 2d, Mary W. Davis, Jan. 20, 1842, who d. Dec. 1, 1870, a. 57.
        3. Charles Austin, b. Dec. 18, 1836 ; m. Mary A. Hill of Barre. Feb. 28, 1864.
        4 Carrie Etta, b. Mar. 26, 1866 ; d. May 9, 1866.
        4. Jennie Augusta, b. Apr 20, 1867.
        4. Cora Bell, b. Aug. 29, 1868.
        4. Charles Henry, b. Mar. 8, 1873.
        4. Catie Viola, b. Aug. 31, 1875.
        3. Ira W., b. Oct. 11, 1844.
        3. William Davis, b. Aug. 7, 1847 ; m. Caroline W. Brooks, July 19, 1868.

I

SMITH.

3. Joel Silas, b. Feb. 4, 1849.
3. Lizzie Ann, b. Mar. 17, 1851 ; m. Rufus Putnam, May 18, 1867.
3. Catherine A., b. Oct. 22. 1853 ; m. Homer Augustus Adams.
2. Lucy, b. Dec. 27. 1813 ; m. Oliver Clark ; m. 2d, John M. Bradshaw of Wayland ; d. Rutland.
2. Ira, b. Dec. 24. 1815 ; m. Abigail Pratt ; rem. Rindge, N. H. ; d. there, 1880.
2. Jonas, b. Sept. 24. 1817 ; m. in Pepperell ; rem. Conn ; d. Kentucky, 1876.
2. Asa, b. Oct. 10, 1820 ; m. Lucy Temple of Shrewsbury ; went to Cal. ; d. on the way home, 1854.
2. Levi, b. June 8, 1824 ; res. Paxton ; m. 2d, Mrs. Sarah (Mason) Brooks.
2. Catherine, b. Oct. 9. 1826 ; m. Franklin Rockwood ; res. Brookline. N. H.
1. Sophia, b. Dec. 30, 1778 ; d. Apr. 3, 1795.
1. Lucy, b. Mar. 1, 1781 ; d. Aug. 6, 1786.
1. Asa, b. May 3. 1783 ; d. Sept. 2, 1786.
1. Catherine, b. Jan. 16. 1786 ; m. Clark Witt.
1. Betsey, b Mar. 29, 1788 ; d Mar. 10, 1846
1. Ira, b. Jan. 25, 1791 ; d. Aug. 19, 1814.

JARED SMITH c. f. Norwich, Ct., 1878 ; m. Clarissa A. Bailey of Warwick, R. I., Dec. 26, 1847.
1. Lorena A., b. Dec. 20, 1851.
1. Dwight J., b. July 11, 1855 ; res. Norwich, Conn.
1. Nelson B., b. Sept. 25, 1860.
1. Clara L., b. Jan. 5, 1863.

SPAULDING.

WARREN SPAULDING c. f. Lincoln, 1872 ; m. Sarah O. Sherman of Lexington, Apr. 25, 1866.
1. Alice, b. Nov. 19, 1875.

STONE.

NATHAN STONE* c. f. Rutland as early as 1768 ; m. Freelove Phillips, who d. July 12; 1826 ; he became blind many years before his death ; (his son Sampson also was blind for many years ;) d. Dec. 19, 1827, a. 81.

STONE.

1. Polly, b. Nov. 8, 1768 : m. Eli Hinds.
1. Nathan, b. May 25, 1770 ; rem. N. Y.
1. Eliphalet, b. Jan. 11, 1772 ; m. Polly Johnson of Barre, Mar. 16, 1794 ; rem. Roxbury, N. H.
1. Jeduthan, b. May 4, 1773 ; m. Azubah Merriam, Dec. 7, 1790 ; rem. Eden, Vt.
1. Euranah, b. Apr. 7, 1774 ; m. —— Earle.
1. Patience, b. Feb. 24, 1776 ; m. Eli Clark.
1. Jotham, b. Apr. 5, 1778 ; m. Lucy Lyon, Aug. 16, 1801, who d. Feb. 8, 1826 ; m. 2d, Diantha (Merritt) Clark, Mar. 31, 1829. who d. July 18, 1841 : he d. June 12. 1831.
2. Betsey, b. Dec. 1, 1801 : m. Sewell Wheeler.
2. Eliphalet, b. Mar. 24, 1805 ; res. Wendell.
2. Lucy, b. Aug. 30, 1807 ; m. Makepeace Clark.
2. Lois, b. Nov. 19, 1809 ; m. William G. Clark.
2. Eliza Ann, b. Apr. 21, 1812 ; m. Jarvis Bates of R. I., Sept. 10. 1838 ; res. Keene, N. H.
2. Jotham. b. June 25, 1814 ; m. Sylvia Roper, Apr. 26, 1838, who d. Dec. 26, 1849 ; m. 2d, Caroline Allen of Lowell, May 8, 1850.
3. Eliza Ann, b. Mar. 13, 1839 ; m. Albert Pond of Keene, N. H., Jan. 1, 1859.
3. Lucy Freelove, b. Nov. 18, 1840 ; m. Baxter H. King of Athol. July 9, 1861, who d. army, Nov , 1863 ; m. 2d. Stuart Dermot, Aug. 3, 1870, who d. June 18, 1880.
3. Alfred R., b. Sept. 17. 1842 ; m. Kitty Cook of Mich.. 1868.
3. Franklin J., b. July 11, 1844 ; d. army Dec. 16, 1862. [See p. 142.]
3. J. Porter, b. Nov. 16, 1846 ; m. Nellie Davis of Princeton, June. 1866 ; res. Worcester.
3. Adam Wheeler, b. Sept. 25. 1848 ; name changed from Stone to Wheeler ; m. Olive Davis of Princeton, June, 1869 ; rem. Worcester.
3. Charles O., b. May 25, 1851 ; m. Lucy E. Hamilton, Jan. 18. 1876.
4. Edward Willis, b. July 4, 1878.
4. Luman Hamilton, b. Aug. 11, 1880.
3. Edward, b. Sept. 1, 1853 ; m. Flora Kendall of Gardner, Oct. 2, 1879. who d. Apr. 29, 1880.

STONE.

2. Asa, b. Oct. 9, 1816; m. Hannah Thompson, Apr. 28, 1846; d. army, June 20, 1864. [See p. 142.]

3. Sylvia L., b. Mar. 13, 1847; m. George Bryant, Nov. 29, 1866; res. N. Brookfield.

3. Roxa T., b. Apr. 17, 1848; m. George R. Miller of West Westminster, Vt., July 3, 1876, who d. Mar. 27, 1878; res. Middletown, Conn.

3. Elnora R., b. Nov. 11, 1851; m. John H. Tyler of N. Brookfield, Mar., 1871.

3. Orrin Franklin, b. Mar. 16, 1860.

2. Freelove, b. Aug 26, 1818; m. Jonathan Gates.

2. Sarah, b. Aug. 31, 1820; m. Spencer Prentiss.

2. Nathan, b. Mar. 4, 1824; m. Lucy Jane Waters; rem. Worcester.

1. Ruth, b. July 6, 1780; m. Abraham Shattuck; rem. Mich.

1. Samuel, b. Nov. 20, 1782; rem. Eden, Vt.

1. Sampson, b. Oct. 2, 1784; m. Lois Waite, Dec. 23, 1805, who d. June 15, 1816; m. 2d, Dolly (Waite) Lamb, who d. Jan. 12, 1842; m. 3d, Lucinda (Underwood) Coleman, Feb. 8, 1843, who d. Medway, 1878; he d. Aug. 12, 1858.

2. Rockwell, b. Mar. 21, 1806; m. Sophia Babbitt of Barre; res. Cal.

2. Louisa, b. Jan. 23, 1808; m. Wm. Morse; m. 2d, Wm. S. Clark.

2. Elmira, b. Nov. 10, 1811; m. John Nelson Gates; m. 2d, John Morse; res. Worcester.

2. Alice, b. Feb. 4, 1814; d. Mar. 6, 1833.

2. Sampson Harrison, b. Mar. 3, 1816; left town.

2. Andrew, b. Jan. 22, 1818; m. Maria L. Woodward of Marlboro', N. H.; d. Nov. 18, 1868; she d. Oct. 14, 1870.

2. Lois, b. Aug. 13, 1819; m. Isaac Williams of Gardner, Nov. 3, 1842; m. 2d, Israel Davis.

2. Albert, b. Feb. 9, 1821; m. Martha Powers; res. Worcester.

2. Mary Amanda, b. Sept. 10, 1823; m. Thomas L. Woodward, May 11, 1843; m. 2d, Jessie W. Graves, Oct. 8, 1847; res. Keene, N. H.

2. Chloe, b. Aug. 3, 1825; m. Samuel K. Savage.

2. Alvin, b. Jan. 22, 1827; res. Cal.

2. Lura, b. Mar. 31, 1829; m. Sumner Frost; res. Brattleboro', Vt.

2. Hepzibah Augusta, b. Jan. 24, 1832; m. Lyman Morse.

1. Freelove, b. Oct. 28, 1786; m. Timothy Phillips of Warwick, Oct. 30, 1804, who d. Warwick; m. 2d, George Ellis of Dorchester.

STONE.

1. Joseph, b. July 21, 1789 ; m. Hannah Heald, Nov. 25, 1810 ; d. Sept. 9, 1853 ; she d. June 8, 1866.
    2. Lois F., b. Feb. 10, 1811 ; m. Austin C. Tenney of Waterford, Vt., Oct. 24, 1828.
    2. Jonas Gilbert, b. Dec. 25, 1812 ; m. Dorcas Allen ; res. Holliston.
    2. Joseph Harrison, b. Mar 2, 1815 ; m. Lucinda L. Page ; res. Holliston.
    2. Hannah Heald, b. Nov. 1, 1821 ; m. Francis Thompson of Holliston.
    2. Augusta Lucretia, b. Mar. 9, 1824 ; m. Daniel H. Fairbanks of Holliston.
    2. Elizabeth Clark, b. Feb. 22, 1827 ; m. Orrin Thompson of Holliston.
    2. Abijah Clark, b. June 4, 1829 ; m. Vera Annie Favor of Dover, Me.: res. Boston.
    2. Helen Smith, b. Jan. 23, 1833 ; m. John P. Wentworth of Northfield.

MILTON STONE c. f. Royalston ; m. Harriet Holden, Mar. 29, 1843.
    1. Albert M., b. Sept. 17. 1845 ; m. Mary Bennett, Feb. 21, 1866 ; d. Sept. 9, 1876.
    2. Addison Milton, b Dec. 4, 1866.
    2. Hattie Melinda, b. Jan. 1, 1869.
    2. Flora May, b. May 3, 1874.

STOWE.

This name was originally, and by a part of the family, is still written *Stow*; but as most of those now living here have added an *e*, their custom is followed in this work for the sake of uniformity.

EBENEZER STOWE c. f. Concord about 1796 ; m. Mary Hartwell, who d. Oct. 15, 1840, a. 85 : he d. May 19, 1841, a. 88.
    1. William, b. Oct. 1, 1776 ; rem. Hillsboro', N. H. ; d. Oct. 26, 1851.
    1. Polly, b. Mar. 25, 1779 ; m. Asa Newton.
    1. Ebenezer, b. Sept. 20, 1780 ; m. Hannah Murdock, Feb. 26, 1807, who d. June 6, 1855 ; he d. Feb. 18, 1875.
    2. Elizabeth, b. Dec. 26, 1807 ; m. Caleb Underwood.
    2. Mary, b. Aug. 21, 1810 ; m. Flint Jennison.
    2. William, b. Oct. 9, 1812 ; m. Mehitable N. Reid, June 3, 1838.

45

STOWE.

3. George W., b. Aug. 5, 1839; m. Lucy Agnes Brigham, Sept. 1, 1862; res. Cambridge.

4. Charles Brigham, b. Mar. 21, 1867; d. Sept. 17, 1867.

4. Gertrude Lucy, b. Aug. 21, 1869.

4. George, b. May, 1871.

3. Maria E., b Sept. 4, 1841; d. Jan. 17, 1867.

3. Charles Reid, b. Nov. 14, 1843; d. army, July 4, 1864. [See p. 142.]

3. Sumner, b. Jan. 9, 1846.

3. Samuel Reid, b. Dec. 11, 1850; d. Cambridge, Aug. 23, 1875.

3. Joseph Edward, b. May 19, 1853.

2. Reuben, b. Dec. 5, 1814; m. Eunice H. Ayers of N. Brookfield, Aug. 10, 1837.

3. Adelia, b. June 18, 1838; d. Nov. 8, 1852.

3. Emma Louisa, b. Apr. 1, 1842; d. May 8, 1842.

3. Charles E., b. Apr. 11, 1843; m. Cynthia C. Johnson of Putney, Vt., Dec. 6, 1865.

4. Willie, b. June 17, 1866.

4. Hattie, b. Aug. 6, 1867.

4. Frankie, b. Dec. 26, 1869; d. May 25, 1876.

2. Sumner, b. Nov. 21, 1816; res. Ind.

2. Harriet, b. Aug. 16, 1819; d. Nov. 22, 1847.

2. Roxa, b. Jan. 17, 1822; d. Oct. 1, 1865.

2. Hannah, b. Dec. 7, 1824; m. Samuel Avery Chamberlain of Worcester, Feb. 18, 1850.

1. Sally, b. Dec. 2, 1782; m. Aaron Grimes.

1. Elizabeth, b. Aug. 7, 1792; d. Aug. 1, 1800.

1. Ephraim, b. May 2, 1797; m. Sally M. Goodspeed, Nov. 20, 1823; d. Mar. 4, 1875; she d. May 25, 1880.

2. John M., b. Sept. 7, 1824; m. Louisa Clark, Sept. 7, 1854, who d. Aug. 16, 1866; m. 2d, Sarah D. Locke of New Ipswich, N. H., Apr. 7, 1868; d. May 9, 1877. [See pp. 168 and 185.]

3. Alfred E., b. Oct. 19, 1855; d. Oct. 24, 1876.

2. Lucy, b. July 4, 1827; d. Oct. 3, 1840.

2. Alfred, b. Nov. 14, 1828; d. Oct. 28, 1840.

2. Sarah, b. July 31, 1831.

2. Mary Amelia, b. Nov. 4, 1838; d. Sept. 13, 1840.

STOWE.

2. Delia Ann, b. May 7, 1840 ; m. Alanson A. Nims of Sullivan, N. H., June 18, 1869.

SWAN.

SAMUEL SWAN c. f. Leicester ; m. Clara Hale, Oct. 29, 1812, who d. Jan. 14, 1860 ; he d. 1863, a. 85. [See p. 183.]

1. Catherine, b. Aug. 16, 1813 ; m. Rev. Abel Brown ; m. 2d, Charles Spear ; res. Brooklyn, N. Y.
1. Clara, b. Feb. 28, 1815 ; d. Mar. 1, 1821.
1. Samuel, b. Mar. 10, 1817 ; d. Kentucky.
1. Reuben, b. July 8, 1819 ; m. Clementine Knight of Newburyport. Feb. 17, 1848 ; res. Worcester.
1. Clara, b. Oct. 30, 1821 ; m. Abijah S. Clark.
1. James, b. Jan. 31, 1825 ; m. Lucy A. S. Merriam of Boston ; res. Passaic, N. J.
1. George, b. Jan. 8, 1826 ; m. Mary D. Goodspeed, Apr. 2, 1857 ; res. Worcester. [See p. 183.]

TAYLOR.

LEMUEL F. TAYLOR c. f. Buckland ; m. Cassandra Dexter, Apr., 1836 ; d. May 29, 1880.

1. Caroline Angelia, b. Mar. 1, 1841 ; m. Darius Parsons.
1. Sarah Arabella, b. June 27, 1856.

TEMPLE.

THOMAS TEMPLE c. f. Westminster ; m. Nancy Greenwood, Nov. 26, 1812, who d. May 26, 1828 ; m. 2d, Rhoda (Pond) Wright. Nov. 5, 1829, who d. Nov. 28, 1878 ; he d. Aug. 1, 1857, a. 70.

1. Nancy, b. Jan. 26, 1814 ; d. Apr. 28, 1815.
1. Lucy, b. Jan. 17, 1816 ; m. Ezra P. Pond.
1. Levi G., b. Jan. 19, 1818 ; m. Persis F. Ball, Dec. 25, 1845 ; res. Princeton.
1. Nancy, b. Dec. 19, 1819 ; m. Elisha Murdock.
1. Harriet R., b. Aug. 4, 1823 ; d. Aug. 5, 1837.
1. Roxa, b. Aug. 7, 1825 ; m. Adam Wheeler ; m. 2d, James Savage.

TENNEY.

ABEL TENNEY c. f. Northboro' ; m. Anna ——, who d. Apr. 28, 1800, a. 43 ; rem. Westminster ; d. Troy, N. H.

1. Chloe, b. July 18, 1776 ; m. Joseph Taber.
1. Molly, b. Mar. 2, 1778 ; m. Joel Adams of Westminster, May 2, 1802.
1. John, b. Feb. 28, 1780.
1. Anna, b. Dec. 28, 1781.
1. Samuel, b. Sept. 16, 1784.
1. Betsey, b. July 28, 1786.
1. Stephen R., b. Apr. 10, 1788 ; m. Ruth Rice ; m. 2d, Polly Jewett, Nov. 21, 1819, who d. Aug. 10, 1869, a. 71 ; he d. Mar. 27, 1860.
   2. Emeline, b. Sept. 16, 1809 ; d. Sept. 12, 1810.
   2. Emerson, b. Apr. 20, 1811 ; d. Sept. 2, 1811.
   2. Emerson, b. June 25, 1812 ; d. May 2, 1820.
   2. Daniel, b. May 7, 1814 ; d. Feb. 10, 1815.
   2. Caroline, b. June 5. 1816 ; m. John J. Joslin of Thompson, Ct., Apr. 9, 1837.
   2. Stephen J., b. June 5, 1820 ; d. Nov. 21, 1845.
   2. Henrietta, b. Dec. 19. 1821 ; d. Aug. 14, 1823.
   2. Mary Davis, b. Apr. 28, 1823 ; m. Edward E. Dunn, Nov. 26, 1846 ; d. Aug. 8, 1854.
   2. Daniel S., b. Jan. 23, 1825 : d. Sept. 23. 1825.
   2. Joseph M., b. Dec. 3, 1826 ; m. Valetta C. Lord of N. Y., Aug. 31, 1860 ; d. Apr. 2, 1877. [See p. 182.]
      3. Albert, b. Oct. 7, 1861.
      3. Charles E. F., b. Oct. 20, 1864.
      3. Cora M., b. Nov. 19, 1867.
   2. Harriet N., b. Nov. 22, 1828 ; d. Feb. 6, 1847.
   2. Ann Judson, b. May 19, 1831 ; d. Jan. 26, 1847.
   2. Daniel W., b. July 20, 1833 ; m. Martha A. Gaut of Princeton : d. Sept. 30, 1878.
      3. Charles J., b. Feb. 18, 1862 ; d. Sept. 9, 1863.
      3. William G., b. Aug. 14, 1864 ; d. Aug. 15, 1864.
   2. Sarah E., b. Aug. 8, 1837 ; m. Israel J. Olmstead ; res. Marlboro'.
   2. George Albert, b. Oct. 22, 1839 ; d. May 14, 1865. [See p. 142.]
   2. Charles F., b. Oct. 24, 1842 ; m. Lucy A. Hobbs, Feb. 1, 1867.
1. Moses, b. May 30, 1790.
1. Aaron, b. May 7, 1792.

TENNEY.

1. David T., b. Apr. 11, 1794.
1. Daniel, b. Nov. 20, 1797.
1. Abel, b. Apr. 28, 1800.

THOMPSON.

JAMES THOMPSON c. f. Holden, 1773 ; m. Elizabeth ——, who d. Apr. 19. 1820, a. 69 ; he d. Feb. 4, 1826, a. 83.

1. Elizabeth, b. Apr. 5, 1769 ; m. Dillington Phelps of Barre, Oct. 15, 1792.
1. Hugh, b. Apr. 2, 1771 ; rem. Maine.
1. James, b. Apr. 7, 1773 ; rem. Marlboro', N. H.
1. Jeremiah, b. Jan. 12, 1776 ; m. Lucy Heald, Jan. 12, 1802 ; both d. Westminster West, Vt. •
   2. William, b. Oct. 27, 1802 ; d. Aug. 2, 1806.
   2. Stillman, b. May 19, 1805 ; d. June 19, 1805.
   2. Stillman, b. Sept. 7, 1806 ; res. Westminster West, Vt.
1. Hannah, b. Apr. 17, 1778 ; m. Joseph Farmer, Apr., 1813. who d. May 8, 1813, a 32 ; she d. Jan. 17, 1842.
1. Polly, b. Apr. 22, 1780 ; m. Joseph Savage.
1. Sally b. June 9, 1782 ; m. Luke B. Osgood of Newfane, Vt., Feb. 17, 1803.
1. Jennie, b. Sept. 15, 1784 ; m. —— Cutler of Newfane, Vt.
1. Joel, b. Oct. 5, 1787 ; d. Nov. 14, 1788.
1. John, b. Jan. 26, 1792 ; rem. Maine.
1. Daniel, b. Dec. 1, 1795 ; m. Sophia Moore, May 20. 1819, who d. July 5. 1826. a. 30 ; m. 2d, Julia McClenathan, Feb 20, 1827 ; rem. Fitchburg, d. Feb. 1, 1872.
   2. Elizabeth, b. Apr. 5, 1820 ; d. Sept. 3, 1843.
   2. George, b. Dec. 25, 1821.
   2. James, b. Apr. 15, 1825.
   2. Daniel, b. July 1, 1826.
   2. Sophia, b. Nov. 21, 1827 ; m. William Coleman of Boston, June 3, 1852, who d. 1864 ; she res. St. Louis, Mo.
   2. John P., b. Nov. 20, 1829 ; m. Elizabeth H. Waite of Deerfield, Mar. 10, 1857, who d. Nov. 24, 1861 ; res. Fitchburg.
   2. Charles S., b. Jan. 16, 1833 ; d. June 1, 1836.
   2. Joseph F., b. Feb. 4, 1835 ; m. Margaret E. McPherson of East Boston, Feb. 21, 1866 ; res. Fitchburg.
   2. Gilbert, b. Dec. 16, 1837 ; m. L. M. Littlehale of Tyngsboro', Nov., 1870, who d. Aug. 5, 1878 ; res. Buffalo, N. Y.

THOMPSON.

2. Julia Ann, b. Mar. 11, 1840; m. Roswell I. Lawton of Fitchburg, Oct. 15, 1868.

2. Mary Adeline, b. Sept. 10, 1842; m. David M. Hollingworth, June, 1860, who d. July 23, 1877; she d. Dec. 22, 1879.

SAMUEL THOMPSON c. f. Holden; m. Anna Waite, June 2, 1791; d. Nov. 29, 1825, a. 59; she d. Dec. 2, 1841.

1. Samuel, b. Mar. 16, 1793; m. Sally Heald, Oct. 16, 1816; d. Aug. 28, 1869.

2. Sarah Augusta, b. Mar. 16, 1817; m. Moses Smith of Rutland.

2. Francis, b. Feb. 23, 1819; m. Hannah H. Stone, Aug. 7, 1843; res. Holliston.

2. Orrin, b. Oct. 24, 1821; m. Elizabeth C. Stone, Oct. 28, 1846; res. Holliston.

2. Hannah, b. Jan. 26, 1823; m. Asa Stone.

2. Mary N., b. Mar. 31, 1826; m. Ethan C. Claflin; res. Holliston.

2. Samuel Jones, b. Aug. 16, 1828; rem. Holliston; m. Sarah Ann Leland of Holliston.

2. Rebecca M., b. Aug. 31, 1833; m. Amasa T. Welch of Princeton.

2. Silas Church, b. July 9, 1835; d. Jan. 31, 1841.

2. Sydney Cook, b. Mar. 16, 1840; m. Laura Rawson; res. N. Y.

1. Anna, b. Jan. 6, 1795; m. William Ware of Oakham, June 12, 1820; d. Oakham.

1. Ira, b. Aug. 9, 1797; m. Sally Pond, Apr. 13, 1823; d. June 30, 1879; she d. Apr. 16, 1879.

2. Cynthia, b. Apr. 14, 1825; d. Oct. 18, 1843.

2. Lucy, b. Feb. 19, 1828; res. Worcester.

2. Lura, b. Oct. 13, 1830; m. Horace G. Pond.

2. Sarah Ann, b. Mar. 31, 1833; m. Charles F. Winn of Worcester.

2. Theodocia Elmina, b. June 3, 1836; m. George Clark.

2. Louisa A., b. 1842; m. James A. Hartwell of Fitchburg, Apr. 5, 1866.

2. Albert Ira Mason, b. Mar. 2, 1844; m. Lizzie Wheeler, June 3, 1867.

1. Hannah, b. May 19, 1800; d. Mar. 28, 1819.

1. Polly, b. Aug. 2, 1802; d. Apr. 1, 1821.

1. Sally, b. Jan. 10, 1805; d. Worcester, Oct. 6, 1864.

THOMPSON.

1. John, b. Apr. 29, 1807 ; m. Mary Harding Clark, Nov. 4, 1835.
   2. Mary Amanda, b. Sept. 16, 1836 ; d. May 30, 1857.
   2. Isaac Clark. b. June 16, 1838 ; d. Sept. 27, 1845. [See p. 167.]
   2. John Charles, b. Oct. 27, 1839 ; m. Emily J. Banford, Mar. 29, 1862.
       3. Leslie E., b. July 20, 1874.
   2. Martha Ann, b. Apr. 13, 1843 ; m. L. Hobart Hale ; m. 2d, Irving T. Hale.
   2. Henry Clark, b. July 6, 1845 ; m. Mary O. Hathaway of Athol, Mar. 7, 1866.
       3. Isaac Hobart, b. Oct. 12, 1867.
       3. John Clark, b. Jan. 13, 1870.
       3. Edward Leonard, b. Sept. 23, 1872.
       3. Mary Cherline, b. Oct. 24, 1875.
       3. Edna Louise. b. Apr. 20, 1877 ; d. Sept. 18, 1880.
       3. William Henry, b. Dec. 26, 1879.
   2. William Fred, b. Oct. 20, 1856 ; m. Josie E. Sargent, Nov. 10, 1878.

TILTON.

ELENEZER TILTON c. f. South Boston, 1853 ; m. Almira Davis of Wellfleet, Sept. 3, 1829 ; d. Feb. 23, 1878, a. 70.
   1. Joseph, b. Aug. 27, 1830 ; m. Phebe E. Morrow of Barre, May 31, 1858.
   2. Edgar P., b. Jan. 27, 1860.
   2. George E., b. Nov. 3, 1865.
   1. Josephine B., b. Nov. 3, 1837 ; m. Alonzo Hartwell.
   1. Amelia A., b. Jan. 7, 1840 ; m. William H. Wilcox.
   1. William Henry, b. Feb. 7, 1847 ; m. Lucy S. Hallett of Boston. Aug., 1869, who d. Apr. 5, 1872, a. 24 ; m. 2d, Ellen M. Rice of Rutland.
   2. Ella L., b. Mar. 10, 1870.
   2. Joseph W., b. Oct., 1871 ; d. Mar. 9, 1872.
   2. William Henry, b. Sept. 10, 1875 ; d. Nov. 7, 1875.

TITUS.

WILLIAM C. TITUS c. f. N. H. ; m. Clara Hartwell, Feb. 14, 1854 ; d. Apr. 21, 1867, a. 35.
   1. Nellie Maria, b. June 18, 1854 ; m. Fred H. Latimer of Olean, N. Y.

TITUS.

1. Henry C., b. Aug. 10. 1856.
1. Stella Adelia. b. Oct. 22, 1861 ; d. Nov. 15, 1866.
1. Cora, b. Feb. 10. 1867.

TOOKER.

SAMUEL N. TOOKER c. f. New York City, 1875 ; m. Frances Kniffin, Jan., 1848; both of Newburg, New York.

TYLER.

NATHAN TYLER c. f. Princeton ; m. Elmira Wheeler, Apr. 5, 1845 ; d. Mar. 31, 1879. a. 63.
1. E. Frances L., b. Aug. 20. 1845.
1. William H. Frederick, b. July 23. 1847.
1. Albert E. A., b. Mar. 20. 1850.
1. Jane M. T., b. Feb. 2, 1852.
1. Lillian P. A., b. Apr. 22. 1854 ; d. Apr. 7, 1874.
1. Mary Ann L., b. Sept. 5. 1856.
1. Edna E. M., b. Dec. 25. 1858 ; m. Llewellyn A. Mariner of Boston. Jan. 31. 1874.
1. Caro E. J., b. July 4. 1861 ; d. Aug. 14. 1877.
1. Orville E. E., b. Aug. 22, 1863.

UNDERWOOD.

TIMOTHY UNDERWOOD c. f. Holliston, 1771 ; m. Lois Parmenter, who d. June 28. 1791 ; m. 2d, Mary Harrington, Oct. 18, 1792; d. Sept. 10, 1820, a. 70; she d. Feb. 24, 1839. a. 79.
1. Molly, b. Nov. 25, 1772 ; m. Abner Adams.
1. Isaac, b. Apr. 16. 1775 ; rem. Jamaica, Vt.
1. Betty, b. Mar. 29, 1777; d. Oct. 31, 1849.
1. Timothy, b. Apr. 29, 1780; d. Dec. 22, 1799.
1. Asa, b. June 29. 1796; m. Anna Goodspeed, Nov. 29, 1821 ; d. Apr. 11, 1880; she d. Dec. 12, 1880.
2. Lyman, b. Jan. 15, 1825 ; m. Susan E. Holyoke of Marlboro', Nov. 7, 1854 ; res. East Boston.
2. Charles G., b. Aug. 12, 1826 ; m. Eunice Bartlett of Princeton, Mar. 6, 1856. who d. Feb. 19, 1859. a. 28 ; m. 2d, Cilena A. Saunders of Perkins, Maine, June 4, 1863 ; res. East Boston.

UNDERWOOD.

1. John, b. Mar. 31, 1799; d. Jan. 21, 1801.
1. Caleb, b. June 12, 1801; m. Elizabeth Stowe, Nov. 29, 1827, who d. Aug. 12, 1858.
    2. Horace, b. Nov. 16, 1828; m. Mary Elizabeth Dunton, Nov. 27, 1851, who d. Sept. 28, 1867; m. 2d, Harriet (Williams) Wilkinson, Sept. 6, 1871.
        3. Willie Alfred, b. Sept. 11, 1853; d. July 27, 1863.
        3. Charles S., b. June 23, 1860; d. May 21, 1874.
        3. George H., b. Sept. 5, 1862; d. July 29, 1863.
        3. Arthur W., b. Sept. 9, 1864.
        3. Alice Elizabeth, } b. Sept. 11, 1866.
        3. Alfred Herbert, }
    2. Mary, b. Sept. 27, 1830; d. Aug. 3, 1835.
    2. Lucy, b. Oct. 4, 1840; m. E. Oscar Holt.
    2. Henry, b. Aug. 5, 1845; d. May 14, 1846.

ISRAEL UNDERWOOD c. f. Princeton as early as 1770; m. Rhoda Newton. Jan. 1, 1789; d. Sept. 26, 1840. a. 78; she d. Sept. 2, 1852, a. 91.

1. Nancy, b. June 8, 1790; d. Apr. 13, 1874.
1. Eber. b. July 23. 1791; m. Dinah Baker, Mar., 1817; d. Oct. 17. 1862; she d. Nov. 10, 1862, a. 72.
    2. Amos Gilman, b. Nov. 29, 1817; m. Nancy Bishop of Warwick. May 9, 1844; d. Jan. 25. 1878.
    2. George Curtis, b. Apr. 15, 1819; m. Susan H. Oaks, Apr. 5. 1842; rem. Gardner.
        3. Sarah M., b. Mar. 1, 1843; m. Calvin Holden of Westminster. Oct. 19, 1862.
        3. Ella Frances, b. June 30, 1845; d. July 2, 1864.
        3. Jane A., b. June 27, 1847; d. Dec. 2, 1865.
        3. Flora A., b. Oct. 4, 1852; m. H. B. Howe of Ashburnham. Mar. 3, 1869.
        3. Nettie, b. Apr. 8, 1858; m. H. E. Nichols of Westminster. May 19, 1878.
        3. George L., b. June 23, 1860; drowned, Aug. 10, 1876.
    2. Dexter, b. Oct. 18, 1820; d. Royalston, May 4. 1866.
    2. Russell, b. Aug. 20, 1823; d Boston, Oct. 6, 1852.
    2. Israel, b. June 19, 1826; rem. Lena, Illinois.

46

UNDERWOOD.

2. Calvin, b. Oct. 24, 1830 ; m. Harriet Augusta Lamb, Jan. 15, 1857. who d. Jan. 7, 1862 ; rem. Templeton.

2. Caroline. b. Aug. 10. 1832 ; d. Royalston, Jan. 9, 1868.

1. Sally, b. Oct. 28, 1793 ; m. Nathaniel Sawyer of Rutland, Mar. 26, 1816 ; d. Jan. 24, 1878.

1. Josiah, b. June 18, 1795 ; m. Betsey Sawyer of Rutland, Jan., 1821 ; d. June 29. 1872 ; she d. Apr. 24, 1878.

2. Lorenzo. b. Nov. 12, 1822 ; res. Gardner.

2. Ira, b. Jan. 8. 1825 : res. Gardner.

2. Sarah P., b. Mar. 28. 1827 ; m. Merlin C. Cobleigh, May 1, 1841.

2. John. b. May 1, 1836 : d. June 9, 1874.

1. Lucy, b. Oct. 15. 1796 ; m. David G. Twitchell of Athol, Nov. 9, 1824.

1. Diodorus, b. July 1, 1798 : rem. Templeton.

1. Rhoda, b. Feb. 10, 1800 : m. Levi Lewis of Royalston, Jan. 19, 1819 : both d. Royalston.

1. Linda, b. Mar. 17. 1803 : m. Hollis Joslin.

1. Eliza, b. Mar. 7, 1804 : m. Ira Davis of Princeton, Jan. 12, 1826 ; m. 2d, James Browning.

WAITE.

Nathaniel Waite† c. f. Leicester about 1766 ; m. Anna Sweetser, May 29, 1866 ; d. Feb. 2, 1815, a. 76 ; she d. July 21, 1840, a. 93.

1. Betty, b. July 7, 1767 ; m. Earl Westgate.

1. Anna, b. Sept. 14, 1769 ; m. Samuel Thompson.

1. Nathaniel, b. Mar. 21, 1772 ; m. Mercy Lamson, who d. Calais, Maine ; he d. Dec. 6, 1846.

2. Nancy, b. Sept. 29, 1793 ; m. Aaron Pond.

2. Benjamin F., b. Dec. 28, 1801 ; rem. Calais, Maine ; d. there.

2. Sally Smith. b. Oct. 30, 1803 ; m. Obadiah Pond.

2. Elizabeth, b. Apr. 13, 1806 ; m. —— Daily of Maine.

1. Jacob, b. Mar. 27, 1775 ; m. Ruth Wright, Nov. 13, 1797, who d July 25, 1818 ; he d. Nov. 14, 1818.

2. Patty, b. Feb. 22, 1798 ; d. July 25, 1800.

2. Charles W., b. Feb. 2, 1800 ; rem.

2. Harriet W., b. Feb. 26, 1802 ; m. Henry Clemence.

2. Chloe Wright. b. Nov. 17, 1804 ; m. Israel Davis.

WAITE.

2. Thomas J., b. Sept. 28, 1807 ; rem Templeton ; d. there.

2. James Madison, b. Jan. 21, 1811 ; m. Maria S. Bennett, Oct. 20, 1836 ; rem. Templeton.

2. Martha W., b. Apr. 30, 1813 ; m. Levi W. Priest of Hinsdale, N. H., May 16, 1836.

1. Sally, b. Mar. 6, 1777 ; m. Levi Smith of Plainfield, N. H. ; d. Jan. 5, 1804.

1. Hannah, b. July 26, 1781 ; m. Cornelius Hinds.

JOSEPH WAITE* c. f. Marlboro' ; m. Hepzibah Sherman ; d. July 26, 1819, a. 65 ; she d. Nov. 5, 1849, a. 89.

1. Moses, b. May 28, 1780 ; m. Phebe Warren, Oct. 11, 1804 ; d. May 19, 1871 ; she d. Oct. 29, 1874.

2. James Alson, b. Dec. 7, 1807 ; m. Elizabeth C. Clark, Oct. 23, 1834 : d. Mar. 9, 1861.

2. Horace, b. Oct. 5, 1809 ; m. Lucy W. Follett, May 24, 1836 ; d. Oct. 15, 1850 ; she d. Aug. 17, 1879.

3. John Gilman, b. Mar. 20, 1837 ; m. Mary H. Clark ; res. Medford.

3. George, b. Nov. 27, 1838 ; d. Aug. 27, 1840.

3. George Sumner, b. May 17, 1840 ; d. Jan. 2, 1843.

3. Albert H., b. Mar. 25, 1845 ; m. Helen E. Morse, June 21, 1870 ; res. Worcester.

4. Albert Morse, b. Feb. 8, 1877 ; d. Feb. 12, 1877.

3. Lucy F., b. May 28, 1850 ; m. James H. Hartwell.

2. John Gilman. b. Jan. 29, 1812 : d. Apr. 8, 1831.

2. Moses, b. Feb. 24, 1814 ; m. Sophronia (Parmenter) Fox of Bernardston ; rem. Walpole, N. H.

2. Amanda, b. Feb. 29, 1816 ; d. June 8, 1816.

2. Harrison, b. Dec. 23, 1817 ; d. Ark., Aug. 6, 1844.

2. Increase Sumner, b. May 1, 1820 ; m. Mary J. Tucker ; rem. Worcester.

3. Ellen, b. Jan., 1845.

3. Jenette, b. Apr. 7, 1851.

3. Mary Jane, b. Aug. 7, 1855.

2. Carlo, b. July 6, 1822 ; name changed to Charles M. ; m. Sarah Mann of Blandford ; res. Blandford.

2. Addison, b. Aug. 16, 1825 ; m. Emily Joslin, Sept. 24, 1855 ; res. Chester.

1. Hepzibah, b. Mar. 31, 1782 ; m. Ebenezer Warren.

WAITE.

1. Dolly, b. July 1, 1784; m. James Lamb: m. 2d, Sampson Stone.
1. Lois, b. Mar. 12, 1786: m. Sampson Stone.
1 Betsey, b. Mar. 22, 1788: m. Russell Morse.
1. Samuel, b. Mar. 8, 1790: m. Lois Brigham of Paxton, Sept., 1813:
    d. July, 1824.
  2. Andrew J., b. Nov. 17, 1814.
  2. Samuel D., b. Dec. 22, 1815.
  2. Lois, b. Jan. 18, 1818; d. Apr. 21, 1818.
1. Susan, b. Nov. 26, 1791; m. George Williams.
1. Joseph, b. May 12, 1794: m. Clarissa Grimes, Mar. 3, 1815, who
    d. Mar. 15, 1863.
  2. Joseph, b. June 16, 1815; d. Dec. 18, 1843.
  2. Clarissa, b. May 1, 1817.
  2. Aaron, b. Nov. 8, 1818; m. Persis Ware of Barre, Nov. 24, 1842,
    who d. Oct. 27, 1874; m. 2d, Mrs. Maria Sylvester, Oct.
    15, 1877.
    3. George Austin, b. Feb. 23, 1846; m. Ella Hatstat of Rutland,
      July 20, 1871; d. Dec. 24, 1875.
    3. L. Anna, b. Apr. 17, 1847; m. John Rice of Templeton, Nov.
      8, 1870.
    3. Aaron Goodhue, b. Mar. 26, 1848; m. Eliza M. Wilson of
      Princeton, Dec. 28, 1870.
    3. Mary Persis, b. Mar. 9, 1850; m. John Holden of Princeton,
      Jan. 1, 1868.
    3. Eddie, b. Dec. 11, 1851.
    3. Luella Josephine, b. Oct. 22, 1877.
    3. Sidney, b. Feb. 28, 1879.
  2. Lucretia Ann, b. Oct. 11, 1820; m. Joseph G. Chandler of South
    Hadley, Oct. 14, 1840; d. Mar. 10, 1868.
  2. Luke, b. Nov. 15, 1822: m. Freelove E. Wright, Dec. 31, 1845,
    who d. Apr. 25, 1860; m. 2d, Harriet Paine of Springfield,
    May 18, 1865.
    3. John Hobert, b. May 21, 1846; res. Boston.
    3. Charles Joseph, b. Jan. 30, 1849; res. Concord.
    3. William Frederick, b. May 14, 1851; m. Jenny Churchill of
      Cornish, N. H., July, 1866; res. Virginia.
    3. James Reuben, b. Jan. 2, 1854.
    3. Hattie Elizabeth, b. July 14, 1871.

WAITE.

2. Rockwell H., b. Oct. 7, 1826; m. Sarah A. Donelson of Coleraine, May 26, 1852.

   3. Reuben Alfred, b. Aug. 30, 1857.

2. Gilman, b. May 1. 1831 ; m. Jerusha Hosmer of Baldwinsville.
May 12, 1856 ; res. Baldwinsville.

1. Clarissa, b. June 25, 1797 ; m. Russell Brown.

1. Alice, b. July 22, 1799 ; d. July 9, 1813.

1. Alvin, b. Nov. 12, 1800 ; m. Mary N Parker, Dec. 22, 1825, who
d. Oct. 15, 1833 ; m. 2d, L. Sophia Gould of Phillipston. Apr.
2, 1835, who d. June 10, 1839; m. 3d. Lydia B. Baker of
Phillipston. Feb. 8, 1842 ; d. Dec. 25, 1856.

2. Elmina Augusta. b. Jan. 22, 1828 ; d. May 18, 1843.

2. Clarendon. b. Dec. 12, 1830 ; m. Hattie G. Baker of Phillipston.
June 16, 1858; d Dec. 16, 1867. [See p. 184.]

2. Mary Parker. b. May 29. 1836 ; d. Mar. 29, 1841.

2. George Alvin. b. June 25, 1838.

1. Mary, b. May 22, 1805 ; m. Horatio N. Bolton of Gardner. Oct.
22, 1829 ; m. 2d, William S. Lynde of Gardner.

WARREN.

EBENEZER WARREN c. f. Rutland ; m. Phebe Garfield, who d. Aug. 1.
1829, a. 73 ; he d. Sept. 17, 1819, a. 65.

1. Ebenezer, b. Jan. 21, 1781 ; m. Hepzibah Waite. Mar. 12, 1803.
who d. June 8, 1852 ; he d. Oct. 15, 1859.

2. Samuel, b. Sept. 3. 1804 ; m. Polly Newton of Westminster, Feb.
22, 1827 ; d. Aug. 28. 1847.

   3. Roxa, b. Aug. 11. 1827 ; d. Dec. 4, 1843.

   3. Levi, b. Oct. 1, 1830; m. Lucretia Browning. Nov. 9, 1853 ;
rem. Gardner.

   3. Rufus, b. Mar. 15, 1832 ; m. Alice Marean, Jan. 10, 1856 :
res. Cambridge.

   3. Mary Ann. b. Mar. 8, 1834 : m. Joseph H. Marean.

   3. Calvin, b. May 21, 1835 ; res. Gardner.

   3. Augustus. b. June 28, 1837 ; m. Josephine S. Upton of Gardner, Nov. 4, 1863.

2. Mary Ann, b. Jan. 23, 1806 ; m. Rufus Holden of Winchendon.
Mar. 19, 1828 ; d. Apr. 14, 1832.

2. Oliver, b. July 27, 1809 ; d. Oct. 29, 1810.

WARREN.

2. Ebenezer Chapman, b. June 19, 1812; m. Olive G. Coleman, Oct. 24. 1833; d. Oct. 18, 1847.

3. Horace b. July 7. 1834; d. Feb. 20, 1837.

3. Gilman, b. Feb. 20, 1836; m. F. Adelaide Johnson of Vernon, Vt., Nov. 7, 1861.

3. Horace S., b. May 3. 1838; m. Helen M. Merritt of E. Templeton, Nov. 1, 1865; res. E. Templeton.

3. Sarah E., b. Feb. 23, 1840; m. Rollin C. White of Cleveland, Ohio, June 3. 1839.

3. Elmira H., b. Jan. 30, 1842; m. Levi Henry Higley, Feb. 28, 1861, who d. U. S. Hospital. Philadelphia, Pa., May 17, 1864; m. 2d, Richard A. Brown of Brattleboro', Vt., Jan. 31, 1866.

3. Elijah A., b. May 19, 1843; m. Eliza H. Wood of So. Gardner, June 3. 1868.

4. Ambrose G., b. Apr. 1, 1873.

4. Asaph W., b. Aug. 4, 1876.

3. Albert, b. Jan. 15, 1845; d. June 20, 1846.

2. Alice W., b. Feb. 27, 1814; m. Benjamin F. Coleman.

2. Sumner, b. Feb. 16, 1816; m. Harriet Bennett, Apr. 21, 1840; d. June 20, 1852.

2. Lois, b. Mar. 7, 1818; m. Luke Sawyer, May 20, 1874; res. Gardner.

2. Joseph Gardner, b. Nov. 22. 1819; rem. Worcester; res. Keene, New Hampshire.

2. Roxa, b. Nov. 30, 1824; d. May 14, 1826.

1. Phebe, b. Jan. 25, 1783; m. Moses Waite.

1. Increase, b. Apr. 7, 1785; m. Patty McClenathan, Dec. 18, 1806; rem. Westmoreland, N. H.; both d. there.

1. Walter, b. May 28, 1787; m. Lucy Moulton, May 27, 1810; d. Jan. 23, 1814.

2. Emily, b. May 20, 1810; m. Abraham H. Wilson, Oct. 6, 1835, who d. Dec. 14, 1876; [see p. 168;] she d. Jan. 31, 1851.

2. John G., b. Feb. 11, 1812; d. Feb. 28, 1819.

1. Sally, b. Feb. 13, 1790; m. Brigham Davis.

1. Nathan, b. Oct, 3, 1792; m. Dolly B. Howe of Templeton, Nov., 1815, who d. Sept. 11, 1821, a. 28; m. 2d, Betsey Davis of Templeton, May 29, 1822; d. Apr. 9, 1841; she d. Aug. 23, 1874.

WARREN.

2. Jane H., b. May 29, 1820; d. Feb. 26, 1825.
2. Dolly Howe, b. May 24, 1823; m. John Davis.
2. Walter, b. June 5, 1824; m. Lydia W. Reid of Rutland; res. Worcester.
   3. Nathan F., b. Apr. 8, 1856.
   3. Nellie A., b. Apr. 17, 1860; d. Apr. 21, 1863.
2. Leander W., b. Sept. 11, 1825; m. Lucy Bowker of Phillipston; d. Aug. 12, 1873.
2. Jane H., b. Aug. 20, 1828; m. Benjamin F. Pond.
2. Hudson, b. May 1, 1830; d. Mar. 21, 1869.
2. Betsey Davis, b. Feb. 27, 1836; m. J. Blake Pierce of Royalston, Jan. 15, 1857; d. Dec. 18, 1857.
1. Samuel, b. Feb. 19, 1795; m. Mary Ann Phillips, Aug. 1, 1816; d. Dec. 6, 1836; she d. Apr. 3, 1874.
2. Chloe, b. Aug. 11, 1816; res. Boston.
2. Abigail, b. Aug. 7, 1817; d. Feb. 15, 1819.
2. Abigail H., m. Charles Conant of Barre, Dec. 6, 1842.
2. Phebe A., m. Addison Ellinwood; m. 2d, Hammet Billings of Boston.
2. Rufus, res. Brookfield.
2. Reuben, b. Apr. 14, 1832; rem.
1. Oliver, b. May 7, 1797; d. Oct. 5, 1800.
1. Elijah, b. Aug. 7, 1800; m. Sally W. Smith, May 6, 1824; rem. Canada.

LUKE WARREN c. f. Northboro'; m. Sarah (Lyon) Matthews, who d. Jan. 30, 1805, a. 38; m. 2d, Eliza Whitney of Westminster, who d. Oct. 30, 1838, a. 68; m. 3d, Polly (Nichols) Newton, Sept. 30, 1841, who d. South Lancaster, 1871; he d. May 7, 1854, a. 82.
1. Lucy, b. June 18, 1799; d. July 15, 1818.
1. Sally, b. June 29, 1803; m. Asa Merriam.
1. Mary, b. May 8, 1807; d. Sept. 5, 1877.
1. Aaron, b. May 11, 1812; d. Apr. 26, 1835.

WHEELER.

ADAM WHEELER c. f. Rutland about 1766; enlisted in the Continental Army in the spring of 1775, and was appointed captain;

WHEELER.

he was a brave and efficient officer during the whole war; for his connection with Shays' Rebellion, see chap. VI; m. Mercy Wheeler of Rutland, Nov. 17, 1763; d. Aug. 24, 1802, a. 70; she d. July 10, 1808, a. 67.

1. Silas, b. Jan. 26, 1763; m. Catherine Morse, Feb. 23, 1786, who d. Dec. 11, 1824; he d. Nov. 3, 1826.

  2. James Harvey, b. June 21, 1786; m. Lucy Woodward, Dec. 18, 1809, who d. Dec. 29, 1862; he d. Feb. 1, 1864.

    3. Betsey W., b. Apr. 3, 1811; m. Ebenezer Murdock; m. 2d, Joseph Raymond.

    3. Lucy, b. Mar. 14, 1813; m. Uriah Balcom.

    3. James S., b. June 13, 1815; rem. Warwick; d. Feb. 15, 1871.

    3. Julia, b. May 24, 1817; m. George W. Hamilton.

    3. Silas, b. Apr. 12, 1820; m. Amanda Rice, Dec. 25, 1845.

      4. S. Theodore, b. Sept. 28, 1846; m. Mary E. Upton of Petersham, May 22, 1868.

      4. William H., b. Sept. 4, 1848; m. Eliza A. Morrison of Petersham, Oct. 4, 1874.

        5. William H., b. Jan. 16, 1880.

      4. Elwyn C., b. July 25, 1851; m. Etta D. Conant, May 25, 1877, who d. Oct. 10, 1879.

    3. Moses C., b. Feb. 14, 1825; m. Mary Ann S. Follett, May 1, 1849; rem. Gardner; d. Sept. 14, 1878.

      4. Everard S., b. July 3, 1850.

      4. Lester Morris, ⎫ b. Mar. 13, 1854.
      4. Morris Lester, ⎭

      4. Clara, b. Oct. 20, 1859; m. Alvin Walker, of Gardner, July, 1878.

  2. Oliver, b. June 25, 1788; m. Anna M. Arntz of Germany, Nov. 30, 1812, who d. Aug. 20, 1863; he d. Nov. 20, 1863.

    3. Mary C., b. Aug. 10, 1813; d. Mar., 1819.

    3. Robert D., b. Aug. 15, 1815; rem. Australia.

    3. Pauline E., b. May 6, 1817; m. Rev. Wareham S. Campbell of Conn., Apr. 12, 1840.

    3. Elmira M., b. Dec. 29, 1818; m. Nathan Tyler.

    3. William H., b. Feb. 14, 1820; d. Apr., 1821.

    3. Albert A., b. July 14, 1823; m. Lucy Jane Young, June 5, 1844, who d. Oct. 18, 1851; m. 2d, Lucinda Young, who d. Sept. 6, 1876.

WHEELER.

3. Orrin F., b. Sept. 9, 1825 ; m. Sarah G. Stickney, Apr. 18,
 1847 ; rem. Boston ; d. July 14, 1873.

2. Caty, b. Apr. 14, 1790 ; m. Elisha Spring, Dec. 26, 1810 ; d.
 Grafton.

2. Silas, b. May 13, 1792 ; m. Susan Browning, Dec. 28, 1815 ; d.
 Aug. 10, 1817.

 3. Lyman, b. June 24, 1816 ; m. Lois Heald, June 30, 1843 ; d.
  Jan. 24, 1846.

2. Sewell, b. Mar. 11, 1795 ; m. Betsey Stone, May 16, 1819, who
 d. Dec. 4, 1869 ; he d. June 9, 1875.

 3. Jennison, b. Sept. 4, 1819 ; m. Myra Ware ; rem. Worcester.

  4. Lizzie, b. Mar. 25, 1847 ; m. Albert Ira Mason Thompson.

  4 Abby M., b. Mar. 4, 1851 ; m. Frank A. Bean of Lowell, June
   2, 1870.

  4. Rhoda, b. Aug. 9, 1857 ; m. Herbert W. Pond.

  4. Harry J., b. Mar. 5, 1863 ; d. July 13, 1867

 3. Adam, b. June 21, 1821 ; m. Roxa Temple, May 8, 1845 ; d
  Jan. 3. 1855.

 3. Elizabeth, b. Sept. 12, 1823 ; d. June 16, 1828.

2. Rhoda, b. Feb. 8, 1797 ; m. Moses G. Cheever of Princeton,
 Apr. 8, 1816 ; d. June 26, 1847.

2. Thaddeus, b. May 29, 1801 ; rem. Dorchester.

2. Harriet, b. Sept. 7, 1803 ; m. Asa Peirce.

2. Elmira, b. Feb. 6, 1806 ; m. Hamilton Wilson of Princeton.

2. Thomas Merrick, b. Jan. 24, 1808 ; m. Emily M. Davis, Nov. 1,
 1837 ; rem. Princeton.

 3. Sewell, b. Mar. 11, 1839.

 3. Isaac Davis, b. Aug. 12, 1841 ; d. Jan. 12, 1843.

 3. Henry M , b. Nov 9, 1843 ; m. Adah M. Harrington, Dec.
  11, 1867 ; rem. Gardner.

 3. Otis P., b. Mar. 10, 1846.

1. Ede, b. Oct. 17, 1766 ; m. Ebenezer Brooks of Rutland, Mar. 10,
 1791.

1. Asa, b. Dec. 12, 1768 ; m. Nancy Muzzy, June 2, 1791 ; d. Nov.
 8, 1831 ; she d. Mar. 19, 1855.

2. Edmund R., b. Aug. 4, 1791 ; d. Aug. 24, 1826.

2. Holly, b. Jan. 2, 1793 ; d. at the mouth of the Yellow Stone River.

2. Asa, b. Nov. 6, 1794 ; d. Sept. 11, 1800.

47

WHEELER.

2. Adolphus, b. Nov. 20, 1797; d. Sept. 11, 1819.
2. Augustus, b. Sept. 11, 1799; m. Sophronia Warren of Brimfield;
   res. Brimfield.
   3. William, b. May 18, 1827; d. Feb. 13, 1829.
   3. Delia, b. 1831; d. Brimfield.
2. William M., b. June 26, 1804; d. Dec. 26, 1805.
2. Louisa, b. Oct. 26, 1805; m. John Goodspeed.
2. William M., b. May 12, 1807; m. Fidelia Goodspeed, Nov. 11,
   1832; d. May 25, 1836.
   3. Adelaide B., b. Aug., 1833: m. Stephen D. Church.
2. Asa, b. Dec. 9, 1810; d. Nov. 13, 1812.
2. Mary C., b. June 3, 1815; m. Stedman Marean.
1. Joel, b. June 5, 1771; m. Martha Lyon, Feb. 13, 1800; rem. Warwick: she d. Johnson, Vt.
1. Rhoda, b. 1774; m. William Joslin: m. 2d, Peter Joslin.
1. Jacob, rem. New York.
1. Daniel, b. 1780; m. Sally Lamb, Sept. 26, 1802; d. May 29, 1810.
   a. 30.
2. Pliny, b. Nov. 2, 1802; rem. Savannah, Ga.
2. Alvin, b. Jan. 9, 1805; d. Calais, Me.
2. James M., b. Aug. 16, 1808; d. Apr. 5, 1829.

WHITTEMORE.

Isaac Whittemore c. f. N. H.: m. Anna Woodward, June 1, 1797, who
   d. June 15, 1816, a. 38; m. 2d, Lucy (Moulton) Warren, May 20, 1819, who d. Aug. 23, 1860, a. 63; he
   d. Oct. 4, 1834. a. 63.
1. Elisha, b. Jan. 7, 1798; m. Betsey Greenwood, Mar. 21, 1821, who
   d. Apr. 17, 1844; m. 2d, Mary (Gleason) Holden; d. June
   24, 1859.
2. Ann W., b. Oct. 12, 1821; m. James Browning.
2. Eliza, b. Sept. 19, 1823; m. Asa B. Browning.
2. Sarah W., b. Mar. 6, 1826; m. Clark W. Marean.
2. Caroline G., b. June 3, 1829; res. Boston.
2. Elisha W., b. Oct. 23, 1831: res. Maine.
2. Cynthia W., b. Dec. 25, 1833; m. Clark W. Marean.
2 William Harrison, b. June 4, 1836; m. Amia M. Brown, Nov. 8,
   1860; res. Worcester.

WHITTEMORE.

3. Helen A., b. July 4, 1863.
2. Charles H., b. Nov. 15, 1838 ; res. Fitchburg ; m. Jane Clifford, of Fitchburg.
1. Elmira, b. Aug. 20, 1800 ; m. Stillman Pond.
1. Elizabeth, b. May 12, 1802 ; d. Aug. 12, 1823.
1. Charity, b. June 7, 1805 ; d. July 29, 1808.
1. William, b. Sept. 22, 1809 ; m. Julia Phillips of Franklin ; m. 2d, Martha Walker ; res. Gardner.
1. Ezekiel Lysander, b. Aug. 15, 1812 ; m. Elizabeth S. Williams, Feb. 15, 1838 ; rem. Rutland ; d. Feb., 1877.
1. Isaac, b. Feb. 23, 1824 : m. Jane Holden of Rutland, who d. July 31, 1846 ; m. 2d, Mary S. Earle of Paxton ; rem. Paxton.
2. Waldo, b. July 23, 1849.
1. Mary Lavina, b. Dec. 18, 1829 ; d Mar. 13, 1839.

WILBUR.

WILLIAMS WILBUR c. f. Raynham, 1810 ; m. Rebecca Browning, Dec. 28, 1815 ; who d. May 17, 1827 ; m. 2d, Lucretia Mann, Apr. 4, 1830. [See p. 172.]
1. Nancy, b. Aug. 28, 1816 ; m. Moses Marean.
1. George B., b. Jan. 13, 1820 ; m. Hannah Reid, May 18, 1845 ; res. Watertown.
2. Mary R., b. Mar. 4, 1846.
2. Charles A., b. Mar. 19, 1850.
2. Clara Maria, b. Aug. 20, 1852.
1. Lucy, b. Mar. 16, 1822 ; m. William Copeland Williams.
1. Lois, b. Sept. 26, 1824 ; m. David L. Johnson.

KEZIAH, sister of WILLIAMS, b. Feb. 16, 1794 ; m. Daniel Hayward, Nov. 3, 1815 ; d. Aug. 29, 1862, a. 68 ; he d. Aug. 28, 1869, a. 84.

EDMUND W., bro. of WILLIAMS, b. May 9, 1796 ; m. Rebecca Rich, Mar., 1819 ; rem. Athol ; d. Feb. 4, 1879.

ABIGAIL W., sister of WILLIAMS, b. Nov. 24, 1798 ; m. Jonas Brown.

MESHACK, bro. of WILLIAMS, b. Oct. 26, 1800 ; d. Ind., Nov., 1863.

WILCOX.

WILLIAM H. WILCOX c. f. New York City ; m. Amelia A. Tilton, Sept. 5, 1860 ; d. Worcester, Sept. 23, 1869, a. 34.

1. Almira J., b. Oct. 4, 1861.
1. William T., b. June 7, 1868 ; d. July 14, 1868.
1. Wilhelmina T., b. Sept. 18, 1869.

WILDER.

NATHANIEL WILDER c. f. Barre ; m. Betsey Marsh, who d. Sept. 10, 1840 ; he d. Sept. 29, 1863, a. 76.

1. Eliza M., b. Sept. 23, 1810 ; m. Isaac Bellows.
1. Addison, b. Mar. 19, 1812 ; d. May 7, 1832.
1. Mary, b. May 26, 1817 ; m. Harvey Brown.
1. Harriet, b. Mar. 18, 1824 ; m. Joseph W. Rice.
1. Henry A., b. Nov. 25, 1827 ; m. Sylvia Walker, Nov. 27, 1856.
  2. George H., b. Sept. 24, 1856 ; adopted ; m. Sarah Allen.
  2. Eva J., b. May 30, 1863 ; adopted.
1. John A., b. Feb. 11, 1831 ; m. Ellen L. Grovesnor of Petersham ; d. Worcester, Nov. 19, 1872.

WILLARD.

JOSHUA WILLARD c. f. Winchendon ; m. Phebe ——, who d. June 30, 1831, a. 85 ; he d. Nov. 9, 1831, a. 80.

1. Simon, ⎱ b. June 20, 1785 ; d. Apr. 24, 1864.
1. Ephraim, ⎰ m. Abigail (Mason) Johnson, Dec. 7, 1821 ; d. Feb. 8, 1875 ; she d. Feb. 16, 1875, a. 89.
1. Salem, b. Aug. 4, 1787 ; d. Baltimore.
1. Phebe, m. Ezra Peck ; rem. Barre.

WILLIAMS.

JOHN WILLIAMS† c. f. Lancaster, 1782 or 3 ; m. Sarah Davis of Holden, who d. Mar. 6, 1830, a. 70 ; he d. Dec. 13, 1832, a. 74.

1. John, b. Jan. 21, 1784 ; d. Sept. 9, 1804.
1. Parley, b. Mar. 7, 1786 ; m. Alice Stearns of Hardwick, who d. Sept. 11, 1847, a. 63 ; he d. July 26, 1861.
  2. Harriet E., b. Apr. 29, 1809 ; m. Horace Morse.
  2. Martha, b. Apr. 12, 1818 ; m. Abel Howe.
1. Sarah, b. June 6, 1788 ; m. Dana R. Parker.
1. George, b. May 29, 1791 ; m. Susan Waite, May 6, 1816, who d. Sept. 27, 1856 ; he d. Nov. 11, 1860.

WILLIAMS.

2. George, b. Aug. 19, 1816 ; m. Mary S. Heald, Sept. 10, 1839 :
      rem. Iowa ; d. 1878.

   3. Helen Carolina, b. May 8, 1841.

   3. Calista Heald, b June 19. 1843.

   3. Christopher L., b. Mar. 15, 1849.

2. Christopher L., b. Oct. 1, 1818: m. Mary Bigelow of Barre : d.
      Feb. 28, 1847.

2. William Austin, b. Aug. 29, 1820 ; m. Esther Houghton of Barre ;
      m. 2d, Hattie Woods of Barre. [See p. 183.]

2. Caroline A., b. Feb. 8, 1823 ; m. Nathan H. Felton.

2. Avaline, b. Apr. 5, 1827 ; res. Worcester.

2. Susan M., b. Oct. 11, 1831 ; res. Worcester.

2. John D., b. July 11, 1833 ; m. Ellen Murdock. Oct. 23, 1856 ; d.
      Oct. 28, 1879. [See p. 168]

   3. Frederick D., b. Sept. 10, 1860.

   3. George E., b. Mar. 6, 1863 ; d. Mar. 12, 1864.

   3. Bessie E., b. Sept. 14, 1866.

   3. Alice, b. Aug. 23. 1868.

   3. George Harry, b. Aug. 23, 1878.

1. Luke, b. Aug. 16, 1794 ; m. Betsey Stone of Peterboro', N. H. ; d.
      Apr. 29, 1871 ; she d. Mar. 30, 1873.

2. Elizabeth, b. Oct. 15. 1817 : m. Ezekiel Lysander Whittemore.

2. John Merrill, b. Sept. 1, 1819 ; m. Elizabeth Tyler of Worcester,
      Mar. 29, 1843, who d. May 5. 1844 ; m. 2d, Abby
      F. W. Baldwin of Cambridge. Mar. 29, 1846 ; rem.
      Worcester.

   3. Merrill Mortimer, b. Feb. 5, 1844 ; d. June 27, 1844.

   3. Josephine, b. Oct. 1, 1848 ; m. Edward Leighton of Orange :
      m. 2d, George Jenner of Worcester ; res. Baltimore.
      Maryland.

   3. Lucy Stickney, b. Sept. 6, 1852 ; m. Edward S. Kenney of
      Worcester, Mar. 9, 1875.

   3. Sarah Jane, b. Jan. 9, 1862.

   3. Minnie Vicksburg. b. July 4, 1863 : d. July 28, 1864.

   3. John Baldwin, b. Mar. 7, 1865.

2. Albert G., b. Sept. 9, 1821 : m. Sarah Tyler of Worcester, Oct.
      19. 1843 ; rem. Worcester.

   3. Nathan Waldo, b. Dec. 14, 1845 : m. Sarah L. Munroe of

WILLIAMS.

Barre, Mar. 30, 1867, who d. Austin, Ill., Aug.
9. 1872, a. 28 ; he d. Chicago, Ill., Apr. 20, 1877.

3. Jane Elizabeth, b. June 17, 1850; d. July 25, 1851.

3. Hattie Emily, b. May 28, 1854 ; d. Aug 19, 1877.

3. Fannie Alberta, b. Sept 7, 1857.

2. Nathan S., b. Oct. 18, 1823 ; d. Mar. 7, 1844.

2. Sarah Jane, b. Aug. 30, 1826 ; m. John W. Earle.

2. Ann Maria, b. Oct. 4, 1828 ; m. Charles Ellinwood.

2. Luke, b. Feb. 18, 1833 ; m. Louisa Brown, Jan. 1, 1861.

3. Nathan A., b. Oct. 1, 1861.

3. Bessie E., b. June 17, 1865 : d. Dec. 5, 1868.

3. Helen Louisa, b. May 26, 1868.

3. Stella, b. Dec. 13, 1872.

2. Harriet, b. Jan. 31, 1835 : m. George Wilkinson, May 1, 1861,
who d. May 5, 1862, a. 27 ; m. 2d, Horace Underwood.

2. Georgianna, b. Dec. 7, 1839 : m. Edward Taylor of Gardner.

1. Henry, b. Sept. 19, 1796 ; m. Keziah Newton, Feb. 12, 1822, who
d. Jan. 9. 1837 : he d. Apr. 30, 1839.

2. Alfred, b. May 21, 1824 : m. Sarah J. Taft of Boston, May 25,
1852 : res. Moline, Illinois.

2. Sarah D., b. July 16. 1826 ; m John Paige of Hardwick ; d.
Jan. 7, 1871.

2. Mary Howe, b. June 4, 1829 : m. Dorrance S. Goddard of Worcester, Mar. 25. 1865.

2. Parley, b Dec. 31, 1831 : m. Maria C. Ball of Holden, Oct. 1,
1854 ; res. Moline. Illinois.

JUDE, bro. of JOHN, m. Dorothy Davis of Holden ; d. Apr. 5, 1834, a. 73.

1. Ann, b. Nov. 9, 1785 : m. John Wiley of Templeton, Feb. 11, 1806 ;
d. May 7, 1855.

1. Bela, b. Apr. 22, 1787 ; m. Mary Parker of Princeton, June 26,
1816, who d. Sept. 20, 1878 ; he d. Barre, Mar. 29, 1864.

2. Mary Maria, b. Apr. 2, 1817 ; m. Charles S. Flint of Paxton, Oct.
9, 1845.

2. Lovell Parker, b. Nov. 29. 1818 ; d. Gardner, Oct. 7, 1853.

2. Salome, b. Mar. 9, 1821 ; m. Warren Phinney of Orange, Oct.
11, 1855 ; d. June 11, 1866 ; he d. Jan. 31, 1866.

WILLIAMS.

2. Moses, b. May 23, 1823 ; m. Elizabeth C. Bragg of Milford, Dec. 9, 1845 ; d. July 15, 1877 ; she d. Dec., 1861.

2. Fidelia, b. Nov. 9, 1825 ; m. Aaron P. Snow of Paxton, Sept. 23. 1851, who d. Oct. 30, 1867 ; m. 2d, William C. Jackson of North Brookfield, Aug. 24, 1869 ; res. Barre.

2. Anson, b. June 26, 1828 ; m. Roena C. Bellows of Westboro', Nov. 30, 1856 ; res. Paxton.

2. Angeline L., b. Sept. 23. 1830 ; m. Willard E. Hemenway of Barre, Jan. 12, 1854.

2. Julia A., m. Carlo R. Bemis of Paxton, Nov. 24, 1853 ; res. North Brookfield.

2. David R., b. July 1, 1837 ; m. Elvira O. Pond ; res. Col.
    3. Harry Falis, b. Jan. 1, 1869.

1. Dolly, b. Sept. 17, 1789 ; m. Phineas Hayward of Barre, Apr. 2. 1816 ; both d. Barre.

1. James, b. Sept. 14, 1792 ; m. Priscilla Rice of Barre, d. Apr. 17, 1833.
    2. Martin Rice, b. 1812 ; m. Priscilla Ballou ; m. 2d, Phebe Flint ; m. 3d, Caroline T. Hopkins of Me. ; res. Worcester.
    2. Ruth Ann H., b. Apr. 15, 1814 ; m. Samuel Austin Parker ; m. 2d, Willard Cook of Chicago, Feb. 2, 1859.
    2. Charles, b. 1816 ; rem. Provincetown.
    2. William Copeland, b. Jan. 13, 1818 ; m. Lucy Wilbur, Nov. 1. 1842.
        3. Delia Ann, b. June 9, 1853.

1. Maria, b. Jan. 9, 1800 ; m. Samuel Fisk of Barre.
1. David, b. Dec. 8, 1808 ; rem.

WILLIS.

GEORGE WILLIS, b. Lincoln ; c. f. Worcester, 1858 ; m. Caroline F. Cutting of Weston, Oct. 9, 1853.

1. Hattie Josephine, b. July 8, 1858.
1. Ella Margaret, b. Apr. 7, 1861.
1. Mary Elizabeth, b. May 28, 1863 ; d. June 23. 1874.
1. George Herman, b. Oct. 10, 1865.
1. Carrie Emma, b. Apr. 19, 1867.

WITT.

OLIVER WITT c. f. Paxton ; settled on farm previously occupied by Israel Green ; at one time he owned the whole farm. 500 acres ; d. Nov. 11, 1807, a. 87 : his wife d. July 13. 1798.

WITT.

1. Daniel*, came about 1788; m. Eunice Flint of Rutland; d. Nov. 12, 1796; she d. Mar. 29, 1820, a. 67.
   2. John, m. Hannah Foster, July 22, 1806; d. Sept. 22, 1832; she d. Mar. 4, 1840, both in Troy, N. Y.
      3. Stillman, b. Jan. 4, 1808; rem. Cleveland, Ohio; d. Apr. 29, 1875.
      3. Lorena, b. Sept. 26, 1810; m. Rev. Wright Hazen of North Adams, Apr. 3, 1837, who d. Nov. 12, 1838.
      3. John Chandler, b. Sept. 5, 1814; d. New York.
      3. Caroline, b. Oct. 17, 1819; m. A. P. Butler of North Adams, Apr. 4, 1837, who d. June 5, 1870.
      3. Eunice, b. Apr. 5, 1823; d. Sept. 27, 1824.
   2. Eunice, b. 1778; m. Samuel Pitcher of Saco, Maine.
   2. Polly, b. Aug. 18. 1780; m. John Brown; m. 2d, Levi Wyman.
   2. Ivory, b. 1786; m. Eunice Foster, Dec. 1, 1808; d. June 27, 1858. a. 72; she d. Oct. 20, 1868, a. 81.
      3. Elisha Foster, b. Nov. 6, 1809; m. Lydia S. Jones; d. Templeton, Apr. 12, 1874.
      3. Sally, b. Sept. 12, 1811; m. Edwin Brown.
      3. Daniel, b. Mar. 21, 1815; m. Rebecca White of Phillipston, Mar. 4, 1838, who d. Oct. 8, 1878.
         4. Harriet W., b. Nov. 3. 1839; d. Sept. 26, 1852.
         4. Ellen J., b. Feb. 10, 1842; d. Mar. 24, 1845.
         4. John C., b. Oct. 12, 1844; d. Oct. 12, 1851.
         4. Clayton, b. June 5. 1846; d. army, Nov. 20, 1864. [See p. 143.]
         4. Everard, b. July 13, 1848; m. Louisa M. Osgood, May 30, 1871; rem. Winchendon.
            5. Mabel Louise, b. Jan. 13. 1875; d. Jan. 13, 1875.
            5. Harlan Everard, b. May 14, 1876.
            5. Frank, b. Aug. 28, 1878.
         4. Mary S., b. Aug. 29. 1853; d. Mar. 17, 1863.
      3. Nelson, b. Aug. 21, 1817; m Betsey Hartwell, Nov. 24, 1842; res. Springfield.
         4. Estus, b. Dec. 12, 1849; d. Aug. 30, 1851.
         4. Ellen E., b. Jan. 15. 1852; d. July 26, 1852.
      3. Albert, b. Feb. 8, 1820; m. Sarah Heald, June 2, 1846; d. Worcester.

WITT.

3. Eurania, b. June 7, 1822; m. Ethan Hemenway; d. Mar. 31, 1851.

3. Jerusha, b. Aug. 31, 1824; m. Norman Rice of Barre, June 2, 1846; res. Hyde Park.

3. Clark, b. Aug. 9, 1826; m. Mary Ann Damon of Phillipston. Sept. 24, 1854; res. Hanover.

3. Hannah, b. Dec. 4, 1828; m. George Bowker.

3. Elizabeth E., b. June 2, 1830; m. C. G. Buffum of Richmond. N. H., Aug. 12, 1856.

2. David, b. 1781; m. Sally (Phelps) Follett, June 1, 1808; d. Dec., 1825.

3. Sophronia, b. Apr. 11, 1809; m. Artemas Brigham of Petersham, Dec. 20, 1827; d. Feb. 2, 1862.

3. Augusta, b. Apr. 28, 1812; m. Cornelius Hinds.

3. Elvira, b. July 22, 1819; m. George Babbitt of Athol, Oct. 22, 1844.

2. Clark, b. 1791; m. Catherine Smith, Jan. 26, 1813; d. Apr. 9, 1827; she d. Jan. 14, 1867.

3. Avaline, b. May 8, 1813; m. George Hoyt, M. D., Oct. 15, 1829; rem. Athol.

3. Albert G., b. Feb. 20, 1815; d. June 3, 1816.

3. Cecelia, b. Dec. 28, 1816; m. William Marean.

1. Oliver, b. 1759; m.; d. Sept. 1, 1802.

2. Alpheus, rem. Acton.

2. Oliver, b. 1792; m. Nancy Pond, Nov. 14, 1830, who d. Feb. 16, 1846; he d. Jan. 18, 1848.

1. Persis, b. July 3, 1763; m. Joel Earle.

1. Rebecca, m. Ebenezer Brown.

WOODS.

JOHN WOODS c. f. Marlboro', 1771; [see chap. VII;] m. Zeruiah Barnes, who d. Dec. 26, 1805, a. 61; m. 2d, Lydia Peirce, Feb. 28, 1810, who d. Oct. 6, 1855, a. 89; he d. May 21, 1819, a. 84.

1. Elizabeth, b. 1767; m. Amasa Bellows; m. 2d, Asaph Bellows.

1. Edward, b. 1769; m. Jemima Robertson, Oct. 15, 1795, who d. Oct. 13, 1842, a. 72; he d. Barre, Sept., 1810.

2. Daniel, b. Jan. 22, 1796; m. Sarah Black of Barre; rem. Medway; d. there.

48

WOODS.

2. John, b. Dec. 3, 1797.
2. Leonard, b. Aug. 15, 1799 ; d. Boston.
2. Achsah, b. Jan. 23, 1801 ; m. Elijah McFarland.
2. Sydney, b. Jan. 10, 1804 ; left town.
2. Edward, }
2. Edwin, } b. Oct. 18, 1805 ; m. Sarah G. Clark, Nov. 27, 1834.
   3. Edward Henry, b. Sept. 19, 1835 ; d. Aug. 5, 1862.
   3. William A., b. Jan. 15, 1838 ; d. Oct. 30, 1842.
2. Alonzo, b. 1808 ; m. Angeline Wyatt of Greenwich ; res. Greenwich.
2. James, b. Apr., 1810 ; d. Aug. 1, 1814.
2. Mary, b. Jan. 25, 1814 ; d. Oct. 15, 1838.
1. John, b. 1765 ; d. Philadelphia, Penn., 1823.
1. Anna, b. Jan. 7, 1772.
1. Nancy, b. 1773 ; m. Windsor Hapgood, June 29, 1800 ; d. Mar. 2,
    1850 ; he d. Dec. 24, 1829, a. 62.
1. Dorothy, b. Oct. 4, 1774 ; m. Abel Thompson, who was drowned
    Dec. 18, 1830, a. 55 ; [see p. 165 ;] she d. Ithaca, New
    York.
1. James, b. Apr. 10, 1781 ; d. Sept. 28, 1853.

WOODWARD.

ELISHA WOODWARD c. f. Newton ; m. Anna Murdock : d. Mar. 18, 1810,
    a. 66 ; she d. Nov. 3, 1822, a. 73.
1. Anna, b. June 19, 1774 ; d. Oct. 20, 1777.
1. Sarah, b. Feb. 27, 1776 ; d. Oct. 24, 1777.
1. Anna, b. May 3, 1778 ; m. Isaac Whittemore.
1. Sally, b. Dec. 13, 1779 ; m. Abner Hinds.
1. Molly, b. July 28, 1781 ; m. Nathan Wright.
1. Elisha, b. Sept. 15, 1783 ; d. Oct. 19, 1784.
1. John F., b. Aug. 31, 1784 ; m. Betsey Lyon, Dec. 7, 1806 ; d. Sept.
    12, 1814.
   2. Elizabeth, b. Mar. 13, 1807 ; d. Sept. 3, 1823.
   2. Samuel, b. Sept. 10, 1808 ; d. Arkansas.
   2. John F., b. Sept. 18, 1812 ; m. Rusha R. Follett, Dec. 29, 1836 ;
     d. Feb. 11, 1880.
     3. Minerva, b. Dec. 15, 1837 ; d. June 14, 1840.
     3. Nathan W., b. May 24, 1841 ; drowned Apr. 19, 1844. [See
      p. 165.]

WOODWARD.

3. Charlotte Ann, b. Mar. 10, 1844 ; m. Henry M. Fairman of
   Conn., June 16, 1869 ; both deaf mutes.
3. Mary, b. Feb. 24, 1846 ; m. William T. Miles ; res. Worcester.
3. Eliza, b. May 18, 1848.
1. Achsah, b. Sept. 14, 1790 ; m. Warner Hinds.

PHILEMON c. f. Newton ; m. Mercy Whitney, May 25, 1773, who d. Nov.
   10, 1821, a. 71 ; he d. Mar. 10, 1826, a. 77.
1. Jason, b. Mar. 1, 1774 ; m. Polly Clark, Sept. 25, 1803 ; d. May
   15, 1822 ; she d. Nov. 1, 1839.
1. Mehitable, b. Dec. 3, 1776 ; m. Aaron Gates.
1. David, b. May 17, 1779, m. Sarah Hoyt, July 8, 1803 : rem. Boston ; d. there.
   2. Mary, b. June 6, 1803.
   2. Adeline, b. Apr. 22, 1806.
   2. William W., b. Nov. 15, 1808; rem. Barre.
   2. John H., b. Mar. 20, 1812.
   2. Aaron G., b. July 1, 1817.
   2. David R., b. Oct. 16, 1820 ; res. Stoneham.
1. Jonathan, b. May 17, 1779 ; d. July 7, 1861.
1. Artemas, b. July 27, 1790 ; rem. Holden.
1. Mercy, b. July 9, 1792 ; m. John Nichols. '

DANIEL.* c. f. Newton ; m. Keziah Newton, Nov. 28, 1784, who d. July
   30, 1851, a. 92 ; he d. Sept. 20, 1853, a. 93. He was in the
   Continental Army at Saratoga, and the surrender of Burgoyne.
1. Betsey, b. Jan. 15, 1785 ; d. Feb. 28, 1795.
1. Lucy, b. Apr. 7, 1787 ; m. James H. Wheeler.
1. Relief, b. July 5, 1789 ; m. Asa Howe.
1. Caty, b. Nov. 18, 1791 ; d. July 29, 1793.
1. Charlotte, b. Sept. 19, 1793 ; d. Aug. 31, 1796.
1. Elisha, b. Aug. 2, 1795 ; m. Mary Greenwood, Apr. 27, 1821, who
   d. Mar. 25, 1865.
   2. Gardner, b. Jan. 17, 1823 ; d. Nov. 17, 1824.
   2. Mary, b. Oct. 13, 1824 ; d. July 4, 1846.
   2. Adelphia, b. Mar. 12, 1829.
   2. Lyman, b. Dec. 6, 1831 ; m. Ann Elizabeth Greenwood, Dec.
      10, 1856.
      3. Alfred Ernest, b. Oct. 29, 1861.

WOODWARD.

   3. Mary Helen, b. Mar. 17, 1866.

1. Asa, b. Apr. 15, 1798 ; d. Virginia, 1849.

1. Rowland, b. Apr. 7, 1800 ; m. Rachel Pond, May 28, 1821 ; d. June 7, 1880.

   2. Catherine, b. Sept. 16, 1821 ; m. Isaac Davis.

   2. Althine, b. Oct. 17, 1824 ; d. Jan. 20, 1826.

   2. Althine, b. Oct. 3, 1825 ; m. Leonard Clark.

   2. Louisa, b. Nov. 9, 1828 ; m. Charles Estabrook of Rutland ; d. Worcester.

   2. Elizabeth, b. June 28, 1831 ; m. Geo. N. Richardson of Holden, Jan. 5, 1856.

   2. Adelaide, b. July 14, 1833 ; m. John B. Church.

   2. Myron C., b. May 27, 1839 ; d. Aug. 29, 1839.

1. Daniel, b. Oct. 3, 1802 ; m. Mary Newton, Nov. 30, 1829, who d. Oct. 19, 1838 ; m. 2d, Anna Newton, July 12, 1842 ; he d. Sept. 25, 1847.

   2. Lucy A., b. Nov. 28, 1830 ; m. Horatio N. Fairbank of Holden, May 1, 1851.

   2. George Gilman, b. Dec. 24, 1832 ; rem. New Albany, Ind.

   2. Nathan N., b. May 1, 1843 ; d. Mar. 5, 1852.

   2. Daniel H., b. Feb. 27, 1845 ; d. army, Camp Nelson, Ky., Sept. 15, 1863.

WRIGHT.

Joseph Wright* c. f. Woburn about 1773 ; m. Martha Eveleth, May 25, 1774, who d. May 6, 1819, a. 63 ; he d. Dec. 17, 1803. a. 57.

1. Joab, b. Apr. 16, 1775 ; d. Mar. 5, 1801.

1. Aaron, b. Dec. 10, 1777 ; m. Lois Lyon, Jan 21, 1802, who d. Feb. 12, 1846 ; he d. Mar. 17, 1851.

   2. Mary, b. Apr. 1, 1803 ; m. Dana Brown.

   2. Joseph, b. Dec. 29, 1806 ; m. Polly (Frost) Phelps ; res. Barre.

   2. Adeline, b. Apr. 9, 1809 ; m. Henry Prentiss.

   2. Lucy, b. Oct. 20, 1814 ; m. Francis Gates.

   2. Stedman, b. Aug. 8, 1818 ; m. Tabitha Brooks of Princeton ; rem. Princeton.

     3. William Herbert, b. July 19, 1843.

     3. John Elliot, b. Aug. 27, 1850.

   2. Lois, b. Mar. 25, 1821 ; m. Justus Woodbury Nims, Dec. 17, 1846 ; res. Keene, N. H.

WRIGHT.

1. Ruth, b. Aug. 1, 1779 ; m. Jacob Waite.
1. Chloe, b. Aug. 6, 1781 ; d. Dec. 2, 1803.
1. Sally, b. Jan. 17, 1783 ; d. Feb. 24, 1801.
1. Nathan, b. June 29, 1784; m. Polly Woodward, Sept. 1, 1805, who d. Nov. 2, 1811 ; m. 2d, Sally (Lamb) Wheeler, Aug. 20, 1812, who d. Mar. 13, 1826 ; m. 3d, Mary Sargent, July 29, 1827 ; he d. Aug. 28, 1864 ; she res. Cambridge.
   2. Sally, b. Feb. 11, 1807 ; m. Sumner Marean.
   2. Dorcas, b. Apr. 20, 1808 ; m. Levi Joslin.
   2. Larkin, b. June 4, 1809 ; d. Nov. 12, 1812.
   2. Polly, b. Oct. 31, 1811 ; m. Lowell L. Hinds.
   2. James Larkin, b. Jan. 1, 1813 ; res. Brighton.
   2. Lucinda, b Jan. 1, 1813; d. Sept. 18, 1813.
   2. Lucinda, b. Apr. 16, 1815 ; m. Augustus Morse.
   2. Chloe, b. July 30, 1817 ; m. A. F. Webb ; rem. St. Louis, Mo.
   2. Salem T., b. Nov. 22, 1819 ; rem. Iowa.
   2. Benjamin F., b. Feb. 19, 1823 ; m. Sarah Hartwell, Jan. 12, 1847.
      3. Alfred, b. Apr. 3, 1848; m. Nellie Alden, Sept. 15, 1874.
      3. Ida E., b. June 30, 1851 ; m. J. Frank Pollard.
      3. George W., b. Nov. 5, 1853 ; d. May 29, 1857.
      3. Chloe Louise, b. June 5, 1857.
      3. Herbert E., b. June 1, 1859 ; d. Apr. 3, 1864.
      3. Etta Clifford, b. Sept. 20, 1861.
      3. William, b. Jan. 14, 1864.
      3. Ellen Bigelow, b. Jan. 12, 1867.
      3. Nathan, b. May 21, 1872 ; d. June 2, 1873.
   2. Avaline, b. Mar. 13, 1828 ; d. Feb. 23, 1831.
   2. Ellen Maria, b. Mar. 30, 1830 ; d. June 25, 1832.
   2. Adelaide E., b. May 24, 1834 ; m. Moses Greenwood.
   2. Edward E., b. Mar. 27, 1837 ; d. Nov. 26, 1840.
   2. Parker S., b. Mar. 10, 1839 ; d. army, June 27, 1862. [See p. 143.]
   2. Hattie P., b. Oct. 24, 1844 ; m. Charles W. Spring ; d. Aug., 1868.
1. Bildad, b. June 20, 1788 ; m. Rhoda Pond, May 27. 1807 ; drowned July 16, 1820. [See p. 165.]
   2. William, b. Aug. 17, 1807 ; rem.
   2. Elvira, b. Mar. 22, 1809 ; m. James Going of Templeton, Mar. 2, 1826 ; rem. Fitchburg.
   2. Martha, b. Feb. 12, 1811 ; m. William C. Goodspeed.

WRIGHT.

2. Susan, b. Dec. 22, 1816 ; m. Jonas Gilman Clark.
2. Benjamin, b. Oct. 11, 1818.
1. Charles, b. Sept. 24, 1789 ; m. Betsey Clark, Nov., 1809 ; d. Dec.
    8, 1847 ; she d. Nov. 13, 1880.
  2. Joab C., b. Jan. 29, 1810 ; m. Lucetta Pond, Apr. 17, 1832.
    3. Worthington V. B., b. Dec. 10, 1832 ; rem. Texas.
    3. Joab Wesson, b. Aug. 11, 1834 ; d. Nov. 24, 1834.
    3. Theodore F., b. Oct. 9, 1835 ; d. Sept. 25, 1837.
    3. Stella L., b. July 20, 1837 ; m. W. Andrews of La. ; d. Dec.
      16, 1873.
    3. Julia Ann, b. Sept. 14, 1839 ; m. George P. Richardson.
    3. Charles J., b. Nov. 20, 1841 ; rem. Texas.
    3. Lucia M., b. Mar. 26, 1845 ; d. July 29, 1864.
    3. Mary E., b. Feb. 9, 1847.
    3. Frank, b. Nov. 17, 1854 ; d. Oct. 6, 1864.
  2. Louisa, b. Nov. 19, 1811 ; m. Bennett Potter.
  2. Charles Jarvis, b. Dec. 11, 1814 ; d. New Orleans, La.
  2. Lucy, b. July 25, 1817 ; m. John H. Heald of Pepperell, Oct.
    7, 1834 ; d. July 27, 1853.
  2. Reuben, b. Sept. 29, 1819 ; res. Ark.
  2. Catherine, b. Feb. 14, 1822 ; m. J. H. Heard of Chelsea, June
    24, 1846.
  2. Freelove Elizabeth, b. Jan. 20, 1825 ; m. Luke Waite.
  2. Adelaide, b. Oct. 16, 1827 ; d. Aug. 22, 1832.
1. Catherine, b. Oct. 2, 1791 ; m. Sewell Phelps ; d. N. Y.
1. Dorcas, b. May 8, 1794 ; drowned May 15, 1808. [See p. 165.]
1. Elizabeth, b. Oct. 13, 1796 ; m. Charles Spring, May 19, 1814 ;
    m. 2d, Lowell Leland.

WYMAN.

Levi Wyman c. f. Chesterfield, N. H., m. Polly (Witt) Brown, Nov.,
    1809, who d. Dec. 5, 1865 ; he d. Aug. 8, 1866, a. 83.
1. Charlotte, b. Sept. 24, 1810 ; m. James Harvey Hartwell.
1. Clara, b. Dec. 5, 1812 ; m. Anson Clifford.
1. Cynthia, b. Feb. 8, 1815 ; d. Apr. 7, 1816.
1. Harrison, b. Feb. 24, 1817 ; m. Celicia Clifford, Nov. 24, 1842.
  2. Charles Torrey, b. Dec. 27, 1846 ; m. Lillie Monroe, July 1, 1876.
    3. Harry M., b. July 19, 1877.

WYMAN.

3. Sadie Gertrude, b. Aug. 6, 1879.
1. Eunice, b. Mar. 14, 1821; m. Merrick D. Raymond of Winchendon, Jan. 30, 1844, who d. Aug. 20, 1880.
1. Cynthia, b. Apr. 18, 1823; m. Benjamin H. Kinney of Worcester, Feb. 25, 1845.

YOUNG.

WILLIAM YOUNG, m. Polly Potter, who d. Jan. 26, 1857, a. 70; he d. Sept. 15, 1859, a. 71.
1. Mary, b. Jan. 28, 1807; m. Noah M. Moore.
1. Phebe, b. May 31, 1809; m. Artemas Baker.
1. Thomas William, b. Aug. 24, 1811; res. Concord, N. H.
1. Allen, b. Jan. 12, 1814; m. Anna D. Barrett of Fitchburg.
1. Hiram, b. Aug. 31, 1816; m. Abigail A. Clark, Oct. 16, 1839; rem.
   2. Makepeace C., b. Aug. 13, 1840; d. army, June 3, 1864. [See p. 143.]
   2. Christopher Sumner, b. Sept. 7, 1842; m. Lucy Jane Leonard, Dec. 19, 1865. who d. July 21, 1872; m. 2d, Emma M. Gates, July 24, 1873.
      3. Stella Abbie, b. June 9, 1867.
      3. Jennie Elizabeth, b. June 28, 1869.
      3. Eunice Maud, b. Nov. 26, 1874.
      3. Alfred Sumner, b. Oct. 9, 1876.
1. Lucinda, b. Dec. 27, 1818; m. Albert Wheeler.
1. Hannah, b. May 4, 1821; m. Henry Stone of Rutland, Apr. 8, 1840; res. Ohio.
1. Sarah, b. Apr. 7, 1823; m. Edwin H. Clark.
1. Elizabeth Jane, b. Feb. 17, 1825; d. Sept. 1, 1825.
1. Lucy Jane, b. Dec. 26, 1826; m. Albert Wheeler.
1. Sumner, b. July 15, 1829; d. Nov. 5, 1841.
1. Nancy E., b. June 30, 1832; d. Nov. 14, 1851.

NOTE. The following names were omitted from their proper place.

PERKINS.

EDWARD PERKINS c. f. Lowell, 1873; m. Eliza J. Hook of Concord, N. H., Dec. 21, 1850.
1. Ella J., b. June 12, 1853.
1. Anna M., b. Dec. 19, 1860.
1. Edward E., b. Feb. 1, 1866.
1. Minnie B., b. Oct. 30, 1870.